Yellowstone Mileposts

The Visitor's Point-by-Point Guide to the World's First National Park

Thomas P. Bohannan

HAYDEN PUBLISHING
New Castle, Delaware

Photographs and illustrations by NPS or the Library of Congress as noted on each.

Library of Congress Control Number: 2013923539
ISBN: 978-0-9854072-2-3 Paperback
ISBN: 978-0-9854072-3-0 EPUB

Front Cover Photo: North Entrance Arch, also known as the Roosevelt Arch. Photo by author, 2011.

Back Cover Photos: Top to bottom: Old road in Yellowstone, ca. 1890s; original Golden Gate viaduct, ca. 1900; Fountain Hotel, circa 1915; Aerial view of the Old Faithful complex, 1968. Photos 1, 3, and 4 courtesy NPS; Photo 2 courtesy Library of Congress.

Disclaimer: The mileage figures and other information contained within this book are believed to be accurate as of the publication date. Road construction is a fact of life within Yellowstone, and at any time, roads may be realigned or modified such that the specific measurements and GPS locations provided herein may become out of date. Therefore, the author assumes no liability for inaccuracies and/or any hardship or financial impacts caused by the information contained within this book. See the text for additional information about anticipated road realignments for further information.

To my wonderful bride of 25 years, Kimberly.
Thank you for sharing your life and your love of
Yellowstone National Park with me.

"*Stay on this good fire-mountain and spend the night among the stars. Watch their glorious bloom until the dawn, and get one more baptism of light. Then, with fresh heart, go down to your work, and whatever your fate, under whatever ignorance or knowledge you may afterward chance to suffer, you will remember these fine, wild views, and look back with joy to your wanderings in the blessed old Yellowstone Wonderland.*"

— John Muir
1898

Preface

In my 2012 book, *Benchmark Hunting in Yellowstone National Park*, I make reference to the book that I had originally planned to write when I arrived to work during the summer of 2011. This is that book.

When I first came to Yellowstone with my wife in 1990, I was attracted not only to the wildlife, the thermal features, and the geology, but the history of the park as well. When you stop and look at the huge stone structures at the park's headquarters in Mammoth, you cannot help but be impressed that these magnificent, century-old edifices of the park's early days are still standing and still being used to make the park work. And though there are occasional interpretive panels and sound bites from tour guides that tell you this building was originally this or that, I wanted to know more about why they were built and what they represented.

As we spent more time in the park over the succeeding years, my fascination with why things were the way they were increased. Why did the road go this way, when it used to go that other way? Why was this structure physically picked up and moved to that spot over there? What's down that gated-off, unmarked gravel road? What happened to the building that was here when I passed through this area 10 years ago? Why was that particular feature given the name it has? My 20+ years in the public safety field (primarily emergency management) imbued me with a drive to learn about the infrastructure - what makes things work the way they do? So I spent a lot of time doing research and investigating the histories of many things most people tend to ignore while they're in the park. I can explain how the 20+ septic systems work anywhere in the park, for example! That will surely come in handy one day.

During my tenure at the bookstore in the Old Faithful Visitor Education Center in the summer of 2011, I'd often encounter people who'd ask about these sorts of things. It was always entertaining to engage in conversation with them and share a bit of the history of the park. There's far more interest about that kind of thing than I think many people realize. And while there are a few books out there that provide some basic road logs giving an overview of what the average visitor will see as s/he passes through the park. I wanted to do something that would appeal to the visitor who has an interest in the whos, whats, whens, and wherefores of why things are the way they are here, there, and out there in Yellowstone. Thus, this book.

There are perhaps a couple of points of interest to keep in mind as you read *Yellowstone Mileposts*. The first involves date disparities. It's not uncommon at all to have two different historians (or other people with some knowledge or authority on a subject) disagree about specific dates regarding when such and such occurred. One thing I found while doing research for this book was that, even in early park memoranda and reports from park personnel, the dates for the same event would be listed differently.

The construction dates of buildings is an excellent example of this. One person might use the date construction began as the "construction date" of building A, while the next person might use the date it opened to the public. If it took two years to build, you'd end up with two different dates listed for the same event. If it took two years to build, and then didn't open until the next season, you may end up with three dates! There's a lot of that in the park's history. So as you read through this and encounter two different dates for the same event (especially if one is from another source), please keep that in mind. I've tried to rectify and clarify these situations when possible, however, to minimize any confusion.

I should also note that the road mileages in this book might differ a bit from those used in many other guides. Most authors round these off to the nearest whole number or use "close to" measurements. The mileages found herein are derived from the very accurate distances for each road as they're laid out in the park's Geographic Information System. Additionally, these measurements are taken from the center point of each junction, whereas those used by others may not be. These distances were verified with a vehicle odometer as well as GPS plots overlaid on top of maps generated in Google Earth. So they are known to be very accurate (not withstanding the occasional typo, of course).

Everything herein is believed to be accurate. However, changes do occur over time, or new information comes to light, or I may have interpreted something I read or overheard incorrectly. Even among the park's historians, disagreement often exists about why something happened, or what happened, who was present when it happened, what year it happened, and so forth. Even with individual historians and authors, it's not uncommon at all to see them disagree with themselves about a nugget of information from one writing to another. So while I've made every effort to ensure the information herein is accurate, it would not surprise me to have someone find an error here or there. If you do find any mistakes, please notify the author via e-mail at yellowstonemileposts@gmail.com so that it can be corrected in the next edition of the book.

Finally, a note about the title of the book. In the park's early days, the roads were constructed and maintained by the U.S. Army Corps of Engineers. Beginning around 1900, as they built and rebuilt these roads, they would install white wooden posts every so often with notations about how many miles you were from the place you'd left and how far you were from the next junction. These were known as mileposts. Thus, the book's name. I should mention that I tried in vain to locate a photograph of these posts, even reaching out to the Corps of Engineer's historian in Washington, DC. Sadly, even they were unable to locate a picture.

Given all of that, I hope you enjoy the book as much as I enjoyed writing it.

Acknowledgments

There are always a great many people to thank when it comes to writing a book like this.

The first group of people I have to acknowledge are the Xanterra coworkers with whom I spent the summer of 2012 (during which I did the bulk of the final research for this book). Park employees, especially those who work for the concession companies, are often the target of a lot of criticism for being lazy, incompetent, and so forth. But I have to say that the overwhelming majority of those who worked at Grant Village in 2012 were hard working people who really, really wanted to do a good job. A lot of people have no idea how difficult it is to serve the thousands of people who come through such a small place every single day, over and over again, 100 days in a row. I gained such a tremendous appreciation for those who clean guest rooms and cook the meals fed to all of these itinerant passersthrough.

There were quite a few individuals who made life in Grant Village, shall we say, more interesting as the summer wore on. This included the Circle of Kings; Megan, Amy, Betsy, and Brianna. And then there was Lisa, for whom we'd never know from one day to the next what kind of trouble she was going to get into. One of the highlights of the summer was getting to meet and talk to people from all over the planet. We ended up with staff members from almost two dozen countries on five continents.

Grant is unlike most of the other work locations in Yellowstone because, rather than a series of dorms or cabins, we just had one large dormitory (with a few satellite cabins). This means that, rather than each dorm having its own residence coordinator, we had a team of four. I was very fortunate in that I was teamed up with three other RCs who were experienced, and it ended up being one of the best groups I've ever worked with. So to Tom Jensen, John Boynton, and Suzanne Schilling, I extend a heartfelt appreciation for your work and your friendship over the course of the summer.

Our security team at Grant was fun to work with as well. The RCs work hand in hand with the Xanterra Security staff to ensure the dorm runs peacefully and that everyone gets along and follows the rules and laws. The Grant Village team included Security Lead Ryan Emerson, and officers Dave Marshall and Brian Cooney.

I also had the opportunity to work with the NPS ranger staff at Grant. And, as has been my experience with every other ranger in the park, they were absolutely nothing less than professional. District Ranger Angela Bowers, Deputy DR Steve Roper, and ranger Ben Welch, and the park's criminal investigator, Les Seano, along with the district's compliment of seasonal rangers all made for a rather interesting summer.

I have to thank cartographic technician Julie Rose of the park's Spatial Analysis Center (the GIS lab) for working with me to produce the data and maps that form the underpinning of much of the information in this book. I've been working with Julie for several years now on multiple projects, and she's always done whatever she could to get me what I needed while working on the more serious stuff she has to do on a daily basis. This book literally would not have been possible without your assistance.

The folks at the park's Heritage and Research Center (HRC) put up with me one or two days a week, every week, for the entire summer (and lived to tell about it). Two people in particular, librarian Jackie Jerla and Archive Technician Shawn Bowden were on the receiving end of a voluminous number of requests for material, and offered to help in any way they could without losing their smiles and senses of humor. I am extremely grateful for the fact that the HRC exists at Yellowstone; it makes doing research for books and other projects so much easier.

I owe a huge debt of gratitude to Xanterra Tour Guide Karen Low for her pre-read and suggestions about changes to various tidbits of information throughout the book. Karen has spent 18 summer and 14 winter seasons in a variety of positions at just about every location within the park and knows the place backwards and forwards. I am grateful that she spent some time proofreading the book for me.

Tobin Roop, Cultural Resources Branch Chief in the park's scientific wing, the Yellowstone Center for Resources, was kind enough to do a pre-read of the book as well to ensure I haven't released too much information about certain aspects of park archeological history. It's a sad testament to the current state of affairs that I have to withhold certain bits of information in order to protect many of the park's sensitive archeological sites and artifacts.

While the vast majority of people would simply view and appreciate things like the old wickiups or poacher's cabins, for example, there are those who would purloin bits and pieces of these important sites simply to have a park "souvenir." After a few people "bits and pieces" a site into oblivion, we'd end up with a situation like what's happened at the now fenced in

Petrified Tree near Tower Junction. At one time there were several of those trees present in that area, but visitors and vandals chipped away at the trees until all but one was gone. And the one that remains has to be protected by a fence to keep people from hauling it away even today.

As much as I believe these things should be shared with those who're interested in them, I also very firmly believe in protecting them for future generations. To that end, I asked Mr. Roop to look over the material I've written to make sure NPS is comfortable that I'm not putting "too much" out there, thereby making it just that much easier for others to damage what you and I cherish. If you're interested in any aspect of park archeology, I highly encourage you to visit the HRC, where you'll find a wealth of information that dates back to the park's founding.

I also have to acknowledge the park's historians, both professional and amateur, past and present. This includes Yellowstone's preeminent historian Aubrey Haines, whose nearly 1,000-page, two-volume set on the park's history is required reading for anyone who's interested in the park's early days, as well as current historian Lee Whittlesey. Mr. Whittlesey has written untold reams of material, much of it unpublished, on not just the park's macro history, but microhistories of developments and even individual structures. Leslie Quinn, Xanterra's Manager of Interpretation has also written extensively on various aspects of park history, especially relative to the Old Faithful Area. And then there's Robert Goss, who compiled a massive, well-documented chronology of park history as it relates to concession operations. I've learned a great deal from reading their writings, attending their lectures and tours, and indirectly absorbing their knowledge over the past 24 years I've spent time in the park.

Finally, of course, there's my lovely bride of 25 years, Kimberly. Words cannot convey what this woman means to me. She's not only allowed me to spend a couple of summers away from home working in Wonderland, but actively encouraged it because she knows of (and shares) my passion for Yellowstone National Park. I look forward to the day she retires from her "real" job so we can work together in the park. She was also gracious enough to proofread and edit much of the textual content here for me. This book is dedicated to her.

TABLE OF CONTENTS

Road segments and developments by map on page xiii

MAP OF ROAD SEGMENTS & DEVELOPMENTS

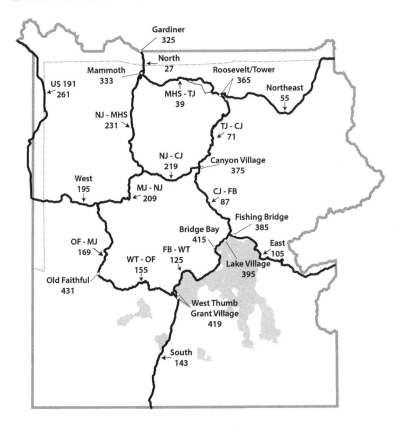

Introduction

On March 1, 1872, President Ulysses S. Grant signed into law an act passed by Congress creating Yellowstone National Park, the world's first national park. And though some small attempts at tourist facilities had begun even before the park was set aside, it would be almost a decade before serious progress was made providing roads and facilities to accommodate visitors. In the succeeding 130+ years, however, the drive to create a road system and infrastructure to facilitate the public's use of Yellowstone has seen its share of twists and turns.

The park's road network has progressed from a series of poorly constructed dirt bridal paths to today's (mostly) modern asphalt road surface that has served as the model for roads in many of our nation's national parks. Over the course of Yellowstone's history, the roads have been realigned and relocated in an attempt to make travel between the various points of interest safer and more efficient, as well as reducing visitor and vehicle impacts on the park's sensitive areas. As these routes have changed, or in some cases completely removed from use, various tidbits of park history have been lost from the public consciousness and relegated to the history books.

Park employees (NPS and concession) are inundated daily by questions from those visiting the park about why places have certain names, where certain events took place, why there are clear cut paths through sections of the forested areas, where the old [insert building name here] used to be, and so forth. And while a vast amount of historical information has been written about the park over the past 50+ years, very little of it has been organized into a manageable collection accessible to the average visitor. This book is designed to bridge that gap and provide some context for what you see as you drive around the park.

Yellowstone Mileposts is broken down into two main sections. The first is a mile-by-mile road log of every significant publicly accessible road within the park. At each point of interest, there'll be a short micro-history of what's at that location or what has happened at that place in the past. The second section is a building-by-building history for all of the major facilities at the park's nine public commercial developments. Almost everyone is familiar with the Old Faithful Inn, but very few people have any clue what the half-dozen or so buildings behind it are for or how they relate to the history of the Inn. You'll find that information within these pages.

Before we get started with the guide, however, it might be a good idea to get a few basic concepts out of the way. If you're an experienced Yellowstone visitor, this may be review material for you. But if you've not been to the park before, the following sections provide you with an overview of the types of activities that are available, as well as some important health and safety guidelines you need to be aware of. These are especially important if you're not used to being in a wilderness or at altitudes above 7,000 feet. Familiarizing yourself with this information will set the stage for the information to come.

ACTIVITIES AVAILABLE WITHIN THE PARK

The following is a summary of the activities and services available throughout the park.

Bicycling: Bicycling is permitted on all park roads and along certain front country trails. While many of the roads have been improved to include sufficient shoulder widths to allow motorists to pass safely, there are a handful where that's not the case (in particular the road between Norris and Mammoth and the North Entrance Road). While helmets are not required by law within the park, you are highly encouraged to wear one. Reflective clothing is also a good idea, especially during the early morning and late evening hours. You must obey all traffic regulations. Approved routes for bicyclists can be found online at the park's website and are marked with the bicycle symbol in this book's Road Log section where appropriate.

If you don't wish to bring a bike with you to the park, Xanterra rents bicycles at the gift shop located in the Old Faithful Snow Lodge. In 2013, rental rates were $8/hour, $25/half day, or $35/full day for an adult bicycle (includes a lock). You can also rent equipment such as helmets, gloves, hip bags, trunk racks, and even bicycle trailers if needed.

Boating: Motorized boating is allowed only on Yellowstone Lake and Lewis Lake, while non-motorized boating is allowed on those and most of the other lakes in the park. The only river where (non-motorized) boating is permitted is the Lewis Channel, which connects Lewis Lake and Shoshone Lake. All boats require a park permit, which can be obtained at the park's backcountry offices. In 2013, the fees ranged from $5 to $20 depending on the type of boat and duration of the permit. You must have sufficient US Coast Guard approved flotation devices on board for every person while out on the water. Note that the park's rangers monitor marine radio channel 16 on Yellowstone Lake.

You can rent a variety of boats from the park's primary concessioner, Xanterra, at Bridge Bay. Rates in 2013 ranged from $10/hr for a four-person rowboat to $47/hr for a boat with an outboard motor (carries up to six people). Scenic cruises of Yellowstone Lake are also offered for $15 per person.

Cell Phone/WiFi Service: Cell phone coverage is spotty at best throughout the park. In most of the developed areas you'll find some service, but once you travel a few miles outside of those, there's generally no signal whatsoever. Currently, Mammoth, Canyon Village, the Lake Village area (which includes Fishing Bridge and Bridge Bay), Grant Village, and Old Faithful have cell towers. You can get some signal about seven miles into the park from West Yellowstone and around the Gardiner area. Cell service is also available at certain places along the Northeast Entrance Road, in Hayden Valley, and along the East Entrance Road. Most of the service is provided by Verizon or one of its CDMA roaming partners (Sprint, Metro PCS, Cricket, & U.S. Cellular), though AT&T and its GSM roaming partners (T-Mobile) work well at Canyon and in the Grant area.

WiFi service is very limited in the park as well. The 3G/4G cellular data connectivity doesn't work very well in the park except in the area immediately surrounding the towers, and then only during non-peak hours when everyone's not trying to use it simultaneously. The park's lodging concessioner, Xanterra, provides fee-based WiFi connectivity for guests at the Mammoth Hot Springs Hotel, the Canyon Lodge, the Grant Village lodges, and the Old Faithful Snow Lodge. Park policy prohibits WiFi provision within the Old Faithful Inn and the Lake Hotel, however.

Fishing: The fishing regulations for Yellowstone are quite complicated and vary depending upon where you're actually fishing. Generally speaking, however, most of the park's rivers open to fishing at the end of May, while the remainder and Yellowstone Lake open in mid-June. Anyone older than 16 who wishes to fish must obtain a park fishing license (state fishing licenses are invalid in the park). These can be obtained at the visitor centers, general stores, and ranger stations, as well as certain vendors outside the park in the gateway communities (license fees vary based on duration). See the park's website for specifics, including a multi-page booklet that details which species may be caught, which must be returned to the park's waters, and what you should do with any invasive lake trout fish you might catch.

Xanterra operates commercial fishing tours out of Bridge Bay. In the summer of 2013, the rates began at $176 for a two-hour tour (for up to six people).

Hiking: Generally speaking, you can hike anywhere in the park that is not closed by signs or regulations. There are over 1,000 miles of maintained trails through the park. If you're going to be hiking into the backcountry, be sure you follow the appropriate safety protocols, including carrying bear spray with you and always hiking in pairs or groups of people. Let others know where you're going and when you should be expected back. If the trailhead has a log book sign it as you enter and leave the trail. If you plan to camp in the backcountry, you'll need to check in and reserve a campsite at one of the park's Backcountry Offices prior to setting out.

Horseback Riding: Guided horseback tours are offered at three locations by the park's primary concessioner, Xanterra. You can take one- or two-hour rides from the Canyon or Roosevelt Corrals, or one-hour rides from the Mammoth Corral. One-hour tours were $40 and two-hour rides were $60 in the summer of 2013. Many other authorized tour providers offer guided horseback tours of certain areas of the park as well. Be sure and examine the park's web site for a list of those authorized to offer such tours.

Junior Ranger/Young Scientist Programs: There are two programs designed to help youngsters learn more about Yellowstone.

Though the Junior Ranger Program is designed for children ages 5 to 12, anyone can participate. Check in with the information desk at one of the visitor centers to get an activity paper that has a series of activities for you to complete. These activities are geared toward helping you understand Yellowstone and its geology, wildlife, and history. Once you've completed the activities, return to the information desk to have your answers checked. If you complete the tasks successfully, you'll earn a junior ranger patch. This program is available during the summer and winter.

The Young Scientist Program is offered at Old Faithful and Canyon Village, and is designed to teach people of all ages about the park's complex geology and hydrothermal systems. You purchase an activity booklet at the visitor center information desk ($5 in 2013) and complete the activities, whereupon you'll be awarded a Young Scientist patch or keychain.

Ranger-led Programs: NPS rangers offer a plethora of talks, presentations, guided hikes, and other programs over the course of each summer, as well as a handful during the winter season. When you enter the park, you should be given an insert with the park newspaper that provides a schedule of these programs. If not, check with the nearest visitor center.

Religious Services: During the summer, there are usually a variety of religious services (most interdenominational) held throughout the park, generally in or near the park's campgrounds. The park's Chapel at Mammoth also hosts services each Sunday morning.

Swimming: There are two officially sanctioned swimming areas in Yellowstone. The first is located at Boiling River north of Mammoth, while the other is located in Firehole Canyon just south of Madison. Though it is not illegal to swim in other park waters, many are too cold to stay in for any length of time. A couple of popular places for wading and swimming include the Firehole River at the Nez Perce Picnic Area and just above the Upper Firehole Cascade south of Madison Junction (these are noted in the Road Logs). Note that it IS illegal to enter or swim in any of the park's thermal features. It is likewise illegal to jump or dive from any of the cliffs, rocks, or trees into any of the park's bodies of water.

Winter Sports/Activities: There are a variety of winter-related activities available in the park during the winter season. This includes snowmobile or snowcoach tours, skiing, snowshoeing, and even ice skating.

Snowmobile and snowcoach tours are available from a variety of locations both inside and outside the park. Park concessioner Xanterra offers tours from Mammoth and Old Faithful inside the park as well as from Flagg Ranch outside the park's south entrance. Several private tour operators provide tours from the park's gateway communities of West Yellowstone, Flagg Ranch, and Pahaska Tepee. Prices vary by tour. Be sure to check the park's website for a list of authorized providers. Up until the early 2000s, it was possible to rent a snowmobile and travel into the park on your own without a guide. However, the park's latest Winter Use Plan has eliminated this, and you now must come in as a part of a guided tour group.

Xanterra also operates Bear Den Ski Shops at Mammoth and Old Faithful during the winter. Here you can rent skis or snowshoes and related equipment, have your equipment repaired, get skiing lessons, and schedule skiing tours. There are over a dozen cross-country ski trails of varying difficulty located throughout the park, and Xanterra operates shuttles to and from the trailheads.

Ice skating rinks are located at Mammoth and the Old Faithful Snow Lodge. Skate rental is free, and there is no admission charge.

HEALTH AND SAFETY IN YELLOWSTONE

Perhaps one issue to be concerned about in Yellowstone, more so than just about any other national park, is safety. Because of the wildlife, the thermal features, and the geology of the area, visitors must remain much more vigilant than they might normally be at home or if they were on vacation in some other area.

Wildlife: Visitors are required to remain at least 100 yards (a football field) away from bears and wolves, and at least 25 yards away from all other wildlife. This includes the park's bison. Many people assume that because they're so large they can't move very fast. Nothing could be further from the truth - bison can hit speeds of 35 mph in an instant. And believe it or not, more people are injured by bison in a typical summer than by bears.

Thermal Features: The thermal features in Yellowstone are driven in large part by hot water, water that is almost invariably at or near the boiling point. People have literally been burned to death after having fallen into the park's thermal pools. You'll want to be especially vigilant with younger children. Note that park regulations require you to stay on boardwalks where they're provided.

Geology: Because of the nature of Yellowstone's geology, falling rocks are quite common throughout the park. This can lead to rocks tumbling down on you from above or rocks slipping out from under you as you hike, resulting in falls. You should be especially cognizant of this along the Grand Canyon of the Yellowstone. In 2012, a new employee on her first day in the park stepped off the marked trail and fell to her death in the canyon when a rock she was sitting on broke loose. Others have been killed when rocks hit them on the head after they fell from above.

Driving: Many of the deaths in the park result from inattentive driving and/or collisions with animals, especially at night. The speed limit throughout the park is 45mph (72kph) unless posted otherwise, though you are encouraged to drive under the speed limit through the Hayden Valley and Lamar Valley areas at night due to the potential presence of the bison. They are extremely difficult to see in the dark, and you likely may not see one standing in the middle of the road until you hit it. Several are killed and injured each year from motor vehicle strikes. Running into a bison will destroy even the largest SUV, often injuring or killing its passengers.

Note that if you're driving slower than the posted speed, you are required to pull over in one of the pullouts and allow traffic behind you to pass (it's also just good common courtesy). Failure to do so often results in other drivers attempting to pass slow vehicles in places where it is dangerous to do so. Several major accidents occur each summer from people who attempt to pass against the double yellow lines.

Boating/Swimming: The water in the park's lakes and rivers is generally very cold most of the year. In Yellowstone Lake, for example, the water temperatures will range from 30°F (-1°C) in June to around 60°F (16°C) in late August. Therefore, it is not safe to spend much time in the water. There are two sanctioned swimming areas in the park, one at Boiling River north of Mammoth and the other just above Firehole Falls south of Madison. Diving into park waters anywhere in the park is prohibited and extremely unsafe.

Park regulations require all boats to have flotation devices for every person on board, and all boats are required to be registered with and licensed by the park. Boats must be in good working order, and you should be cognizant of the weather outlook, especially during the latter part of the summer. It is not uncommon at all for sudden storms to come up over Yellowstone Lake. There have been dozens of people killed through drownings and boating accidents throughout the park's history (in fact, drowning is the second leading cause of fatalities within the park behind auto accidents).

In the event of an emergency on Yellowstone Lake, if you're equipped with a marine radio, the park rangers monitor Marine Channel 16. Also note the safety information about swimming outlined above. See the park's boating guide for additional safety information and regulations regarding the operation of boats and other watercraft on the park's waterways.

Altitude Sickness: Given that the average elevation of the park is around 8000 feet (2438 m) above sea level, it is not uncommon for visitors to experience what is known as high-altitude sickness. Largely the result of reduced oxygen in the atmosphere, it usually manifests itself in the form of headaches, muscle weakness, a bodywide dull pain, fatigue, nausea and vomiting, appetite loss, rapid heartbeat, and shortness of breath. It may take a few days to acclimate to the higher elevation. This can best be treated by staying hydrated, getting plenty of rest, and taking things easy your first few days in the park. If possible, spend a few days at a slightly lower elevation such as in Jackson, Bozeman, or Cody prior to arriving in Yellowstone. If you suffer from a history of cardiac or respiratory problems, seek advice from your doctor before traveling to Yellowstone.

Pets: As a general rule, it's a good idea to leave pets at home. If you do bring animals with you, however, you are required to keep them on a leash at all times when they're outside a vehicle. They're prohibited on the trails and boardwalks, and may not be taken into the backcountry. You are also required to clean up after your pet. Keep in mind that if your little puppy or kitty bolts and runs off into the woods, the coyotes or bears are liable to find it snackworthy. Pets are not allowed to stay in the lodge and hotel rooms, but may stay with you in a cabin at any of the park's lodging facilities for an additional fee. See Xanterra's Yellowstone web site for details.

First Aid/Medical Emergencies: Basic and advanced emergency medical services in the field are provided by the park's law enforcement rangers (all are required to be EMTs or paramedics). There are eight ambulances deployed throughout the park. If you are sick or injured and need medical assistance, contact the park's Communications Center at 9-1-1 and someone will be dispatched to assist you.

The park also has three medical clinics. The clinic at Mammoth is open year round, while the satellite clinics at Old Faithful and Lake Village area open during the summer only. If you become sick or have a minor medical issue, you may seek treatment at one of these facilities. The park's medical service provider, Medcor, accepts many insurance policies, but you may be required to pay up front for some treatments. And though the clinics do have basic pharmacy services available, you may need to travel to one of the gateway cities in order to fill some prescriptions (the closest pharmacy is in West Yellowstone).

If you experience a life-threatening emergency, the clinics will stabilize you and arrange for you to be transported to a hospital in Idaho Falls or Jackson. This may be via ground ambulance or via helicopter. Check with your insurance company before you travel to Yellowstone to determine whether a helicopter transport is covered, as these can be extremely expensive.

Firearms: As of 2010, it is legal to carry or transport firearms in and through Yellowstone National Park. Those who do carry are required to comply with the law of whichever state they're in at the time, however. Since the vast majority of the park is in Wyoming, those are the laws you'd need to be familiar with.

Wyoming law allows for open carry of handguns, as well as concealed carry if you are a Wyoming resident or have a permit from another state recognized by Wyoming. You are allowed to carry firearms into the backcountry.

Note that almost all facilities in the park specifically prohibit bringing firearms into the building, including the visitor centers, hotels, lodges, restaurants, stores, etc. See the park's website for specific information about this law and how it is applied within the park.

Weather: You'll often hear park employees state that there are three seasons in Yellowstone: July, August, and winter.[1] And while it is not terribly common, it's certainly not unheard of for it to snow in July or August. You are very likely to see the white stuff and its attendant cold temperatures in the park during June and September, as well as the other months of the year. Conversely, it is relatively rare for temperatures to climb above 90°F even during the hottest times of the year. During the summer, itinerant, pop-up thunderstorms are quite common, especially on the eastern side of the park and around the lake. These often bring strong winds and hail, as well as lightning. A lightning strike in the summer of 2010 injured over a dozen people at Old Faithful. If you see lightning in the area, get indoors and out of the open immediately.

The sun is another thing that many people don't factor into their visit. Since you're at a higher altitude than most of the rest of the country, you'll receive a much greater exposure to the sun. Always wear sunscreen, especially if you're out hiking. The humidity levels are typically very low in Yellowstone as well, so you'll want to use plenty of lotion and lip balm.

It is a good idea to bring clothing that can be layered. This way when you leave your hotel in the morning, you can be dressed for the 30-degree temperatures, but also be prepared for the 70s or 80s later that afternoon. This is especially important if you're going hiking into the higher elevations (including Mt. Washburn). Take rain gear with you (emergency ponchos are an excellent idea!) and be prepared by checking the weather forecast at the nearest visitor center or ranger station before you head out for the day.

The park has two NOAA Weather Radio transmitters. One is located in the Mammoth area (162.425MHz), while the other is located at Grant Village (162.450MHz).

Children: Keep your children with you at all times, and ensure they are aware of the dangers present in the park (consistent with their ability to understand the world around them). Many children have been scalded (and a handful killed) by falling into hot pools. Children may not have a full understanding of the dangers of approaching wildlife, either. And every summer, rangers deal with dozens of kids who end up getting separated from their parents. Don't let this happen to you!

PRIVACY OF PARK EMPLOYEES

Because of the lack of formal planning that took place during the park's early days, many structures within Yellowstone are right alongside park roads. Many of these are not public buildings and indeed may be residences for park staff. Unless a building is designated or marked as a public facility, do not enter any building without specific authorization from the National Park Service or the responsible concessioner. You are, of course, free to photograph the buildings, but please respect the privacy of those living and working in these facilities; it's their home.

PROTECTION OF ARCHAEOLOGICAL INFORMATION

The park is awash with archaeological sites. Any site where one of the early camps was established, where a road camp existed, where Native Americans camped, where old hotels existed, or where any human activity might have occurred may be considered to be of actual or potential historical significance. The NPS has asked that I not publish information about the specific locations of these types of sites, and I have wholeheartedly agreed not to do so (with the exception of material that is widely published in other books, documents, or on the Internet).

The sad reality is that, while the vast majority of people would be content with simply visiting a site and enjoying its historical context, others would seek to steal and pilfer material that might be found at those locations. Like many others with a deep attachment to the park, I believe that every aspect of the park should be protected from such intrusions where possible, and so we must resort to dealing with the lowest common denominator.

As a result, you'll see references to the general locations of old camps, old buildings and developments, and other such sites. I've not provided GPS coordinates or other information necessary to afford the average person the ability to locate most of these places. If you're interested in conducting research into the archaeology of the park, you should contact the park's Cultural Resources Branch at the Yellowstone Center for Resources.

MATERIAL NOT COVERED IN THIS BOOK

The intent of this guide is to provide information about the various features found along the park's roadways and in its developments, and provide some historical context behind them. As a result, little time is spent covering material that is easily found in other books or materials widely available elsewhere. Adding in-depth discussions on all of these features would result in a book three to four times the size of this one, and would be unnecessarily duplicative. Here are some books I highly recommend on those subjects:

Geology: While some minor details of the park's geology are discussed where a particular feature is geologic in nature, there is no attempt to discuss the rich geologic underpinnings of Yellowstone or its related volcanic and seismic infrastructure. The 311-page *Roadside Geology of Yellowstone Country*, by authors William J. Fritz and Dr. Robert C. Thomas, provides an outstanding reference on this subject. The book can be found in the park's bookstores.

Thermal Features: While this book provides some details on how many of the park's thermal areas and thermal features are named, as well as basic information about their temperature, eruption cycles (for geysers), and the like, there are other books and guides produced by the NPS and various authors that are better suited for gaining an in-depth understanding of these geologic wonders. Perhaps the most robust and well-known book is T. Scott Bryan's *The Geysers of Yellowstone, Fourth Edition*. It, too, may be found in stores throughout the park.

Trails: A basic summary of each trail is provided where the trailheads are found along the park's roadways. Detailed information about the hundreds of trails can be found in numerous books, however, including *Hiking Yellowstone National Park*, by Bill Schneider, and *Yellowstone Trails: A Hiking Guide*, written by Mark and Joy Marschall (both former Yellowstone rangers) and published by the Yellowstone Association.

History: Much of the material herein is historical in nature. In fact, the entire idea of this book is to provide a micro-history of many of the points of interest that can be found along the park's roads and within its developed areas. If you're interested in a more robust, general history of the park, there are several books and publications you might find of interest. The first is *The Yellowstone Story, Volumes I & II*, by the park's first and longest-serving historian, Aubrey Haines. Haines traces the park's history from its pre-existence (Volume I) through its founding and development up through the 1970s (Volume II). Current historian Lee Whittlesey has also been a very prolific writer, and you can find many of his books on Yellowstone in any of the park's bookstores and gift shops, as well as on Amazon's website.

NPS historian Mary S. Culpin has produced three fascinating documents relative to park history. One is a history of the development of the road system within the park (*A History of the Construction of the Road System in Yellowstone National Park, 1872-1966*), another is a history of the development of the administration of the park (*Managing the "Matchless Wonders." A History of Administrative Development in Yellowstone National Park, 1872-1965*), and the third is a history of concession operations within the park (*For the Benefit and Enjoyment of the People: A History of Concession Development in Yellowstone National Park, 1872-1966*). All three of these can be found online, and all were used rather extensively in the research for this book.

Popular Features: There is also little in-depth discussion of the more common "primary" features within the park (e.g., the major waterfalls, mountains, etc.). There are reams of material produced by the NPS and others that discuss these and there is little purpose served by repeating that information here.

HISTORICAL SOURCES/DISAGREEMENTS

A variety of sources were used in the production of this book. These include everything from the bible of Yellowstone history, Aubrey Haines' two-volume set, to material produced by a number of amateur historians with some connection to the park. Reams of material from the park's archives were also used.

Even within material produced by the same authors and sources there is often some disagreement on dates, facts, and figures. This has confounded park historians for years. In much of Lee Whittlesey's material, he frequently notes that even original sources differ regarding the facts when it comes to matters of historical note. Material produced by Haines himself has been found to be less than 100% accurate. Much of this can be attributed to a lack of good recordkeeping by early park managers and concession operators.

I've attempted to explain the discrepancies where necessary (usually via endnotes), and have relied on material produced by Whittlesey, or Xanterra Interpretation Chief Leslie Quinn (who's responsible for teaching their tour guides), followed by material produced by Haines or Culpin or that discovered through my own personal review of archive material (which is occasionally at odds with all of the aforementioned sources). Basically, I have assumed that the park's current historians are more knowledgeable about any specific set of facts, given that they've been able to digest older material and examine newer material within that context to come up with a more accurate picture.

Symbols Used in this Book

⬤	Amphitheater	🔭	Overlook
🔧	Auto Repairs	P	Parking Area/Lot
🚗	Auto Tour	🏕	Picnic Area
🚲	Bicycling Trail	🏕	Picnic Area - Covered
🛥	Boat Launch	✱	Point of Interest
⛺	Campground	✉	Post Office
✚	Clinic/First Aid	🏠	Ranger Station
🎣	Fishing	♻	Recycling Center
🍴	Food/Restaurant	🚻	Restrooms - Public
⛽	Fuel/Gas Station	🚐	RV Campground
🛒	Groceries	🚍	RV Dump Station
🚶	Hiking Trail	🚤	Scenic Boat Cruises
🐎	Horse Rental/Tours	🚶	Self-Guided Tour
H	Hospital	🚿	Showers
ⓘ	Information	⛷	Ski Trail
🛶	Kayak/Canoe Launch	🍴	Snacks/Snack Bar
📷	Laundry	🏊	Swimming
🛏	Lodging	☎	Telephone
⚓	Marina	♿	Wheelchair Access
🔭	Observation Tower	🔭	Wildlife Viewing

Road Logs

Anyone who works in Yellowstone and has a job that involves contact with the public is invariably on the receiving end of a variety of questions about what lies along the park's roadways. These range from, "Which geyser basin are we in?" to "What's down that gated-off road just north of here?" With almost 400 miles of publicly-accessible roadway throughout the park, there are hundreds of points of interest that capture the imagination of visitors and employees alike. So it is helpful to have a guide that explains what each of these is and provides a small tidbit of history behind them where possible.

The following sections provide a mile-by-mile guide to the park's public road system. This includes the nine segments of the Figure-8 Grand Loop Road (GLR), the five entrance roads, U.S. Highway 191 through the park's northwest corner, and several scenic side roads. The book assumes an initial entrance into the park at the North Entrance at Gardiner, and proceeds around the park in a clockwise fashion. Each of the other entrance roads is included where they intersect with the Grand Loop Road, and there is a special section dedicated specifically to the side roads.

Mileage figures for each road begin at zero based on this paradigm. Mileage for each GLR segment is measured from the end of the last segment. For each of the entrance roads, the originating mileage is shown from the boundary of the park so that a visitor entering via those roads can instantly pick up reading from that point and begin clockwise travel from its intersection with the Grand Loop Road. Reverse mileage is also provided so the guide can be used regardless of which direction you're traveling. The only exception to this is where the road is designated as one-way.

Global Positioning System (GPS) coordinates are also provided in decimal degrees for each reference point. For those features or turnouts with two entry points less than ¹⁄₁₀ of a mile apart, the GPS coordinates are provided for the midpoint between the two. A directional indicator is used where necessary to indicate which side of the road a particular point of interest is located.

Mileage is indicated from the center point of each junction, so you'll want to zero out your odometer as you travel through the middle of the intersection. Given that each individual might reset an odometer at a slightly different point, and the need to round off mileage measurements to a usable figure, you may find that a specific feature is located slightly before or slightly past the indicated mileage in these logs. Keep this in mind as you approach each point. If in doubt, rely on the GPS coordinates.

The indicated mileage may differ slightly from figures provided in other guidance or other guide books. The figures used herein are based on precise measurements obtained from the park's Geographic Information System and verified with a second mapping system, then confirmed through being overlaid on top of Google Earth and re-measured. A typical entry would look like this:

1.7 / 3.5 GPS: 45.01038, -110.69391
North End of Gardner Canyon
Eagle's Nest Rock (E)
Split Rock (W)

In the example above, you'd be 1.7 miles from the junction you just left and 3.5 miles from the next junction (or the reverse of that if you were traveling from the other direction). At this point, you'd be at the north end of Gardner Canyon, Eagle's Nest Rock would be on the east side of the road, and Split Rock would be on the west side of the road. The latitude and longitude would be as indicated.

A Brief History of Road Development in Yellowstone

In order to better understand why some points are located where they are, or why some features are named as they are, it is helpful to have a basic understanding of how the road system as we know it today came to be. What follows is a very brief overview of the history of the park's road network. National Park Service historian Mary S. Culpin prepared a voluminous backgrounder on the park's roads as a prelude to the massive rebuilding program undertaken by the Federal Highway Administration in the late 1980s. Her work was also used to support the preparation of the documentation necessary to have the Grand Loop Road designated as a National Historic District in 2003. The document and related material can be found on the National Park Service's web site.

The first roads into Yellowstone National Park were built by private individuals. The original road to Mammoth Hot Springs was a toll road built from Bozeman through Yankee Jim Canyon. Completed in 1873, James "Yankee Jim" George charged travelers a toll (which varied according to his mood at the time) to pass through to the park. He was able to continue this for almost 20 years before Park County bought the road from him for $1000 and removed the requirement to pay for the privilege of passing through.

Also that year, the town of Virginia City, then the capitol of the Montana Territory, hired rancher Gilman Sawtell to build a road into the west side of the park. This road passed along what is today the route of the West Entrance Road to Madison Junction, and then followed the Firehole River south to the Fountain Flats area where George Marshall had constructed a hotel and mail station. In contrast to the road to Mammoth, there were no tolls along this new route and the road became known as the Virginia City and National Park Free Road. There are some who assert that the lack of tolls was not the result of any real benevolence, but rather the fact that it was impossible to keep travelers from circumventing any toll booths that would have been erected. This would have made any attempts to impose a toll a waste of time.

Following the creation of Yellowstone in 1872, the park's first superintendent, Nathaniel P. Langford, requested funds from Congress to build roads inside the park. He had envisioned a "circuit road" that connected all of the park's major points of interest. Despite repeated requests, however, no monies were appropriated for any purpose. But while no official roads were constructed, several bridal paths and makeshift roads from one point to another popped up around the park. This included a dirt path from what became known as the town of Gardiner to the Cooke City mines via what is today the Northeast Entrance. It was along this trail that C. J. "Jack" Baronett constructed his toll bridge over the Yellowstone River.

In 1877, the park's second superintendent took charge. Philetus W. Norris would have more success than his predecessor in securing funding and began construction of some primitive roads. This included roads between Mammoth Hot Springs and the Upper Geyser Basin. Norris also believed in the concept of a circuit road connecting the park's major features.[1]

The year 1877 also saw the Nez Perce flight through Yellowstone. To support his pursuit of the Native Americans through the park, General O. O. Howard constructed a road from the west side of the park to the east side. As the road crossed over Mary Mountain (which, along with a

Old road in Yellowstone, ca. 1880s.

lake of the same name, was named after Mary Clark, a young woman who was a member of a tourist party that passed through the area in 1873), it became known as the Mary Mountain Road. In the aftermath of the short-lived incursion, the road was used by tourists who wished to see the lake and the waterfalls in the Grand Canyon of the Yellowstone. The road was used until the early 1890s when the new road between Old Faithful and West Thumb was constructed. Today, the old road is a foot trail known as the Nez Perce Creek Trail or the Mary Mountain Trail.

Norris was able to secure $10000 from Congress in 1878, and immediately set out building a primitive road between Mammoth and the Upper Geyser Basin. Though this was done primarily to support movement of the military from Fort Ellis (MT) to eastern Idaho and the Henry's Fork area (Norris was tremendously concerned about Indian attacks, given the recent incursion by the Nez Perce), it also afforded access to the thermal areas for the visitors who were able to find their way to the park.

This first road traveled along Clematis Gulch, up through Snow Pass and onto Swan Lake Flat, then southward to the Beaver Lake area generally along the route of the current road. From there, it traveled east of today's road, past Lake of the Woods and along what is today a foot path known as the Solfatara Creek Trail to Norris Geyser Basin. It would continue south along the east side of Gibbon Canyon, then on to an area south of present day Madison Junction along what has become known as the Mesa Service Road. From there it headed south to Fountain Flat, where it intersected with the road from Virginia City built by Sawtell. Continuing south, one would pass the intersection with the Army-built Mary Mountain Road, and then through the geyser basins, finally arriving at Old Faithful.[2]

Norris would also go on to explore the possibility of constructing a road between Tower Fall and the Canyon area. His travels would take him along the eastern face of Mt. Washburn, and though there'd always be a foot trail along this part of his route, the new road would eventually be built through the pass along the western flank of the mountain (today's Dunraven Pass Road). The westernmost pass was picked because it would be easier to build a road through it, and would allow for the construction of a road to the summit of Washburn, something that was desired at the time.

In 1880, Norris, in concert with the private enterprise that held the mail delivery contract between Virginia City and Mammoth, would construct a new route between the west entrance and the Lower Geyser Basin. This new road would depart from the existing road approximately four miles east of the park boundary and would travel southward over the Madison Plateau before terminating near the site of the old Marshall Hotel (which at the time also included a mail station). The new road had the advantage of not being waterlogged for much of the year and would be used until the U.S. Army Corps of Engineers constructed a new road through Madison Canyon in 1900.

For the next couple of years road work was limited primarily to maintenance of existing roads or the construction of bridges and minor bypasses. In 1882, Norris would be replaced as superintendent and with the exception of a short stretch of road near the canyon's waterfalls, no significant road work was done until the following year when the U.S. Army Corps of Engineers (USACE) was placed in charge of all road building and maintenance activities within the park. This would set the stage for the development of the road system in Yellowstone as we currently know it, and would establish design principles used to integrate roads into national park landscapes to this day.

In August of 1883, Army Engineer Lt. Daniel Kingman arrived in the park and set out immediately repairing old roads. He would also begin surveying routes for a road system that would connect the park's major attractions, much as what Nathaniel Langford had described during his tenure as head of the park. This road design would, with a few minor exceptions, go on to become the Figure-8 Grand Loop Road still in place today. Kingman also believed the roads should "lay lightly upon the land," a design tenet that is reflected throughout the national park system to this day.

First Golden Gate Viaduct, constructed by Lt. Dan Kingman, ca. 1900

Among Kingman's many accomplishments within the park is the road through Golden Gate Canyon south of Mammoth. At the time, stagecoaches had to climb a rather steep hill to get through Snow Pass, and this often resulted in teamsters (and often passengers) having to stop and unload supplies and luggage from the coaches so the horses could pull the wagons up the hills. Kingman designed and built the first (wooden) viaduct around the canyon wall. Though the bridge has been replaced a couple of times since, the path through Golden Gate is still considered to be one of the most spectacular parts of a trip through Yellowstone. The pass is named Kingman Pass in his honor.

A series of engineers would follow Kingman over the next four years until 1891, when Lt. Hiram M. Chittenden would be assigned to the park for his first tour of duty. He'd serve for two years, leave, and then return (as a Captain and later Major) from 1899 until 1906. Chittenden would go on to be associated with many major improvements and road construction projects throughout the park. These include the road to the summit of Mt. Washburn, completion of the road over Dunraven Pass, the road between Old Faithful and West Thumb, the East Entrance Road, and the construction of the first bridge over the Yellowstone River just above the Upper Falls (the replacement for which is named in his honor).

He'd also instigate several programs to improve the management of the roads, including the use of distributed road camps. These camps, later known as "engineering stations" once the NPS took over management of the park, housed work crews and equipment, and were spaced every 8-10 miles along the park's major roads. These crews would ensure the sections of road assigned to them were kept clear, sprinkled or oiled (to reduce the dust), and ice/snow free during the park's random snowfall events. Chittenden was also the first to install mileposts indicating the distance between major points of interest throughout the park. This book is named for those posts.

A sea change in road construction and maintenance came about in 1916 when automobiles were allowed into the park. Though horses and autos were both allowed to use the roads during that first season, it soon became obvious that was not going to be a tenable solution (horses didn't react well to the spitting and sputtering of the cars, and the road design just didn't accommodate vehicles very well). With the advent of the creation of the National Park Service that year, and its subsequent assumption of the management of the park a couple of years later, the improvement of the roads and tourist support facilities took on a more central focus. But with the exception of a few realignments, the vast majority of the road projects during this period were improvements to existing sections of road or construction of appurtenances tangential to the roads themselves.

In 1923, the U.S. Bureau of Public Roads (BPR), a division of the Department of Agriculture at the time, conducted a survey of the entire road system throughout the park.[3] This was done as part of a nationwide survey of roads on all federally-owned lands. Shortly after this, the BPR and NPS began a series of discussions about the former assuming responsibility for the road system in the western parks. Yellowstone Superintendent, and Deputy Director of the National Park Service, Horace Albright was initially opposed to this idea. He was concerned that, because BPR road construction standards were higher than those of the NPS, it would cost much more to build them in the parks than the NPS had been used to spending. On top of that, BPR had little experience building roads that meshed with a national park landscape. Eventually, the two agencies reached an agreement whereby BPR would allow NPS to approve design specifications and perform landscaping work. Thus, in 1926, the BPR and NPS signed a memorandum of agreement (MOA) that allowed the highway agency to manage the major road construction projects in Yellowstone and other western parks.

This MOA remains in force today with BPR's successor organization, the Federal Highway Administration (FHWA), now within the Department of Transportation. The FHWA has a field office in Yellowstone, in fact, that oversees all major road construction projects within the park (and Grand Teton). Under the agreement, FHWA designs the roads and manages the projects to build them, while NPS handles the landscaping and other adjunct projects that allow the road to harmonize with the natural landscape present in the park.[4]

With the newly minted agreement in place, BPR set out developing plans to reconstruct the entire road system throughout the park, a process that began in earnest in the late 1920s and wasn't completed until just before World War II. Many of the projects involved realignments of major segments of roads; many of the scars from these old roads remain visible today and are pointed out in the road logs that follow. A large pool of funding for these projects came from Roosevelt's various "New Deal" agencies created in the midst of the Great Depression, and with road crew and Civilian Conservation Corps camps spread out all over the park, Yellowstone was quite the busy place. The final segment wasn't completed until 1941 with the paving of the road between Old Faithful and West Thumb. Upon its completion, the Figure-8 Grand Loop Road as you drive it today was largely completed (with a few minor realignments discussed below).

There'd be no further modifications to the roads within the park until the late 1950s, when NPS Director Conrad Wirth conceived of and implemented a major road and facility building program known as Mission 66. It was designed to improve the facilities in the nation's parks in time for the 50th anniversary of the National Park Service in 1966. In Yellowstone, the first manifestation of the program was Canyon Village. Two other commercial developments were supposed to have been completed as part of this as well. One of these, Grant Village, began as part of the program, but financial and political issues delayed its completion until well into the 1980s. The other, Firehole Village, which was designed to relocate the development at Old Faithful away from the thermal area, never made it off the drawing board.

In addition to the new buildings and facilities, the Mission 66 Program saw the reconstruction of many intersections and the removal of roads from thermal and other sensitive areas throughout the park. The road through Norris Geyser Basin was relocated eastward; bypasses were constructed at Old Faithful, Lake Village, and West Thumb; and new road segments were built away from problem areas such as Firehole Canyon Drive and Virginia Cascade Drive. And of course, the new Canyon Junction was created to facilitate traffic flow into and out of the new commercial development there. And though the Mission 66 Program was cancelled in 1964, many of these projects weren't completed until well into the 1970s.

In the late 1980s, the Federal Highway Administration began another survey of the park's roads and undertook planning to rebuild the road system to meet new design standards. The existing road network was largely a product of 50-year old technology and was having trouble keeping up with the increasing traffic loads. The process culminated in a plan known as the *Parkwide Road Improvement Plan*, a 20-year project to rebuild the park's primary road network. Despite taking several years longer than anticipated (almost entirely due to budget issues), most of the roads are now in decent shape. There are two segments that have yet to be rebuilt. The first is the road between Norris Junction and Mammoth Hot Springs. Though it has been resurfaced several times, the road itself is still the remnant of the 1930s rebuild that took place under the old BPR. The project to reconstruct it will begin in 2014 and last from six to eight years. After that, the next road to be rebuilt will be the North Entrance Road.

As you drive around the park, you'll see remnants of the old road system here and there if you know what you're looking at. This book is intended to help explain what those are and why other places of interest exist where they do. Almost all of it can be traced back to a piece of road history in one form or another, and knowing why things are where they are helps you appreciate the park's robust history just a little bit more.

TERMINOLOGY

There are several terms used throughout this book that you should be familiar with.

Pullouts vs. Turnouts: These terms, though often used interchangeably in many documents, have specific meanings herein. Pullouts are basically single- or double-lane areas on the side of the main road designed to allow a vehicle(s) to pull off the road and allow traffic to pass. A turnout, on the other hand, is a larger, more formal area designed to allow for parking of multiple vehicles, and is usually (though not always) separated from the main traffic pattern by a berm or barrier of some type.

Road Camps vs. Engineering Stations: From the early 1900s through the late 1930s, a series of road camps was established throughout the park, at intervals of roughly eight to ten miles or so. These camps housed men and equipment necessary to maintain sections of roadways, ensuring they were graded, cleared of snow or debris, and for many years, sprinkled with water or oil to help keep the dust down. For a period of time, the NPS referred to these as "Engineering Stations," and some maps from the 1920s-1930s use that term in lieu of "Road Camp." They are one and the same, however, and the term "Road Camp" is used herein to indicate where those camps were located.

Road camps were used to house road crews and equipment in the days before mechanized road machinery was widely available. Without the capabilities we have today, it was necessary to have a contingent of men spaced every few miles so they could perform the almost continual maintenance activities necessary to keep the roads passable. Once the various road segments were rebuilt and paved with asphalt, and modern road building equipment became available, it was no longer necessary to house the crews every 8-10 miles. The camps were abandoned and the buildings torn down. Little evidence can be found of these camps today, but their locations are noted on the road logs in the following sections.

Snow Poles

As you travel through the park from opening day through June, you'll notice the thin fiberglass poles sticking out of the ground along the roadside. These are snow poles, used to delineate the sides of the road and obstructions for the road maintenance crews as they plow and maintain the roads during the winter (and clear them in the spring). These poles will disappear for a couple of months, and then begin reappearing in mid- to late-August as crews prepare for the upcoming winter. It takes several weeks to deploy the tens of thousands of poles all over the park and the seasonal road crew personnel leave Yellowstone by the first of October, so they have to get an early start in order to get as much done before the season comes to an end, and the park's maintenance staff is reduced to a bare minimum.

The poles are different colors depending on what they're being used to mark. The orange poles delineate the edge of the road; yellow poles mark obstructions such as signs, rocks and small boulders, curbs, raised sidewalks, etc.; blue poles mark water system valves, meters, and other equipment, and so forth.

Mileage Chart

On the following page, you'll find a chart showing the mileage between all of the major intersections within the park. The figures assume the shortest route possible is used to move from one point to the other.

Yellowstone Mileage Chart

	North Entrance	Mammoth Hot Springs	Tower Junction	Northeast Entrance	Canyon Junction	Fishing Bridge	East Entrance	West Thumb Junction	South Entrance	Old Faithful	Madison Junction	West Entrance	Norris Junction
North Entrance		5.2	23.3	51.9	41.6	57.0	82.9	77.6	99.0	55.3	39.4	53.3	26.1
Mammoth Hot Springs	5.2		18.1	46.7	36.4	51.8	77.7	72.4	93.8	50.1	34.2	48.1	20.9
Tower Junction	23.3	18.1		28.6	18.3	33.7	59.6	54.3	75.7	59.0	43.1	57.0	29.8
Northeast Entrance	51.9	46.7	28.6		46.9	62.3	88.2	82.9	104.3	87.6	71.7	85.6	58.4
Canyon Junction	41.6	36.4	18.3	46.9		15.4	51.3	36.0	57.4	40.7	24.8	38.7	11.5
Fishing Bridge	57.0	51.8	33.7	62.3	15.4		25.9	20.6	45.0	52.6	40.2	54.1	26.9
East Entrance	82.8	77.7	59.6	88.2	51.3	25.9		46.5	67.9	64.1	66.1	80.0	52.8
West Thumb Junction	77.6	72.4	54.3	82.9	36.0	20.6	46.5		21.4	17.6	33.5	47.4	46.8
South Entrance	99.0	93.8	75.7	104.3	57.4	45.0	67.9	21.4		39.0	54.9	68.8	68.2
Old Faithful	55.3	50.1	59.0	87.6	40.7	52.6	64.1	17.6	39.0		15.9	29.8	29.2
Madison Junction	39.4	34.2	43.1	71.7	24.8	40.2	66.1	33.5	54.9	15.9		13.9	13.3
West Entrance	53.3	48.1	57.0	85.6	38.7	54.1	80.0	47.4	68.8	29.8	13.9		27.2
Norris Junction	26.1	20.9	29.8	58.4	11.5	26.9	52.8	46.8	68.2	29.2	13.3	27.2	

North
Entrance Road
—————————⊸○⟆⟊⟦○⊸—————————

The North Entrance Road is five miles (8 km) long from the Roosevelt Arch to its intersection with the Grand Loop Road in front of the Mammoth Hot Springs Hotel. The current road takes you through Gardner Canyon and along the Gardner River, one of the many scenic waterways to be found within the park.

As this route was among the earliest used to access the park by visitors, it is rich with history. The current road generally follows the third road built between what is now Gardiner, Montana, and the park's headquarters at Mammoth. The second route, now known as the Gardiner High Road, remains accessible as a scenic side road, affording high views of Electric Peak, Mt. Everts, Bunsen Peak, and the other scenery that rings the area. There's a 1000-foot (304 m) drop in elevation as you leave the little development at Mammoth and arrive at the arch, regardless of which path you choose.

In the early days of the park, this entrance was easily the most used route into Yellowstone. The Northern Pacific Railroad Depot, first in Cinnabar and then in Gardiner, brought visitors by the thousands each summer to see the park known around the world as *Wonderland*. The government established a headquarters at Mammoth (later used and greatly expanded by the U.S. Army), and began building a series of roads into the depths of the park to allow visitors access to its thermal features, canyons, lakes, and other points of interest.

Today, this is the third most used entrance into the park (the West Entrance is the most popular, followed by South). As you travel along the road, keep your eyes open for elk, pronghorn antelope, and, as you travel through Gardner Canyon, bighorn sheep. This road is winding and steep in places, and there's a section known as Soap Hill because of how slick it gets when it's wet. So while you're driving, be sure and keep your eyes firmly on the road. If you see something you wish to examine more closely, pull off the road where it is safe to do so to avoid interfering with the flow of traffic.

As you begin your trip to Mammoth, one of the first things you'll notice is the large complex on the north side of the road just inside the arch. This is the old Yellowstone Park Transportation Company complex, much of which was constructed in the mid-1920s. This was the area from which the concession tour buses would leave to pick up tourists arriving at the Gardiner Railroad Depot. From here, they'd take the tourists to the Mammoth Hot Springs Hotel to begin their journey through the park. Today, this complex is used primarily by Xanterra, the park's lodging, restaurant, and tour concessioner, and is the check-in point for as many as 3000 seasonal park employees every spring. See the Gardiner and North Entrance Development Section for additional details on these buildings.

From here, you'll pass through the north entrance gate, travel along the Gardner River, and pass the site where a garden was operated to supply U.S. Army personnel and the park's hotels with fresh vegetables year round. You'll also pass Boiling River, a hot spring that is one of only two sanctioned swimming areas in the park. From there, you'll continue up past the Mammoth Campground and a large employee housing complex, and arrive in Mammoth Hot Springs.

0.0 / 5.2 GPS: 45.02963, -110.70888 ELEVATION: 5318 FEET
NORTH ENTRANCE – ROOSEVELT ARCH 🏞
ARCH PARK (N) 🏕🖼
XANTERRA HEADQUARTERS AND WAREHOUSE COMPLEX (E)
GARDINER MEADOW (W) 🚶

The imposing **Roosevelt Arch** marks your entry into Yellowstone National Park at its north boundary. Built in 1903, it is slightly skewed so that it faces what is now the Heritage and Research Center (HRC), necessitating a somewhat awkward, blind turn if you're approaching from the east. At the time of its construction, the Northern Pacific Railroad Depot was located where the small Park County building is today (south of the football field), and the Arch was built as the grand entrance for those arriving via train. No one envisioned the automobile becoming the primary means of travel into and through the park, or that train service would eventually be discontinued (the depot was razed in 1954). At the time, it was believed the relatively bland and uninspiring northern entrance to the park needed a grand visual statement for arriving visitors, so the concept of the grand arch was developed.[1]

The 50-foot tall Arch gets its name from President Theodore Roosevelt, who laid the cornerstone for the structure on April 24, 1903, while he was vacationing in the park. You can easily pick out the cornerstone, located on the inside of the right column (looking at it from the Gardiner side); it bears the inscription "April 24, 1903."

A common question asked of rangers and other employees is what lies behind the doors on either side of the vehicle passageway. The answer is nothing. These were originally walkthroughs for pedestrians, but they were closed for safety reasons after a rape occurred in one in the 1930s. The center roadway opening is 25 feet wide by 35 feet tall.

The small park/picnic area located across the road to the north of the arch is known as **Arch Park**. It is a restoration of the original park that was located here when the arch was constructed. It re-opened in 2000 and now has seven picnic tables, and a covered picnic shelter.

The small pullout on the west side of the road after you pass through the Arch was the site of the first check-in stations for the park. The original station (built in 1921, to replace a tent that was being used) burned in 1937, and a replacement was constructed on the same site. These early stations presented a somewhat awkward situation for those entering in automobiles. Since the station was on the right side of the vehicle, the driver had to lean across the passenger seat to transact business with the ranger. Over time, the entrance stations have been relocated to a variety of sites until 1991 when the present kiosk was constructed.

The large field on the east side of the road is known colloquially as **The Triangle**. For a period of time after the Arch was built, this area was used to grow alfalfa to feed the bison, pronghorn, and other wildlife. This practice has long since been discontinued, however. In the 1890s, this area was the home to a horse racing track built by early park concessioner James McCartney (see the entry for the McCartney Hotel in the Mammoth Hot Springs Development section of Part II).

On the opposite side of the Triangle is a building complex that houses two of the park's primary concession operators, Xanterra (hotels and lodges, campgrounds, restaurants, transportation, and several other services) and the Yellowstone Park Service Stations (YPSS). The complex includes warehouses, offices, a bunkhouse for employees, and several residential structures that house senior managers of the concessioners and NPS staff. See the Gardiner and North Entrance Development section in Part II for details on these buildings and their history. Most of these structures date to the mid-1920s when one of Xanterra's predecessors, the Yellowstone Park Transportation Company, built the complex to house and manage the buses and other vehicles they used to transport visitors around the park. The area is now a historic district.

As you drive the quarter of a mile between the Arch and the North Entrance Station, keep your eyes open for the pronghorn antelope, elk, and bison that frequent the flats on the west side of the road (known as **Gardiner Meadow**). If you wish to stop and photograph them, be sure to pull off to the side of the road so that others can pass unhindered.

0.4 / 4.8 GPS: 45.02571, -110.70151
ROBERT REAMER AVENUE - SERVICE ROAD (N)

The service road that runs north from here is known as **Robert Reamer Avenue**, named after the famous architect of the Old Faithful Inn and several other buildings within the park (including several of the structures located along this road). This is primarily an access road for employees of the concession companies that have offices in the building complex described above.

By the way, if you try to go around the line of cars backed up at the North Entrance Station via this road during the summer, you'll usually be asked to turn around and come back up the North Entrance Road from the Arch.

0.5 / 4.7 GPS: 45.02528, -110.70083
NORTH ENTRANCE STATION 🏠
OLD GARDINER HIGH ROAD (W) 🚲

This the **North Entrance Station**, where you'll be greeted by a uniformed visitor services representative of the National Park Service, and asked to pay your entrance fee or show your pass. Once you've paid, hang onto your receipt – you'll need it to get back in the park (and may be asked to show it on the way out). You'll be provided with the park's newspaper, a map, and any other relevant information related to road construction, road closures, or any other situation that might impact your ability to move about the park efficiently. You are welcome to ask any questions, but be mindful of any traffic behind you, especially during the busy summer season.

The small building here was constructed in 1991, the latest in a long series of buildings used to control entrance into the park at this location. During the peak of the summer season, another, smaller temporary structure is added to help facilitate traffic flow and cut down on congestion. Current plans call for a reconfiguration of the entire area, and include an expanded entrance complex to help alleviate these problems.

Just past the Entrance Kiosk, on the west, is the exit from the old **Gardiner Road** (also known as the Gardiner High Road because it went over higher ground en route to Gardiner). This is a one way road (two-way for bicycles) that comes from Mammoth (behind the hotel), and is only open during the dry months of the summer season. It was one of the original routes people used to get from one place to the other, but was relegated to back up status once the road through Gardner Canyon (roughly today's road) was constructed in 1884.

If you walk out into the field immediately to the east of the Entrance Kiosk, you can still find traces of the very first road leading from (what would become) Gardiner up into Shooting Range Flat (see below), and would connect into the old Turkey Pen Road as it took traffic toward Cooke City. See the section on the Mammoth to Tower Falls Road for more information about Turkey Pen Road (at the entry for Blacktail Deer Creek Trailhead).

0.8 / 4.4 GPS: 45.02096, -110.69714
MIGRATING ANIMALS PULLOUT (E) 🔭 🧍

This turnout has a couple of interpretive panels about Yellowstone's Northern Range and the migration of wildlife through the area. The Northern Range includes the Yellowstone River Valley from this area through the Lamar Valley in the northeastern section of the park.

1.1 / 4.1 GPS: 45.01770, -110.69385
RESCUE CREEK WEST TRAILHEAD (E) 🥾
SHOOTING RANGE FLAT/McMINN BENCH (E)

The **Rescue Creek Trail** has its western terminus here. It is a 7.7-mile (12.5 km) trail that connects with the Blacktail Creek Trail, which has its trailhead on the Mammoth to Tower Road east of the Wraith Falls Trailhead. Much of the trail is what remains of the old Turkey Pen Road, a miner's road that led from this area to Cooke City at the park's northeast entrance.

Rescue Creek got its name through a misunderstanding. It was the mistaken belief of Ferdinand Hayden that Truman Everts had been found along this creek (which is a couple of miles up the trail), when in actuality he was found near Tower Creek on the park's eastern side. Everts became lost on one of the early expeditions through the park, and wandered the wilderness for 37 days before being found.[2] His story is told in the book, *Lost in the Yellowstone: Truman Everts' "Thirty-Seven Days of Peril."*

The large expanse of flat land across the river from you was originally a rifle range for the U.S. Army during its tenure in the park (1886-1916). When the Army left, the land was used as a golf course for park employees from 1920-1940 (known as the Antelope Golf Course). Today, locals know the area as **"Shooting Range Flat."** If you hike about a third of a mile out on the Rescue Creek Trail, you'll still be able to see the trenches used by the target operators in the fields to the north. To the south from the Flat, you see a ridge known as **McMinn Bench.** It is named after Silas McMinn, a gentleman who operated a coal mine at its base from 1883 until 1920. The NPS rehabilitated the mine in 1993, however, so little trace of it remains.

1.7 / 3.5 GPS: 45.01038, -110.69391
NORTH END OF GARDNER CANYON
EAGLE'S NEST ROCK (E) 🔭🥾
SPLIT ROCK (W) 🔭

This is the north end of **Gardner Canyon.** As you pass over the bridge (built in 1957), notice the tall rock spire on the east side of the road (look high up). This is **Eagle Nest Rock.** Like many other features of the park, it got its name early on. In reality, the birds that build nests on these spires are osprey, or fish hawks, not eagles, though. Check to see if birds are nesting there, and if so, you might have the opportunity to watch them dive into the river below to catch fish.

On the opposite side of the road in the river, you'll see a large boulder that rolled down the hill and into the water, splitting down the middle. It should come as no surprise to you that the rock is often referred to as **Split Rock.** On July 4, 1887, this point on the road was the scene of the first of the park's five stagecoach robberies. You can see a few vestigial remnants of the old road on the other side of the river here as well.

1.9 / 3.3 GPS: 45.00683, -110.69351
SLIDING HILL (W) 🥾

On the west side of the road, you'll notice evidence of several landslides and mudslides along the face of Sepulcher Mountain. This stretch of roadway has caused tremendous problems for the park's road crews over the years, especially when the road was on the opposite side of the river (1901-1921). Debris would often roll down into the roadway, occasionally causing damage to the tires of passing vehicles. Even today it is not unheard of for a major rockslide to occur along this road, shutting down the roadway.

The rocks above you to the east are prime territory for bighorn sheep; you'll often see them moving about the sides of the steep cliffs. During the early and late seasons, the sheep can often be found grazing along the side of the road as well.

2.2 / 3.0 GPS: 45.00317, -110.69233
45TH PARALLEL PULLOUT (E) 🔭

At this point, you are almost exactly halfway between the North Pole and the Equator. The actual line is about 800 feet south of here, but there is no place to build a pullout at the exact location where the parallel crosses. Up until a few years ago, it was believed the line was considerably south of this point near Boiling River. And contrary to popular belief, this is not the Montana/Wyoming State Line. That is approximately one mile to the south (see below).

2.7 / 2.5 GPS: 44.99652, -110.69324
SOUTH END OF GARDNER CANYON
CHINAMAN'S GARDEN (W) 🔭

This is the south end of Gardner Canyon. In 1879, a garden was established in the large flat area to the west of the road to provide fresh produce for the park. When the U.S. Army assumed control of the park, the garden was expanded and improved (i.e., irrigation ditches added).

From 1907 until at least the late 1910s, an Oriental man named Sam Wo operated the garden to provide produce for the hotels. Sam's residence, which was removed in 1931, was designed by Robert Reamer, the same man who designed the Old Faithful Inn and many other important buildings in the park.

3.0 / 2.2 GPS: 44.99287, -110.69276
BOILING RIVER TURNOUT (E) 🚻 🏊
GARDNER RIVER PICNIC AREA (W) 🪧

Boiling River is a hot stream of water emanating from the rocks along the edge of the Gardner River. It is believed to be runoff and drainage from the springs and terraces in Mammoth and is one of only two places where swimming is officially authorized within the park (the other is in Firehole Canyon).

Up until the mid-1980s, this spot was little known outside the park employee community, but it is now one of the most popular places in the park during the summer. Park in the lot and take the ½ mile hike to the mouth of the river. Nudity is not permitted, and the only place to change is the vault toilet at the head of the trail, so you may wish to come prepared if you plan to dip into the water. You can also continue south along the trail another mile and connect into the Lava Creek Trail. The water here doesn't really boil, as it averages between 115°F-125°F (46°C-52°C).

During the late May and early June time frames, the water levels are often too high to allow for safe swimming so the NPS will close this area during that time. The small building on the north end of the parking lot at the river's edge is a U.S. Geological Survey gauging station that monitors water levels and flow rates at this point on the Gardner River.

Boiling River was the site of Matthew **McGuirk's Medicinal Springs** when the park was created in 1872. Mr. McGuirk had established the camp in 1871, approximately 150 yards above the river's mouth; it was designed to offer invalids and others who believed the water had "healing powers" a place to stay on site. The government closed the camp in 1874, used the structures to house government employees for a brief period, and then removed all of the facilities (house, bath house, barn, fence) in 1889. McGuirk later received $1,000 from the federal government to compensate him for the property.

The **Gardner River Picnic Area** (also known as the Montana/Wyoming State Line Picnic Area or the Forty-Fifth Parallel Picnic Area) the on the south side of the road has two tables. There's no toilet at the picnic area, but you can walk across the street to use the vault toilet at the Boiling River Parking Lot. During the busy July/August time frame, people often use this to park for the swimming area, so the parking lot is often full.

Just north of this the road crosses over the Gardner River on a bridge built in 1958 as part of the Mission 66 Program.

3.0 / 2.1 GPS: 44.99232, -110.69239
MONTANA/WYOMING STATE LINE
SOAP HILL

Surveyors originally intended to set the Montana/Wyoming border at the 45th Parallel, but they made a slight miscalculation. As a result, the state line is here, several hundred feet south of the Parallel. The sign was erroneously placed up until a few years ago.

The hill you begin climbing at this point (or that you just descended if you're coming from Mammoth) is **Soap Hill**, so named because it is quite steep and can become "slick as soap" when it gets wet.

4.0 / 1.2 GPS: 44.97863, -110.69228
LAVA CREEK NORTH TRAILHEAD (E) 🚶

This is the north trailhead for the **Lava Creek Trail**. It is a 4.5-mile (7.2 km) trail that follows Lava Creek back to Undine Falls and ends near the Lava Creek Picnic Area (both accessible off the side of the road on the Mammoth to Tower Road east of Mammoth Hot Springs). About 1500 feet from this trailhead, the Lava Creek Trail turns south. Alternatively, you can turn north and walk approximately ½ mile to Boiling River. This is an excellent alternative to the bathing area's actual parking area on busy days during the summer.

There is an interpretive display here regarding Mt. Everts. The trail skirts Everts until the last half mile or so, when it climbs up onto the small bench over which Undine Falls drops.

4.3 / 0.9 GPS: 44.97528, -110.69300
LOWER MAMMOTH HOUSING AREA SOUTH SERVICE ROAD (N)
DUDE HILL (N)

This is a service road that leads to a residential and maintenance area used by NPS personnel. Much of the housing in this area was constructed by the Civilian Conservation Corps in the 1930s as part of the Emergency Conservation Work Program implemented by Franklin D. Roosevelt during the Great Depression. Another group of housing was added in the early 1960s as part of the Mission 66 Program.

The large building you see on the north side of the road as you drive by is the old Yellowstone Elementary School, constructed in 1962 as a part of the Mission 66 program. The building originally had five classrooms and a gymnasium, but another classroom and office space were added in 1972, and an addtional expansion occurred in the mid-1980s. Up until 2008, this was where the children of NPS employees attended elementary school, but it is now the Mammoth Community Center. Today, all students of employees in Mammoth attend school in Gardiner. The school sits on the site of a small housekeeping cabin complex (three dozen or so cabins) that were constructed by the Yellowstone Park Company in conjunction with the old campground (1926-1958; many were removed to other locations in the park).

The hill to the immediate north of the school is referred to by locals as "**Dude Hill**". The "dudes" from the Mammoth Campground often walk to the top of this hill to get a good view of the area around Mammoth (you can see the worn foot trails up the hill in several places).[3] The hill is a moraine - a collection of debris that accumulated from a landslide or debris slide off a glacier.

4.4 / 0.8 GPS: 44.97288, -110.69308
MAMMOTH CAMPGROUND/AMPHITHEATER (W) ▲ ♨ ♦♦

The **Mammoth Campground** is the only campground inside the park that is open year round. It's located within the hairpin turn here just below Mammoth Hot Springs and has 85 sites, an amphitheater, and five comfort stations with running water and flush toilets. The campground was constructed in 1937-1940 by the Civilian Conservation Corps. This occurred at the same time as the initial portion of the housing complex across the street was being developed. The campground's amphitheater was added in 1953.

The daily rate for 2014 is $20 per night. Just before you get to the entrance to the campground, there's a small turnout for one of the comfort stations on the west side of the road, making it accessible to those traveling along the highway. The campground is built across an extinct hot spring known as Cedar Terraces. You can still see the old travertine deposits in the hill to the west of the campground (the terraces were apparently still issuing forth water in the 1880s, memos from that era suggest).

Across the street from the roadside restroom at the campground's entrance was the location of three small stores used to serve campers (a delicatessen, general store, and a Haynes photo shop). Though constructed in 1924-1929 during the days of the second campground, they remained in place for a number of years to serve campers in the current campground as well. The buildings were removed in the late 1950s. After the stores and the housekeeping cabins were removed (see note about the school site above) and the housing area was expanded, the NPS created a man-made berm along the east side of the road to block views of the residential area from the campers.

4.5 / 0.7 GPS: 44.97229, -110.69328
LOWER MAMMOTH HOUSING AREA NORTH SERVICE ROAD (E)

This is another service road into the NPS residential complex. The area east of the road here was the site of the previous Mammoth Auto Camp and a small housekeeping cabin area, complete with a Haynes Photo Shop and a small cafeteria. Once the campground was moved across the road to its present location, the area was adapted for housing park employees. The houses in this complex were constructed beginning in the late 1930s through the 1960s.

The original road up to Mammoth actually traveled through the old campground and what is today the housing complex prior to 1938 (it connected with the road to Tower just east of the old Guardhouse, which is now Residence #8 - see the Mammoth Development Section for more details on it). The NPS constructed the new, steeper road up Cedar Terraces in conjunction with the creation of the Esplanade that year (the split road in front of the Post Office and Justice Center).

From 1929 to 1931 this area was also home to a short-lived fish stocking operation. The water was of poor quality and millions of fish died before they could be stocked in the park's streams, however, so it was closed down.

5.2 / 0.0 GPS: 44.97666, -110.70036 ELEVATION: 6245 FEET
MAMMOTH HOT SPRINGS JUNCTION 🏠

From here, you can head 20.9 miles (33.6 km) south to Norris Junction and the Norris Geyser Basin, east 18.1 miles (29.1 km) to Tower Junction, or north 5.2 miles (8.4 km) to Gardiner.

Mammoth Hot Springs is the park's headquarters. The large development on the east side of the road is known as "Fort Yellowstone," and houses most of the administrative operations that are necessary to allow the park to function on a daily basis. Most of the buildings in this area were constructed from the late 1800s through 1916 when the U.S. Army was responsible for the park. This is also a National Historic District.

On the opposite side of the road are the hotel, general store, service station, dorms and support facilities for concession personnel, and the park's Justice Center. See the Mammoth Hot Springs Development section for a walking tour of these buildings and their history, as well as background on some important buildings that are no longer here.

The roadway in front of the Clinic, Post Office, Justice Center, etc., was constructed in 1936-1938. Prior to that, entry into upper Mammoth area was via a road that connected near the Chapel.

Mammoth Hot Springs
to
Tower Junction
⟶∘⟨⟩⟨⟩∘⟵

This 18.1-mile (29.1 km) road between Mammoth and Tower Junction has its roots in an old trail used to afford travel between what is now Gardiner and the mines in Cooke City. Known in the park's early days as Turkey Pen Road, the old path connected into the Bannock Indian Trail near Blacktail Deer Creek.[1] After the development of Mammoth as the park's headquarters, a new road from the west was constructed and became the primary route between the Gardiner/Mammoth area and Cooke City. Today's road deviates very little from its predecessor, with the exception of a six mile stretch at Blacktail Plateau Drive (see below).

The road takes you through an area of the park known as the Northern Range. For more than 80 years this large grassland area has been the subject of intense scrutiny over its ability to sustain the populations of wildlife found there. Some scientists have been concerned about the number of ungulates, primarily elk and bison, who use the area to forage for food, and fear that the current populations are too large and overgraze the area. Others believe the ecosystem itself regulates the number of animals it can sustain and thus there is no issue. Throw into the mix the wolves who prey on the ungulates and the other animals that rely on the types of trees and other vegetation that exists here, and things get even more heated. Debate and study continue to this day.

About five miles (8 km) east of Mammoth, the road begins to parallel and/or travel along the old Bannock Indian Trail. The Bannock's way of life was centered around the American Bison, and its extirpation in much of the west forced the natives to migrate to other areas of the country in search of the animals. One of their primary trails passed through the Yellowstone area. The trail enters the park on its west side, passes by Mount

Holmes, and then enters the Northern Range in the area around Lava Creek. From here, it roughly follows the road to Tower Fall and crosses the Yellowstone River at Bannock Ford, just east of the waterfall. You can still see some evidence of these trails today, as is pointed out in the mile-by-mile guide below.

Blacktail Plateau Drive is an old remnant of the original stagecoach road between Mammoth and Tower Junction. This undulating dirt road is closed until late in the season and once open is subject to being closed at a moment's notice because of poor road conditions. It, too, followed the original Bannock Trail, and is worth the side trip if you have the time and the desire to see an area very few visitors ever see. The road affords some of the grandest views of the Northern Range.

There are two popular secondary park features along the road. The first is Undine Falls, a gorgeous 60-foot waterfall that once graced the cover of National Geographic magazine. It is located right alongside the road four miles (6.4 km) east of Mammoth. Just past that to the east is the trailhead for Wraith Falls, another popular waterfall.

The second feature is Petrified Tree, the remains of which can be seen at a turnout just west of Tower Junction. Though there were several petrified trees at this location when the park was created, vandals have made off with all but one of these specimens. It is now protected by a fence and is worth the short side trip if you have the time.

The road between Mammoth and Tower Junction has not been rebuilt to meet current road standards and is therefore narrow and subject to washouts in some locations. There are several turnouts, however, and you should make use of them if you find yourself holding up traffic.

0.0 /18.1 GPS: 44.97634, -110.70094 ELEVATION: 6250 FEET MAMMOTH HOT SPRINGS JUNCTION ⌂

From here, you can head 5.2 miles (8.3 km) north to Gardiner, 18.1 miles (29.1 km) east to Tower Junction, or south 20.9 miles (33.6 km) to Norris Junction.

This area tends to be quite congested during the busy summer months, so keep your eyes peeled for people, elk and even the occasional bison darting out into the traffic pattern from any direction. See the section on Mammoth Hot Springs for information about the buildings and services in this area.

0.1 / 18.0 GPS: 44.97442, -110.70025
AVENUE A (S)

Along this dead end road, which is shown on some maps as **Avenue A**, you'll find, from east to west the old Haynes Photo Shop (which is now used for storage by NPS), and the former residences of Jack Haynes, Huntley Child, and Harry W. Child, all important figures in early concession operations of the park. These residences are used still used today to house senior executives of the park's primary concession operator. See the section entitled Mammoth Hot Springs Development for additional information about the history of these structures.

The "Avenue A" designation comes from the early 1900s when Army Engineer Capt. Hiram Chittenden laid out and constructed a new road network for the Mammoth area. All of the roads had letter designations, (though this is the only one for which the old name is still commonly used).

0.2 / 17.9 GPS: 44.97362, -110.69924
EXIT FROM OFFICER'S ROW (AVENUE C) (N)

The road exiting from the west here is **Officer's Row**, so-named because the large houses on this road were originally for the senior officers of the U.S. Army when they were responsible for the park (it's official designation is Avenue C). This road is a one-way road from the other end, so don't make the mistake of trying to turn into the entrance here.

0.4 / 17.8 GPS: 44.97258, -110.69819
MAMMOTH CHAPEL (N) ✴

The **Mammoth Chapel** was constructed in 1912-1913 and remains in use today. Interdenominational services are held every Sunday throughout the year; there's a schedule posted on the announcement board in front of the building. You can also get married here if you wish (see the park's web site for details). There is a small parking lot across the street from the church for use by visitors (this was the site of the original 200-seat campground amphitheater at Mammoth as well from 1934-1968). See the Mammoth Hot Springs Development section for more information about this structure.

The large patch of mostly bare land behind (to the southeast) of the chapel was the site of the third Mammoth Hospital from 1911 until 1964, when it was torn down and replaced by the Lake Hospital (now clinic).[2] The road just to the east of the Chapel is a service road and is for employee use only.

0.5 / 17.6 GPS: 44.96912, -110.69717
Bluff Creek/Lost Creek Crossing

Bluff Creek passes under the road here. This creek drains the terraces via the old reservoir at a rate of about 500 gpm; it was given its name by Superintendent Philetus W. Norris for the small bluff over which it drains on this side of Capitol Hill. Many people erroneously refer to this creek as Lost Creek, as it drains into/through a small seasonal lake in the Lower Mammoth Housing Area referred to colloquially as Lost Lake.[3] The creek empties into the Gardner River. Bunsen Peak is visible to the south, and Mt. Everts to the north.

0.6 / 17.5 GPS: 44.96737, -110.69360
Old Powerhouse (N) [Westbound Only]
Mount Everts (N)

As you drive toward Mammoth, down below you to the north, you'll see the old **Mammoth Powerhouse** (and Mammoth's lower residential area). This structure, constructed in 1910-1911, was once used to produce electricity to operate many of the facilities in Mammoth before commercial power lines were routed into the park in the late 1950s. The building housed three large generators capable of generating almost 800KW of power. Today, electrical service is provided to most of the park by Northwestern Energy (formerly the Montana Power Company). The powerhouse was taken offline permanently in 1963.

The powerhouse was located below the hill and out of sight of the main headquarters area to keep the sound of the generators from being heard in town and to take advantage of the gravity to allow the water to power the generators. At the time it was constructed, none of the housing was present.

The large mountain to the north is Mt. Everts, named after Mr. Truman Everts, a member of the Washburn-Langford-Doane Expedition of 1870. Everts got lost and wandered in the wilderness for 37 days before being found near Crescent Hill, several miles east of this area. The mountain was given its named because of a misunderstanding of where his rescue took place (as did Rescue Creek along the North Entrance Road).

1.1 / 17.0 GPS: 44.96446, -110.68718
Lowest Point on The Grand Loop Road [※]

This spot is the lowest point on the Grand Loop Road, with an elevation of 6005 feet (1830 m). The small, informal pullout on the south side of the road just to the west of here affords an excellent view of Mt. Everts (7846 ft/2391 m).

1.3 / 16.8 GPS: 44.96276, -110.68528
Soda Lake (E)

The small, seasonal lake on the east side of the road here is known as **Soda Lake**. It was given its name for unknown reasons in 1904 by members of the Hauge Expedition.

1.7 / 16.4 GPS: 44.95817, -110.67915
Gardner River/Sheepeater Canyon Bridge ⛟

The Gardner River makes its way from the Gardner's Hole/Swan Lake Flat area south of Mammoth through Sheepeater Canyon to this point and eventually along the North Entrance Road into Gardiner, Montana. This 805-foot (245 m) long, steel-truss bridge dates to 1939, though it was reconstructed in 1979. When it was built, it was said to be the highest bridge in the state of Wyoming (200 feet above the river), though the state doesn't keep such details, so such claims are unsubstantiated. The bridge is often referred to as the Gardner River Trestle.

The existing structure replaced the original bridge built across the river in 1904-1905. If you look closely, you can still see the approach landings for the old bridge a few hundred feet south of the existing bridge. Several options for building the new bridge were proposed, but the "high bridge" was selected because it was more "preferable from a landscape standpoint."[4]

3.2 / 14.9 GPS: 44.94610, -110.65477
Old Road Bed (S)
Creek Crossing

You'll have to look closely as you're traveling eastbound, and probably won't be able to see it if you're heading west, but there's an old road bed that heads up the hill here on the south side of the road. This was a section of the original road between Mammoth and Tower.

You'll see a utility box on the south edge of this road bed. This is where the underground electrical cable between Mammoth and Tower is located (installed in 1987). When you get to Undine Falls ahead, you can walk across the street and up a small hill to see more of this old road. This is also the crossing for an unnamed seasonal tributary of Lava Creek.

3.8 / 14.3 GPS: 44.94554, -110.64437
VIEW OF MAMMOTH TERRACES [WESTBOUND ONLY]

If you're traveling westbound, you'll get your first sight of Mammoth's travertine terraces in the distance at this point.

4.0 / 14.1 GPS: 44.94330, -110.64048
UNDINE FALLS / LAVA CREEK CANYON (N) 🅃
UNDINE FALLS SKI AREA & OLD ROAD BED (S)

One the prettiest falls in the park, **Undine Falls** (pronounced: "*UN deen*") was named for a mythological female water fairy that was said to be able to gain a soul by marrying a mortal. The falls is a three-tiered, 60-foot plunge/fan-type waterfall on Lava Creek in the Lava Creek Canyon. A photo of the falls appeared on the cover of the July, 1977, issue of *National Geographic* magazine.

Due to the steepness of the walls, a technical descent is required to get to the bottom of the canyon or the falls. At least one person has died falling into the canyon while trying to get a photograph, so be careful if you elect to explore this area.[5] An excellent close up view of the falls can be had by walking a short distance up the Lava Creek Trail on the other side of the river (see 4.4/13.6 below).

Across the street from the parking lot is a dirt path that climbs a few dozen feet to the top of a hill above the existing road. If you climb this, you'll be at the base of what was known as the **Undine Falls Ski Area**. From 1942 until 1992, the 250-foot hill on your right was used as a ski slope by park staff, ski clubs in the Gardiner area, and by school children from the park's elementary school. Originally, a rope tow was used to transport skiers to the summit (up the hill to the ski slope's west). This method was deemed unsafe in 1992, and the park planned to install a Poma Lift the following winter.

When environmentalists complained (largely because the park was cutting down very old trees for the towers necessary to operate the lift), park administrators decided that a ski area was not appropriate for Yellowstone and shut it down. The ski building and comfort station that existed here at the time were removed in the summer of 1994.

When you climb up this trail, you land on a section of the old road that used to travel through this area. The utility boxes you see are for the underground electrical wires that carry electricity from Mammoth to the

Tower and Mount Washburn areas. The other end of this section of the old road can be found west of here at 3.2/14.9 (see above).

4.4 / 13.7 GPS: 44.94075, -110.63283
LAVA CREEK CROSSING
LAVA CREEK PICNIC AREA(S) 🅿 🚻
LAVA CREEK EAST TRAILHEAD (N) 🚶

The **Lava Creek Picnic Area** has five tables and a handicap-accessible vault toilet. It is usually quite busy during the summer season because of its proximity to Mammoth, the natural beauty of its setting, and the fact that it's the only picnic area along the Mammoth to Tower Road. Unfortunately, the picnic area itself is not easily accessible to those in wheelchairs. This area used to be the site of a small campground that could accommodate ten vehicles (known as the Lava Creek Campground).

Across the road from the picnic area, the **Lava Creek Trailhead** will take you to the brink of Undine Falls (½ mile), and then about four more miles (6.5 km) on to its north trailhead, which is located one mile north of Mammoth Hot Springs on the North Entrance Road. The trail follows Lava Creek along the base of Mt. Everts.

Lava Creek got its name from the fact that it passes over and through a series of old lava flows. The original stagecoach road through this section of the park followed Lava Creek, as did the old Bannock Indian Trail. The bridge here was built in 1932.

4.9 / 13.2 GPS: 44.94239, -110.62351
WRAITH FALLS TRAILHEAD (S) 🚶

Wraith Falls is a 90-foot (27 m) cascade-type waterfall on Lupine Creek; it is reached via a half mile (0.8 km, each way) trail from the parking lot. The short hike is a favorite of wildflower fans. A wraith is a type of ghost or ghostlike image. The waterfall was probably given this name because of its sudden, almost ghostlike appearance over the cliff.

6.2 / 11.9 GPS: 44.95308, -110.60264
BLACKTAIL PONDS (N) 🌱

These small lakes (during the spring/early summer, these may be one lake) are all that remains of a huge glacial lake that once existed in this area. The sign at the turnout says "Blacktail Lakes," but the official name of the little bodies of water is "**Blacktail Ponds**." The ponds get their name from the nearby creek (see below), which in turn is named after the blacktail deer, a subspecies of the mule deer.

6.7 / 11.4 GPS: 44.95527, -110.59259
BLACKTAIL DEER CREEK TRAILHEAD (N) 🚶
BLACKTAIL PATROL CABIN SERVICE ROAD (S) 🚻
BLACKTAIL DEER CREEK CROSSING

The **Blacktail Deer Creek Trail** (sometimes referred to as the Blacktail Creek Trail) is a four-mile (6.5 km) long trail that will connect you to the Yellowstone River Trail (you'll cross a long suspension bridge just before you get to that trail). From there, it's only a mile and a half more to Knowles Falls, a 15-foot cascade-type waterfall on the Yellowstone River. This trailhead is (was) also the terminus for Turkey Pen Road, an old road that has its origin at Gardiner and skirts Turkey Pen Peak (thus the name). It was the first route of travel from the Gardiner area to the Cooke City mines, and was the route the Washburn-Langford-Doane Expedition took to enter what would become Yellowstone. In later years, it was used as a fire access and utility road.

A couple of hundred yards east of the trailhead is a service road that leads to the **Upper Blacktail Patrol Cabin** (there's also a Lower Blacktail Patrol Cabin on the banks of the creek just above its mouth at the Yellowstone River). The cabin is still referred to by some locals as "Mary's Cabin," for Mary Meagher, a park biologist who lived in the cabin for much of each year and used it as a base for her research on park wildlife.

This particular cabin was constructed in 1931 by the Yellowstone Park Transportation Company to replace one they'd built on the site in 1900. It was used to house the manager for the corrals and pastures where the company kept their horses during the summers when they weren't being used in various services around the park (first to pull carriages, and later to offer guided horse tours to park visitors).

In 2010, the NPS installed a vault toilet at the turnout. In the 1910s-1930s, there was a road camp co-located with the cabin and corrals.

Blacktail Deer Creek crosses under the road just east of the service road. From here, one can see the Washburn Mountain Range to the southeast (from north to south, Prospect Peak, Folsom Peak, and Cook Peak) and the Gallatin Range to the west. The creek was named for the blacktail deer that inhabit the park. The creek does not drain into the Blacktail Deer Ponds. Quite the opposite, in fact. The ponds drain into the creek to the east, and the creek runs north into the Yellowstone River just above the suspension bridge on the trail.

7.4 / 10.7 GPS: 44.95582, -110.57822
OLD ROADBED CROSSING

Looking off to the northeast and southwest, you can see hints of another section of an old road that passed through this area of the park.

8.1 / 10.0 GPS: 44.95775, -110.56865
BANNOCK TRAIL CROSSING ⁕

Here you can see the old Bannock Indian Trail cross from the west side of the road to the east side. It is much more pronounced here than in other places because equipment went through here years ago to lay telephone wire. Blacktail Plateau Drive (see below) follows this old trail as well.

The Bannock Indians traveled through the northern section of Yellowstone in their hunts for bison. As the animal was extirpated in their ancestral hunting grounds, they were forced to make longer treks to find the bison upon which much of their livelihoods depended. They entered Yellowstone on the west side and traveled north through the Mammoth area, along Lava Creek, and through this section of the park into Lamar Valley and out through what is now the Cooke City area. Some of the park's early explorers and the first road through the northern range followed this trail as well.

8.2 / 9.9 GPS: 44.95909, -110.56646
FORCES OF THE NORTHERN RANGE SELF-GUIDING TRAIL (N) 🚶
FROG ROCK SERVICE ROAD/SKI TRAIL (S) 🎿

This one-half mile, wheelchair-accessible, self-guiding trail explores the nature and geology of what's referred to as the park's Northern Range, which includes the Lamar River and lower Yellowstone River valleys.

Across from this trail is a service road that leads to a construction equipment and materials staging and dumping area used by the NPS. The area is known as the **Frog Rock Pit** because of the large boulder that sits at the east side of the entrance road. To many people it resembles a crouching frog. The rock itself is what's known as a glacial erratic, a rock different from those in the bedrock in the area, and that was deposited by the withdrawal of glaciers from an area. These are common throughout much of Yellowstone. If you park in the large parking area north of the gate, you'll notice an old roadbed running off to the east. You can walk a few hundred feet in that direction and still see asphalt from the original road through this area. This portion of the old highway followed the Frog Rock Service Road (used as a ski trail in winter) roughly parallel to the existing highway, and connected into what is now the Blacktail Plateau Drive further to the east.

9.5 / 8.6 GPS: 44.95812, -110.54179
BLACKTAIL PLATEAU DRIVE ENTRANCE (S) 🔭 🎿 👀

The **Blacktail Plateau Drive** used to be part of the main road from Mammoth to the Tower area from 1905 until the 1930s. When the asphalt road was constructed, however, this dirt road became a side road. This tortuous, winding road takes you along the high plateau (with incredible views of the Northern Range) and then descends through a canyon known as "The Cut" (once referred to as "Devil's Cut") and a lightly forested valley before reconnecting to Grand Loop Road at 16.6/1.5. Sections of this drive, which also follows the old Bannock Indian Trail, have a grade of 8%.

The road is one-way and is only open during daylight hours between June and September, and may be closed after rainstorms. Since it is a dirt road it can become very muddy and rutty, and is not recommended for vehicles with low clearance. Trailers and RVs are not permitted, nor is travel off the road.

During the winter, this road is a popular ski trail (the ski trail actually begins at the Frog Rock Service Road parking lot to the west; shuttle service is usually available from Xanterra during the winter). See the Miscellaneous Road section for an in-depth exploration of this drive.

10.2 / 7.9 GPS: 44.95584, -110.52813
PHANTOM LAKE (S) 🔭
OXBOW CREEK CROSSING

On the south side of the road is **Phantom Lake**, so-named because it tends to dry up during the latter part of the summer. The lake is fed by runoff and by Oxbow Creek, a seasonal creek that enters the lake from the east. The creek crosses the road just west of the lake and eventually empties into the Yellowstone River near an oxbow bend, and thus its name.

11.6 / 6.5 GPS: 44.95509, -110.50129
GEODE CREEK CROSSING

Geode Creek crosses here. It was given its name for the prevalence of geodes in the area. The creek drains into the Yellowstone River.

12.9 / 5.2 GPS: 44.95439, -110.48022
HELLROARING CREEK OVERLOOK (N) 🐦

This overlook affords a view of the **Hellroaring Creek** to the northeast. From here the creek runs southwest to the Yellowstone River, which is hidden from view. You'll also see several small ponds in the valley below. These are known as "glacial kettles," areas where chunks of ice are left behind after a glacier retreats. The ice melts and the hole is filled with (and later captures additional) water and becomes a small pond or lake. You'll see those at several locations along this road and the Northeast Entrance Road.

According to park historian Lee Whittlesey, the creek got its name when a prospector, who'd gone ahead of his party, returned and was asked how the creek was. He exclaimed that it was a "hell roarer," and the name stuck.[6]

13.3 / 4.8 GPS: 44.94957, -110.47606
GARNET CREEK CROSSING

Named for its proximity to Garnet Hill, a small hill east of here north of the road. This seasonal creek empties into the Yellowstone River.

14.4 / 3.7 GPS: 44.947482, -110.45371
HELLROARING CREEK TRAILHEAD (N) 🚶

The **Hellroaring Creek Trail** (called simply the "Hellroaring Trail" by some) is one of the more popular trails in the park, especially so with horse or stock parties and those heading further into the backcountry of northern and northeastern Yellowstone or wanting to explore the Black Canyon of the Yellowstone.

The trail leads to a suspension bridge over the Yellowstone River. The trail has seven miles (11.4 km) inside the park and then crosses into the Gallatin National Forest. It affords access to the Buffalo Plateau/Buffalo Ford Trail (which terminates at the Slough Creek Campground 22 miles/35 km to the east), the Yellowstone River Trail, and the Coyote Creek Trail.

14.9 / 3.2 GPS: 44.94205, -110.44922
FLOATING ISLAND LAKE (S) 🔭 🏛
CRESCENT HILL (S)
GARNET HILL (N)

Floating Island Lake, named for the little patch(es) of land in the middle of it that appear to be "floating," is home to many different types of waterfowl, including Canada geese, sandhill cranes, and the occasional Trumpeter Swan. At one time this was a popular spot to find and watch beaver, but the lake has gotten shallower in recent years, and there are no longer any beaver present. Note the signs asking you to remain in the turnout and not walk down to the lake, as this contributes to predation of the fowl here (human scents attract predators).

As you approach the lake (from the west), **Garnet Hill** is to the northeast and **Crescent Hill** is to the southwest. Crescent Hill is famous for being the location where Truman Everts was found after his 37 days lost in the Yellowstone wilderness (See the note back at 0.6/17.5 about the naming of Mt. Everts). Garnet Hill is composed of rock estimated to be around 48 millions years old. It was the site of a suicide in 2010.

16.2 / 1.9 GPS: 44.92666, -110.44709
ELK CREEK CROSSING

Named in accordance with the early practice of assigning names based on local wildlife, **Elk Creek** follows the southern base of Garnet Hill and drains into the Yellowstone River.

16.6 / 1.5 GPS: 44.92200, -110.44410
EXIT FROM BLACKTAIL PLATEAU DRIVE (S)

This is the exit from the Blacktail Plateau Drive. It's a one-way road, and if you're approaching from Tower Junction the entrance is about seven miles (11.2 km) ahead.

16.7 / 1.4 GPS: 44.92125, -110.44118
PETRIFIED TREE ROAD (S) ✴
LOST LAKE WEST TRAILHEAD (S) 🚶
YANCEY CREEK CROSSING

The half-mile **Petrified Tree Road** takes you back to a petrified redwood tree. The tree is behind a protective fence constructed in 1907 to keep people from picking it apart. At one time there were several other petrified trees in the area, but vandals and souvenir hunters completely removed them before they could be protected. Because of the limited space at the parking lot, buses and RVs are prohibited from entering this road. In the park's early days, people were allowed to camp in this area.

The **Lost Lake Trailhead** is found at the east end of the parking lot. This 1.5-mile (round trip, if you head to the lake and back to this trailhead) trail takes you to Lost Lake and, if you continue on eastward, to the Roosevelt Lodge and another short trail to Lost Creek Falls (if you want to take just the trail to Lost Creek Falls, it begins behind the Roosevelt Lodge).

Just before you get to the Petrified Tree turnoff, **Yancey Creek** crosses the road. This creek is named after John F. "Uncle John" Yancey, an early concessioner who operated a hotel, saloon, and mail station nearby. It flows northward and joins with Lost Creek and Elk Creek, eventually draining into the Yellowstone River.

The portion of road from here to Tower Junction is known locally as "bear alley" or the "bearmuda triangle" because of the prevalence of black bears (and the attendant traffic jams) in the area during the summer.

16.8 / 1.3 GPS: 44.92163, -110.43857
"Winds of Change" Fire Turnout (N)

This exhibit describes and explains the effects of the 1988 fires on the Douglas fir forest that existed here. The fire was so hot in this area it literally sterilized the soil.

17.0 / 1.1 GPS: 44.92191, -110.43723
Buildings in Pleasant Valley (N)

Down below the road, through the little valley, you can see a couple of small buildings. This is the site of the old five-room Pleasant Valley Hotel, constructed by "Uncle John" Yancey in 1884. Yancey operated the hotel, a saloon, a mail station, and had a residence in the valley until he died in 1903 (after becoming ill while attending the ceremony at the Roosevelt Arch). The room rates were $2 per day at the time, and his primary customers were miners traveling back and forth to/from the mines in Cooke City.

When he passed away, his nephew Dan continued the business for another three years until the hotel burned down (the saloon survived!). Dan requested permission to rebuild, but by that time Camp Roosevelt had been constructed just a mile away, so his request was denied.

Camp Roosevelt, of course, would go on to become today's Roosevelt Lodge complex. Today, this area is where the Old West cookouts are held by Xanterra during the summer. The small buildings you see are picnic shelters and cookout platforms.

17.9 / 0.2 GPS: 44.91712, -110.41937
TOWER RANGER STATION/TOWER ADMINISTRATIVE AREA (S) 🏠
LOST CREEK CROSSING

The **Tower Ranger Station** is a small building located near the front entrance to the Tower Administrative Area. The station is staffed during the summer by an interpretive ranger who can answer questions and provide guidance about what to see, wildlife sightings, etc. Here you can obtain backcountry permits, fishing licenses, trail guides, and other information.

The structure at the front of this complex is a reconstructed 1907 soldier station from the U.S. Army's tenure in the park. It was remodeled in 1923, and today it serves as a residence for one of the rangers at Tower. It is the oldest of the original soldier stations to remain standing.

The area behind the ranger station is the **Tower Administrative Area**, home to maintenance and ranger operations and a residential area for NPS staff based in the district. This was the site of the Roosevelt Road Camp in the 1910s-1930s.

Just east of the driveway into the Ranger Station, **Lost Creek** crosses the road. From here it flows across the open meadow to the north and west, then connects with Elk Creek and empties into the Yellowstone River.

18.0 / 0.1 GPS: 44.91667, -110.41789
TOWER JUNCTION SERVICE STATION (S) 🚰 ⛽ 🚻 🚹 ♻️

The **Tower Junction Service Station** is typically open from June to September, though you can buy fuel 24/7 with a debit or credit card. No repair services are available here, however. The station was built in 1962 by the Conoco Oil Company. Adjacent to the service station are recycling bins and a couple of vault toilets.

18.1 / 0.0 GPS: 44.91598, -110.41581 ELEVATION: 6270 FEET
TOWER JUNCTION
ROOSEVELT LODGE (S) 🛏️ 🍴 🐎 📷 ⛽ 🥾

From this point, you can continue eastward to the Tower Fall area and then on to Canyon Village via Dunraven Pass (18.3 miles/29.4 km), or you can head through the Lamar Valley to the Northeast Entrance, Cooke City, and Beartooth Highway (28.6 miles/46.0 km to the northeast boundary of the park). You can also head back to Mammoth Hot Springs (18.1 miles/29.1 km).

This area was originally the site of one of the park's "permanent camps" operated by W.W. Wylie. Wylie opened his camp here in 1906 and in 1913 rechristened it Camp Roosevelt in honor of the President's stay. Contrary to common mythology, however, Roosevelt did not camp here, but rather two miles up the road near the Calcite Springs Overlook.

The existing **Roosevelt Lodge** itself was built in 1919 and has a dining room and gift shop. The lodge has a number of cabins for rent, though the majority are what's considered "rustic" in that they have no running water or bathing facilities in them, and are heated by wood stoves. Fourteen of the "Frontier" cabins do have running water and electric heat, however.

There are comfort stations located throughout the cabin area. These facilities have showers and toilet facilities. It can be quite dark in the middle of the night when you need to go take care of your personal business, so be sure and bring a flashlight (and bear spray!) with you if you plan to stay here.

There is a small General Store in front of the Lodge, but aside from that, there are few other services. The concession company operates horse rides and stagecoach rides/cookouts during the busy part of the summer season.

See the Roosevelt/Tower Development section for details and historical background on the buildings and development in this area.

Northeast
Entrance Road

The Northeast Entrance Road stretches 28.6 miles (46 km) from the park's boundary to Tower Junction. It is one of the most scenic and wildlife-rich roads in the park. You're likely to see bison, elk, bighorn sheep, wolves, grizzly bears, badgers, coyotes, eagles, osprey, and possibly even a mountain goat if you're lucky. Though this area is not as popular as some of the "feature" attractions such as Old Faithful or the Grand Canyon of the Yellowstone, there are people for whom this stretch of roadway is their sole reason for visiting the park.

The original Northeast Entrance Road was constructed in the 1890s by U.S. Army Engineer Lt. Hiram Chittenden. Chittenden considered it a "side road" and never intended for it to be, nor believed it would be an entrance road.[1] It was built primarily to allow easier travel from Yancey's hotel in Pleasant Valley to the mines in Cooke City. The road was reconstructed in 1905 and again in the 1930s. Small portions of it have been realigned over time, but even now it generally follows the path of the original road. During the harsh winters that impact the area, the road through the park between Cooke City and Mammoth is kept open to wheeled vehicles, as it is the only way for residents of that area to reach the outside world. The roads to the east are closed the entire winter due to massive snowfalls.

Probably the highlight of a trip along this road is the Lamar Valley, referred to by many as America's Serengeti because of the vast amount of wildlife that can be found here. It was in this area in 1995 that the gray wolf was returned to the park, restoring a significant portion of the park's natural ecosystem. One of the park's primary bison herds can be found here just about all year, and the area is rich with elk.

The road is in pretty good shape, and turnouts, picnic areas, and trailheads are plentiful. There are two campgrounds in this area as well. One of them, the Slough Creek Campground, is considered among the best in the national park system for the robust fishing and hiking possibilities nearby.

If you're traveling eastbound and depart through the gate, you may wish to travel up along the Beartooth Mountains via the Beartooth Pass, one of the most scenic drives in the entire country. Note that it can and does snow at any time of the year up there, however, and be prepared for inclement weather.

0.0 / 28.6 GPS: 45.00347, -110.00178 ELEVATION: 7370 FEET
YELLOWSTONE BOUNDARY

The park boundary is almost one-half mile east of the entrance station, and this is only one of two park entrances that are open year round to automobiles (the other being the North Entrance at Gardiner). This is necessary because, once the road over Beartooth Pass and the other eastern routes into this area are closed, travel through the park is the only way for residents of Silver Gate and Cooke City to get to other services not available in their respective cities.

0.4 / 28.2 GPS: 45.00447, -110.01039
NORTHEAST ENTRANCE STATION 🏠 👫

This is the **Northeast Entrance Station**, where you'll be greeted by a uniformed visitor services representative of the National Park Service, and asked to pay your entrance fee or show your pass. Once you've paid, hang onto your receipt – you'll need it to get back in the park (and may be asked to show it on the way out). You'll be provided with the park's newspaper, a map, and any other relevant information related to road construction, road closures, or any other situation that might impact your ability to move about the park efficiently. You are welcome to ask any questions, but be mindful of any traffic behind you, especially during the busy summer season.

This building was constructed in 1934-1935 and is listed on the National Register of Historic Places.

0.5 / 28.1 GPS: 45.00391, -110.01222
NORTHEAST GOVERNMENT AREA (N)

The **Northeast Government Area** is an NPS housing and maintenance complex. It dates to the mid-1930s when the ranger's residence and several other buildings were constructed, around the same time as the existing entrance station. In 1968, the ranger station, barn, and another building burned to the ground. The ranger station was later replaced.

The National Park Service bases an ambulance here year round, and in fact, the NPS is the only source of EMS assistance to the residents of Cooke City and Silver Gate during the winter.

1.5 / 27.1 GPS: 45.00434, -110.03155
WARM CREEK PICNIC AREA (S) 🌲 🚻

The **Warm Creek Picnic Area** has seven tables and a vault toilet, and most of the sites are handicap accessible. The picnic area gets its name from a nearby creek (located outside the park) that drains into Soda Butte Creek.[2]

1.6 / 27.0 GPS: 45.004511, -110.03337
WARM CREEK TRAILHEAD (N) 🥾

The **Warm Creek Trail** is basically the eastern terminus of the Pebble Creek Trail some 12 miles (19 km) distant. You can also access the Bliss Pass Trail via this route.

2.3 / 26.3 GPS: 45.00367, -110.04697
WYOMING/MONTANA STATE LINE

Although there is no sign here, you pass into Wyoming if you're heading west, or into Montana if you're heading east.

3.0 / 25.6 GPS: 44.99529, -110.05422
ABIATHAR PEAK (S) 🌟

The large mountain visible to the south is **Abiathar Peak**, named by the Hague Expedition in 1885 for Charles Abiathar White, a paleontologist. White provided technical assistance to various USGS projects in the western portion of the country, but was never in Yellowstone (and the naming of the peak for him has therefore generated some controversy).[3]

3.3 / 25.3 GPS: 44.99169, -110.05653
SODA BUTTE CREEK CROSSING
BARONETTE SKI TRAIL EAST TRAILHEAD (N) ⛷️

Soda Butte Creek crosses back to the south side of the road where it remains (if you're headed east). The bridge here was built in 1934 when the road was realigned to the south side of the creek.

The old roadbed on the north side of the creek is now the Baronette Ski Trail, a 3.5-mile (5.6 km) long trail that has its western terminus at the next crossing of the Soda Butte Creek (see 6.8/21.8 below). The easy, scenic trail passes through thick conifer forests at the base of Baronette Peak.

4.2 / 24.4 GPS: 44.97930, -110.06268
BARRONETTE PEAK PULLOUT (N) ✳

This turnout provides a view of the spectacular **Baronette Peak**. The 10404 foot (3171 m) peak is named for John "Yellowstone Jack" Baronett, a rather robust figure in the early days of the park. He built the first bridge (a toll bridge, in fact) over the Yellowstone River along the route to the Cooke City mines. The bridge was burned by the Nez Perce as they fled the U.S. Army in 1877, but was rebuilt by Baronett shortly thereafter. Later, he was an important guide for others exploring the area. Baronett's name has been misspelled in a variety of ways, and the peak's name was left as it was originally notated by the Hayden Survey team in 1878. It's not uncommon to see mountain goats moving about the face of the peak.

This mountain was once known as Hermit Mountain, according to the late park historian Aubrey Haines, and is part of the Absaroka Mountain Range. In the spring when the snow melt begins, you can see several waterfalls cascading down its face; none of these have names.[4]

6.8 / 21.8 GPS: 44.94510, -110.08231
SODA BUTTE CREEK CROSSING
BARONETTE SKI TRAIL WEST TRAILHEAD (N) 🎿

Soda Butte Creek moves from the south side of the road to the north side of the road. The bridge here was built in 1934. This is also the western trailhead for the Baronette Ski Trail. See notes at 3.3/25.3 above.

7.5 / 21.1 GPS: 44.93484, -110.08400
SODA BUTTE PICNIC AREA (S) 🏔 👫

The **Soda Butte Picnic Area** has four tables, as well as a handicap-accessible vault toilet. The road cuts through here are volcanic breccias, possibly a slide down the slope of an old volcano.

8.1 / 20.5 GPS: 44.92707, -110.08858
ICE BOX CANYON (S) ✳

There's a very small, informal pullout along the ½ mile canyon here. You can park and walk along the canyon wall, but be mindful of traffic and the danger of sliding off into the canyon.

Ice Box Canyon is part of the larger Soda Butte Canyon. The position and narrowness of the canyon make it tough for sunlight to penetrate the canyon and melt the ice. As a result, ice lingers until well into the summer. Thus, the name.

8.7 / 19.9 GPS: 44.92162, -110.09552
Thunderer Turnout (S) ⛅ 🧍

This is the western trailhead for the **Thunderer Cutoff Trail**. This trail is 17 miles (27.4 km) long and terminates at Cooke City via Chaw Pass and Republic Pass. The **Thunderer** (10544 ft/3214 m) was given its name because early explorers felt it was a good vantage point from which to watch thunderstorms.[5] Amphitheater Creek empties into Soda Butte Creek just to the south of this pullout.

9.4 / 19.2 GPS: 44.91594, -110.10925
Pebble Creek Trailhead (N) 🧍

The **Pebble Creek Trail** is 11 miles (19 km) long and takes you through the Pebble Creek Valley to the Warm Creek Picnic Area. The bridge over the creek here was built in 1934. Across the road from the pullout is the massive Thunderer (see above). Parking here is somewhat limited, but you can also pick up the trail from the campground driveway just to the west.

9.7 / 18.9 GPS: 44.91444, -110.11324
Pebble Creek Campground (N) 🔺
Pebble Creek Crossing

Nestled at the base of Mount Hornaday, the **Pebble Creek Campground** has 36 sites and vault toilets. The daily rate for 2014 is $15. You can also pick up the Pebble Creek Trail from the campground's entrance road.

Just east of the campground entrance road you cross over **Pebble Creek** which, during the early days of the park, was known as Tate Creek.[6]

10.2 / 18.4 GPS: 44.90780, -110.11553
Round Prairie (S)

The large expanse of meadow along Soda Butte Creek you see spread out to the east here is **Round Prairie**. Round Prairie was the site of a saloon built in 1885 by a Mr. "Red" Siwash for those traveling to/from the mines in Cooke City. He (allegedly) believed that this area was outside the park boundaries, but the federal government determined otherwise; he was evicted in 1887 by the U.S. Army.[7] No sign of the saloon building remains (though a spring box may still be present). The building itself was up against the hillside to the south of the creek, where the trees thin out.

Lee Whittlesey, in his book, *Death in Yellowstone*, states that there's a grave here that may hold the remains of a gentleman who died in 1910 after he was thrown from his horse.[8]

10.9 / 17.7 GPS: 44.89916, -110.12293
TROUT LAKE TRAILHEAD (N) 🥾 🏕

This trail is a half-mile long, and takes you to **Trout Lake;** it was once used as a fish hatchery for the park (1922-1951) and as a fish supply for the workers in the mines in Cooke City. It was known as Fish Lake for a period of time (prior to the existence of the hatchery). It is one of the best places in the park to see otters (and occasionally moose).

If you hike north of Trout Lake a few hundred feet, you'll find Shrimp Lake, and if you hike a few hundred feet northeast, you'll find Buck Lake. The small stream that serves as the outlet for Trout Lake is known as Fish Creek; it drains into Soda Butte Creek across the road and to the west of the trailhead.

11.7 / 16.8 GPS: 44.89113, -110.13657
DRUID PEAK (N)

The steep mountain to the north of the road is **Druid Peak,** (9583 ft/2921 m) the namesake of one of the most famous of the original wolf packs in 1995, the Druid Peak Pack. The NPS has a radio repeater located on this mountain to provide coverage to this portion of the park.

If you're headed eastward, you're entering the Absaroka Mountain Range, which forms much of the northeastern and eastern boundaries of the park.

13.0 / 15.6 GPS: 44.87798, -110.15287
SODA BUTTE (S) 🌸
SITE OF SODA BUTTE SOLDIER STATION (N)

Soda Butte is a nearly extinct hot spring and is unique in that it is the only thermal feature in the area for miles. It was mistakenly named for

Soda Butte Soldier Station, ca. 1905.

the material that was used to clean chimneys (Soda Ash) by A. Bart Henderson, one of the area's early prospectors.[9]

Across the road at the foot of the hill was the **Soda Butte Soldier Station,** one of the outposts originally used by the U.S. Army to guard and patrol the park. The building and its associated structures were removed and relocated to the Buffalo Ranch in 1938 (since razed, however).

This area had also been the site of a mail station for a brief period before the Army built their soldier station. The mail station was constructed in 1882, and the following year was commandeered by the park superintendent for use as a residence for one of his assistants.[10]

13.9 / 14.7 GPS: 44.86918, -110.16655
LAMAR RIVER TRAILHEAD/DEAD PUPPY HILL (S) 🚶

This trailhead is for use by those hikers not going in with horses or other stock. It is often referred to by the locals as the "Footbridge" turnout because of the small footbridge over the creek on the trail. The **Lamar River Trail** serves primarily as a connector for several other trails in this part of the park, including the Cache Creek, Miller Creek, and Cold Creek trails. This is also the eastern terminus for the Specimen Ridge Trail.

The hill across the creek is known colloquially as **Dead Puppy Hill**. It was given this name after a dead coyote pup was found there shortly after the Druid Peak wolf pack was released into the wild in 1995, marking the beginning of what would become that pack's infatuation with hunting and killing coyotes in their territory.

If you hike up the Lamar River Trail approximately 1.5 miles (2.4 km, just prior to the Lamar River itself), you'll come across the vestigial remains of Harry Yount's cabin. Yount was a gamekeeper from 1880-1881, but resigned because of the lack of enforceable authority (this was pre-Lacey Act). In 1883, a man named Billy Jump was allowed to operate a mail station out of the cabin, but a year later he was evicted from the park and the cabin burned. All that remains are some debris from the chimney and an old spring box.

Just over the hill to the north of the road is a small lake known as Foster Lake, named after Fred J. Foster, the gentleman in charge of the park's fish hatcheries in 1930.

14.3 / 14.3 GPS: 44.86872, -110.17442
LAMAR RIVER TRAIL – STOCK TRAILHEAD (S) 🚶 🚻

This **Lamar River Stock Trailhead** is for use by those using stock (horses, etc.) from July 1 to September 15. The pullout is known colloquially as "Hitching Post" because of its association with horses. The trailhead for regular hikers is located ⁴⁄₁₀ of a mile up the road. There are a couple of vault toilets here.

15.0 / 13.6 GPS: 44.87079, -110.18722
ELK TRAP (S)
CONFLUENCE EAST PULLOUT (N)

This area (in the V between the creek and the river back near the tree line) is the site of an old elk trap, used to capture the animals in the days when culling the herds was believed to be an appropriate management tool for maintaining healthy populations. Nowadays, of course, the wolves help control these populations. The pullout is on the east side of the confluence of the Soda Butte Creek and the Lamar River, and is known colloquially as the **Confluence East Pullout**.

15.3 / 13.3 GPS: 44.87020, -110.19301
CONFLUENCE OF SODA BUTTE CREEK AND THE LAMAR RIVER (S)
JACKSON GRADE / CONFLUENCE WEST PULLOUT (N)

The Lamar River is on the right and Soda Butte Creek enters its stream from the left (looking from the little pullout on the north side of the road).

As this is the confluence of the two streams of water, the entire area is known collectively as "the confluence."

On the hill above the road here (and to the northeast somewhat) is what is known as **Jackson Grade**. This is a portion of the original road through this area, and was named for a squatter found in the area in the early 1880s.[11]

The pullout here is known as the **Confluence West Pullout**, or by some as the Jackson Grade pullout.

15.9 / 12.7 GPS: 44.87149, -110.20531
FENCED IN VEGETATION (N)

On the north side of the road here you can see an example of a fenced in enclosure used to study animal effects on park's vegetation. The enclosure is designed to keep animals away from the plants, thereby allowing scientists to compare the flora inside and outside the enclosure to determine the effects of the animals eating the plants. There are several of these throughout the park, most of which were put in place in the early 1960s.

There is a small, informal pullout along the north side of the road here that is known locally as the "Enclosure Pullout," for obvious reasons.

16.2 / 12.4 GPS: 44.87458, -110.20948
BUFFALO FENCE PULLOUT (S) 🔭

There's an interpretive sign here that describes the efforts to preserve the last remaining herd of wild bison in the park's early days. This pullout is known colloquially as the "Geriatric Pullout." Across the valley from you is Specimen Ridge, upon which a vast collection of petrified forests exists. See below at 26.6/2.0 for details.

16.4 / 12.2 GPS: 44.87640, -110.21189
AMERICAN EDEN PULLOUT (S) 🔭 🎣

This turnout has an interpretive sign about Lamar Valley and the bison and elk herds that call it home. The Lamar Valley area is often referred to as America's Serengeti because of the vast array of wildlife and vegetation here.

The pullout is known locally as the "Old Picnic Area" pullout. Until 1998, there was a four-table picnic area nestled among the trees along the river. It was removed because it was almost continuously threatened by high water or flooded outright during the first half of the season.

17.1 / 11.5 GPS: 44.88473, -110.22083
MIDPOINT PULLOUT (S)

This pullout is colloquially known as "**Midpoint**" because it is (roughly) midway between the ends of the Lamar Valley.

18.0 / 10.5 GPS: 44.89430, -110.23518
BUFFALO RANCH (N) ✶ 🏠
ROSE CREEK CROSSING

In 1907, the (acting) Superintendent of the park, Major John Pitcher, established the **Buffalo Ranch** in this area to help preserve and restore the Yellowstone bison herd. A small group of Plains bison from Texas and Montana was brought in, and were mixed with offspring from a small native herd that had been held in a pen at Mammoth. These two groups bred with one another, so the herds that exist in the park today are hybrid animals. The first building constructed here was added in 1915 when a cabin was built for the buffalo keeper, and the original Soda Butte Soldier Station was relocated here in 1938 (neither of which remain standing).

Today, the site is used for the Lamar Ranger Station and by the Yellowstone Association to hold many of its Yellowstone Institute classes. There are several cabins, a washroom, messhouse, classrooms, and a small store. Additionally, the two buildings nearest the road are residences for rangers assigned to this area. The one closest to the roadway was built in 1922, and the building behind it, which was originally a bunkhouse, was constructed in 1937. The barn and the classroom building were also constructed in 1937. These four buildings comprise the Lamar-Buffalo Ranch Historic District. There is an interpretive sign across the highway explaining the purpose of this area and its importance in preserving the American Bison.

In 1994, sixteen residential cabins were built to replace older units that had originally been relocated here from Fishing Bridge in the 1980s (they'd been built in the 1930s). The ranch is somewhat unique in that there is no commercial electrical power. All of the electricity is provided through the solar array you see on the east side of the complex, or via generators located in a shed at the rear of the compound.

The creek that runs under the road just east of the entrance to the Ranch is **Rose Creek**, named after the flower. One of the three original acclimation pens used to reintroduce wolves into the park was located approximately ¾ of a mile north of the Buffalo Ranch along this creek (just below the west face of Druid Peak).

19.3 / 9.3 GPS: 44.90760, -110.25165
DOROTHY'S KNOLL PULLOUT (S) 👀
JASPER BENCH (S)

This little pullout is an excellent spot to watch wildlife in the Lamar Valley. The pullout is colloquially known as **"Dorothy's Knoll,"** for a woman who conducted research on the park's coyotes from this location.

The ridge of land across the river is known as **Jasper Bench**, named for the creek that drains into the Lamar River on the ridge's east side. The creek, in turn, was named for the mineral.

19.7 / 8.8 GPS: 44.91199, -110.25878
COYOTE PULLOUT (S) 👀

This small pullout is colloquially known as **"Coyote Pullout."** It is an excellent place to observe coyote as you might suspect from the name.

20.3 / 8.3 GPS: 44.91471, -110.26876
LAMAR RIVER OVERLOOK (S) 📷
BISON PEAK (N)

This turnout affords a wide, expansive overlook of the Lamar River. It is known colloquially as "Fisherman's Turnout." To the north of the road here is **Bison Peak**, an 8294 foot (2528 m) peak named after the American Bison.

21.0 / 7.6 GPS: 44.91464, -110.28287
LAMAR RIVER CANYON - EAST END

If you're traveling westbound, you're entering the **Lamar Canyon** (if traveling eastbound, of course, you're leaving the canyon).

The canyon is named for the river that flows through it and is home to some of the oldest rock in the park. Many of the rocks here have been estimated to be 2.7 billion years old.[12]

22.0 / 6.6 GPS: 44.91963, -110.30312
LAMAR RIVER CANYON - WEST END

See note above at 21.0/7.6.

22.7 / 5.9 GPS: 44.92073, -110.31689
Slough Creek Campground (N) △ ⌑
Slough Creek Trailhead (N) 🚶 ♦♦

The **Slough Creek Campground** has 29 sites and vault toilets. The 2014 rate is $15 per night. The sites are available on a first-come, first-serve basis only. The campground is at the end of a two-mile (3.2 km) dirt and gravel road.

There's a vault toilet in a small parking area just after you turn off the main road. The large expanse of land to the northwest toward the river is known as **Slough Creek Flats**. There's an old gravel pit service road that runs west out of this small parking area and around the small butte you see off to the west at the bend in the river (just north of the bridge).

On the east side of the road (northeast of the intersection itself), is a small knoll known as "**Dave's Hill**." This has been a popular spot for watching wolves in the past. The granite ridge west of Slough Creek is known colloquially as "**Mom's Ridge**," as it was the home of a couple of the park's early alpha female wolves and their pack (Rose Creek pack).

NPS has a barn at the end of a short service road running west off the campground entrance road. This is where they keep their horses when the rangers are not in the backcountry during the summer in this part of the park.

The **Slough Creek Trailhead** is located across the intersection from the NPS service road. The trail is very popular with horseback riders and fishermen, and is the remnant of an old wagon road that lead from this are to the Silver Tip Ranch outside the park's northern boundary eleven miles (17.5 km) to the north. The trail intersects with the Buffalo Fork Trail and the Bliss Pass Trail. You can make a circuit by hiking north on the Slough Creek Trail, taking the Buffalo Fork Trail to the Soldier's Trail, and following it back to the campground.

23.3 / 5.3 GPS: 44.91485, -110.32324
Lamar River Bridge/Turnouts (E & W)
Crystal Creek (S)

This new bridge opened in the fall of 2012, replacing one constructed in 1938 and reconstructed in 1988. Turnouts on either end allow you to park and walk down to the bridge and/or the river. **Crystal Creek** empties into the Lamar River just below the bridge on the south.

23.6 / 5.0 GPS: 44.91187, -110.32782
Specimen Ridge - Central Trailhead (S) 🚶
Little America/Horseshoe Valley 🔭

From the pullout here, there's an old roadbed here that led to a corral at one point. If you follow this road and the trail at the end of it, you'll get up into Specimen Ridge where the petrified trees are located. It is very steep and hard to follow in some places, but it affords one of the best ways to access the trees. Check in with the Tower Ranger Station before attempting this, as the trail is not marked well.

The **Little America** area gets its name from the old Civilian Conservation Corps Camp that was built on the north side of the roadway about a half mile to the west of here. Several of these work camps were built in national parks all across the country in the 1930s, and they were often referred to as "little Americas" because the workers stationed there represented a cross-section of America.[13] The area had also been the site of an NPS Road Camp during the 1910s-1930s. The entire flat between Junction Butte (ahead to the west) and the Lamar River crossing is known as Little America Flat.

This small valley to the south of the road is known as **Horseshoe Valley**, or simply, "The Horseshoe." This area, colloquially named for its shape, is a major calving spot for bison.

23.8 / 4.8 GPS: 44.91012, -110.33243
Aspen Turnouts (N)

There's a small photogenic stand of aspen trees on the north side of the road here. The two turnouts along the road on either side of the trees are known colloquially as the West and East **Aspen Turnouts**.

25.4 / 3.2 GPS: 44.90886, -110.36412
Boulder Pullout (N)

This pullout is colloquially named the "**Boulder Pullout**" for the large glacial erratic on the east end of it. The seasonal pond north of the pullout is unnamed.

25.6 / 3.0 GPS: 44.91018, -110.36858
Fenced in Area (N)

This is one of several small areas fenced off to allow park ecologists to study the effects of large ungulates grazing in this portion of the park.

26.6 / 2.0 GPS: 44.91229, -110.38720
SPECIMEN RIDGE TURNOUT (N) 🌼
SPECIMEN RIDGE WEST TRAILHEAD (S) 🚶

Specimen Ridge is the ridge of mountains you see to the south; they separate Horseshoe Valley from Mirror Plateau. Specimen Ridge is estimated to hold over 27 individual petrified forests, some of which date back as far as 50 million years. It's important to note that you can't see the trees from this trail, however. You'll need to use the trail at 23.6/5.0 above. Again, check with the Tower Ranger Station to get the best information based on what you're interested in seeing.

The **Specimen Ridge Trail** is a 17.5-mile (28 km) long trail that takes you along Specimen Ridge. The trail's eastern terminus is at the Lamar River Trailhead near Soda Butte. You have to ford the Lamar River just before the end of this trail, so if you'd rather do that early on rather than after you've been hiking all day and are tired, you may wish to consider starting at the eastern end.

26.9 / 1.7 GPS: 44.91338, -110.39254
RUDDY DUCK POND (N)
JUNCTION BUTTE (N)

This small, seasonal pond has two colloquial names. The body of water was christened Lake LaCombe in the early 1930s because one of the park's rangers, a gentleman by the name of Bob LaCombe, drove his (personal) vehicle into the lake after a night of partying at the Tower Ranger Station. Historian Lee Whittlesey notes that this pond is now more commonly known as the **Ruddy Duck Pond**, and was given the name by local NPS personnel in the 1970s.[14]

The large mass of land that rises beyond the lake is **Junction Butte**, named not for its proximity to Tower Junction, but rather its being located just southeast of the junction of the Yellowstone and Lamar Rivers.

27.4 / 1.2 GPS: 44.91728, -110.39983
YELLOWSTONE RIVER PICNIC AREA (S) 🪑 🚶
YELLOWSTONE RIVER OVERLOOK TRAIL (S) 🚶 🥾

The **Yellowstone River Picnic Area** has nine tables, and a handicap-accessible vault toilet. The **Yellowstone River Overlook Trail**, which departs to the east from the picnic area, is a two-mile (3 km) trail that affords an excellent view of the Grand Canyon of the Yellowstone along

The Narrows, the narrowest portion of the canyon. It terminates at the Specimen Ridge Trail (and you can continue on from there if you're so-inclined). This area, including the small turnout to the north of here, is a good place to see bighorn sheep.

27.6 / 0.9 GPS: 44.92121, -110.40024
WRECKER TURNOUT (N) 🔭

This turnout is known colloquially as "**Wrecker Turnout,**" and is a good jumping off point if you'd like to hike the one-half mile north to see the confluence of the Lamar and Yellowstone Rivers. You'll also pass the vestigial remains of the old Baronett Bridge (see below), as well as a couple of old service roads that were used to access gravel pits on the north side of Junction Butte (the large mound of land to the east; see note above).

27.9 / 0.7 GPS: 44.92032, -110.40409
YELLOWSTONE RIVER 🔭

This 604-foot (184 m) **Yellowstone River Bridge** was completed in 1961. The bridge is known to some locals as the "Tower Bridge" for its proximity to Tower Junction. About one-half mile north of this location are the vestigial remnants of the old Baronett Bridge, built by Scotsman John H. "Jack" Baronett. Baronett had come to the area as a prospector along with many others. He made his riches by building a toll bridge across the Yellowstone here, however. Just north of the existing bridge, the river is only 100 feet wide. As the only place to cross the river in this part of the state, anyone headed to make their fortune in Cooke City was obligated to pay Mr. Baronett for the privilege of crossing his bridge. He also constructed a cabin for himself and a couple of outbuildings (none of which remain standing).

The bridge was constructed in 1871, before the park existed. In 1877, the Nez Perce burned the bridge while fleeing the Army forces commanded by General O. O. Howard. The bridge was reconstructed, and Baronett (or his associates) operated it as a toll bridge until the government bought it and the cabin from him for $5,000 in 1899. Four years later, the bridge was destroyed when a new one was built.[15]

28.3 / 0.3 GPS: 44.91974, -110.41252
GARNET HILL LOOP CROSSING

The 7.5-mile (11.8 km) **Garnet Hill Loop Trail** takes hikers and horse riders around Garnet Hill, the small peak seen to the northwest. Garnet

Hill is named for the presence of small crystals of garnet in the rock comprising the hill. The rock is believed to be as much as 48 million years old.[16] The trailhead for this trail is located in front of the Roosevelt Corral.

28.6 / 0.0 GPS: 44.91598, -110.41581 ELEVATION: 6270 FEET
TOWER JUNCTION

From here, you can travel east to the Tower Fall area and then on to Canyon Village via Dunraven Pass (18.3 miles/29.4 km), west to Mammoth Hot Springs (18.1 miles/29.1 km), or head back to the Northeast Entrance (28.6 miles/46.0 km).

You could also, of course, stop in at Roosevelt Lodge to rent a cabin, have a meal in their dining room, or rent a horse or take a stagecoach ride to Pleasant Valley and the site of John Yancey's old hotel for an outdoor cookout. See the Roosevelt/Tower Junction Development section for more details on the facilities located here.

Tower Junction
to
Canyon Junction

The road from Tower Junction to Canyon Junction is 18.3 miles (29.4 km) long, and takes you through some of the most spectacular scenery in the park. The highest point accessible to the public via automobile lies along this route, and there are several pullouts that afford wide, sweeping vistas of the peaks and valleys of the Washburn Mountain Range.

Dunraven Road, as it is often called, is the first primary road in the park to close each season, and the last to open due to the deep snow that accumulates during the harsh winters. It typically takes park maintenance crews until Memorial Day each year to get it open, and it generally closes after the first weekend of October. The seasonal staff is mostly gone by this time, and to allow crews that are still in the park to concentrate on other, more traveled routes, the road between Canyon and Tower is closed, and snow is allowed to accumulate until the following spring.

The road over Dunraven Pass follows an old Indian trail that existed long before early American explorers arrived. Interestingly, the original path mapped out for a road between Tower and Canyon was around the east face of Mt. Washburn via Rowland Pass, which would have had the added benefit of taking you to Washburn Hot Springs (much of today's Glacial Boulder Trail follows what would have been that road). The path via Dunraven Pass was selected because it was slightly lower in elevation and allowed for the building of a road to the summit of Mt. Washburn, which is something both park engineer Hiram Chittenden and the superintendent at the time wished to accomplish.

This was the last segment of the Grand Loop Road to be completed, due in large part to the challenges associated with building a road at these elevations and the fact there was such a short construction window each year. Work began on the road in 1903 and was largely completed by 1906, including a one way side road up the south face of Mt. Washburn to its summit and down its north face.

Chittenden laid out a route for the man he left in charge of surveying the southern portion of this road when he departed from the park in 1905. However, the engineer felt that Chittenden's path traversed too much marshland and would make construction of the road too difficult. So he unilaterally altered the path of the road, building it higher up on the sides of the hills (the east face of Dunraven Peak). This resulted in a much more difficult time clearing the roads each season because of the higher elevation.[1]

The road was reconstructed along its current path (the one Chittenden originally intended to be used) in the mid-1930s by the Bureau of Public Roads. At both the north and south ends, the road was moved to lower elevations. The old north end is now an abandoned roadbed between Chittenden Road and the Tower Fall Campground, while the old south end can still be seen in places along the hills on the west side of the road between the Dunraven Picnic Area and Dunraven Pass.

For many years, from Dunraven Pass itself, it was possible to drive up to the summit of Mt. Washburn if you had an automobile that could handle it (each vehicle was checked prior to heading up to ensure its brakes worked!). This ended in 1947, though concession bus service to the top of the peak resumed in 1959 and continued until 1972. Today, the old road bed on the south face of the mountain is one of the more popular foot trails in the park, while the road on the north face is open to the public as a foot path but is also used by NPS and concession vehicles to supply the fire lookout tower and access the vast array of communications equipment that exists there.

The north half of the road takes you along the lush Amphitheater Valley (also known as Antelope Creek Valley), home to a great many grizzly bears. The south half affords views of the Grand Canyon, Washburn Hot Springs, and a lush assortment of wildflowers. It has been named by many publications as one of the most scenic drives in the national park system.

The road between Tower and Canyon is in excellent shape, but it is quite curvy so you'll definitely want to keep your eyes on the roadway. Unlike the other main roads, the speed limit is 35, due in large part to the winding nature of the road. There is a plethora of turnouts and overlooks, and a couple of well-placed vault toilets in case nature calls while you're in traffic.

0.0 / 18.3 GPS: 44.91598, -110.41581 ELEVATION: 6270 FEET
TOWER JUNCTION
ROOSEVELT LODGE & CABINS/STORE (S) 🛏 ⏀ 🐴 🚻 🍴
LOST CREEK FALLS/LOST LAKE TRAILHEAD (S) 🥾

From here you can drive 28.6 miles (46 km) to the Northeast Entrance, 18.1 miles (29.1 km) to Mammoth Hot Springs, or 18.3 miles (29.4 km) to Canyon Junction.

In 1906, the Wylie Permanent Camping Company constructed a tent camp on the site south of the junction. Several years later it would go on to become Camp Roosevelt, and would eventually become known as the **Roosevelt Lodge**. See the Roosevelt/Tower Development section for details on the history and background of the facilities found in this area.

Lost Creek Falls, a 40-foot plunge waterfall into a deep canyon, is reachable via an almost ½ mile hike, though it requires hiking a rather steep and narrow trail. The creek gets its name from Geologist William Holmes, who thought that it "[sank] from sight" at its lower end. You can also hike one mile to **Lost Lake**, which gets its name from the fact that it feeds the creek of the same name.[2]

0.2 / 18.1 GPS: 44.91485, -110.41220
ROOSEVELT CORRAL (S) 🐴
SITE OF NYMPH SPRING BATH HOUSE (S)

The **Roosevelt Corral** is located on the south side of the road here. The park concession operator offers horse rides from the corral, as well as stagecoach rides and cookouts.

Located on the hill just to the east of the corrals is a small set of four hot springs. Around the time that Camp Roosevelt was constructed, a small bath house was erected here (known as the **Nymph Springs Bath House** or the Roosevelt Pool). Guests were allowed to bathe in the warm waters of the spring for several years. A new, larger bath house was built in 1926, but it and another structure built near it were removed in the 1930s by Civilian Conservation Corps crews.

0.9 / 17.4 GPS: 44.90901, -110.40273
RAINY LAKE (N) ❄
BUMPUS BUTTE (N)

Rainy Lake was given its name because of underground hot springs bubbling up through it. The bubbling water makes it appear as if it's raining on the lake.

In 1903, during President Teddy Roosevelt's visit, his entourage camped on the east side of this lake up against the hill. The president himself camped up the road at the old Tower Soldier Station at the behest of his Secret Service detail. Roosevelt had come to be president after the assassination of William McKinley, and the Service was concerned for his safety. It was felt having him at the military outpost would afford him much more protection than he would have had if he'd camped at the lake.

Bumpus Butte is the large butte to the east of the lake, named for Dr. Hermon Bumpus, the gentleman who supervised the construction and outfitting of the park's new museums in 1929-1930.

1.4 / 16.9 GPS: 44.90206, -110.39617
SITE OF ORIGINAL TOWER SOLDIER STATION (S)

On the south side of the road at this point, during the early part of the century, stood the **Tower Soldier Station**, one of the outposts the U.S. Army constructed and used to protect and patrol the park during its tenure. This site is remarkable for the fact that Teddy Roosevelt camped here during his 1903 visit to the park (see the notes above at Rainy Lake).

In 1907, the Soldier Station was removed and a ranger station was erected at the site of the present day Tower Ranger Station at Tower Junction. The outpost was relocated primarily because this section of road was only seasonally used and it was felt having the station at the junction would afford the soldiers easier access to the park's roads.

The original station consisted of three buildings, two solider quarters and officer quarters, plus a small corral for the horses. Constructed in 1901, it was razed in 1907 after new station was built at Tower Junction. After the soldier station was removed, the area was used briefly (1913-1916) as a Shaw and Powell campground, and then became the first sanctioned campground in the Tower area in 1922.

1.6 / 16.7 GPS: 44.90173, -110.39318
CALCITE SPRINGS OVERLOOK (N) 🏛
THE NARROWS (N)

This overlook allows you to look down into the Grand Canyon of the Yellowstone just east of Bumpus Butte to see a small thermal area on the river's bank known as **Calcite Springs**. This area is referred to as **The Narrows** because it is the narrowest section of the canyon. There is an interpretive sign here explaining the formation of the canyon walls.

The parking area for this was enlarged and improved in 2013, and the road relocated some 150 feet south of its original alignment. The hill here (around which the overlook platform sits) is known as Midway Hill, for its position midway between Overhanging Cliff and Bumpus Butte.

From this point eastward to Devil's Den you'll quite often see a small herd of big horn sheep. The narrow road and the limited number of turnouts can often make traffic in this area a nightmare when the sheep are present, however. Vehicles have been damaged by rocks kicked off from above by the animals moving about on the cliffs, by the way. Head's up!

2.0 / 16.3 GPS: 44.89702, -110.38949
OVERHANGING CLIFF (S) 🌠

You can't help but notice **Overhanging Cliff** as you continue your drive eastward. The rock in this cliff is columnar jointed basalt, believed to be over 2.2 million years old, and is identical to the short basalt columns you can see across the canyon at The Narrows.

The road through here has slowly been tilting and sinking toward the river. A 2012-2013 road project dug out much of the existing road, added a reinforced substrate, and then rebuilt the road over the top of that. With this work the road is expected to last from 20-30 years before needing to be rebuilt again.

2.2 / 16.1 GPS: 44.89453, -110.38818
DEVIL'S DEN OVERLOOK (N)

From this small pullout you can peer down into **Devil's Den** (the small canyon) and across the top of Tower Fall as Tower Creek tumbles over its edge. The large pinnacle in Devil's Den is known as Devil's Hoof.

2.4 / 15.9 GPS: 44.89192, -110.38731
TOWER CREEK CROSSING
TOWER FALL/TOWER GENERAL STORE (N) 🧋 🍴 🚻 🏪
TOWER FALL CAMPGROUND/RESIDENTIAL AREA (S) ⛺ 🪧

Tower Creek crosses under the road just north of the store and its parking lot. The creek is rather robust in the early part of the season during the spring snow melt, and is supposedly the coldest creek in the park with an average temperature of 45°F (7°C). The historic bridge over the creek was constructed in 1935 when the road through here was realigned.

Tower Fall is a 132-foot plunge-type waterfall named for the towering pinnacles looming above it in the small canyon known as Devil's Den. It was given its name in 1870 by members of the Washburn Expedition.[3]

Today's **Tower General Store** is basically the same building that's been here since 1959. The first store on this site was constructed in 1936 after the road was relocated along its current alignment, but in 1959 it was completely remodeled (you can see hints of the "modern" style that was common with other Mission 66-type structures built in the park during this time frame). Much of the original store still exists behind the façade you see now, however. The small comfort station was added by NPS in 1975.

Prior to 1936, the Grand Loop Road took a somewhat different path to this point. It actually passed through the (existing) Tower Fall Campground; you can still see the old roadbed on the campground's eastern side. In fact, you have to walk across it to get from the camp sites to the amphitheater. The history of stores in this area goes back to 1912, however.

The first building constructed in this area was a stage station, built in 1912 by the Monida and Yellowstone Stagecoach Company. In 1917, following the demise of the horse and stagecoach operations and the use of the park roads by automobiles, park concessioner Jack Haynes (who had been a partner in the stage company) converted the building into a store where he sold his photographs and developed film for tourists. The NPS approved this contingent upon him selling brake shoes and other parts for automobiles. The early vehicles would wear their brakes out coming down the steep incline from the summit of Mt. Washburn, and would need some place to buy new brake shoes. Haynes agreed, and operated his store at the site of the present day employee dorm north of the campground (see below).

In the mid-1930s, with the realignment of the road network through the area, Haynes built a new store on the site of the present day building, and used his old store as a dormitory for his employees. A new dorm would later be constructed and is still in use today. The older store was razed in 1958, however. When the Haynes family sold its assets to Hamilton Stores in 1967, the building became one the park's General Stores, and is still operated as such today. There are plans (and have been for some time) to raze this building and build a new store at Tower Junction two and a half miles to the west, primarily to cut down on the congestion in this area.

On the south side of the road you'll find the entrance to **Tower Fall Campground**, a small, primitive campground operated by the National Park Service. Its 32 sites fill rather rapidly during the summer, and are available on a first-come, first-serve basis. There are three vault toilets and an amphitheater here, and in 2013 the daily rate was $15 per night. Many experienced Yellowstone campers consider this to be a less than desirable campground because the sites are so closely situated and therefore lacking in relative privacy. Others prefer it because of its proximity to Lamar Valley and one of the most bear-rich areas of the park.

This campground was constructed in the 1950s, and a previous campground due west of here (just east of the old soldier station, known as the Tower Falls Public Automobile Camp, built in 1922) was removed and the area rehabilitated. On the north side of the campground is the dormitory and a few RV spots for employees who work at the General Store, and a small employee recreation hall.

On the east side of the campground you'll find an old road bed. This is the north end of the original road used by vehicles traveling from Mt. Washburn and Dunraven Pass to get to the Tower Fall area. The Dunraven Service Road as it is officially known, it is still often referred to as the "Model T Road" because that was the primary vehicle that made use of it when it was first opened. The road was used up until the mid-1930s when, as a part of the road reconstruction in the park by the federal Bureau of Public Roads, it was relocated away from the campground (see the notes above about the store).

Up until a couple of years ago you could hike this road or take a bicycle to its other end after July 15th (prior to this, the area was closed for bear management purposes). Today, however, the NPS has put a carcass disposal area near its south end, so it remains closed to all traffic for much of the season (check with the Tower Ranger Station for its status).

The **Tower Creek Trailhead** is located in the southwest corner of the campground. It is a 2.8-mile long (4.5 km, each way) trail that takes you along Tower Creek. The eastern terminus of the Roosevelt-Tower Fall Trail is here as well.

2.7 / 15.6 GPS: 44.88788, -110.38672
Exit from Tower Fall Campground

This is the exit from the Tower Campground/Employee area. It's tough to get a larger RV out of here during the busy season.

3.7 / 14.6 GPS: 44.87358, -110.38231
ANTELOPE CREEK PULLOUT (E)

This small pullout allows you to walk down alongside Antelope Creek. The creek has its headwaters on Mt. Washburn and slowly winds its way through the valley down to the Tower area, where it empties into the Yellowstone River just a few yards downstream from a point known as Bannock Ford. This is the location where the Bannock crossed the Yellowstone River on their travels through the park. See the entry at 8.1/10.0 in the Mammoth to Tower Junction section for more information on the Bannock Indian Trail.

4.7 / 13.6 GPS: 44.86438, -110.39618
BUFFALO PADDOCK PARKING AREA (S)

In the 1930s, bison were corralled into the valley here for visitor viewing. The area had been fenced in and pens added (a four-acre show corral, plus 300-acre pasture), and the parking area was for tourists to afford them a view of the bison. Those pens were closed and removed in 1944, and the area now affords a great view of the lower Antelope Creek Drainage. This parking area also afforded access to a section of the old Howard Eaton Trail when it was being maintained.

For a while, this was the Antelope Creek Picnic Area. Though it was originally supposed to have six tables, it never had more than one, and they removed it in the late 1990s. The original plans for the rehabilitation of the Canyon to Tower Road called for reconfiguring this into the Buffalo Paddock Picnic Area with as many as ten tables, but as of late 2013 that had not been accomplished.

5.4 / 12.9 GPS: 44.86831, -110.40645
OLD DUNRAVEN SERVICE ROAD - SOUTH END (W)

This is the south end of the old **Dunraven Service Road**, which has its north end in the Tower Fall Campground (See 2.4/15.9 above). An area near this end of the road is used to dispose of carcasses now and civilian access to the area is often prohibited due to bear danger.

The brown metal box you see beside the roadbed is an electrical box. There is an underground electrical cable that runs from Tower Junction up to the summit of Mt. Washburn; it follows the old road to the new road and then up to the summit alongside the north trail. These boxes are spaced periodically to allow for service on that cable. Do not attempt to open or play with these.

6.7 / 11.6 GPS: 44.85334, -110.41684
AMPHITHEATER VALLEY PULLOUT (S) 🔭 🏛

This small pullout provides an excellent overlook of **Amphitheater Valley**. Though many people refer to this valley as Antelope Creek Valley (Antelope Creek has its headwaters on Washburn and drains through this valley just below the turnout), the legitimate name for it is Amphitheater Valley, so-named because of its resemblance to an amphitheater as it descends the north face of Mt. Washburn.

This area was the site of the park's ski area from 1935 to 1941. Consequentially, it is known to many locals as the "ski slope" pullout. After World War II, the park built a new area across from Undine Falls (see the 4.0/14.1 entry in the Mammoth to Tower Junction section).

7.1 / 11.2 GPS: 44.85139, -110.42268
GRIZZLY HABITAT PULLOUT (E) 🏛

There's an interpretive sign here with information about the grizzly bear, given that this is prime grizzly territory. Hiking off road through much of this area is prohibited year round because of that.

8.3 / 10.0 GPS: 44.83851, -110.43710
MAE WEST CURVE

This hairpin turn is known as "**Mae West Curve**." It was given this moniker by early park concession bus operators. Mae West was a mid-20th century actress and sex symbol, and was known for her curvaceous figure.

8.5 / 9.8 GPS: 44.84063, -110.43901
CHITTENDEN ROAD/MT. WASHBURN TRAIL (E) 🚗 🥾 🔭 🧗 🚻

Chittenden Road is a 1.3-mile (2.1 km) gravel road that leads to a parking area part ways up the side of Mt. Washburn, with an elevation gain of about 600 feet. From the parking area, you can hike (or bike) three miles along a gravel service road (Mt. Washburn North Trail) to the 10243 foot (3122 m) summit. This trail has few trees for shade, and is a bit steeper than the trail from the Dunraven Pass side, but is about ⁷⁄₁₀ of a mile shorter.

This road was originally the exit for the (one-way) Mount Washburn Road, which originated at Dunraven Pass (see entry at 13.5/4.8 below). This road took first stagecoaches then automobiles to the summit, and then brought them down this side of the mountain. Near today's parking area, the road split in two, with one leg taking the traveler back toward the Canyon area (see 11.2/7.1 below), and the other (today's Chittenden Road) carrying visitors on toward Tower. The Canyon leg was built to keep travelers from having to reclaim so much lost elevation once they descended from the summit. Today, the dirt/gravel road to the summit is used by NPS to service and supply the fire lookout atop the mountain, and by telecommunications personnel who manage and maintain the vast array of communications equipment located there.

The road over the summit was initially completed in 1905, and was known as the Mount Washburn Road. In 1913, however, to honor the engineer who built it, it was renamed as Chittenden Road.[4] The road was seven miles in length, 18-20 feet wide in most place, though it narrowed to ten feet in some, and had grades of 12-15% in places.

The first fire lookout was built atop the summit in 1921. It cost $3,000 to construct, and was built from stone taken from the mountain and cement mixed with water made from melting snow. A sign placed on the lookout at the time read, "Mount Washburn, Altitude 10,317 Feet" (sic) along with a quote from Isaiah: "And I shall make all of my mountains a way, and my highways shall be exalted."

IMAGE COURTSEY NPS

Mt. Washburn Lookout, early 1920s.

The current fire lookout was constructed in 1939, and consists of three main levels. The top level is the lookout and residence, while the middle level houses communications equipment for the NPS and other agencies along with cellular equipment. The bottom level contains bathrooms and a panoramic viewing room for visitors (added in 1980) above a radio room that houses communications equipment for CenturyTel. Keep in mind that this is a park employee's residence during the summer and respect his/her privacy. Do not climb on the non-public areas of the lookout.

For a great many years, the park staffed three lookouts throughout the summer (Mt. Sheridan and Mt. Holmes were the other two), but today with the advent of a variety of technologies that make detecting fires easier in general, this is the only lookout that is permanently staffed inside the park. A lookout is based here from mid-June until the first significant snowfalls reduce the park's fire danger (usually in late September or early October). There are two webcams mounted on the tower that allow you to see what the fire lookout sees year round. You can access them via the park's web site at www.nps.gov/yell. There are toilets located at the parking area and at the summit.

8.7 / 9.5 GPS: 44.83857, -110.44180
Cook Peak Overlook/Chittenden Vault Toilet (W) 🚻 🚽

This turnout is located in a meadow surrounded by an area of lodgepole pines that were burned in the 1988 fires, and provides a view of the western side of the Washburn Mountain Range, with **Cook Peak** (9742 ft/2969 m) off in the distance to the west. The peak is named after Charles W. Cook, who was with the 1869 expedition to the park, and who co-wrote one of the first magazine articles about the area.

At the turnout, you look down into the small valley drained by Carnelian Creek (named after a form of quartz). There is a vault toilet located at this turnout.

10.5 / 7.8 GPS: 44.81698, -110.45014
Blister Rust Turnout (W)

The pullout is named for its being located near one of the blister rust camps that housed crews battling white pine blister rust on pine trees in the area. This is an excellent place to see wildflowers in the spring and summer.

11.2 / 7.1 GPS: 44.80865, -110.44285
Old Chittenden Road - South End (E)

This small pullout looks rather innocuous, but if you look about 10 feet above your head (parked in the pullout facing north), you'll see the south end of part of a leg of the old Chittenden Road that used to bring visitors down from the summit of Mt. Washburn.

Approximately 1.3 miles from the end of Chittenden Road, coming down from the summit, travelers had the option of going straight and heading toward Tower, or turning south and taking a road back toward Dunraven Pass. This second route prevented them from losing a significant amount of elevation and having to reclaim it on their way back up to the pass. This road has been abandoned and is no longer used. If you are traveling north from Dunraven Pass, you can see the road cut in the side of the mountain as you head toward Tower.

11.6 / 6.7 GPS: 44.80474, -110.44767
OLD CHITTENDEN ROAD VIEW [NORTHBOUND ONLY]

If you're traveling northbound, you'll notice a road cut along the southwestern slope of Mt. Washburn at this point. Many people mistakenly believe this is part of Chittenden Road as it ascends the peak, but it is really an abandoned portion of the original road descending from the service road that leads to the fire tower from the Chittenden Road parking area. See the 11.2/7.1 entry above for notes about the road and the pullout ahead.

11.75 / 6.55 GPS: 44.80275, -110.44693
HIGHEST POINT ON THE GRAND LOOP ROAD ⛰

Despite common perception and often-repeated anecdote that Dunraven Pass is the highest point on the Grand Loop Road, this point approximately 1.7 miles north of the pass is around 9-10 feet higher, and is technically the highest point.

13.5 / 4.8 GPS: 44.78463, -110.45403
MT. WASHBURN SOUTH/DUNRAVEN PASS TRAILHEAD (E) 🥾 🚻
OLD ROAD BED (W)
DUNRAVEN PASS ⛰

Dunraven Pass, 8878 feet (2706 m), is a pass between Mt. Washburn on the east and Dunraven Peak on the west. Though this is often billed as the highest point commonly traveled by vehicles on the Grand Loop Road, there's a spot some 1.7 miles north of here that is slightly higher (see section above). The pass (and the peak) is named for Windham Thomas Wyndham-Quin, the Fourth Earl of Dunraven, who visited the park in 1874, and later wrote a book about his travels, thus introducing Europeans to the wonders of Yellowstone.[5]

On the east side of the road is the south trailhead for the 3.2-mile (5.1 km) trail to the summit of Mt. Washburn. The trail follows the old Mount Washburn Road, which was constructed in 1905 and, until 1947, allowed visitors to drive to the summit. Beginning in 1959 and lasting until 1972, the park's concession operator took tourists up this road via their buses, though no private vehicles were allowed.[6] As you hike along this route, you'll still see sections of asphalt in many places, in fact.

Though this trail is somewhat longer than the north trail, it is not as steep and has plenty of shade along the way. It is widely considered to be the more scenic of the two main paths to the top. This section is no longer used by vehicles, unlike the Chittenden Road trail (see 8.5/9.8 for information about the other trail and this road, as well as the fire lookout at the summit). This trail is one of the most popular in the park, and the parking lot is usually full by lunch time in July and August. Prior to it being rebuilt, people would park along the sides of the road and traffic through the area was a nightmare. There is a vault toilet here (as well as at the summit).

You can still see remnants of the original road to the pass from the Canyon area on the west side of the road, especially if you hike a couple hundred yards up the trail. The other end of this old roadbed can be found behind the Dunraven Road Picnic Area (see 15.8/2.4 below). Today's road follows the path originally recommended by Capt. Hiram Chittenden when he designed the road system in this area. His road engineer at the time, however, elected to deviate from Chittenden's specifications (to avoid some marshy areas), much to the Captain's chagrin. The road was built at a much higher elevation than originally outlined and this resulted in much greater effort and expense in maintaining the road, especially with respect to snow removal and getting the road opened each season. In the 1930s, the road was realigned to follow (generally) that which exists today.

Dunraven Pass was also the site of a ranger station/check station in the park's early days. The U.S. Army constructed a checking station here to monitor the flow of traffic through the area, and to serve as an outpost for patrolling this section of the park. When they left, the NPS used it as a road camp until the 1930s, and then as a ranger station until World War II. Most of the buildings were removed in the early 1940s, though the last one wasn't gone until 1958.[7]

13.9 / 4.4 GPS: 44.77971, -110.45676
SULPHUR CREEK OVERLOOK (E) 🅟 🚻

Another view of Washburn Hot Springs (see below) and Mt. Washburn to the north, and **Sulphur Creek** below the parking area. The creek gets its name from the presence of sulfur in the water (the creek was named in the early days of the park using the old spelling). This pullout has a vault toilet.

14.9 / 3.3 GPS: 44.76787, -110.45539
WASHBURN HOT SPRINGS/CALDERA TURNOUT (E) 📷 🏔

This turnout affords a view of **Washburn Hot Springs**, a small thermal area on the southern face of Mt. Washburn. The area includes a group of dark-colored mud pots, including the Devil's Inkstand and Inkpot Spring, along with about a dozen other unnamed hot springs. The dark color of these comes from a black pigment created by a sulfide of iron called pyrite (FeS^2). There is an interpretive sign here that provides some background on the Yellowstone caldera.

15.8 / 2.4 GPS: 44.76183, -110.47119
DUNRAVEN ROAD PICNIC AREA (W) 🌲 🚻

The **Dunraven Road Picnic Area** area has 12 tables and a handicap-accessible vault toilet.

Exiting to the west from the rear of the picnic area is the remnant of the original road that took vehicles from this area up to Dunraven Pass. This is the other end of the road you saw (or will see) across from the Mt. Washburn South Trailhead (see the entry at 13.5/4.8 above). As you drive north you'll occasionally see signs of the old road on the hills above you to the west. The road made an almost 90 degree bend here and crossed the current road onto the other side just south of the existing driveway - you can see a slight clearing in the trees on the east side of the road where the old road went through. For the next couple of miles or so (traveling south), the old road crossed back and forth over the existing road.

17.0 / 1.3 GPS: 44.75151, -110.48596
CASCADE LAKE PICNIC AREA (W) 🌲 🚻

The **Cascade Lake Picnic Area** is one of the larger ones in the park, having 16 tables, five grills, and a handicap-accessible vault toilet.

You can take a trail from the picnic area's south end to connect to the Cascade Lake Trail, though this section is no longer maintained. Up until about 2007, this was the primary trailhead for that trail, but traffic and parking for those wishing to use the trail interfered with the use of the area as a picnic spot. Therefore, if you plan to do no picnicking here, consider using the trailhead ³⁄₁₀ of a mile to the south.

17.3 / 1.0 GPS: 44.74994, -110.49152
CASCADE LAKE TRAILHEAD (W) 🚶

The **Cascade Lake Trail** is a 2.2-mile (3.5 km, each way) trail to Cascade Lake. You can also reach Observation Peak, one of the park's old fire lookout towers (built in 1937 by the Civilian Conservation Corps, and still used by rangers as a patrol cabin), and the Howard Eaton Trail (also known as the Chain of Lakes Trail in this section of the park). This trail

connects you to Grebe Lake, Wolf Lake, and Ice Lake, and then on to the
Solfatara Creek Trail north of the Norris Campground. The lake contains
a population of cutthroats and grayling (catch and release only), and is
the headwater for Cascade Creek. The creek used to supply water for the
facilities in the Canyon area before 1957.

17.8 / 0.5 GPS: 44.74249, -110.49407
GOVERNMENT AREA SERVICE ROAD (W)

This road leads into the NPS maintenance and governmental residence
area for Canyon Village.

18.3 / 0.0 GPS: 44.73591, -110.49325 ELEVATION: 7924 FEET
CANYON JUNCTION ▣ ⁄ ▵ △ ¶¶ ⑦ ▣ ⊨ ⊠ ♠ ♻ ♦♦♦ ▨ ¥ ₪

From here you can travel 18.3 miles (29.5 km) north to Tower Junction,
11.5 miles (18.5 km) west to Norris Junction, 15.4 miles (24.8 km) south
to Fishing Bridge Junction, or you can turn east into the Canyon Village
Development.

Just north of the junction itself you can turn into the Canyon YPSS
Service Station.

Canyon Junction
to
Fishing Bridge Junction

The road from Canyon Junction to Fishing Bridge is 15.4 miles (24.8 km) long, and passes through Hayden Valley, one of the most wildlife-rich areas of the park. The north and south ends of this road travel through richly-for

ested areas, while the middle two thirds of it pass along/through an area that was once a part of Yellowstone Lake.

The prevailing theory these days suggests that this massive lake was trapped behind a dam made of glacial ice and that, at some point, it melted, releasing all of that water. The existing Yellowstone Lake is all that remains. As it was a former lake bed, the soils in the valley are rich in clay, and do not permit water to sink into the soil. Therefore, trees cannot grow here. The lush grasses of the area are perfect for the bison, many of which inhabit this area year round. Many others migrate to different areas of the park (including the Madison Valley on the opposite side of the park), and return here in August specifically for the rut (mating season).

The present day Canyon Junction is the fourth iteration of the intersection of the Grand Loop Road and the road from Norris, commonly known as the Norris Cutoff Road. The junction has been moved as development of the Canyon area occurred over time. Its current iteration is the result of the development of the existing Canyon Village as part of the Mission 66 Program in Yellowstone in the late 1950s. The previous three junctions were further south (see the mileage log below for details on one of those).

This road is one of the more heavily traveled stretches in the entire park, and the presence of bison, wolves, grizzly bears, and waterfowl on any given day ensure that traffic will be backed up. During the busy August bison rut, it's not uncommon for these backups to be measured in miles and the time needed to travel the 15 miles measured in hours. So if your plans call for a visit to this area during this time frame, be prepared. There are no toilets in the heart of the valley, so utilize one at the picnic areas or at Mud Volcano if you're traveling north, or stop in at Canyon Village if you're headed south.

If you're going to be traveling this road at night, pay special attention to the speed limit, and you may even wish to drive a few miles per hour under it. Bison are very hard to see at night, and every year, more than a dozen are hit and killed by automobiles along this road. In almost every case, an impact with a bison will total even the largest SUV, and it's not uncommon at all to have people injured or occasionally killed in one of these accidents. This section of road has the highest number of motor vehicle vs. wildlife accident rates in the park, not surprisingly.

There are a huge number of turnouts along the valley and the river, as well as several picnic areas, but keep in mind that the Yellowstone River is closed to all fishing (and watercraft!) through Hayden Valley.

0.0 / 15.4 GPS: 44.73591, -110.49325 ELEVATION: 7924 FEET
CANYON JUNCTION 🔌 ⚡ ♨ ⛺ 🍴 ⑦ 🗑 🛏 ✉ 🏠 ♻ 👫 🎒 🥤 📷
CANYON VILLAGE (E)

From here, you can travel 18.3 miles (29.4 km) north to Tower Junction, 11.6 miles (18.7 km) west to Norris Junction, 15.4 miles (24.8 km) south to Fishing Bridge Junction, or you can turn east into the Canyon Village Development.

Canyon Village was constructed as part of the Mission 66 program. Work began in 1956 and much of it was completed in time for at least a portion of the area to be open for the 1957 summer season. See the Canyon Village Development section for details on the history and background of the buildings in this area.

0.1 / 15.2 GPS: 44.73386, -110.49341
CANYON VILLAGE SERVICE ROAD (E)
CASCADE MEADOW/DOLLAR LAKE (W)

The road running east here is a service road for employees and deliveries to the stores and the Visitor Education Center and is not open to the public.

Cascade Meadow can be seen to the west. Cascade Creek flows through this area and was once the primary source of potable water for many of the facilities that existed in this area before the late 1950s. This was the site of a Washburn Expedition camp on August 30, 1870.[1] The small, seasonal lake on the west side of the road is known colloquially as Dollar Lake.

0.7 / 14.7 GPS: 44.72626, -110.49390
LOCATION OF OLD CANYON TRANSPORTATION COMPLEX (E)

The flat expanse of meadow on the east side of the road was the site of the old **Canyon Transportation Complex** maintained by Xanterra's predecessor concession operator, the Yellowstone Park Transportation Company (YPTC). At its height, there were some two dozen buildings here, including bus barns, maintenance shops, employee housing, and other support facilities.

Prior to that, beginning in 1908, there were facilities for housing and maintaining the stagecoaches that provided transportation for guests from the nearby hotels. Most of the buildings were removed in the 1960s, though one, a small tin shed, did linger to 1996. Three of the buildings here were designed by Robert Reamer (architect of the Old Faithful Inn), including a hay barn, which was converted into a driver's dorm once the transition to buses was made. The remodeled facility became known locally as the Cody Bunkhouse because it housed the drivers who transported tourists between Canyon and the Cody train depot.

0.9 / 14.5 GPS: 44.72337, -110.49422
CANYON CORRALS (W) 🐎 🚻
SITE OF THE OLD GRAND CANYON HOTEL (W)

The **Canyon Corral** hosts about 70 horses during the summer, and visitors can avail themselves of one- and two-hour guided rides. There are several barns and related structures here. The house on the hill north of the corral is known as the "Winterkeeper's Residence." It is where the maintenance manager for the concession company lives during the summer, and the winter keeper (person who shovels snow off the roofs of the buildings) lives during the winter. Off to the east, you can see a couple of buildings at the Canyon Wastewater Treatment Plant.

This area was also the site of the gargantuan **Canyon Hotel** until 1960. In 1889, a 250-room hotel was built at the south end of the current site of the Canyon Corrals to replace an older structure located at what is today the Brink of the Upper Falls parking lot. Despite known problems with the stability of the foundation, a third hotel was built here in 1910-1911.

The third Canyon Hotel, ca. 1941. Note the section near the top below the structure built at a 45° angle from it. This was the second Canyon Hotel, originally constructed in 1889.

Designed by Robert Reamer, who'd also designed the Old Faithful Inn and updates to the Lake Hotel, the building incorporated the 1889 structure. Over 250 men worked seven days a week for months in temperatures as low as -40°F (-40°C) to get the hotel ready in time to open for the 1911 summer season. Successive additions eventually led to a structure that was almost one mile in circumference, containing 430 rooms and capable of housing almost 1,000 guests. Structural problems would haunt the facility throughout its life, however.

In the late 1950s, as part of the Mission 66 Program, NPS required the primary park concessioner, the Yellowstone Park Company (YPC), to build a cabin and lodge operation at the new Canyon Village. YPC had wanted to keep the hotel open as well, but when it was determined that the structure would require extensive foundation repairs, the company lacked the funds to make that happen, having invested so heavily in the new facilities up the road. As a result, the hotel was sold to a salvage company for a mere $25. It closed after the 1959 season, and the salvage company began disassembling the building.

On August 8, 1960, what was left of the hotel mysteriously caught fire and burned to the ground. No official cause was ever determined, though there were many theories about how the fire started. Some thought the salvage company burned it so they didn't have to tear the building down or that YPC employees were having a party in the building and started the fire accidentally. One theory held that the Grand Old Lady spontaneously combusted, preferring to go out in a blaze of glory rather than suffer the indignity of being taken apart piece by piece and sold as scrap.[2]

Today, if you get out and walk around the area, you can still see remnants of the old hotel's footprint in many places. One of the original men's dorms for the old hotel was converted into the large hay barn you see at the rear of the corral.

1.2 / 14.2 GPS: 44.72059, -110.49962
NORTH RIM DRIVE (E) 🚗

The **North Rim Drive** is a 2.2-mile long scenic drive that affords access to the brink of the Lower Falls and several observation points along the Canyon. This includes Inspiration Point. See the Miscellaneous Road Section for the road log.

1.5 / 13.9 GPS: 44.71839, -110.50449
CASCADE CREEK CROSSING

The road crosses over **Cascade Creek** here. The stream has its headwater at Cascade Lake (from whence it gets its name) northwest of today's Canyon Village. Until the new village was developed an impoundment diverted water into a reservoir near the north end of the creek. This reservoir provided potable water to the old hotel and other facilities located in the canyon area.

The creek continues on to the edge of the Grand Canyon and falls over its side as Crystal Falls, visible from the Upper Falls Overlook at Uncle Tom's Trailhead. Until 1959, raw sewage from the Canyon Hotel emptied into the creek just above the waterfall.

1.6 / 13.8 GPS: 44.71707, -110.50483
BRINK OF UPPER FALLS ROAD (E) 🚗 🚻 ♀♂
CANYON ELECTRICAL SUBSTATION SERVICE ROAD (W)

The **Brink of the Upper Falls Road** carries you to a parking area where you can take a short, paved trail down to the brink of the 109-foot Upper Falls of the Yellowstone. This area was where the original road between Lake Village and the Canyon area connected together. Prior to the development of Canyon Village, this is where you'd find all the stores, the ranger station, gas station, and other support buildings that made up the development at Canyon.

As soon as you turn into today's road just before you get to the parking lot, the old Whittaker Store (built in 1921) and gas station (1924) were on the left-hand side of the road. The ranger station (1921) was where the small island with the "one way" sign is today. The Haynes Photo Shop

(1924) was immediately north of the present day comfort station. There's an old spur road off to the right of the parking lot entrance (still visible). As you drove down that road, the auto camp was on the right, and the housekeeping cabins (forerunners of today's cabins) were on the left. The first auto campground replaced the second Wylie Camp in the Canyon area.

The first Canyon Hotel (1886) was north of the auto camp, and replaced a tent camp that had been there since 1883. The new hotel had a large structure that housed office, kitchen and dining room, and several small rooms for up to 45 guests, supplemented by a series of tents for additional capacity (likely left over from the tent camp the new hotel replaced). The total capacity was about 70 guests (plus employees).[3]

The trail from the road that leads south from the brink takes you along the original road through this area, terminating at Chittenden Bridge. It was abandoned for vehicular use when the existing Fishing Bridge to Canyon Road was constructed. This old segment is known locally as the Crystal Falls Road now. One of its more unique features is the large arch bridge over Jay Creek. This bridge was built in 1915 by the U. S. Army Corps of Engineers. It is no longer used for vehicular traffic, but is part of the North Rim Trail.

As you can see, all of this development was right on the edge of the canyon at this point, and this was the impetus for relocating everything northward and away from this area. The Canyon Village Development section has an aerial view of the cabins and other structures that used to exist here so you can see how they were placed relative to what's here now.

The dirt road leading to the west from this point is the east end of what was the original road to the Canyon area from Norris Junction prior to 1957. Today, it is a service road that leads back to the Canyon Electrical Substation, as well as a carcass disposal area. Due to safety concerns, this road is closed to public travel (foot or bicycle). Across the road from this entrance you can still see a hint of the old road that led to the auto campground referenced above.

1.8 / 13.5 GPS: 44.71406, -110.50437
OLD CANYON CAMPGROUND (W)

On the west side of the road here was the third iteration of the Canyon Campground, which existed up until the current campground in Canyon Village was built in the late 1950s. The previous two campgrounds were located immediately to the north of this area on the same side of the road.

2.1 / 13.2 GPS: 44.70971, -110.50507
GRAVEL PIT/INCINERATOR SITE (W)
NPS CORRALS/FIRE CACHE/SITE OF OLD ROAD CAMP (W)

This service road leads back to an area where construction materials are staged, as well as a helicopter landing site, and is home to an NPS fire cache and barn/corral where rangers' horses are kept when they're not patrolling the backcountry. Both the barn and the fire cache building were built in 1934 by the Civilian Conservation Corps.

From 1903 through the early 1930s, this area was a huge garbage dump, used by the area's hotels, campgrounds, and other facilities to dispose of trash. In 1929, the NPS constructed an incinerator here that remained in service until World War II when manpower was too short to allow them to continue operating it. The incinerator and its bunkhouse were razed in 1949. The concession companies continued disposing of trash in this area until 1932 when the new "bear feeding ground" was constructed at Otter Creek (see 2.7/12.7 below).[4] NPS also operated a road camp here in the 1910s-1930s.

2.3 / 13.1 GPS: 44.70814, -110.50376
SOUTH RIM DRIVE (E) 🎞️

The 1.6 mile **South Rim Drive** takes you to Uncle Tom's Trail and to Artist Point, one of the most photographed (read: busiest) areas of the park during the summer. See the Miscellaneous Roads section for the road log.

2.7 / 12.7 GPS: 44.70244, -110.50580
OTTER CREEK BEAR FEEDING AREA SERVICE ROAD (W)
OTTER CREEK CROSSING

The Grand Loop Road crosses **Otter Creek** here, named for the river otter, an indigenous inhabitant of the park. The bridge over the creek was built in 1934 during the reconstruction of this section of roadway.

The service road leads back to the old **Otter Creek Bear Feeding Area**. Constructed in 1930-1931, this area was used to feed the park's bears as a form of entertainment for tourists until World War II. As many as 600 vehicles would line up each evening bringing hundreds of tourists to watch the bears rummage through the garbage and fight with one another. People would sit on a series of benches arranged in an amphitheater style constructed on a hill across from the feeding platform. Though the seating capacity was 250 people, there'd often be far more than that, with the hillside literally covered with human beings, watching as many as 67 bears feed over the course of one evening. There was a special bunker with portholes for photographers to get good, up-close shots, and the area was patrolled by rangers armed with 30.06 rifles to protect the spectators. This practice stopped in 1941, and the facility was razed in 1946.

This area was also used as one of two "group camps" from the 1960s until 1982 (the other was at Indian Pond on the East Entrance Road). These camps were set aside for groups like the Boy Scouts or large family reunions, and had a capacity of about 200 people. The camp was in the meadow over the spectator hill, a meadow referred to by the locals as Tesinsky Meadow, after Bill Tesinsky, a photographer who was killed by a grizzly bear there in 1986.

This area was also the site of a skirmish between tourists and the Nez Perce in 1877, as the Nez Perce were fleeing the U. S. Army. The Helena Party had camped on the hill upon which the spectator seating was later built. When the warriors raided the camp, they shot and killed one member of the party and wounded another. The man who was killed was buried in the area initially, but later disinterred and moved to Helena.[5]

3.0 / 12.4 GPS: 44.69845, -110.50326
OTTER CREEK PICNIC AREA (E) 🎪 🚻

The **Otter Creek Picnic Area** has eight tables, but no toilet facilities. Over the past few years, this has been a fairly popular spot to watch the Canyon wolf pack at times. The picnic area is generally pretty busy during the summer, being very easy to get to and situated alongside the river.

4.2 / 11.2 GPS: 44.68349, -110.49383
MARY MOUNTAIN EAST TRAILHEAD (E) 🥾

This is the eastern terminus of the **Mary Mountain Trail**, a 20-mile (32.2 km) trail that has its western end on the other side of the park just south of the junction of the Nez Perce Creek and the Firehole River. The trail takes you past Highland Hot Springs, a thermal area of about 50 unnamed thermal features, before making its way to Mary Lake. From that point westward, the trail is also known as the Nez Perce Creek Trail. This area is for day use only, and no overnight camping is permitted.

It is important to keep in mind that this area is heavily used by grizzly bears, especially in the late summer, and has been an area where a substantial number of human-grizzly encounters have taken place, a few of which have been fatal. Use caution, hike in groups, and carry your bear spray with you if you plan to hike this trail. It is not at all uncommon for rangers to close this area for public safety reasons. This also marks the north end of Hayden Valley.

4.6 / 10.8 GPS: 44.67901, -110.48805
River Feast Turnout (E) ✷

This pullout has an interpretive sign explaining the prevalence of waterfowl and other wildlife that live in and around the river.

4.8 / 10.6 GPS: 44.67759, -110.48577
Alum Creek Crossing

Alum Creek was given its official name in the park's early days for its taste. Park historian Lee Whittlesey has a lengthy history of the creek's name and other monikers under which it has been known in his book, *Yellowstone Place Names*.

5.0 / 10.4 GPS: 44.67537, -110.48218
Unnamed Turnouts (E & W)
Old Crater Hills Road (W)
Crater Hills Thermal Area/Sulphur Mountain (W)

At the southern end of the western turnout here you may notice a couple of depressions that form what appears to be a vehicle path heading off to the south. This is a remnant of the old **Crater Hills Road**.

From 1880 until around 1894, the primary route from the west side of the park to the Canyon and Lake areas was via the old Mary Mountain Road, today known as the Mary Mountain Trail (or, at least, much of it). The road came across from Porcupine Hills to Mary Lake, up to Highland Hot Springs, then headed southeasterly along Trout Creek until it got to just south of what we know today as the **Crater Hills Thermal Area** (the thermal area visible at the foot of the hill, known as **Sulphur Mountain**, to the south from this pullout). At that point, stagecoaches could head north to the Canyon area along the path you see here or south to the Lake area.[6]

In 1894, the U. S. Army Corps of Engineers (USACE) completed a new road between Lake and Canyon, generally following today's Hayden Valley Road, and the Mary Mountain Road connected to it just south of the big bend along Trout Creek (a parallel road was later constructed to the Trout Creek Dump, terminating at the same location. See the entry at 7.7/7.5

below). With the completion of the new Hayden Valley Road and the road between Old Faithful and West Thumb, the Mary Mountain Road and its spur here were no longer necessary and fell into disuse. However, because of continued interest in the Crater Hills thermal features, in 1895, the USACE constructed a new side road to the area, much of the northern portion of it along the same path as the original stagecoach road, which is what you're seeing here. This road remained in use until 1929, when it was closed and abandoned.

5.2 / 10.2 GPS: 44.67401, -110.47962
Sulphur Spring Creek crossing

Here you cross over **Sulphur Spring Creek**, though it has no sign announcing its name as the other major streams in the area do. Originating in the Crater Hills Thermal Area, it empties into the Yellowstone River here.

Crater Hills is a small thermal area of approximately 70 features of varying types, the majority of which remain unnamed. Among the named features are Blue Mud Pot, Turbid Blue Mud Spring, Foam Spring, and Sulphur Spring, the headwater for the creek. The area was quite popular in the early days of the park, as the primary road from the west passed right by it (see entry above). The moderate-sized hill you see the steam rising from is known as Sulphur Mountain. This area is very popular with grizzly bears in the summer, so if you go hiking to the mountain/thermal area, be sure to take the proper precautions.

5.8 / 9.6 GPS: 44.66814, -110.47015
Grizzly Overlook (E) 🧍 🔭

Grizzly Overlook is perhaps one of the best wildlife viewing platforms in the park, sitting atop a 100,000 year old rhyolitic outcropping within Hayden Valley. You have a panoramic view of the entire valley from here, and will often see bison, bears (including, of course, the grizzly, for which the turnout is named), and the gray wolf, in addition to the waterfowl and a variety of other animals.

In May and early June, the floor of the valley is often still covered with snow, making spotting wildlife quite easy. When wildlife is active in the valley below this overlook, the traffic around this area can get quite busy, so please keep an eye out for people darting in and out of the parking area. The parking area was reconfigured in 2013, reducing the number of vehicles that can park in the turnout. During the busy parts of the summer, there is usually an interpretive ranger stationed here.

Walk up and over hill on the west side of the road and down into the valley to see remnants of the original 1894 road through this area. There are several sections of this road visible along the west side of the existing road between Alum Creek and the Mud Volcano area.

6.3 / 9.1 GPS: 44.66273, -110.46442
UNNAMED TURNOUT (E)

The steam you might see coming from the hills off in the distance to the north is from the Forest Springs Thermal Area, a collection of about 200 unnamed hot pools due east of the Lower Falls.

7.5 / 7.9 GPS: 44.64597, -110.45867
TROUT CREEK CROSSING

Trout Creek crosses the road here. It was named by the Hague Expedition of 1885 in accordance with the practice of naming park features after indigenous wildlife.[7] As you head north, on a clear day, you can see the fire lookout tower atop Mt. Washburn.

Located near here (and to the west) is the area where bison were relocated into Hayden Valley in the mid-1890s. This was done to help preserve the park's herd, and was paid for by the Smithsonian Institution.

Just to the north of the crossing, on the west side of the road, was the site of the old Trout Creek Road Camp from 1908 into the 1930s. The buildings were removed in 1938.[8]

This was also the south end of the old Crater Hills Road (see 5.0/10.4 above), as well as the original Mary Mountain Road that allowed travelers to get to this side of the park from the geyser basins on the west side. Along this road, a few miles west of here, was the Trout Creek Lunch Station, which served to provide hot meals to travelers on their way between the two sides of the park. It operated from 1888 until 1891, and was relocated to West Thumb when the road over Craig Pass opened.

7.8 / 7.6 GPS: 44.64259, -110.45674
OLD TROUT CREEK DUMP ROAD (W)

Barely discernible along the edge of the small depression here, this road led 2.5 miles (4.0 km) west to the **Trout Creek Dump**, one of the sites where the park disposed of much of its garbage from 1951 (after the old incinerators were shut down) through 1970. The majority of the debris generated during the building of Canyon Village was dumped here in the late 1950s, and the dump was used to dispose of debris generated by operations at Canyon, Fishing Bridge, Lake, and Bridge Bay until it ceased operation.

This practice was stopped in the early 1970s, primarily because the park's bears had come to rely on obtaining food at these sites, and that was deemed (appropriately) unnatural. The park's garbage is now sent to West Yellowstone, and much of it is recycled or composted.

7.9 / 7.5 GPS: 44.64089, -110.45531
Elk Antler Creek Turnout (E)

Elk Antler Creek crosses under the road just south of turnout. It was named by Superintendent Horace Albright for the prevalence of antlers throughout the park.

8.5 / 6.9 GPS: 44.63466, -110.44817
American Bison Turnout (E) 🚶 🔭

This turnout affords an excellent view of Hayden Valley and the Yellowstone River. There are three interpretive panels here that explain the American Bison and its migration, calving, and mating cycles, as well as its role in the park's ecosystem.

9.1 / 6.3 GPS: 44.63031, -110.43922
Hayden Valley Turnout (E) 🚶

If you're headed north this is your first good look at **Hayden Valley**, and if you're headed south, then it's your last good look. There's an interpretive panel here that explains how Hayden Valley was formed. Hayden Valley is named for Dr. Ferdinand V. Hayden, the medical doctor turned USGS geologist who led several exploratory expeditions into Yellowstone in the 1870s.

At one time, this entire area was part of Yellowstone Lake. As a result, the floor is composed of a thick, clay-rich sediment and therefore water has a hard time soaking into the ground.[9] Trees also have a hard time taking root, so you won't see many of those in the floor of the valley. The thick, lush grasses here make it the home and breeding grounds for one of the park's major bison herds. As a result, Hayden Valley is one of the best places to see the bison rut each August.

9.5 / 5.9 GPS: 44.62710, -110.43277
SULPHUR CAULDRON TURNOUT (E) ⬛
SOUR CREEK DOME (E)

Sulphur Cauldron sits below the turnout here on the east side of the road. Several sources say this is the most acidic feature in the park, with a pH of around 1.3 to 1.8. The park's thermal features database, however, lists its pH as 2.4, still strong enough to eat human skin.

The ridge across the river from Sulphur Caldron is the **Sour Creek Dome**, one of two resurgent domes found in Yellowstone today (the other is the Mallard Lake Dome just east of the Old Faithful area). These domes are formed by the swelling or rising of the floor due to movement in the magma chamber beneath it.

From 1923 to the mid 1980s, surveyors noticed a rise of almost one meter in this area, and thus discovered that Yellowstone was "breathing."[10] Sometimes the ground also recedes, however - all part of the geologic processes that make Yellowstone what it is. Scientists have a vast array of seismic and ground deformation monitoring equipment deployed throughout the park, and monitor these processes very closely.

9.5 / 5.8 GPS: 44.62585, -110.43310
MUD VOLCANO PARKING LOT (W) ⬛ ⬛ ⬛

The **Mud Volcano** area includes approximately 60 thermal features, including those at Sulphur Cauldron to the north and the 15 or so unnamed features across the river. They include the infamous Black Dragon's Caldron, Dragon's Mouth Spring (which has had more than a dozen different names since it was discovered), Sour Lake (with a pH of 2.7), Churning Caldron, and Mud Volcano itself.

In contrast to most of the other thermal basins in the park, this area uses primarily surface water (i.e., from snow melt, rain runoff, etc.) to provide the liquid for the actions of its features. As a result of a lack of significant ground water, there are no actual geysers here; most of the features are either mud pots or hot springs. There are some noisy features here to be sure. And in fact the 1870 Washburn Expedition made note of hearing what sounded like distant artillery as they approached the area.[11]

Note that you can only enter the parking area from the north driveway. Portions of this trail are wheelchair accessible, and there are four wheelchair-accessible vault toilets in the parking lot.

On the east side of the road is a very small pullout from which you can view a few other thermal features located across the river from the Mud Volcano area.

9.9 / 5.4 GPS: 44.61973, -110.42567
COLD WATER GEYSER PULLOUT (E)

Though there are no signs here, there are two small features of interest. The first is a small cold water pool located about 150 feet off the side of the road (over the small hill). It is a perpetual spouter of about 6 inches.

The second is **Cold Water Geyser,** located along the riverside (follow the informal trail to it). It erupts sporadically to heights of about 1.5 to 3 feet.[12] Neither of these is a true "thermal" feature, but rather are driven by carbon dioxide escaping from underground.

10.2 / 5.2 GPS: 44.61924, -110.42432
NEZ PERCE MEADOW PULLOUTS (E & W)

These pullouts look out onto **Nez Perce Meadow** and seem rather innocuous, but are perhaps one of the best places to park to watch the bison rut in August. You can sit here for hours and watch the big bulls fight one another alongside the road for the right to mate with the females.

10.4 / 5.0 GPS: 44.61838, -110.42086
NEZ PERCE FORD PICNIC AREA (E)

The **Nez Perce Ford Picnic Area** is one of the largest in the park, with 17 tables and a handicap-accessible vault toilet.

This area got its name from the route the Nez Perce Indians took during their flight across the park on August 25, 1877; they forded the river here. The area was also referred to as Buffalo Ford for a period of time, after a small herd of bison was found frozen to death at the crossing in the winter of 1946.

10.5 / 4.9 GPS: 44.61797, -110.41853
TROUT SPAWNING/MIGRATION TURNOUT (E)

This pullout has three interpretive panels describing the importance of the river to the ecosystem, whirling disease, and the migration and spawning of Yellowstone Cutthroat Trout along the river. The trout is considered one of the most critical species of wildlife in the park.

10.6 / 4.8 GPS: 44.61681, -110.41664
CASCADE PICNIC AREA (W) 🏕 ♦♦ ℂ
SITE OF THE MUD VOLCANO SOLIDER STATION (W)

The **Cascade Picnic Area** has six tables, a handicap-accessible vault toilet, and a holdover from the 1970s - a public pay phone. These phones were placed in strategic locations throughout the park after an oil tanker turned over and burned in 1970. Most have been removed, but this one and one near the Norris Campground remain.

This area was the site of the old **Mud Volcano Soldier Station**, originally known as the Mud Volcano Safety Station when it was first constructed in the mid-1890s. The station was placed here to allow soldiers to protect the small bison herd that existed in Hayden Valley at the time (see the entry at 7.5/7.9 above).

Later, the area was converted to a moderate-sized auto campground, capable of hosting about 54 vehicles. Although there were plans to convert the campground into a large, more "official" campground (to be known as the Hayden Valley Campground, with 111 spaces, part of the Mission 66 Program[13]), those plans were never realized, and it became a picnic area in the late 1960s.

11.3 / 4.1 GPS: 44.61081, -110.40747
LEHARDY PICNIC AREA (W) 🏕 ♦♦

The **LeHardy Picnic Area** has six tables and a handicap-accessible vault toilet. There's also a riverside pullout on the east side of the road.

12.3 / 3.1 GPS: 44.60768, -110.38696
NORTH LEHARDY RAPIDS TURNOUT (E) ⭐ 🏕 ♦♦ ♿

LeHardy Rapids is named after Paul LeHardy, a topographer who accompanied the expedition of Capt. William Jones in 1873. The Jones Expedition is not as widely discussed as many of the others that sought to explore the area, but Jones' exploration was an attempt to locate a suitable route from the Wind River Mountain Range to Montana as a part of his duties to develop military defenses of the area. Jones Pass, north of Sylvan Pass, is named for him, and was considered for a time as a possible route for the East Entrance Road before Hiram Chittenden decided the route via Sylvan Pass would be easier to construct and more scenic. LeHardy had a particularly frightening encounter here when he lost his raft (and much of his equipment) in the rapids.

There are a couple of picnic tables alongside the river here, though it is not an official picnic area and does not show up on any maps as such. Much of the walkway/boardwalk here is wheelchair-accessible.

12.6 / 2.8 GPS: 44.60588, -110.38364
SOUTH LEHARDY RAPIDS TURNOUT (E) 🔭 🏛

LeHardy Rapids is a section of water cascades over a series of northeast trending fault lines where hard rock has been uplifted, forming a dam that holds back the water that creates Yellowstone Lake. In fact, geologists and ecologists consider this to be the northern boundary of the lake and the beginning of the Yellowstone River.[14]

This is an excellent spot to watch the annual trout migration, as the fish attempt to swim upstream over these rapids. There is a substantial boardwalk here that affords riverside access.

12.8 / 2.6 GPS: 44.60309, -110.38524
DIRT SERVICE ROAD (W)

The dirt service road running west into the woods here allows crews from Northwestern Energy to access the power lines running between Canyon and Fishing Bridge.

13.0 / 2.4 GPS: 44.59966, -110.38702
SITE OF OLD LEHARDY RAPIDS CAMPGROUND (E)

The large meadow here is the site of an old, informal campground known as the LeHardy Rapids Campground, which was used until the late 1960s.[15]

13.5 / 1.9 GPS: 44.59194, -110.38623
OLD ROADBED (E)

This pullout is innocuous, and it appears as if nothing's here. However, if you walk southeast into the woods a short distance, you'll find the remnants of the old road that used to lead from this point down to what was the old Fishing Bridge Junction prior to its realignment in 1972. When the road was constructed around Lake Village, the junction was moved to the west about 200 yards, and the road from where you are to the existing Fishing Bridge Junction was constructed.

The old road bed was abandoned to history, and now has a stand of lodgepole pine trees growing on it. There is an old benchmark from 1923 cemented into the top of a small boulder along the trail (used primarily by bison now). The road came out about 200 yards east of the present day Fishing Bridge Junction near another benchmark sitting on a concrete pedestal visible from the roadway.

14.9 / 0.5 GPS: 44.57435, -110.38257
FISHING BRIDGE MICROWAVE SERVICE ROAD (W)

The gravel road headed west into the woods here is a service road that allows crews to access a microwave tower used to transmit radio and telecommunications signals to Mount Washburn.

15.1 / 0.3 GPS: 44.57122, -110.38586
FISHING BRIDGE RESERVOIR SERVICE ROAD (W)

The service road on the west side of the highway leads back to a cold spring, pumping station, and a water reservoir that supplies potable water for the Fishing Bridge area. Water is captured from these springs, treated, and then pumped to the reservoir, which is connected to those at Lake and Bridge Bay to help balance the water supply for the entire area. When the supply system was initially constructed in this area, there was a huge redwood tank that held the water. This was replaced with the existing 250,000 gallon concrete reservoir in the 1930s.

15.4 / 0.0 GPS: 44.56810, -110.38829 ELEVATION: 7832 FEET
FISHING BRIDGE JUNCTION

From here, you can go 25.9 miles (41.7 km) east to the East Entrance, 15.4 miles (24.8 km) north to Canyon Village, or head south 20.6 miles (33.2 km) to West Thumb Junction.

East
Entrance Road
—◦∞◦—

The East Entrance Road is 25.9 (41.6 km) miles long from the park boundary to Fishing Bridge Junction. The road takes you into Yellowstone via Sylvan Pass, and through some of the most spectacular forested scenery in the park.

The original East Entrance Road was built by U.S. Army Engineer Capt. Hiram Chittenden. It was completed in 1903, and included the large log bridge that came to be known as Fishing Bridge. The route over Sylvan Pass was selected over a proposed route via Jones Pass some six miles to the north due to it being approximately 1000 feet (304 m) lower in elevation and having much better scenery. Chittenden stated he selected the route because, "[Sylvan] is one of great scenic beauty and will be an important addition to the attractions of the park."[1]

In 1927, immediately after the Bureau of Public Roads (BPR) assumed responsibility for major road projects within the park, work began on rebuilding the road. This included the rerouting of a segment that originally passed along Turbid Lake, and building a new road along the sides of the mountains above the old road from Sylvan Pass eastward. The rerouting of the road from Turbid Lake to its current path along the shore of Yellowstone Lake was done because the newer route was perceived to be much more scenic. And, in hindsight, the old road also passed through some very critical grizzly bear habitat. Had it existed today, it would likely have become a candidate for being rerouted for that reason alone.

The new road east from the pass itself was completed higher up on the side of the mountain, which alleviated some of the issues with steep grades and unstable roadbeds causing a lot of maintenance problems. It also eliminated the need for the Corkscrew Bridge, the remnants of which can still be seen below a turnout just east of the large parking area on the pass.

The East Entrance Road parallels Middle Creek from the park's border back to its source just below the pass at the base of Top Notch Peak. For the first few miles, you'll come across several itinerant waterfalls cascading down the rock walls built to protect the road from falling debris.

You'll pass two of the prettiest lakes in the park, Eleanor Lake (named after engineer Hiram Chittenden's daughter), and Sylvan Lake, and then continue westward to Yellowstone Lake, the largest high-altitude lake in the United States.

Until you get to the lake and the Fishing Bridge area, the only wildlife you're likely to encounter along this road is the occasional grizzly bear digging for meals alongside the road. You might see the random bull bison sauntering along the roadway as well, and perhaps the occasional pika or marmot in the rocks along the road.

The road is in excellent condition, having been reconstructed over the past decade and a half. There are some significant grades, and if you're driving a larger vehicle, you'll want to use the numerous pullouts to allow faster traffic to pass you when appropriate. During the early and late parts of the season (i.e., through June and from late September on), Sylvan Pass is subject to significant snowfalls and may occasionally close for brief periods until park road crews can get up there and plow the roads.

There are vault toilets at the East Entrance and at several points along the road between the entrance and Fishing Bridge.

0.0 / 25.9 GPS: 44.48947, -110.00167 ELEVATION: 6942 FEET
YELLOWSTONE BOUNDARY

The Yellowstone sign marks the eastern boundary of the park, approximately ¹⁄₁₀ of a mile east of the entrance station.

In 1923, just inside the east boundary on the north side of the road was a small auto campground, perhaps having as few as 12 sites. The campground was apparently removed in the 1940s, or at least, not used again after the war.

0.1 / 25.8 GPS: 44.48862, -110.00388
EAST ENTRANCE STATION 🛖

This is the **East Entrance Station,** where you'll be greeted by a uniformed visitor services representative of the National Park Service, and asked to

Sylvan Pass Lodge, ca. 1930.

pay your entrance fee or show your pass. Once you've paid, hang onto your receipt – you'll need it to get back in the park (and may be asked to show it on the way out). You'll be provided with the park's newspaper, a map, and any other relevant information related to road construction, road closures, or any other situation that might impact your ability to move about the park efficiently. You are welcome to ask any questions, but be mindful of any traffic behind you, especially during the busy summer season.

The Sylvan Pass Soldier Station was erected on the south side of the road here in 1904 right after the road was opened to traffic. It remained in place until the original East Entrance Station and the Ranger Station (still standing) were constructed in 1924, along with the Sylvan Pass Lodge (see below). The East Entrance Station was replaced in 1932, and then again in 1969 with the building you currently see.

The government area on the north side of the road was the site of a short-lived Wylie Permanent Camp Company tent camp from 1913 to 1917. It was closed when all of the camping companies in the park were merged into a single company and their operations consolidated.[2]

In 1924, a new building was constructed here and operated as the Cody Lunch Station initially. Shortly thereafter, it became the Sylvan Pass Lodge, (see photo above) providing bus passengers arriving from Cody with a lunch stop and a minimal number of overnight accommodations. The building closed after the 1934 season due to relatively low utilization, and was torn down in 1940 when the road was realigned and paved.

0.2 / 25.7 GPS: 44.48808, -110.00547
EAST GOVERNMENT AREA ACCESS ROAD/VAULT TOILETS (N) 🚹🚺

There are two vault toilets here, as well as the entrance road into the government housing and maintenance area. A couple of law enforcement rangers are based here as are the personnel who staff the Entrance Station.

1.4 / 24.5 GPS: 44.48164, -110.02686
LICHEN PASS

This lesser known pass through this section of the Absaroka Mountains is known as **Lichen Pass**, so-named for the presence of lichens on the rock walls along the north side of the road. The pass sits at roughly 7050 feet.

1.9 / 24.0 GPS: 44.47902, -110.03568
MIDDLE CREEK ACCESS ROAD (S)

The short dirt road to the south affords access to **Middle Creek**. This was the site of an old contractor's camp during the construction of the original road (1900-1903), and later an informal campground, which was closed in the 1960s.

If you're traveling east, you'll begin the climb out of Middle Creek Valley. The original road through this section of the park was a bit to the south and more closely followed the creek. If you walk down to the creek and head west a couple hundred feet, you'll see evidence of the old road.

3.7 / 22.2 GPS: 44.46830, -110.06721
"SYLVAN FALLS" TURNOUT (N) 🔭 🚹🚺

The waterfall at this turnout is on an unnamed tributary of Middle Creek. In their book documenting many of the waterfalls of the park, Whittlesey, et. al., has suggested the name "Sylvan Falls" for this particular 20-foot plunge, for the fact the waterfall is shaded by trees (the word *sylvan* means "forested area") and its proximity to Sylvan Pass.[3] There is a vault toilet here.

5.1 / 20.8 GPS: 44.46601, -110.09374
UNNAMED TURNOUT W/ WATERFALL (N)
MIDDLE CREEK CANYON

The unnamed 35-foot waterfall here is on an unnamed tributary of Middle Creek. The main road is passing through **Middle Creek Canyon** at this point. You are halfway through it, regardless of whether you're headed east or west. As you head west, you'll likely see several roadside waterfalls cascading down the face of the rocks on the north side of the road, especially during the early part of the season when runoff from the snowmelt is at its peak.

6.1 / 19.8 GPS: 44.45925, -110.11284
SIX MILE CORNER

This almost 90-degree bend in the road and the small pullout here are known colloquially as "Six Mile Corner," since it is six miles from the East Entrance Station.

6.4 / 19.5 GPS: 44.46139, -110.11811
CORKSCREW BRIDGE VIEW PULLOUT (S) 🔆

The pullout on the south side of the road here is above the remnants of the old **Corkscrew Bridge**, constructed in 1919. This earth and concrete structure replaced a wooden bridge built in 1903 when the entrance road was first constructed. These bridges allowed early stagecoaches and motor vehicles to descend the steep grade here more easily.

Just below this area is where the road picks up Middle Creek (specifically, its north fork here), and follows it until it leaves the park at the East Entrance. The creek's source is a cold spring known as Mammoth Crystal Spring just below the pass to the east. The spring's name was given to it for unknown reasons by a tourist in 1905.[4]

7.0 / 18.9 GPS: 44.46460, -110.12766
SYLVAN PASS PARKING AREA (N) P
AVALANCHE CONTROL AREA/OLD ROADBED (S)
"TALUS FALLS" (S)

Sylvan Pass, 8524 feet (2598 m), is a passageway between Hoyt Peak to the north (10506 ft/3202 m) and Top Notch Peak to the south (10245 ft/3123 m). The pass is named for its proximity to Sylvan Lake (see below), while Hoyt Peak is named for Dr. John Wesley Hoyt, a territorial governor of Wyoming (1878-1882) and Top Notch Peak is named for the prominent "notch" at its summit.

The rock pile at the base of Hoyt Peak is andesite talus, which is generated by frost action spalling the material off the face of the cliffs here. This area has been the source of a great deal of rock used in many of the road construction projects throughout the park.

On the south side of the pass is a large platform upon which you may notice a large military-grade Howitzer (seasonally). This gun is used for avalanche control purposes during the winter and early spring. During the winter, this is a very high avalanche hazard area and the pass is often closed due to the danger levels becoming exceptionally high.

Under the howitzer platform is small pullout for an old roadbed that leads down to Corkscrew Bridge. This old road was used until the late 1930s when the existing road was constructed. You can walk down to the old bridge from here, but the road is blocked with a massive amount of trees in a couple of locations.

During the early spring and summer runoff season, you may notice a tall (100-foot) slender column of water cascading down the side of the mountain face. Whittlesey, et. al., has dubbed this *"Talus Falls"* for the prevalence of talus at the pass.[5]

7.6 / 18.3 GPS: 44.46939, -110.13863
Eleanor Lake East Pullout (S)
Crecelius Cascade (S) 🏞

The small body of water is **Eleanor Lake**, named by Hiram Chittenden for his daughter. The lake hosts a small population of cutthroat trout.

During the spring and early summer, you'll likely see **Crecelius Cascade** falling down the face of the mountain. This is a 75-foot seasonal cascade on Clear Creek, and was given its name by Chittenden for his construction foreman on this section of roadway. Clear Creek flows into Eleanor Lake and then out the other side to parallel the road for several miles to the west.

7.8 / 18.1 GPS: 44.47067, -110.14264
Eleanor Lake Picnic Area (S) 🏕
Avalanche Peak Trailhead (N) 🥾

The small **Eleanor Lake Picnic Area** has two tables, but no toilet or other facilities. It is almost always busy during the summer. This area was the site of one of the park's road camps in the 1910s-1930s.

The **Avalanche Peak Trail** is about two steep miles (3 km) in length, making it one of the park's more difficult hikes. In spite of its difficulty, it is one of the more popular trails in the park, however, affording an impressive view from the top (10566 ft/3220 m). If you hike it before mid-July, you can expect to encounter some snow fields.

8.9 / 17.1 GPS: 44.47832, -110.15822
SYLVAN LAKE (S) 🔭
SYLVAN LAKE PICNIC AREA (N) 🌲 🚻

The large lake on the south side of the road here is **Sylvan Lake**, given its name for the lush forest surrounding it (the word *sylvan* means "forested"). You can fish in this lake, but it is catch and release only (the lake hosts a population of cutthroat trout and longnose suckers).

The **Sylvan Lake Picnic Area** has two parts. The larger area is on the north side of the road; it has eight tables and a vault toilet. The smaller lake overlook across the road has two tables only, but inarguably the much more scenic view. You may also notice the geological benchmark on the concrete pedestal here, one of about 500 or so that can be found throughout the park. More information on this and other benchmarks can be found in my book, *Benchmark Hunting in Yellowstone National Park*.

In 1906, a Cody-based tour guide named Tex Holm began guiding tours through the east entrance, and would set up camp at Sylvan Lake. Eventually, in 1912, Holm would construct a Lodge building here as a stopover. It operated for two years before the company declared bankruptcy and ceased operation. In 1912, The Wylie Permanent Camping Company also operated a lunch station at the lake, but the following year it was relocated to the east entrance as a part of its camp there.

If you look to the east, you'll see Top Notch Peak, and can easily see why it was given its name. This is the site of one of the park's radio repeaters, which is rather unique because there's no electrical service at the summit. The repeater is powered via solar cells and wind turbines.

As you head to the west, you'll pass through the relatively short Clear Creek Canyon, with Clear Creek itself occasionally visible on the south side of the road. The creek, an important spawning ground for the park's signature cutthroat trout, empties into Yellowstone Lake; its mouth was the site of one of the park's fishery operations for a number of years.

10.0 / 15.9 GPS: 44.48934, -110.17510
GRIZZLY PEAK (S)

The large peak to directly south of you here is **Grizzly Peak** (9915 ft/3022 m), named after the grizzly bear. On the northwest aspect of the mountain you'll notice a cirque (French for "arena"), an amphitheater-shaped gouge cut into the mountain by the action of glaciers.

12.4 / 13.5 GPS: 44.50409, -110.19560
CUB CREEK CROSSING

Cub Creek crosses under the road here. It was named for its proximity to Bear Creek, which flows into Turbid Lake and is located approximately one mile to the north. The historic bridge over the creek was built in 1922, and reconstructed in 1995.

The open space to the north of the hairpin turn was the site of the Cub Creek Road Camp from the days of the road's construction (ca. 1903) until the early 1930s. In its later days, the camp was quite extensive with mess halls, bunkhouses, stables, a small house/ranger station, several outhouses, and a bath house over a hot spring in the area. Most of the buildings remained well into the 1940s after the parkwide paving of the roads was completed.

There are some sources that indicate the area was used as an auto campground afterward, but former park historian Aubrey Haines said there was never a campground there to his knowledge.[6] There was a Mission 66 Program proposal to construct a small campground on the site, however, with a capacity of about 35 people, but that never came to fruition.

There was a 12-table picnic area (known as the Cub Creek Picnic Area) here from the early 1960s until the late 1970s. It was removed because of the prevalence of bears in this part of the park.

14.4 / 11.5 GPS: 44.50261, -110.23130
CUB CREEK THERMAL AREA (S)

The are several small ponds and hot pools off the south side of the road here. All of these exist along an unnamed creek for which the source is a large 200ft x 200ft hot spring located about 1000 feet south/southeast of the pullout. The spring is a part of the **Cub Creek Thermal Area**, which consists of about a dozen unnamed, mostly acidic hot springs spread out over a square mile of land. The creek eventually empties into Yellowstone Lake.

14.9 / 11.0 GPS: 44.50445, -110.24072
TETON POINT TURNOUT (S) 🏕

The **Teton Point Turnout** affords the eastbound traveler the first view of Yellowstone Lake as well as the Grand Teton Mountains some 60 miles (96.6 km) to the south.

15.2 / 10.7 GPS: 44.50677, -110.24507
UNNAMED LAKE (S)

The small lake south of the road here has no official name.

15.6 / 10.3 GPS: 44.50965, -110.24959
OLD ROAD BED (N)

This is the east end of the old **Turbid Lake Road** segment. See below at 22.5/3.4 for additional information about this road. The Turbid Lake Trail begins at the Nine Mile Trailhead (see below at 17.1/8.8) and connects into this old road just north of the bend here.

16.4 / 9.5 GPS: 44.50457, -110.26345
LAKE BUTTE OVERLOOK (N) 🔭 🚻 📷 🚹

This ¾ mile road takes you to a viewing area on the west side of Lake Butte, some 300 feet above Yellowstone Lake. From this point you have an excellent view of lake and surrounding mountains, and, on a clear day, the Grand Tetons to the south. There's a vault toilet adjacent to the parking lot.

From the lookout you can often see a small rocky "island" in the lake just off shore, especially during the latter part of the summer. This is known as Pelican Roost, named for the propensity of the birds to use it as a resting spot. During the early part of the season, the water is usually high enough to completely cover it.

17.1 / 8.8 GPS: 44.50661, -110.27618
NINE MILE TRAILHEAD (S) 🚶

Though this is the trailhead for the Thorofare Trail, the trailhead itself is often referred to as the **Nine Mile Trailhead** because it is about nine miles from Fishing Bridge Junction. It provides access to the southeastern portions of the park, including the Thorofare Ranger Station some 32 miles (51 km) south. This part of the park is the most remote area in the lower 48 states, being some 20+ miles from the nearest roadway (as the crow flies).

Across the road from the parking area is the eastern trailhead for the Turbid Lake Trail, which will eventually take you along the old original road through this area. The trail climbs the hill and makes a right turn at the remains of an old NPS corral, and then crosses the Lake Butte Road and follows the existing road up to the hairpin curve where it connects to the old road. From here, it's another 4.5 miles (7.2 km) to Turbid Lake.

18.1 / 7.8 GPS: 44.52072, -110.27882
SEDGE BAY CANOE LAUNCH / PICNIC AREA (S) 🏕 🚻 ⛴
BUTTE SPRINGS THERMAL AREA (N)

This small beach on **Sedge Bay** is one spot where you can officially launch non-motorized boats. There's also a small picnic area here with three tables and a handicap-accessible vault toilet.

There was a large rock-crushing operation here during the 1930s when the bypass (existing road) replacing the old Turbid Lake Road was being constructed.

Across the road from the boat launch/picnic area is a small collection of about three dozen unnamed thermal features known as **Butte Springs** (for their proximity to Lake Butte). This area is closed to hiking for safety reasons.

18.4 / 7.5 GPS: 44.52351, -110.28131
SEDGE CREEK CROSSING

Sedge Creek is named for the plant prevalent throughout the park. For a period of time in the early days of the park, the creek was known as Turbid Creek, as it passes through Turbid Lake on its way to its mouth here at Sedge Bay. The bridge over this creek was constructed in 1997.

19.3 / 6.6 GPS: 44.52893, -110.29642
STEAMBOAT POINT EAST TURNOUT (S)

This is the easternmost turnout for Steamboat Point. See the next entry below for additional details.

19.4 / 6.5 GPS: 44.52990, -110.29723
STEAMBOAT POINT WEST TURNOUT (S)

This is the westernmost turnout for **Steamboat Point**, an outcropping on the northeastern shore of the lake, named for the presence of a small thermal area known as Steamboat Springs. The area consists of about three dozen mostly unnamed thermal vents, mud pots, and hot springs. One hot spring in particular was given the name "Steamboat Spring" for the continuous puffs of steam emanating from it, while one of the more active steam vents was named Locomotive Vent. Both of these are located just below the turnout on its north side.

19.6 / 6.3 GPS: 44.53248, -110.29638
STEAMBOAT POINT PICNIC AREA (W) 🏕 🚻

The small **Steamboat Point Picnic Area** overlooks the lake here; it has two tables and a vault toilet.

19.9 / 6.0 GPS: 44.53684, -110.29460
HOLMES POINT (W)

Holmes Point, so-named because of a boulder here with the initials, "W.H.H." carved into it, for William H. Holmes. Holmes was a geologist and topographer who accompanied the Hayden Survey of 1878, and who generated some of the most accurate and detailed maps of the park for their time.[7]

Mt. Holmes on the western side of the park (in the Gallatin Range) was named for him as well. This point marks the south end of Mary Bay.

20.8 / 5.1 GPS: 44.54671, -110.29426
MARY BAY (S)
BEACH SPRINGS LAKE (N)

Mary Bay is named after Mary Force, a girlfriend of a member of the Hayden Survey of 1871. Mary Bay doesn't freeze in the winter and is an excellent place for observing waterfowl if you're in the park in the winter. In fact, this area is still home to many thermal vents under the water, and the highest temperature recorded in the lake was taken here (212°F/100°C)

Scientists posit that a tsunami helped create Mary Bay approximately 13,800 years ago. The belief is that some seismic fault action occurred under Yellowstone Lake, resulting in a wave washing over the area which, at the time, was a series of steam vents, probably part of the same system that exists on the north side of the road today. The resulting cold water invasion of the steam vents resulted in an explosion that created Mary Bay.[8]

Mt. Sheridan and the Red Mountains are visible to the south of the Lake. There was at one time a picnic area here with a solitary picnic table.

Beach Springs Lake (lagoon, really) is the large pool on the northern side of the road, and is named for its proximity to Beach Springs (see next item below). The much smaller lake just to the west of this is unnamed, though some locals refer to it as "Baby Beach Springs Lake" or "Little Beach Springs Lake."

21.5 / 4.4 GPS: 44.55276, -110.30467
BEACH SPRINGS (N)

This series of thermal springs is collectively known as "**Beach Springs**," so named for their location on the "beach" of Mary Bay. The small lakes are quite acidic, on the order of 2-3 on the pH scale.

On the west side of Mary Bay is a small cove known as Concretion Cove. It was given its name by Supt. P. W. Norris for the various irregularly shaped rocks, known as concretions, found there at the time (most of which have long since been carried off by tourists). The Storm Point Trail runs along the shore of this cove for a short distance.

22.3 / 3.6 GPS: 44.55900, -110.31943
OLD ROAD BED (S)

If you look to the south here, you can see the vestigial remains of the old road that led to the Indian Pond Group Camp on the south and east side of Indian Lake. It's perhaps barely discernible, but look for the smaller trees and the cut through the wooded area. This campground was one of two "group camps" in the park until the 1970s (the other was at Otter Creek), and was used by groups such as the Boy Scouts, family reunions, and stock parties. This camp's capacity was approximately 75 people.

22.5 / 3.4 GPS: 44.55984, -110.32224
INDIAN POND TURNOUT (S) ⊻⋇

Indian Pond was given its name because the Nez Perce camped next to the lake on August 26, 1877, during their flight through the park. From the 1920s up until 1981, this body of water was known as Squaw Lake. Many park documents and (older) maps produced by the USGS still refer to this body of water by that name, in fact. The lake was formed from the crater of a hydrothermal explosion believed to have occurred approximately 3,000 years ago. You may see steam rising from a small thermal area on the hills north of Indian Pond. This is Vermilion Springs, a small thermal area of about a dozen mostly unnamed features lying along Pelican Creek.

22.6 / 3.3 GPS: 44.56002, -110.32390
PELICAN VALLEY TRAILHEAD (N) 🏃
OLD TURBID LAKE ROADBED

The old road bed that takes you back to the trailhead is a remnant of the original road that took travelers past Turbid Lake and connected back into today's main road east of Lake Butte (see the entry at 15.6/10.3 above). The old road was closed to vehicle traffic in 1939 and for years was accessible as a trail. Much of it still is, but the portion between this parking area and the lake was rehabilitated and closed to all travel just within the past few years. You can still hike north on the Pelican Valley Trail a couple of miles and then swing back south toward the lake, however. Once you arrive, you'll find a large, cloudy, foul-smelling pool of water with a series of hot springs on its eastern shore.

The **Pelican Valley Trail** takes you north through the Pelican Valley, and on to other trails such as the Turbid Lake, Astringent Creek, Mist Creek, and Pelican Cone (an old fire lookout tower built in 1937; still in use today as a patrol station) trails.

The trails into this part of the park are for day-use only, (9AM to 7PM) and it is recommended that you hike in groups of four or more. These trails take you through some of the most grizzly-dense portions of the park. The area was designated for day use only in late 1984 following the fatal, unprovoked grizzly attack on a 29-year old Swiss woman who'd camped alone near White Lake.[9] All of the backcountry campsites in this area were closed as well. Even today, the entire valley is closed for bear management purposes until July 4th. Occasionally, there are scheduled ranger-led hikes through this area during the summer, budget permitting. Check the park's newspaper or the Fishing Bridge Museum ranger desk for the schedule.

22.7 / 3.2 GPS: 44.55971, -110.32665
STORM POINT TRAILHEAD (S) 🚶
OLD SQUAW LAKE DUMP N)

The **Storm Point Trail** is a short, 1.5-mile (2.4 km) trail out to Storm Point on Lake Yellowstone. This location was named for its excellent viewpoint of the storms that roll in over the lake in the afternoons during the latter part of the summer. This trail is often closed due to bear activity, so be sure and check in with one of the ranger stations or the Fishing Bridge Museum prior to heading out. There's another small parking area just to the west of this one as well.

Across from the trailhead, behind the clump of trees, is the old **Squaw Lake Dump** (sometimes referred to as the Turbid Lake Dump). The dump was used to dispose of old tree stumps and burnable debris during the construction of this segment of road. You can barely make out the old road that led back to it.

23.2 / 2.7 GPS: 44.55826, -110.33613
Abandoned Trail (S)

The old roadbed (that now looks like a trail) leading off to the southeast toward Storm Point was referred to at one time as the "party road." Back in the day, rangers would send large parties back to the end of that road to "get them out of the way." [10]

24.0 / 1.9 GPS: 44.55795, -110.35276
Entrance to old Pelican Creek Campground (N)

The 115-site **Pelican Creek Campground** opened in 1959 and operated until 1972. It was originally intended to accommodate overflow during periods when the campground at Fishing Bridge was full (which was happening quite a bit during the busy summers at that point). The primitive (no facilities) campground area was located in prime grizzly habitat, however, and it was eventually closed off (even to foot travel) to preserve that habitat. You can't really even make out the old roadbed now. In the 1910s-1930s, this area was home to one of the park's road camps.

24.1 / 1.8 GPS: 44.55853, -110.35482
Pelican Valley (N & S) 🔭

Pelican Valley is one of the most pristine grizzly habitats in the lower 48 states, and is recognized as perhaps the most ecologically diverse area of the park. As a result, use of this area is highly restricted. These turnouts make excellent platforms for watching wildlife in the area, especially the bald eagles and a variety of waterfowl.

24.2 / 1.7 GPS: 44.55907, -110.35683
Pelican Creek / Pelican Flats

Pelican Creek is named for the pelican, which is omnipresent in this area, and indeed uses a pair of small islands in the southern end of the lake as its primary nesting ground. The large expanse of flat land over which the bridge passes is known as **Pelican Flats**. The 1500-foot bridge itself was constructed in 1934 when the road through this area was rebuilt.

24.4 / 1.5 GPS: 44.56021, -110.36069
Pelican Creek Nature Trailhead (S) 🚶

The **Pelican Creek Nature Trail** is a short (½ mile or ⁸⁄₁₀ km), easy hike through an area rich in wildflowers and opportunities for birdwatchers.

Much of the trail, which passes through some marshy areas, is boardwalked for your convenience. There are occasionally ranger-led walks along this trail, so be sure to check out the park's newspaper or visit one of the nearby ranger stations for a schedule.

24.9 / 1.0 GPS: 44.56296, -110.37011
FISHING BRIDGE RV PARK (N) 🚐 🏕 🔫 🧺

Fishing Bridge RV Park is the only campground inside Yellowstone that has full hookups for RVs, including water, sewage, and 50-amp electrical service. The daily rate for 2014 is $46.50. Built in 1963-1964 as a part of the Mission 66 Program, the campground has been restricted to hardside units since 1977 due to the heavy presence of bears in the area. The campground has several comfort stations, and the Camper Services Building has showers and a laundry for visitor use.

25.1 / 0.8 GPS: 44.56389, -110.37334
YGS EMPLOYEE DORMITORY & ICE KIOSK (N)

The larger building here is an employee dormitory for those working at the General Store. The building was relocated to this area and converted into dorm space in 1950. See the Fishing Bridge Development section for more details. The small building is an ice vending machine.

25.2 / 0.7 GPS: 44.56428, -110.37479
FISHING BRIDGE GENERAL STORE (N) 🛍 ⛽ 🚻
WARMING HUT/TOILET (S) 🚻
OLD CAMPGROUND ENTRANCE (S)

The **Fishing Bridge General Store** was built in 1939. It has a small grill, grocery store, souvenirs and clothing, wine, etc. There is an ATM in the store as well. More details on this building can be found in the Fishing Bridge Development section.

The large flat area behind the General Store was once home to over 300 cabins which were rented out to guests, a practice that stopped in 1975. The cabins were constructed in 1935-1936, and most were removed in groups between 1980 and 1985. Only five remain today, all of which are used by the Yellowstone Park Service Stations (YPSS) to house employees. The vast open space is now home to a softball diamond for employee recreation, as well as a construction material staging area, and a staging area for firefighting resources for use when there are major fires in progress within the eastern portions of the park.

On the south side of the road is a small building, vault toilet, and the entrance to the old **Fishing Bridge Campground**. The campground here was one of the busiest in the park from the time it was built in 1957 until it was closed after the 1989 season. In 1977, use of it, too, was restricted to hard-sided units. The small building was the original Ranger Station, constructed in this area in 1928. The building is now used as the **Fishing Bridge Warming Hut** during the winter and for storage during the summer. There's also a new vault toilet at the pullout here.

25.3 / 0.6 GPS: 44.56480, -110.37666
Fishing Bridge Museum/Amphitheater (S) 🛖 ⑦ 🛷
Fishing Bridge Picnic Area (S) 🌲
YPSS Service/Repair Station (N) 🏪 🔧

The **Fishing Bridge Museum** was built in 1931, along with those at Norris, Madison, and Old Faithful (since removed). The museum has interpretive displays about the lake and waterfowl and other animals that inhabit the area. It also has a small Yellowstone Association bookstore. Rangers present daily talks here, as well as evening programs at the adjacent amphitheater, which was added in 1932. See the park newspaper or the ranger desk in the museum for a schedule.

The structure next to the museum is known as the Naturalist's Residence. It was built concurrently with the museum to serve as a residence for the naturalist who staffed the museum (at the time of construction, only one staff member worked there). Today it's the office for the rangers who're based at the Museum. There's a comfort station located in the woods to the north and east of the museum, in what used to be the old campground. It was built in 1936, and is still in use.

On the south (lake) side of the museum is Diamond Beach, the stretch of beach along the lake shore between the lake outlet at Fishing Bridge and Mary Bay. The **Fishing Bridge Picnic Area**, located on the west side of the parking lot, has 11 tables.

On the north side of the road you'll find the **Fishing Bridge Service Station**, which sells gasoline, diesel, and propane, as well as snacks and small sundry items, along with the old **Fishing Bridge Repair Garage**. The garage's roof collapsed from the weight of snow in early 2011 and the building has yet to be rebuilt (it was a historic structure, and rebuilding one of those takes quite a bit of time and coordination among a variety of different agencies). YPSS has opened a temporary repair operation in the parking lot for the time being, however.

See the Fishing Bridge Development section for additional details on all of the structures located in this area.

25.4 / 0.5 GPS: 44.56546, -110.37889
Fishing Bridge East Parking Lot (N) [P]
Howard Eaton Trailhead (N) [⚲]
Old RV Park (S)

This section of the Howard Eaton Trail takes you from Fishing Bridge to Canyon Village, specifically to the Wapiti Lake Trailhead, some 15 miles (24 km) north. This particular portion of the trail is often referred to as the Hayden Valley Trail, in fact. It winds along a route parallel to the Yellowstone River, and through the lush Hayden Valley, with its rich abundance of wildlife. Approximately four miles (6.5 km) north of here you'll come upon an outstanding overlook of LeHardy Rapids.

For the past few years, there have been intermittent closures of sections of this trail due to its proximity to wolf dens in Hayden Valley. Check with the rangers at the Fishing Bridge Museum for current closures. The initial part of the trail follows a service road north from the old Fishing Bridge cabins area and up along the road leading to the wastewater treatment plant prior to forking off to the left and picking up the river. You'll also pass near old Fishing Bridge Incinerator site, a relic from the park's past, if you care to make a detour of a couple of hundred yards (take the east fork along the service road rather than the west one).

On the south side of the road you'll see vestigial remnants of the original RV park at Fishing Bridge. It was closed in 1964 when the new (existing) Fishing Bridge RV Park opened.

25.6 / 0.3 GPS: 44.56669, -110.38219
Fishing Bridge [⚲][♙]

You are passing over what is perhaps the most famous bridge within the park, **Fishing Bridge**. The existing bridge was constructed in 1936-1937 to replace the original, which was built in 1903 along with the remainder of the East Entrance Road (it was reconstructed in 1919). The 532-foot (162 m) span cost just over $150,000, and was rehabilitated in 2001. The bridge is showing its age, however, to the point of complete erosion of the surface deck in some places. These holes are often covered with steel plates, which have a bad habit of causing motorcycle accidents. The original span crossed the outlet just south of this one; you can still see the old pilings in the shallower waters.

The bridge was given its name in 1914 because people would line up along its edges and fish off its sides. This went on for decades. As a result, the newer bridge was built with sidewalks to protect the fishermen from being hit by passing automobiles.

In 1973, the National Park Service banned fishing from the bridge to protect the park's native cutthroat trout population. They were being removed from the lake at such a high rate the NPS believed it might negatively impact their ability to survive in the lake (which was quite prescient, given their current battle with the invasive lake trout). Safety was also a concern; there are many photographs showing people lined up shoulder to shoulder across both sides of the bridge, and it wasn't uncommon for someone to "hook" other people fishing from its edges.

On the west bank on the north side of the bridge, you'll notice a small USGS stream gauge building. This is used to monitor the river's level and flow rate. From 1935 until 1973, there was a boat house and a small dock here from which boats and canoes were rented. You could take one of these small craft out and fish or just enjoy the waters between the bridge and LeHardy Rapids some two miles to the north.

The boat house itself was designed by Robert Reamer, the architect of the Old Faithful Inn and several other buildings within the park. The structures were removed around the same time as the new policies about fishing from the bridge were enacted, all as a part of an attempt at better wildlife management policies. Today, boating north of the bridge is not allowed.

The two small islands north of the bridge near the eastern bank of the river are known colloquially as the Bridge Islands. Prior to the construction of the existing bridge, these did not exist. Scientists believe the pilings break up the ice flows that travel downstream during the spring melt. In the past, the ice would pass through in larger, heavier sheets and scour the river bed. Now, however, the bridge supports break up this ice, resulting in much less scour, and thus, much more sand and silt deposits accumulating in places where it hasn't happened in the past. One of the more visible results of this are these two small islands, and thus, their name. The trees on these islands date to 1938, which further supports this theory.

Many people erroneously believe that this is the headwater (source) of the Yellowstone River. However, its true source lies on Younts Peak, a 12156-foot (3705 m) mountain in the Teton Wilderness southeast of the park's boundary. The river flows into Yellowstone Lake, and then resumes its course as it flows north from the outlet here at Fishing Bridge. The peak was named for Harry Yount, who was Yellowstone's first gamekeeper, and considered by many to be the first park "ranger."

25.7 / 0.2 GPS: 44.56757, -110.38429
Fishing Bridge West Parking Lot (N) [P]

This parking lot affords easy access to the walkway across Fishing Bridge, and along the western bank of the river to the north.

Across the street, there is a trail, known as the Lakeshore Trail, that leads to the Lake Village area. Over the past few seasons, however, NPS has kept it closed due to erosion and instability concerns.

25.8 / 0.1 GPS: 44.56799, -110.38634
Old Roadbed (N)

If you look closely at the ground on the north side of the road here, you'll notice an area that is a darker shade than the rest of the grass (especially noticeable in the spring and fall). This is where the original road from Canyon used to intersect with the East Entrance Road.

In 1972, when the bypass road around Lake Village was constructed, the junction was moved to its present location some 200 yards west of here. The old road was reclaimed and only a faint hint of it is visible now. The other end of this old roadbed is at a pullout 1.9 miles north of the current Fishing Bridge Junction (see the entry at 13.5/1.9 in the Canyon Village to Fishing Bridge section).

25.9 / 0.0 GPS: 44.56810, -110.38829 Elevation: 7832 Feet
Fishing Bridge Junction

From here, you can go 25.9 miles (41.7 km) east to the East Entrance, 15.4 miles (24.8 km) north to Canyon Village, or head south 20.6 miles (33.2 km) to West Thumb Junction.

Fishing Bridge Junction
to
West Thumb Junction

The road from Fishing Bridge Junction to West Thumb is 20.6 miles (33.1 km) long and generally parallels the shore of Yellowstone Lake for much of its length. It is the second longest segment of the Grand Loop Road. and though it affords outstanding views of the lake and the Absaroka Mountains to the east, many consider it one of the more tedious drives in the park because of its length and the relative lack of variations in scenery.

Most of your travels will be through thick, lush forests, with the exception of the Arnica Creek area where a large wildfire burned through in 2009. There are a great many pullouts for both scenic and fishing purposes, two of which have vault toilets. Once you reach Pumice Point, you'll be traveling around West Thumb, the blown out crater of a volcanic vent dating as far back as 180,000 years. This area is lined with a variety of thermal features.

The original road between West Thumb and Fishing Bridge was constructed in the early 1890s, and basically followed a path similar to today's road, albeit a little closer to the lake shore. This was done to prevent having to cut a path through the thick forests, but resulted in the road being washed out or under water quite often. At one particular location just north of West Thumb, the road traveled over a sandbar which was often completely covered with water during the early part of the spring (during the lake's high season). This caused the stagecoaches to get bogged down and often stuck, giving the segment a reputation for being a hard road to travel.

In 1904-1905, the U.S. Army Corps of Engineers constructed a bypass between Arnica Creek and Natural Bridge. This resulted in shorter travel times, but a much less scenic drive, and required some steep climbing in one section. Therefore, in 1926, the Bureau of Public Roads reconstructed the lake shore road, albeit a further distance from the edge of the water to prevent the washing out experienced in earlier years. Since that time, the road has generally remained in its current alignment, with the exception of the segment between Lake Village and Fishing Bridge, which was rerouted in the early 1970s to move through traffic around the commercial area, and the junction at West Thumb, which was remodeled in the late 1970s.

The road is in excellent shape, and there are plenty of pullouts along the route, including several picnic areas. You're liable to see bison and elk along this stretch of road, especially between Fishing Bridge and Bridge Bay, and near West Thumb (elk, primarily). You may also see the occasional grizzly bear.

0.0 / 20.6 GPS: 44.56810, -110.38829 ELEVATION: 7832 FEET
FISHING BRIDGE JUNCTION

From here, you can go 25.9 miles (41.7 km) to the East Entrance, 15.4 miles (24.8 km) north to Canyon Village, or head south 20.6 miles (33.2 km) to West Thumb Junction.

0.2 / 20.4 GPS: 44.56578, -110.39011
UNNAMED PULLOUT (E)

This innocuous pullout used to be the site of a couple of outhouses, right alongside the road. They were removed several years ago, but the wood-covered vaults are still visible east of the pullout.

0.5 / 20.1 GPS: 44.56154, -110.39341
LAKE ADMINISTRATIVE (GOVERNMENT) AREA ROAD (W)

The **Lake Administrative Area** is a complex of NPS and concession housing and maintenance facilities. The area was developed after World War II, and was originally in the "rear" of the Lake Village until the bypass was constructed in 1972. There are no public services/facilities in this area.

0.7 / 19.9 GPS: 44.55889, -110.39564
NPS CORRALS PULLOUT (W)

You'll notice a large pasture surrounded by a wooden fence on the west side of the road here. This is part of the **NPS Corrals** where the Lake District rangers keep their horses when not in the backcountry. You can occasionally see the horses grazing out in the pasture, and it's not uncommon to see other animals, especially elk and deer grazing here as well.

1.0 / 19.6 GPS: 44.55722, -110.39929
OLD BARN OFF THE SIDE OF THE ROAD (E)

This building attracts a lot of attention from people who're new to the park, largely because it seems so out of place along the side of the road. This was originally a barn used to house stock, built long before the road was routed on its current alignment. The building, constructed in 1930, is now used as for storage. Even with as close to the road as it is, this area is closed during the early part of the season because bears use Lodge Creek (which runs between the road and the barn; see next entry) to fish.

1.0 / 19.6 GPS: 44.55688, -110.40080
LODGE CREEK CROSSING

Lodge Creek crosses the road here; it was named by local personnel for its proximity to Lake Lodge. The creek is an important food source for bears in the early part of the season, and the area is closed to foot travel. Several cabins that abut the creek in the Lake Lodge cabin complex are closed until July because of this as well.

1.1 / 19.5 GPS: 44.55669, -110.40172
ELEPHANT BACK TRAILHEAD (W) 🚶

The Elephant Back Trail is a four-mile (6.5 km) trail that takes you to the summit of a small hill (8600 ft/2621 m) with an incredible vista of Pelican Valley, Yellowstone Lake, and the Absaroka Mountains. This is a popular trail for "moonlight hikes" because of that. The ridge reminded someone of an elephant's back, thus the name. This area is pretty popular with grizzly bears in the early part of the summer, so be sure you have your bear spray with you, and hike in groups. Shortly after you start the hike, you'll pass an old spring box and piping that was once part of the water supply system for the Lake and Lake Utility Areas. There's a small pullout on the east side of the road just north of the trailhead for hikers to use as well (this trail is very busy in the summer). A dirt trail on the east side of the road will lead you to the rear of the Lake Lodge Cabin complex.

1.3 / 19.3 GPS: 44.55541, -110.40585
HOTEL CREEK CROSSING

Hotel Creek is named for the fact that it crosses near the Lake Hotel south of where it crosses the road here. The creek empties into Yellowstone Lake, and until the mid-1930s the hotel's raw sewage was drained into the creek (the area's first sewage treatment plant came online in the 1930s).

1.6 / 19.0 GPS: 44.55170, -110.40872
HATCHERY CREEK CROSSING
LAKE VILLAGE/LAKE JUNCTION ROAD (E)

Lake Village Road takes you into the Lake Village commercial area, where you'll find the Lake Hotel, Lake Lodge, Lake Ranger Station, the Lake General Store, the Fish Hatchery area, and the Lake Clinic.

Just north of the intersection is the crossing of **Hatchery Creek**, which passes alongside the old Lake Fish Hatchery, and thus its name. During the heyday of the hatchery, this creek was used to harvest fish eggs as the trout spawned. Originally called Boathouse Creek because it also passes alongside the big boathouse in front of the hatchery (and existed before the hatchery was constructed).[1] The original hatchery was built in 1911, but replaced in the 1930s with the current structure. See the Lake Village Development section for more details on these structures.

1.7 / 18.9 GPS: 44.55064, -110.40971
SERVICE ROAD (W)

The dirt road you see heading into the woods on the west side of the road here is a service road to allow Northwestern Energy crews to access their power lines.

2.2 / 18.4 GPS: 44.54749, -110.41794
DIRT SERVICE ROAD (W)

Another dirt service road running southwest off the main road affords Northwestern Energy access to power lines. There are also water and sewer lines that run through this area.

2.3 / 18.3 GPS: 44.54550, -110.41822
LAKE VIEW PULLOUT (E) 🚶 🚲 📷

This pullout has an excellent view of the lake, but you'll also notice the remnants of an old road that runs off to the northeast along the shore (may be tough to see if you're headed south – stop in the pullout). The main road through here used to pass in front of the Lake Hotel, but in 1971, the bypass was constructed (the road you're on) to divert traffic away and reduce congestion in the area. The east end of this section of the road can be found between the old boathouses and the Lake Fish Hatchery just west of the hotel. Today, the old road is open only to hikers and bicyclists, though it is closed for bear management purposes until July 15th.

2.4 / 18.2 GPS: 44.54389, -110.41929
LAKE TRANSFER STATION SERVICE ROAD (W)
WELLS CREEK CROSSING

The **Lake Transfer Station** is where garbage collected from the east side of the park is taken to be sorted and loaded up and taken to the appropriate disposal facility outside the park. This is one of only two such facilities in the park (the other's at Mammoth).

Wells Creek crosses under the road just south of the entrance drive. According to Lee Whittlesey, the creek is named after a gentleman who was an assistant engineer for the Northern Pacific Railroad.[2] Many of the locals who've been around for some time refer to it as South Incinerator Creek, however. It was given this name when the old incinerator occupied the site of today's transfer station. The small creek that runs under the road just north of here is known colloquially as North Incinerator Creek.

2.9 / 17.7 GPS: 44.54019, -110.42602
BRIDGE BAY FLATS (W & E) 🏕

This large meadow along both sides of the road here is known colloquially as **Bridge Bay Flats**. There are four pullouts to allow you to view the lake. It's not uncommon to see bison, elk, and even grizzlies here.

3.3 / 17.3 GPS: 44.53626, -110.43252
BIKINI BEACH (E)

This road is technically a service road to allow maintenance personnel access to the sewage pumping station found at its west end, but it is quite popular with visitors enjoying the lake as well. The pumping station moves raw sewage from the campground and marina up to the Fishing Bridge area where it is treated and disposed of. The area is known colloquially as **Bikini Beach** because campers from the Bridge Bay Campground often come down and lay out on the beach here. The access road along the shoreline was part of the original road through here prior to 1961.

3.4 / 17.2 GPS: 44.53479, -110.43415
BRIDGE BAY ENTRANCE (W) 🏕 ⛴ 🚤 🚻 ⚓ ⚓ 🏠 🚹🚺 ⚓
MARINA, CAMPGROUND, GENERAL STORE, PICNIC AREA (W)

The **Bridge Bay Marina** complex was constructed in 1962-1964 as one of the park's major projects under the Mission 66 Program. It consists of a Marina, Ranger Station, Marina Store, concession operation, Picnic Area, and the largest campground in the park. Bridge Bay gets its name from the nearby Bridge Creek (see entry below at 3.8/16.8), not the bridge that now takes traffic over the entry to the bay as many believe.

The **Bridge Bay Marina** is operated by the park's primary concession operator and offers a wide variety of marine-related services. This includes slip rentals (about 100), boat rentals (motorized, canoes, etc.), guided fishing tours, and scenic lake tours. The NPS also docks its research and lake patrol watercraft here.

The **Bridge Bay General Store** is a small, marine-oriented store where you can buy snacks, small sundry items, souvenirs, gear, and some basic grocery items. The building that houses the store also includes the ticket and rental counter for the marina, as well as the **Bridge Bay Ranger Station**.

The **Bridge Bay Picnic Area** is in the wooded area adjacent to the Marina and is the largest picnic area in the park. Here you'll find 23 tables, three grills, and a comfort station with running water and flush toilets. Handicap accessible.

The **Bridge Bay Campground** was completed in two stages. The first section (162 sites in Loops A through D) was constructed in the late 1950s, with the remaining 269 sites (Loops E through J) and the Amphitheater being completed in 1969. This area has long been utilized as a camping spot. It was the site of a Shaw and Powell Camp in the early 1900s, then known as the Lake Night Camp. The original auto campground in this area was also here from the 1920s through the 1950s.

3.6 / 17.0 GPS: 44.53210, -110.43496
Bridge Bay Bridge

The **Bridge Bay Bridge** was constructed in 1961 when the road was rerouted and rebuilt as part of the Mission 66 Program to build the marina complex. The original bridge was a few hundred feet to the east, closer to the bay's outlet.

3.7 / 16.9 GPS: 44.53055, -110.43596
Gull Point Drive North Entrance (E)
Natural Bridge Trailhead (W) 🚶 🚴
Arnica Creek-Natural Bridge Service Road (W)

Gull Point Drive takes you onto a small outcropping of land into the lake known as Gull Point. It is a scenic drive, and at the south end you'll find the Gull Point Picnic Area, one of the larger picnic areas in the park. It has 21 tables and a vault toilet that is handicap-accessible. The road runs along the lake shore and is often closed in the early part of the season due to high water. See the Miscellaneous Roads section for a road log.

The **Natural Bridge Trail** takes you back approximately one mile to a natural bridge formed by Bridge Creek cutting its way through a rhyolite lava cliff. In the early 1880s, the bridge was considered as a potentially viable path for horses and carriages through this part of the park, but it was never actually used for that purpose.[3]

This first mile of trail is paved and was once part of the main road between West Thumb and the Lake area. See the entry at 13.8/6.8 below for a detailed examination of what transpired with the road system here. This was once part of the old Howard Eaton Trail system. Currently, however, the NPS uses an area near the north end of the old trail as a carcass disposal site and as a result, the entire road/trail is now closed to all travel once you reach Natural Bridge.

3.8 / 16.8 GPS: 44.53009, -110.43616
BRIDGE CREEK CROSSING

Bridge Creek crosses under the road here. It was given its name by the Hayden Expedition in 1871 because it flows under the "natural bridge" referenced above.

3.9 / 16.7 GPS: 44.52862, -110.43654
YELLOWSTONE LAKE PARKING AREA D (E) P 🛉

This turnout affords access to lake views, and has a couple of picnic tables, even though it's not an official picnic area. It's used primarily as a turnaround for visitors when the gate just south of the turnout is closed.

After you leave the parking lot heading south, you'll soon find yourself climbing and then descending Gull Point Hill.

In the 1986 plan for the removal of the Fishing Bridge development (which was never fully implemented), there was a proposal to build a new campground on the west side of the road roughly halfway between the north and south entrances of Gull Point Drive. The campground was to be known as the "Lodgepole Campground," with 310 sites, and was one of three proposed to help offset the loss of the huge campground at Fishing Bridge.[4]

5.3 / 15.3 GPS: 44.51536, -110.41904
GULL POINT DRIVE SOUTH ENTRANCE (E) 🏕

This is the south entrance to Gull Point Drive and is the quickest route to the Gull Point Picnic Area. See the entry at 3.7/16.9 above for specifics regarding this road. As you head north from here, you begin climbing and then descending Gull Point Hill.

5.4 / 15.1 GPS: 44.51352, -110.41758
UNNAMED PULLOUT (E)
WEASEL CREEK CROSSING

If you park in this pullout facing north, you'll notice a stand of younger trees along the shoreline to the north. This is the path of the original road through here before the current Bridge Bay development existed. The road crossed a bridge a couple of hundred feet east of the current bridge and continued across onto the road that leads down past the sewage lift station (the Bikini Beach Service Road referenced at 3.3/17.3 above). The new bridge and rerouting were required to allow boats traveling to and from the new marina to pass under the bridge deck.

Weasel Creek crosses under the road here as well, and empties into the lake. The original Lake Incinerator was located along Weasel Creek in this area prior to the reconfiguration of the roads. It was used until 1949, and then all traces of it were removed in the 1960s as the new road was being constructed.

6.0 / 14.6 GPS: 44.50583, -110.42082
STEVENSON ISLAND PULLOUT (E)

This small pullout affords an excellent view of **Stevenson Island**. The island was named for James Stevenson, one of Ferdinand Hayden's assistants in 1871. In the 1930s-1940s, the Yellowstone Park Company held "Island Picnics" there. For $3 a person, you'd be taken by "speed boat" to the island where you could fish and then cook whatever you'd caught.

The remnants of the old steamship *E. C. Waters* are also located on the island. Named after the park concessioner who built her, the ship was never actually used to transport passengers between its intended destinations of West Thumb and the dock in front of the Lake Hotel. Waters had wanted to boat to be certified to carry as many as 600 passengers, but the government would only allow it to carry 125, so Waters beached it on the far side of Stevenson Island in 1905. In 1924, the ship's boilers were removed and used to heat the Lake Hotel, and the remainder burned. Today, all that is left is the keel of the old boat. You can see it by taking Xanterra's SceniCruiser tour from Bridge Bay.

6.5 / 14.0 GPS: 44.49818, -110.42035
SAND POINT PICNIC AREA (E) 🏕️ 🚻

The **Sand Point Picnic Area** is one of the larger picnic areas in the park, having 18 tables and a pair of handicap-accessible vault toilets.

8.9 / 11.7 GPS: 44.47416, -110.45159
HIDDEN ROAD BED TO OLD GRAVEL PIT (W)

Though it's hard to see from the road, there's an old road bed in the woods to the west. It takes you back to an old, unnamed gravel pit. If you walk off the road into the trees and turn north, you'll see the smaller trees growing along what used to be the road to the pit.

9.4 / 11.2 GPS: 44.47000, -110.45860
UNNAMED TURNOUT (E)

Though this turnout technically isn't named, and there are no tables present, it is the site of the old **Spruce Point Picnic Area**.

9.8 / 10.8 GPS: 44.46765, -110.46680
SPRUCE-FIR EXHIBIT (E) 🔭
CONTRASTING FORESTS PICNIC AREA (E) 🏕️ 🚻

There is a large interpretive station here that explains the contrast between the vast forest of spruce and fir trees found here with the lodgepole pine forests found in much of the remainder of the park. The **Contrasting Forests Picnic Area** has four tables, and there is a handicap accessible vault toilet in the northern half of the pullout.

10.9 / 9.7 GPS: 44.45909, -110.48425
DOT ISLAND PICNIC AREA/SPRUCE POINT (E) 🏕️

Though this area doesn't show up on any official maps or lists, it is the **Dot Island Picnic Area**, located on a point known as Spruce Point. There are four tables here, but no toilet facilities.

From the beach, you'll be looking at Dot Island, so-named because it appeared as a mere "dot" on the maps of the day. Dot Island is the small island located directly to the east. The larger island further out in the lake and a bit more to the south is Frank Island, the largest of the lake's eight islands.[5]

Dot Island was the site of a small "zoo" operated by one of the park's early concessioners, E. C. Waters, from 1896-1907.[6] He kept a small herd of bison and elk, plus at least one bighorn sheep here, and would ferry tourists out on one of his tour boats. The government made him close it down due to the squalid conditions of the pens.

11.5 / 9.1 GPS: 44.45478, -110.49474
YELLOWSTONE LAKE PARKING AREA B (E) P

This is another small parking area designed to provide quick access to the lake. This is also a favorite spot for the rangers to set up a radar and catch speeders since it's located along a lengthy straight section of roadway.

11.9 / 8.6 GPS: 44.45300, -110.50349
PUMICE POINT TURNOUT / PICNIC AREA (E) 🐻 🏕

Pumice Point is a large rounded point on the lake that marks the northern reach of West Thumb Bay. See the entry below at 18.0/2.6 for an explanation of how this bay was created. If you look to the south from here, you can see the steam rising from Potts Hot Spring Basin and the West Thumb Geyser Basin.

The **Pumice Point Picnic Area** is a small one, with only two tables and no access to toilet facilities.

12.3 / 8.3 GPS: 44.45691, -110.50840
YELLOWSTONE PARKING AREA C (E) P

This is the third parking area (from the north) designed to provide easy access to the lake.

12.7 / 7.9 GPS: 44.46146, -110.51192
FISHERMAN'S ACCESS PICNIC AREA (S) 🐻 🚻

The drive leads to a parking area. At the end of the parking area is a short walk to a 30-foot lake overlook where you'll find three picnic tables. There is a handicap-accessible vault toilet at the parking lot. Some sources have this listed as Park Point Picnic Area, but its official name is the **Fisherman's Access Picnic Area**.[7]

12.9 / 7.7 GPS: 44.46335, -110.51440
PUMICE PIT SERVICE ROAD (W)

This gated service road leads back to an area used to store and stockpile construction material and debris, as well as one of the park's three law enforcement shooting ranges (referred to locally as the "Arnica Range.").

13.2 / 7.4 GPS: 44.46729, -110.51705
SAND BAR TURNOUT (E)

You can walk out onto the sand bar that was part of the first stagecoach road through this area (see the entry below). During the summer, it's not uncommon to see people sunbathing out on the sandbar.

13.8 / 6.8 GPS: 44.47349, -110.52584
HARD ROAD TO TRAVEL TURNOUT/PICNIC AREA (E) 🐾 🚻

The **Hard Road to Travel Turnout** gets its name from the sandbar you see out in the lake. This natural sandbar forms Arnica Lagoon, so-named because Arnica Creek drains in to it just west of this location (see the next entry down). The extensive burned out area you see through here is the result of the Arnica Fire in 2009. It closed this stretch of roadway for several days late that summer.

The "hard road to travel" moniker comes from the early days of the park when the first road between West Thumb and the Lake area traversed the sandbar. That original road hugged the shoreline of the Lake, much like the existing road does today. At the time it was built, however, this area was thick with trees and to reduce construction time and costs, engineers elected to take the road over this sandbar.

During the spring and early summer the high water of the lake would erode the sand and make the entire path mushy, resulting in stuck stagecoaches and an often impassable section of road. And thus it became known as a hard road to travel. Most of the rest of the road between the two locations had also been constructed along the lakeshore and was often swamped during high water as well or washed out by wave action.

In 1904-1905, the U.S. Army Corps of Engineers rebuilt much of the road, and constructed a "bypass" that took travelers directly across this peninsula rather than along its edge. You can find the south end of this old road below (see the entries at 14.8/5.8 and 15.1/5.5), and the north terminus at the end of the Natural Bridge Service Road. Today, it is referred to locally as the "Arnica Bypass." Not only did it make the road much more favorable for vehicular use, it shaved four miles off the distance between here and Bridge Bay.

Over time, however, the new bypass was deemed "featureless" and lacking in any significant sight-seeing features. Additionally, it had a significant hill to climb just as the bypass began (or a steep descent if you were coming from the north), and it lacked a water source for sprinkling, which was a common method of keeping dust down during that time period.

In 1926, the decision was made to reconstruct the road along the shoreline once again, this time moving it far enough back so it would not be exposed to high water and wave action. There is a small interpretive sign here that explains a bit more about the old road and the obstacle it presented to early visitors.

Once the new road was opened to traffic, the old cutoff became part of the Howard Eaton Trail. Today, however, most portions of that trail through this section of the park have been abandoned altogether by trail maintenance crews, and the old cutoff road is now closed due to the presence of a carcass disposal area at its north end. One interesting feature along the bypass was a section of woods where much of the ornate, twisted timber used in the construction of the Old Faithful Inn was obtained in 1904.

The **Hard Road to Travel Picnic Area** has three tables, and there is a handicap-accessible vault toilet here (which, remarkably, survived the burnover during the Arnica Fire). The picnic area was originally known as the "Sand Bar Picnic Area."

14.8 / 5.8 GPS: 44.47738, -110.54311
Arnica Creek Turnout (E)
Arnica Bypass Service Road (W)
Arnica Creek Crossing

This turnout gets its name from **Arnica Creek**, which flows under the road just east of the easternmost exit. The creek is named for the species of flower commonly found in this part of the park.

The gated drive on the west side of the road is for the **Arnica Bypass Service Road,** and exists primarily to allow utility crews to access power lines that can be found several hundred feet to the west. The utility corridor runs along the old Arnica Bypass Road. See the entry above for details about this old road. An old trail to Beach Lake can also be found here.

15.1 / 5.5 GPS: 44.47554, -110.54889
Old Roadbed Termination (W) [Northbound Only]

This is the south end of the old highway that took visitors from West Thumb to the Bridge Bay area (see the entry above at 13.8/6.8). It is difficult to see if you're heading south, but if you're headed north, you'll see just a quick opening in the trees on the hill just above the road here. Blink and you'll miss it.

15.2/ 5.4 GPS: 44.47511, -110.55030
Little Arnica Creek Crossing

Little Arnica Creek passes under the roadway here. It's named for its proximity to Arnica Creek approximately ½ mile to the north.

16.1 / 4.5 GPS: 44.46433, -110.55579
Howard Eaton Trail (W)

You'll have to watch closely for the faded orange marker on a tree just as you enter the curve if you're traveling northbound. This is part of the now largely abandoned **Howard Eaton Trail**. From here it travels west, then northward until it reaches the old roadbed at Arnica Creek, from which point it traveled on northward to the Natural Bridge area. Since the roadbed is now closed by the NPS due to bear management concerns, this section of the trail is no longer maintained. This area was also the site of a Shaw and Powell "Lunch Camp" from 1913 to around 1917.[8]

16.6 / 4.0 GPS: 44.45759, -110.55868
Carrington Island (E)

Carrington Island is visible in the lake just off the eastern shore. It was named after E. Campbell Carrington, a zoologist with the first Hayden Expedition in 1871. During the spring and early summer, it's not uncommon to see a single tree standing in the water here because the rest of the tiny island is under water. There is no real pullout here, so you'll have to catch a glimpse of it as you pass by.

17.4 / 3.2 GPS: 44.44667, -110.56313
Bluff Point Pullout (E)

This small pullout is located at **Bluff Point** on the lake. It was given its name in 1878 by the Hayden Survey team because it is located on a high bluff above the lake. There are no signs or other information here.

18.0 / 2.6 GPS: 44.44090, -110.57217
Exploded Bay Pullout (E)

There is an interpretive sign here that explains the basics of how West Thumb was created. West Thumb is a small caldera resulting from an eruption that occurred some 180,000 years ago and is home to some of the deepest waters in the lake (almost 400 feet in some places).

18.1 / 2.4 GPS: 44.44049, -110.57397
No Name Lake (W)

The small body of water on the west side of the road here is known colloquially as "No Name Lake." It has no official name and isn't a true lake, however.

18.5 / 2.1 GPS: 44.43744, -110.57962
Little Thumb Lagoon Pullout (E)

The small **Little Thumb Lagoon** is formed by a sandbar where Little Thumb Creek empties into the Lake

18.6 / 2.0 GPS: 44.43680, -110.58093
Little Thumb Creek crossing

Little Thumb Creek is named because of its proximity to Big Thumb Creek.[9] It was known originally as "Fisheries Creek" because of the old fish hatchery constructed here in 1903. By 1906, the hatchery consisted of three buildings, but in 1913 it ceased operations with the opening of the Fish Hatchery near the Lake Hotel.

18.7 / 1.9 GPS: 44.43538, -110.58294
Little Thumb Creek Pit Service Road (W)

The **Little Thumb Creek Pit Service Road** provided access to an old gravel and materials quarry, and is still used by utility crews to access power lines located in this area. The road to the pit area is approximately $\frac{4}{10}$ of a mile long and is largely overgrown by small trees today. Just before it reaches the pit itself, the road crosses Little Thumb Creek, for which the pit was named. This quarry was used to provide construction materials for a number of road projects in the southern half of the park from the 1930s through the 1960s. The pit itself is about 12 acres in size and has a vertical wall 150 feet tall by 1200 feet long. The area was remediated in 1997.

18.9 / 1.7 GPS: 44.43310, -110.58485
POTTS HOT SPRING BASIN (E) ✳

On the east side of the road is a long, slender pullout that brings you alongside the **Potts Hot Spring Basin**, a small thermal area of about 200 mostly unnamed features. There are about a dozen, however, that do have official names, including Resurgent Geyser, Corner Pocket Geyser, and Mezzanine Pool.[10]

You can take a short walk to the edge of the fence surrounding the area, but there are no boardwalks or trails here, and no access to the thermal basin itself. Despite it being very unsafe to enter, rangers issue several citations to people who climb over the fence illegally every summer. The original road through this area ran between the thermal features and the lake shore, and was relocated to its present alignment outside the basin in 1972.

The basin was named for trapper Daniel T. Potts, who made his way through the area in 1822. Upon his return home, he wrote a lengthy letter to his brother describing the unusual features he'd encountered. This is believed to be the earliest known description of thermal features in Yellowstone, and so park officials gave the basin its name in 1956.

19.9 / 0.7 GPS: 44.42218, -110.57454
WEST THUMB - LAKESHORE GROUP (E)

This narrow pullout brings you alongside a portion of the West Thumb Geyser Basin known as the Lakeshore Group. This area has about two dozen features, including Occasional Geyser and Overhanging Geyser, both of which are visible from the road.[11]

20.3 / 0.2 GPS: 44.41659, -110.57539
DUCK LAKE TRAILHEAD (W) 🏃

The trailhead for the **Duck Lake Trail** can be found here. This half-mile (each way) trail takes you up to the rim and down into the crater of Duck Lake, a moderate-sized lake formed in the caldera of a hydrothermal explosion that occurred between 6000 and 8000 years ago.[12] Once you get to the bottom, you can hike around the shore of the lake. Duck Lake once hosted a population of brown trout, but they were eradicated in 1967 because of fears that the non-native fish might somehow find their way into the nearby Yellowstone Lake. Running off to the west from this point is an old road bed that was a turn lane from this road onto the road to Old Faithful prior to 1991.

West Thumb Hamilton Store, ca. 1983. Hamilton operated this store along with a "mini-store" he'd acquired when the Haynes family sold their photo shop enterprise to Hamilton in 1967.

20.5 / 0.1 GPS: 44.41564, -110.57656
WEST THUMB GEYSER BASIN (E) [icons]
WEST THUMB PICNIC AREA (E)
UNNAMED HOT SPRING (W)

Access to the **West Thumb Geyser Basin** is on the east side of the road. The driveway leads into a two-section parking lot, with ample space for large RVs and buses. The basin itself is home to approximately 150 thermal features, some 30 or so of which have official names. There is a half-mile long boardwalk trail that winds its way through many of these features. Pick up a guide map at the trailhead for details on the more well known features, or see Scott Bryan's *The Geysers of Yellowstone* for an in-depth discussion of many of the named features.

Though it's hard to tell today, West Thumb was home to a fairly large commercial development until the 1970s. It hosted over 300 cabins, a 170-site campground, full size and smaller General Stores, a cafeteria, a gas station, a ranger station, post office, and employee housing and other support buildings necessary to allow all of that to function. The development was removed, and much of it replaced at Grant Village in the 1960s-1980s. See the West Thumb/Grant Village Development section for more details on the various structures that used to be here.

The lone structure here today is the small building used as a bookstore by the Yellowstone Association during the summer, and as a Warming Hut during the winter. The sales staff of the store is very helpful if you have questions, as there often isn't a ranger here to answer questions (though there are usually several ranger visits throughout the day). The building itself was constructed in 1931 and was originally a ranger station.

On the east side of the parking lot is the **West Thumb Picnic Area,** which has five tables. In the parking lot, you'll find four vault toilets, two of which are handicap-accessible.

The bubbling spring on the west side of the road is unnamed, as is the spring in the middle of the parking lot at the basin.

20.6 / 0.0 GPS: 44.41402, -110.57852 ELEVATION: 7818 FEET WEST THUMB JUNCTION

From this point, you can drive 20.6 miles (33.2 km) north to Fishing Bridge, 17.6 miles (28.3 km) west to Old Faithful, or 21.4 miles (34.4 km) south to the South Entrance.

South Entrance Road

The South Entrance Road is 21.4 miles (34.4 km) long from the south boundary of the park to West Thumb Junction. Much of the southern half of the road takes you along Lewis Canyon and the Lewis River, but the balance is through thick, richly forested areas. If you're heading south, the two-mile long segment of road just north of the south entrance is known locally as Teton Straight. When you're leaving the park, the drive affords you a gorgeous preview of the Grand Tetons.

The initial route between Jackson, Wyoming, and West Thumb was cut by General Philip Sheridan in 1881. Construction of a legitimate road wouldn't begin until the late 1880s, and it would be 1892 before visitors could enter the park via this route. For a great many years, this was the least used entrance road into the park. With the increasing population south of Yellowstone, and the rise in popularity of the Jackson Hole Airport, however, it has become the second most used entrance behind that at West Yellowstone. On busy days, traffic can back up as much as half a mile or more from the entrance kiosks.

The road today generally follows the same path it did when it was initially constructed, though there have been some modifications. The original road ran west of the hills that form the western edge of Lewis Canyon, whereas today the road runs along the canyon's western wall. This was done to afford a more scenic drive for tourists. The road has also been realigned between Grant Village and West Thumb.

There are vault toilets at the south entrance, at the Heart Lake Trailhead, and the Lewis Lake Campground, but other than that, there aren't many to be found. Plan accordingly. This drive is not known for its abundance of wildlife, though you may get lucky and see the occasional moose, especially in the Lewis Falls area. As you approach West Thumb you're liable to encounter a small herd of elk that makes its home in the area, as well as the occasional grizzly bear.

The road has not yet been rebuilt to current road standards and is very narrow and potholed in places, and there are a limited number of turnouts, especially if you're heading north. Use caution and be especially attentive to your driving as you're driving along Lewis Canyon.

0.0 / 21.4 GPS: 44.13335, -110.66522 ELEVATION: 6892 FEET
YELLOWSTONE BOUNDARY

As you drive up to the gate, you're leaving the John D. Rockefeller, Jr., Memorial Parkway. This space between Yellowstone and Grand Teton National Park was left out of the latter when it was created in 1929 so that the new park would not be seen as "Yellowstone South" or simply an extension of Yellowstone National Park. The eight mile (12.9 km) road and some 24,000 acres surrounding it was designated as a memorial parkway in 1972 for John D. Rockefeller, Jr., who purchased much of the land that eventually became Grand Teton National Park, and provided many other generous gifts to the NPS to help preserve land and wilderness.

0.0 / 21.4 GPS: 44.13339, -110.66526
GOVERNMENT SERVICE AREA (W)
BESSIE ROWBOTTOM GRAVE (W)
SOUTH BOUNDARY TRAILHEAD (W)

The driveway to the west takes you into the **South Entrance Government Area** where those who work in this part of the park live while they're here. This area is generally closed to public travel, so please respect the privacy of those who make their homes here. The area dates to the 1930s, with the original barn and fire cache, both built by the CCC in 1934, still standing.

The grave of **Bessie Rowbottom** is located in the housing complex behind and to the southwest of the corral (immediately behind the weather station). Ms. Rowbottom was the child of a tourist family visiting Yellowstone. For unknown reasons, she died in the park and was buried here in 1903. The Snake River Ranger Station has a binder of information about the child and her grave if you wish to learn more. You should check in with the ranger station prior to driving into the complex to view this grave.

The western **South Boundary Trailhead** takes you west along the southern border of the park and, eventually, into the Bechler area. The trailhead is located on the north side of the corral.

0.2 / 21.2 GPS: 44.13577, -110.66680
ENTRANCE KIOSKS
SNAKE RIVER RANGER STATION (E) 🏠 🚻
EASTERN SOUTH BOUNDARY TRAILHEAD (E) 🚶

This is the **South Entrance Station**, where you'll be greeted by a uniformed visitor services representative of the National Park Service, and asked to pay your entrance fee or show the pass you obtained when you entered Grand Teton National Park (the passes are valid for seven days in both parks). Once you've paid, hang onto your receipt – you'll need it to get back in the park (and may be asked to show it on the way out). You'll be provided with the park's newspaper, a map, and any other relevant information related to road construction, road closures, or any other situation that might impact your ability to move about the park efficiently. You are welcome to ask any questions, but be mindful of any traffic behind you, especially during the busy summer season. As the South Entrance is the second busiest during the summer, traffic can get really backed up here.

On the right as you pass through the entry point, you'll see the **Snake River Ranger Station** (built in 1989) and a couple of vault toilets. At the ranger station, you can stop in and ask questions, as well as obtain fishing licenses and backcountry camping permits.

Behind the station is the eastern trailhead for the **South Boundary Trail**. This trail heading east will take you to the Harebell Patrol Cabin some 12 miles (19 km) out, and will require you to ford the Snake River. From Harebell, you can continue on to the Fox Creek Patrol Cabin and then on to the Thorofare area, the most remote section of the park.

0.3 / 21.1 GPS: 44.13704, -110.66777
SNAKE RIVER PICNIC AREA (E) 🧺 🚻

The **Snake River Picnic Area** has 15 tables, eight grills, and a vault toilet that is handicap accessible. In recent years, the gravel road through this area has been in terrible condition, so drive gingerly through it so you don't damage your car.

Until 1972, this area was a small 11-site campground. It was converted into a picnic area following the construction of the new facilities (including a campground) at Flagg Ranch just two miles to the south.

As you drive north, you'll notice a small, unnamed lake off in the woods on the east side of the road.

0.9 / 20.5 GPS: 44.14571, -110.66979
SOUTH ENTRANCE PIT SERVICE ROAD (W)

This service road leads back to the **South Entrance Pit,** an area used by the NPS to stage construction materials and to store old equipment, buildings, etc.

1.4 / 20.0 GPS: 44.15210, -110.67382
CRAWFISH CREEK CROSSING
MOOSE FALLS TRAILHEAD (E) ⃰ 🏃

The parking areas on both side of the road here provide access to the **Moose Falls** area. The 30 foot, plunge-type waterfall is located along Crawfish Creek, which passes under the bridge (built in 1934) just south of the trailhead and eventually empties into the Lewis River approximately one half mile to the east. Even though the falls is just a short walk from the trailhead, few people actually take the time to stop and look at this gorgeous water feature. The falls was given its name in keeping with the policy of naming natural features after wildlife or flora found within the park.

Crawfish Creek gets its named from the presence of small crayfish that live in its thermally-heated waters. The source of the creek's water is a small area of hot springs known as the Crawfish Thermal Area, as well as Spirea Creek, named for a shrub. Spirea Creek is also fed by a thermal field known as the Spirea Creek Thermal Area. Both are located about a mile to the northwest of the waterfall.

If you're headed north, as you come out of the 90-degree bend in the road just north of the Crawfish Creek, you'll be on one of the longest straight stretches of road in the park. At about two miles in length, it is known colloquially as Teton Straight and is one of the few places to pass slower vehicles for the next 20 miles.

1.9 / 19.5 GPS: 44.15842, -110.67166
OLD ROAD BED (E) [SOUTHBOUND ONLY]

You have to be traveling south to pick this one out; it appears as a small path through the woods heading south on the east side of the road. This is an old road bed that was part of the original South Entrance Road. The old road through here moved slightly east of the current alignment, then crossed the existing road 1/10 of a mile north of Crawfish Creek and crossed the creek itself on a bridge approximately 50 yards upstream of the existing bridge. This road was realigned in the mid-1930s.[1]

2.4 / 19.0 GPS: 44.16472, -110.66671
OLD ROAD BED (W)

This is the south entrance/exit to another segment of the original South Entrance Road. When the road was first constructed in 1895, it was routed to the west of Lewis Canyon. Reconstruction in the mid-1930s moved the road to its present alignment along the canyon's wall, and this section of road was closed. This old segment was at one time maintained as a bike and ski trail, but has long since been abandoned. The north end of the road can be found at 7.4/14.0 below.

4.3 / 17.1 GPS: 44.19056, -110.65582
LEWIS CANYON PULLOUT (E) 🏛

This short, skinny pullout affords an excellent view of the south end of the deepest part of Lewis Canyon, named after the river that runs through it. Do not climb over the rails here. It is very dangerous, and several people have been injured from falls. Lewis Canyon is several miles long, 300 feet deep, and 1,800 feet wide at its widest point.

6.6 / 14.8 GPS: 44.22183, -110.65541
LEWIS CANYON FIRE PULLOUT (E) 🏛

As is the case in many other areas of the park, Lewis Canyon was heavily impacted by the 1988 fires that burned almost a third of the park's surface area. This interpretive display describes the damage to the area inflicted by the Snake River Complex and its impact on the canyon.

As you travel north, approximately ²⁄₁₀ of a mile ahead of you, you'll see the Upper Lewis Canyon Falls, an 80-foot cascade type waterfall along the Lewis River. There aren't any pullouts along this stretch of the roadway, so you'll have to slow down and look at it as you drive. If you do find a place to get out and look, be very careful, as the footing along the canyon wall can be tenuous. A tourist died when he fell into the canyon here in 1974.[2] There is a Lower Lewis Canyon Falls about ²⁄₁₀ of a mile south of here, but it is generally not visible from the roadway.

7.4 / 14.0 GPS: 44.23239, -110.65329
NORTH END OF OLD SOUTH ENTRANCE ROAD (W)

You'll have to look closely as you drive southward, but the vestigial remains of the original South Entrance Road can be seen heading off to the south here as the current road curves eastward (see 2.4/19.0 above for more).

8.2 / 13.2 GPS: 44.24326, -110.64721
Pitchstone Plateau Trailhead (W) 🚶

The **Pitchstone Plateau Trail** is an 18-mile (29 km) long trail that takes you through some of the most remote areas of the park, including through areas covered in thick, black, glassy pitchstone (lava). This lava is some of the youngest in the park, around 70,000 years old.[3]

This is a fairly difficult hike, primarily because portions of the trail are hard to find, and water is scarce. Approximately 4.5 miles (6 km) into the hike you'll come upon Phantom Fumarole, so-named because it is tough to find unless you are in the area early in the morning when the steam clues you in to its existence. The trail itself has its south terminus at the Grassy Lake Reservoir west of Flagg Ranch.

8.6 / 12.8 GPS: 44.24861, -110.64556
Enter Avalanche Danger Zone

This zone, which extends from here to ³⁄₁₀ of a mile north, is known for high avalanche danger during the winter and during early spring. Signs are posted indicating NO STOPPING for this area during those portions of the year when the danger of avalanche conditions might exist. The northern end of the zone is at 8.9/12.5.

8.9 / 12.5 GPS: 44.25284, -110.64409
North end of Avalanche Zone

9.4 / 12.0 GPS: 44.25842, -110.64050
Site of the old Lewis River Road Camp (W)

The flat patch of land to the west of the roadway here was the site of the old Lewis River Road Camp in the 1910s - 1930s.

10.0 / 11.4 GPS: 44.26729, -110.63503
Lewis Falls South Pullouts (W & E) 📷🏞️

Parking pullouts on both sides of the road here afford access to the **Lewis Falls** area. This 30-foot, cascade-type waterfall on the Lewis River is one of the most popular waterfalls in the park given its proximity to the road. Lewis River drains Lewis Lake, located approximately one mile to the north, and eventually empties into the Snake River just north of the South Entrance Station. Here the water falls over the edge of the Yellowstone Caldera from atop the Pitchstone Plateau.

While you can remain at the viewing area alongside the parking pullout, or on the bridge (built in 1960) over the river to view the falls, there is a short trail on the south side of the river that takes you back to an excellent overlook of the falls itself.

The falls, river, and lake are named after explorer Meriwether Lewis, who along with William Clark, led one of the most famous expeditions to explore the west. Though Lewis never visited the area that would become Yellowstone, these features were named in his honor as one of the most important explorers of his time.

10.2 / 11.2 GPS: 44.26814, -110.63334
LEWIS FALLS NORTH TURNOUT (E) 🚶 ⛰

This turnout is located just north of the bridge over the Lewis River and affords additional access to the Lewis Falls (see above). The large marshland to the east is the confluence of Aster Creek and the Lewis River, and is a popular spot to see moose.

11.3 / 10.1 GPS: 44.28327, -110.62654
LEWIS LAKE CAMPGROUND/PICNIC AREA (W) ⛺ 🏕 🚤 🚻 🛖

The **Lewis Lake Campground** has 85 sites, with vault toilets only. The 2014 summer rates is $15 per night. The campground was opened in 1961 as one of the park improvements undertaken as part of the Mission 66 Program. Because of the small size of the sites, there is a 25-foot limit on RVs and trailers. The campground is usually the second to last to open each season (mid-June or so), primarily because much of it is under water early in the season. However, it remains open until the last weekend the park is open (typically the first weekend in November).

The **Lewis Lake Picnic Area** is located at the entrance to the campground itself, down the short access road. The area has nine tables and access to vault toilets that are handicap accessible. There's a small ranger station here as well, though it is often closed while the ranger is out on patrol. When staffed, you can obtain boating permits and fishing licenses.

12.2 / 9.2 GPS: 44.29196, -110.61726
LEWIS LAKE OVERLOOK SOUTH (W)

This is the **Lewis Lake Overlook South** pullout. It is designed for traffic heading south, so if you drive into it from the south, you may encounter oncoming traffic in the narrow pathway.

12.9 / 8.5 GPS: 44.30127, -110.61053
LEWIS LAKE OVERLOOK NORTH (W)

This is the northern **Lewis Lake Overlook** pullout. Lewis Lake, at 2716 acres in size, is the third largest lake in the park. It has a maximum depth of 108 feet (33 m). The lake supports populations of brown, lake, and brook trout.[4]

13.7 / 7.7 GPS: 44.31045, -110.60183
LEWIS LAKE SHORELINE PULLOUT (W)

This pullout will get you right alongside the shore of Lewis Lake. Get out and get your feet wet (though it is usually too cold to swim).

14.0 / 7.4 GPS: 44.31370, -110.60066
LEWIS LAKE WEST PIT SERVICE ROAD (W)

The **Lewis Lake West Pit** is used by NPS to stage construction materials and equipment. and is one of two former sites for previous iterations of the Lewis Lake Campground. It was home to an old picnic area as well.

14.2 / 7.2 GPS: 44.31697, -110.59944
HEART LAKE TRAILHEAD (E) 🚶 �

The **Heart Lake Trail** is a 7.5-mile (12 km) trail that takes you to the western shore of Heart Lake, passing through the Heart Lake Geyser Basin and the Witch Creek Thermal Area along the way. These two areas consist of about 400 mostly unnamed thermal features. The trail ends at the Heart Lake Patrol Cabin. From there, you can continue around the north side or the western side of the lake.

If you continue along the western shore, the trail will connect you to the Mt. Sheridan Trail, a difficult 4.5-mile (7.2 km, each way) climb to the summit of Mt. Sheridan. Though it is a pretty tough trail, you are rewarded at the summit with an outstanding panoramic view of the southern half of the park, as well as views of the Grand Tetons to the south. If you continue past the Mount Sheridan Trail to the south, you will eventually connect to the South Boundary Trail.

Mt. Sheridan is the site of one of the park's three primary fire lookout towers. This particular one is normally unstaffed, but is equipped with video cameras that allow the wildland fire staff in Mammoth to keep an eye on things. This is also the site of one of the park's main radio repeaters.

There is a single handicap-accessible vault toilet in the trailhead parking area. You'll notice an old road running east out of the parking area. This leads to the old Heart Lake Trailhead Gravel Pit, which was used as a source of aggregate material for a variety of road construction projects in this part of the park, as well as material used to construct the existing Lewis Lake Campground in the 1960s. The pit is no longer used.

14.4 / 7.0 GPS: 44.32026, -110.59831
LEWIS CHANNEL/DOGSHEAD TRAILHEAD (W) 🚶 👫
OLD ROADBED (W)

The **Lewis Channel Trail** is a seven-mile (11 km) trail that takes you along the northern shore of Lewis Lake and then up along the 3.5-mile (5.6 km) Lewis Channel, the river that connects Lewis Lake to Shoshone Lake (the park's second largest lake). This channel is the only river in the park where boating is allowed, and then only canoes or other self-propelled boats (no motorized craft).

This trail is pretty heavily used by fishermen, but is a scenic trail very much worth your time if you have a day to kill in the area. You can come back the same way, or you can walk a few hundred feet north at the end of the trail to come back along the **Dogshead Trail**, which will cut your return trip by about three miles (4.8 km). This trail is four-miles (6.4 km) long and provides the shortest path to Shoshone Lake from the South Entrance Road. The first mile or so follows part of the original road built through this area. The trail is named for a nearby creek of the same name (the origin for which is unknown).

Coming in from the north is the old roadbed (originally constructed in 1895) used up until 1915 when the road was relocated eastward. The north end of this old segment can be found at the end of the Grant Incinerator Service Road at 20.2/1.2 below.

16.7 / 4.7 GPS: 44.34993, -110.58519
OLD SERVICE ROAD (W)

The logs you see staked into the ground on the west side of the road here mark the entrance to an old service road that led to the Riddle Lake Trail Gravel Pit, used to provide aggregate and sand for road construction along the South Entrance Road. The old road is barely visible, and the pit is almost impossible to get to since it has long been abandoned and is now largely overgrown with trees.

17.3 / 4.1 GPS: 44.35850, -110.58201
RIDDLE LAKE TRAILHEAD (E) 🧍

The **Riddle Lake Trail** is a five-mile (8 km) round trip that takes you to the small Riddle Lake. This trail typically doesn't open until the middle of July (for bear management reasons), though it is not uncommon for rangers to cite people who use the trail prior to its opening each year.

Park historian Lee Whittlesey tells us that the lake's name came about from a combination of a mapping error and fur trapper stories about a lake that drained into both the Pacific and Atlantic oceans.[5] For the record, the lake drains into Yellowstone Lake via its outlet at Solution Creek, and therefore into the Atlantic Ocean.

17.4 / 4.0 GPS: 44.35975, -110.58129
RIDDLE LAKE DIVIDE PULLOUT (E) ⚊

This small pullout is known locally as the **Riddle Lake Divide Pullout**. Here, just north of the Riddle Lake Trailhead, is where the South Entrance Road crosses the Continental Divide, marking the boundary between water drainage to the Atlantic Ocean (often via the Gulf of Mexico) and the Pacific Ocean. The park's roads cross the Continental Divide in three places (the other two are along the road from West Thumb to Old Faithful).

18.1 / 3.3 GPS: 44.36910, -110.58084
SANDY CREEK CROSSING
TWIN MEADOWS (E & W)

There are two small meadows on opposite sides of the road here, known colloquially as **Twin Meadows** because of their similar size and appearance. **Sandy Creek** traverses the meadows from west to east and flows north through the Grant Village area to Yellowstone Lake.

Lee Whittlesey indicates this stream was named in honor of the original name assigned to Big Thumb Creek by early surveyors of the Northern Pacific Railroad (who were surveying the area for a potential rail line in the early 1880s).[6]

19.6 / 1.8 GPS: 44.39094, -110.57178
GRANT VILLAGE ENTRANCE (E) 🏠 ⑦ ✉ ⛺ 🪧 🍴 🛏 🚆 📷 ⛽ 🎿

Grant Village, named in honor of President Ulysses S. Grant, who signed the legislation that created Yellowstone on March 1, 1872, is a development that was in large part designed to replace facilities and services once located at West Thumb. Begun in the early 1960s as part of the Mission 66 Program, its campground and visitor center opened in the mid-1960s. Additional services and facilities were added over time through the mid-1980s. Today there are two general stores, a service/repair station, post office, two restaurants, a large campground, picnic area, amphitheater, ranger station, visitor center, and employee housing and maintenance areas located here. For more information on the history of this area see the West Thumb/ Grant Village Development section.

The village got its name in 1945 during discussions and planning about the relocation of facilities away from the West Thumb area, though other names would continue to be floated around for it until work was actually started (e.g., Thumb Bay, Grant's Thumb, etc.).

20.2 / 1.2 GPS: 44.39851, -110.57012
GRANT INCINERATOR SERVICE ROAD (W)

Though it has now been removed, this area once housed an incinerator where NPS burned much of the waste produced in the southern portions of the park. Today, most trash is hauled off to recycling centers or composted. The area is now used as a storage and staging area for maintenance supplies and equipment.

This service road is also the north end of a segment of the original road constructed in 1895 and used until 1915 when a new road was constructed to replace it (roughly following the existing road). The south end of the old road is at the Dogshead Trail listed at 14.4/7.0 above.

On the east side of the road, you may notice a line of smaller trees if you're looking due north as the road begins to curve to the west slightly. This was the path of the original road through the area - the one that took you right through the West Thumb Geyser Basin. The road was relocated to its current alignment in the 1970s.

20.7 / 0.7 GPS: 44.40528, -110.56938
BIG THUMB CREEK CROSSING

Big Thumb Creek passes under the road here and empties into West Thumb Bay. The creek was originally known simply as Thumb Creek, but in the early 1960s, it was given the name Big Thumb and its little cousin on the Fishing Bridge to West Thumb Road the name Little Thumb to prevent confusion of the two (Little Thumb Creek was also called Thumb

Creek up to that point). The creek is one of the major trout spawning areas in this part of the park., and it's not uncommon to see grizzlies in and around this area, especially in the early part of the spring.

The bridge here was constructed here in 1972 when the new road alignment was built; it replaced one located closer to the mouth of the creek.

20.8 / 0.6 GPS: 44.40732, -110.57101
WEST THUMB SERVICE ROAD (E)

The **West Thumb Service Road** takes you back to an old utility area where the West Thumb Electrical Substation and a storage building (originally a powerhouse, built in 1935) are located now, as well as softball/baseball field used for recreation by Grant Village employees. This area was the site of the old West Thumb Incinerator as well (ca. 1932). In the winter, the road is open to snowmobile use.

20.9 / 0.5 GPS: 44.40864, -110.57281
UNNAMED CREEK CROSSING

The creek that passes under the bridge here has no official name, though it is known locally as "Unnamed Creek." The bridge was constructed in 1972 at the same time as the Thumb Creek Bridge referenced above.

21.4 / 0.0 GPS: 44.41402, -110.57852 ELEVATION: 7818 FEET
LAKE OVERLOOK TRAIL/SAVAGE HILL (S) [𝕥]
WEST THUMB JUNCTION

From here, you can go 20.6 miles (33.2 km) north to Fishing Bridge Junction, 17.6 miles (28.3 km) west to Old Faithful, or 21.4 miles (34.4 km) back to the South Entrance.

Just to the southeast of the junction is the crossing for the **Lake Overlook Trail**, which takes you up a one-mile (1.6 km) trail to the summit of **Savage Hill**, affording an excellent view of Yellowstone Lake and the Absaroka Mountains. You'll pass by a small handful of unnamed thermal features as well. The hill gets its name from the fact that the "savages," an old name for park concession employees, used this hill for recreation and courting in their off hours during the days when the large West Thumb development was here. See the West Thumb/Grant Village Development section for more details about what this area used to look like.

West Thumb Junction
to the
Old Faithful Interchange

The road from the junction at West Thumb to the Old Faithful Interchange is 17.6 miles (28.3 km) long. Much of the route passes through heavily forested area with little variation in scenery. You cross the Continental Divide twice, including at Craig Pass, one of the park's three high-altitude mountain passes. The pass is also where you'll find Isa Lake, which has the unique distinction of being the only lake in the United States that drains to both the Pacific and the Atlantic Oceans.

U. S. Army Engineer Lt. Hiram Chittenden originally laid out a route for the road between Old Faithful and West Thumb through Norris Pass, along the north shore of Shoshone Lake, and then roughly up the same route used by today's South Entrance Road to West Thumb. In 1891, however, Congress passed a law requiring Chittenden to complete the road via "the shortest practicable route."

Chittenden would go onto survey a new route himself, and he ended up with a proposed path that roughly parallels today's existing road. The west end would travel south to Lone Star Geyser before heading east, however, and then would follow Spring Creek through its namesake canyon before connecting into the existing road near the present-day Spring Creek Picnic Area. On the east end, the original alignment was further to the north and much more of a straight line alongside Dry Creek to West Thumb. The road was completed in 1892.

For some 40 years, this was a one-way road (west to east). In the 1930s, however, the road was re-engineered to realign it along its current path, and widened to permit two-way traffic. The new alignment shaved 2.7 miles off the original route.[1] The work began in 1935 and took six years to complete.

In 1946-1947, it became the last section of the Grand Loop Road to be paved with asphalt. The entire route was rebuilt again beginning in the late 1980s.

You won't see much wildlife along this stretch of road except the occasional lone bison and a handful of elk in the West Thumb area. The road itself is in excellent condition, but given its winding, hilly nature, there are very few opportunities for passing along the entire stretch. As this is a primary route to Old Faithful from the South Entrance, it is heavily used and the slower traffic often does not make use of the pullouts. Patience is definitely a virtue when driving along this stretch of highway.

The road travels over Craig Pass, which is subject to receiving considerable snowfall at any time of the year. Therefore, it is not uncommon for it to be closed periodically, especially in the May-June, and late September-October time frames. Rest assured that, when the park is open, plow crews do work to re-open the road, so waiting in the Grant/West Thumb or Old Faithful areas is usually much more efficient time wise than driving all the way up to Norris, over to Canyon, and then back down through Hayden Valley and the Lake areas (or vice vsersa) to get to the other side of the pass.

There are three picnic areas along the route, each with a vault toilet, as well as a toilet at the Lone Star Geyser Trailhead. The picnic areas are usually snowbound during the early part of the season, however, so if you're heading west during this time period, stop in at West Thumb, or if you're heading east, stop at Old Faithful prior to getting on the road.

0.0 / 17.6 GPS: 44.41402, -110.57852 ELEVATION: 7818 FEET
WEST THUMB JUNCTION

From here you can drive 20.6 miles (33.2 km) north to Fishing Bridge Junction, 17.6 miles (28.3 km) west to Old Faithful, or 21.4 miles (34.4 km) south to the South Entrance.

The current design of this intersection took shape in 1973 when the entire West Thumb area was reconfigured. Since then the only significant change has been the 1990 removal of the curving turn lane for traffic heading westbound from the Fishing Bridge to West Thumb Road.

The remnants of the old road beds around West Thumb can still be seen in various places between here and Grant Village and just west and north of this intersection. See the West Thumb/Grant Village Development section for more details on this history of this area.

0.3 / 17.3 GPS: 44.41723, -110.58234
ELK VIEW PULLOUT (N) 📷

The pullout here is known as the "**Elk View Pullout**" because it's often clogged with people who've stopped to watch the elk, bears, and other wildlife that tend to gather in this area from time to time. This is also a popular spot for rangers to stop speeders coming off the hill to the west.

0.4 / 17.2 GPS: 44.41827, -110.58416
BARRICADE PULLOUTS (N & S)
DUCK LAKE (N)

This pair of pullouts is known collectively as the "**Barricade Pullouts**" because they're at the Duck Lake Barricade, which closes off traffic going westbound when Craig Pass is closed (usually for snow and ice). You do have an excellent view of both Yellowstone Lake and Duck Lake from the north pullout. The mountains in the distance are part of the Absaroka Range which forms the eastern boundary of the park.

Duck Lake, on the north side of the road, was the potable water supply source for the old development at West Thumb. Today, there's only a bookstore/warming hut there, but from the mid 1930s until the late 1970s, there was a substantial number of guest cabins, a campground, stores, and other facilities there. After Grant Village was completed, all of the structures at West Thumb were removed, as was the old pumping station located on the west end of the Duck Lake (you can still see the foot print of the pumping station in the wooded area just to the west of the barricade on the lake side of the road).

Duck Lake once hosted a population of brown trout, but they were eradicated in 1967 because of fears that the non-native fish might somehow find their way into the nearby Yellowstone Lake (either via a large flood of Duck Lake or via a bird carrying one from one lake to another). The lake itself is in a crater formed by a hydrothermal explosion some 6000 to 8000 years ago.

0.7 / 16.9 GPS: 44.42169, -110.58657
PANORAMA POINT (N) 📷

This turnout is known colloquially as **Panorama Point** for its panoramic view of the Yellowstone Lake and Absaroka Mountain Range. On a clear day, this is one of the best spots in the park to get a full panoramic photograph of Yellowstone Lake, and so it is also known as Lake View.

1.2 / 16.4 GPS: 44.42152, -110.59215
Old Road Bed (W)

You'll have to take a quick look to the west here as you drive by, but you'll see a clearing going through the trees back to the west just after you come out of the first (easternmost) Duck Lake Curve. This is the end of the original road to this area from Old Faithful (the other end is at the westernmost crossing of Dry Creek at 7.8/9.8).

Approximately five miles west of here, the old road passes through a quarry (known as the Dry Creek Pit) used to provide materials to build the original road. The quarry itself was remediated in 1997.

An old garbage dump used to dispose of refuse from the former development at West Thumb is located along this abandoned road as well.

1.7 / 15.9 GPS: 44.41714, -110.59751
Enter/Exit Duck Lake Curve

If you're headed westbound, you've just come out of what is colloquially known as **Duck Lake Curve**. If you're headed east, then you'll just be entering the wide, sweeping S-curve that marks the final approach to the West Thumb area.

2.6 / 15.0 GPS: 44.42388, -110.61301
East crossing Little Thumb Creek

This is the eastern crossing of the **Little Thumb Creek** along this section of roadway. The creek is seasonal and is often dry late in the summer.

3.3 / 14.3 GPS: 44.42877, -110.62501
West crossing of Little Thumb Creek

This is the western crossing of the Little Thumb Creek along this section of roadway.

3.7 / 13.8 GPS: 44.43243, -110.63298
East Divide Picnic Area (N) 🏕️ 🚻

The **East Divide Picnic Area**, located near the eastern Continental Divide crossing on this road (and thus it's name), has 14 tables and a vault toilet that is handicap accessible.

4.1 / 13.4 GPS: 44.43402, -110.64087
EAST CONTINENTAL DIVIDE PULLOUTS (N & S) ✻

There are pullouts on both sides of the highway to allow people to take photos of the Continental Divide sign. If you park on the north side, be careful crossing the highway as people tend to speed through this area.

4.7 / 12.9 GPS: 44.43372, -110.65073
DRY CREEK EAST CROSSING

Dry Creek crosses from the south side to the north side of the road here. The creek gets its name from the fact that it's dry most of the season, and usually only active during the snow runoff in early spring.

7.8 / 9.8 GPS: 44.45220, -110.68637
DRY CREEK WEST CROSSING

See the note above regarding **Dry Creek**. In the original (1892) road alignment, the road from here to West Thumb followed Dry Creek from this point eastward, rather than taking the current southern alignment. In fact, that segment of road was often referred to as "Dry Creek Road." The other end of this road segment can be found at 1.2/16.4 above.

8.2 / 9.4 GPS: 44.44845, -110.69198
SHOSHONE POINT (S) 🎑

From the turnout, you have an excellent view of Shoshone Lake three miles to the south, as well as the Grand Teton Mountains 50 miles to the south.

Shoshone Lake (*Shō shō nè*), at over 8000 acres, is the second largest lake in the park, and was named in 1872 for the tribe of Indians who frequently visited it.[2] Prior to that, the lake had been known by as many as a half-dozen other names. It is the largest lake in the contiguous 48 states that isn't reachable via a road. In 1914, **Shoshone Point** was the site of the 4th of the park's five stagecoach holdups. A lone robber stopped 15 coaches and relieved dozens of passengers of money and other valuables. The thief was later caught and imprisoned.

8.6 / 9.6 GPS: 44.44777, -110.69758
DeLACY CREEK PICNIC AREA (N) 🌲 🚻

The **DeLacy Creek Picnic Area** has nine tables and a vault toilet. Most of the table sites are not terribly friendly to wheelchairs.

If you walk 50 yards toward the back of the picnic area, through the woods and downed trees, you'll come to a small dropoff atop an old road cut. If you look down from this cliff you'll see part of the original stagecoach road built through here in 1892.

8.7 / 8.8 GPS: 44.44663, -110.70091
DeLacy Creek Trailhead (N) [🚶]

The **DeLacy Creek Trail** is a three-mile (5 km) path to Shoshone Lake, and is therefore the shortest way to get to the lake. The large parking area is located on the north side of the road, while the trailhead itself is on the south side.

The trail exists along a portion of an old dirt road once used by fishermen to travel to Shoshone Lake for fish for the hotels in the early days of the park. The creek itself winds through a lush meadow known as DeLacy Park all the way to the lake.

Once you reach the lake, you can head west along the northern shore trail, or you can continue along the DeLacy Creek Trail around the eastern shore of the lake, connecting to the Dogshead Trail to take you out to the South Entrance Road.

The creek and its trail were named for Walter DeLacy, a surveyor who passed through the park in 1863. Had he published the maps he drew of the area during his travels, he would have been credited with discovering Yellowstone. As it is, he has this creek named after him thanks to Superintendent Philetus W. Norris.

DeLacy Park was one of the sites the Shaw and Powell Camping Company set up its portable tent camps to house tourists as they traveled through the area from the early 1900s until 1913 (that year they established permanent camps and no longer used the portable camp model). And from 1910 until the 1930s, it was the site of an NPS Road Camp.

9.1 / 8.5 GPS: 44.44784, -110.70773
Herron Creek

Many people assume that **Herron Creek** was named for the bird (heron), given that so many other features in Yellowstone have names associated with local fauna. However, it was actually named after William H. Herron, a topographer who accompanied Arnold Hague on one of his surveys in 1885-1886.[3]

If you're headed west, you'll begin the climb up Corkscrew Hill to Craig Pass. If you're eastbound, you've just come down from the Hill (see below).

9.8 / 7.9 GPS: 44.44270, -110.71630
CORKSCREW HILL

Corkscrew Hill is the moniker given to the one mile downward grade from Craig Pass, ending (beginning) at Herron Creek. This name was given to the stretch of roadway by early stagecoach drivers in the late 1890s, and was made official in 1937. The name refers to the winding nature of the original road that existed at the time. The present road is significantly less winding than the original, but the hill retains its name nonetheless (deservedly so). It was said that the (original) road was "...so crooked that you pass one place three times before you get by it, and then meet yourself on the road coming back."[4]

9.9 / 7.7 GPS: 44.44149, -110.71884
CRAIG PASS / CONTINENTAL DIVIDE ⛰
ISA LAKE (N & S)

Craig Pass sits at the western crossing of the Continental Divide along this road. At 8290 feet (2527 m), it is the lowest of the three passes through which the park's roads commonly carry visitors.[5] The pass is named for Ida M. Craig Wilcox, the first white woman to pass through the area after the road was constructed in 1891.[6]

Isa Lake, which straddles Craig Pass, has the unique distinction of draining to both the Pacific Ocean and the Atlantic Ocean. In fact, it drains backward, and is likely the only lake in the world to do so. Sitting atop the Continental Divide, the easternmost portion of the lake drains westward to the Pacific, while the westernmost portion drains eastward to the Gulf of Mexico. The lake is named for the first lady to visit the area, a Ms. Isabelle Jelke, about whom little else is known according to park historian Lee Whittlesey.[7] The bridge here was constructed in 1936, and plans are underway to replace or rehabilitate it beginning in late 2014 (which will significantly affect travel through this area!).

10.2 / 7.4 GPS: 44.43858, -110.72372
RED ROCK (N)

The red coloring of the rock on the north side of the road (and in other places around the park) comes from iron oxide in the rhyolite that makes up the rock here. This spot is colloquially known as "**Red Rock.**"

10.4 / 7.2 GPS: 44.43694, -110.72720
Norris Pass to the south (S)

Norris Pass was the first route used to travel from the Upper Geyser Basin to the West Thumb area. Discovered in 1879, only saddle horses could use it, but it allowed travelers to get to the Thumb area via Shoshone Lake before the existing roads were cut through the trees. This route was used until the first road was completed in 1892.

The pass itself is about a mile south/southwest of Craig Pass, and this pathway through the two hills here was the easiest way to get to it prior to the existence of the road you're on now.

10.7/ 6.9 GPS: 44.43807, -110.73109
Spring Creek Crossing

Spring Creek crosses from the north side to the south side of the road here. From this point it roughly parallels the existing road for a couple of miles, then bends southwestward toward the Lone Star Geyser area where it empties into the Firehole River. The creek is named for the numerous cold springs that exist along its path.

11.0 / 6.6 GPS: 44.43486, -110.73493
Divide Trailhead (S) 🚶

The **Divide Trail**, sometimes referred to as the Divide Mountain Trail or the Divide Lookout Trail, is an almost two-mile (3.2 km, each way) trail that leads to the summit of Divide Mountain. From 1958 to 1968 this peak was the site of a fire lookout tower; the lookout was abandoned and eventually removed in two sections by helicopter in 1991. There are some decent views as you climb the trail, but the view at the top is rather limited given the dense forest.

Approximately a half mile down the Divide Trail is the Spring Creek Trail, which follows an old portion of the road through this area (see below at 12.3/5.3). Today it is a ski trail and is not maintained for summer use, but it is possible to walk it.

12.0 / 5.6 GPS: 44.43079, -110.75303
Spring Creek Picnic Area (N) 🚻 🚶 🚹

The **Spring Creek Picnic Area** has 10 tables, two grills, and a vault toilet that is handicap accessible.

The picnic area takes its name for the nearby Spring Creek, which runs roughly parallel to the existing roadway several hundred feet to the south. You can walk down to the creek from the picnic area and catch the Spring Creek Trail (see below).

Interestingly, the NPS had a bypass lane added to the road so westbound vehicles waiting to turn into the picnic area would not hold up traffic.

12.3 / 5.3 GPS: 44.43159, -110.76009
SPRING CREEK SKI TRAIL TRAILHEAD (S) 🚶 ⛷️

Though this trailhead is unmarked, if you park here and look into the woods to your south, you'll see a spur leading to the **Spring Creek Trail**. This trail largely follows what was the original road through this section of the park. In fact, you'll occasionally see areas of old asphalt and gravel, as well as bridge remnants from the old road as you make the trek.

The path follows Spring Creek westwardly through Spring Creek Canyon, and connects into the Lone Star Geyser Trail approximately ⅔ of a mile north of the geyser (two miles south of the trailhead at the road). Up until 1936 when the existing road alignment was established, visitors drove toward Lone Star Geyser, then connected to the road along Spring Creek to begin their travel to the West Thumb area. Today, this is primarily a ski trail and isn't maintained during the summer, but it is very passable.

Approximately a half mile into the trail from this point you'll come upon a rock formation that bears a strong resemblance to a snapping turtle with its head raised up. Not surprisingly, this was known as "Turtle Rock" during the days when the road passed through here. It was here that the third of the park's five stagecoach robberies occurred. On August 24, 1908, a robber managed to waylay 17 stagecoaches, relieving their occupants of about $2,000 worth of money and other material possessions. The bandit was never caught.

12.5 / 5.1 GPS: 44.43132, -110.76240
CONGRESS LAKE (S)

Congress Lake is a small, seasonal lake that was given its (colloquial) name because "it just sits there and does nothing," much like the U.S. Congress. This area was the site of an old NPS Road Camp in the 1920s. Don't confuse this lake with Congress Pool, which is a thermal pool located in the Norris Geyser Basin.

12.7 / 4.9 GPS: 44.42988, -110.76618
SCAUP LAKE (N)

Scaup Lake is named for the scaup, a type of duck that is occasionally found in the park. The lake itself is devoid of fish (but does support a healthy population of leeches - enjoy your swim!).

13.8 / 3.8 GPS: 44.43370, -110.78863
UNNAMED LAKE (S)

The small seasonal lake on the south side of the road here has no official name.

15.0 / 2.6 GPS: 44.44530, -110.80451
LONE STAR TRAILHEAD (S) 🚶 🚴 🚻

The **Lone Star Geyser Trail** is a 2.5-mile (4 km), mostly paved trail, though the road surface is in less than pristine condition in many places. At one time it was possible to drive an automobile back to the geyser, but the NPS closed the road to vehicular travel and now permits only hikers and bicyclists to use it. The trail itself continues south past Lone Star along the Shoshone Lake Trail, off of which splits the Bechler River Trail, which leads into the remote southwestern portions of the park.

At more than nine feet tall, Lone Star Geyser has one of the larger cones in the park. It erupts on average about every three hours or so to a height of 45-50 feet. Each eruption lasts about 45 minutes. The steam phase of its eruptions can be heard for quite some distance. If you happen to catch an eruption, be sure and record it in the logbook located on the post near the geyser.

Shortly after the trail leaves the trailhead, you'll notice a short spur leading to the Firehole River with some mechanical equipment at the river's edge. This is the small diversion dam that is used to funnel water to the Old Faithful Water Treatment Plant, and provides potable water for the Old Faithful area.

The original alignment of the road between Old Faithful and West Thumb brought traffic down to near Lone Star, and then took a turn to the east, traveling through Spring Creek Canyon. Today this is a ski trail that is largely unmaintained (see the entry above at 12.3/5.3). One early proposal for additional roads in the park had a road going from Lone Star to the Bechler area via the Three Rivers Junction area.

Until 1995, there was an four-table picnic area here. There was also a small, unofficial campground near the geyser at one point.

15.1 / 2.5 GPS: 44.44610, -110.80554
KEPLER CASCADES (S) 🛉

Kepler Cascades is a pair of cascades of 100 and 150 feet, and are formed by water washing over a rhyolite lava flow. They were named for the son of the Wyoming Territory governor John Hoyt (for whom Hoyt Peak along the park's east entrance road is named).

Just downstream from the cascade is a deep, narrow canyon known as "Devil's Gate" (visible looking to the west from the overlook platform). In 1976, a park concession employee fell to his death while climbing the walls of this canyon.[8]

15.7 / 1.8 GPS: 44.45334, -110.81332
OLD FAITHFUL WATER TREATMENT PLANT SERVICE ROAD (N)

An underground pipeline leads from the dam on the Firehole River, across the Grand Loop Road, and to a water treatment plant on the north side of the road here. The water is treated and pumped to an underground reservoir in the government area, and then gravity fed to places such as the restaurants, stores, lodging facilities, dorms, etc.

Just west of this (about ⅒ of a mile) is where the old original road through the Old Faithful Area left the Kepler Cascade area and traveled northwest through the woods toward the development (just as the existing road begins to curve southward. You can easily see this road on Google Earth). The old road is used as a ski trail during the winter.

16.1 / 1.5 GPS: 44.45391, -110.81965
FIREHOLE RIVER CROSSING (UPPER FIREHOLE BRIDGE)
BEAR'S PLAYGROUND (N)

Here the **Firehole River** crosses under you as it makes its way up to the Upper Geyser Basin. The bridge was built in 1970 as a part of the construction of the bypass around the Old Faithful area (prior to this, everyone drove right through the development, between the geyser and the Inn).

Just west of the bridge, on the north side of the road hidden somewhat in the woods, you'll see a small lake and meadow. Up until the mid-1930s the Old Faithful Bear Feeding Area was located at the southeast of what is today the eastern parking lot. Each evening the bears would come out to rummage through the garbage. Quite often, before the crews brought the refuse out, some of the bears would "play" in this little lake. So the lake is occasionally referred to as "**Bear's Playground**" by some who've been around the park for a while.

16.7 / 0.9 GPS: 44.45412, -110.82962
HOWARD EATON TRAILHEAD (W) 🚶 🎿
FERN CASCADE LOOP TRAILHEAD (W) 🚶
RESERVOIR HILL (S)
MYRIAD CREEK

This section of the **Howard Eaton Trail** takes you to Lone Star Geyser via a 3.1-mile (5 km) trail. The trail is not very scenic, however, and is really only of use if you want to hike to the geyser from the Old Faithful area without having to use a car. The 157-mile Howard Eaton Trail was developed in 1922 to parallel the park's road system for horses and hikers, and was named in honor of park guide Howard Eaton, who led many pack tours of the park. Today, only fragments of the trail remain viable, including this one.

The **Fern Cascade Loop Trail** also starts here. It is a 1.7-mile (2.7 km) loop that takes you near a small, three-tiered cascade on Iron Spring Creek (though you only have a clear view of the top two tiers of 10- and 20-feet. The bottom 70-foot tier is hard to get to).

The gated road that heads south takes you to the cell tower site up on **Reservoir Hill** behind the Old Faithful Government Area. The hill is colloquially named for the underground reservoir below the tower that provides water to the Old Faithful development.

Just to the east of the trailhead, **Myriad Creek** runs under the road. The creek has its origin southeast of Reservoir Hill, flows under the pavement here, across the entrance and exit roads for the Old Faithful Development, behind the ranger station, behind the Old Faithful Inn, and under the road to empty into the Firehole River just west of the oxbow bend. The collection of thermal features behind the Inn are known as the Myriad Group, and the creek is named for its proximity to this area. The stream is also known as Zipper Creek by locals due to its running past the old laundry building behind the Old Faithful Inn. In the early days of the park it was known as Crystal Creek (in fact, many early park lease agreements use Crystal Creek as a point of reference).[9]

16.9 / 0.7 GPS: 44.45537, -110.83425
PEDESTRIAN CROSSING TO GOVERNMENT AREA
OLD HAYNES PHOTO SHOP BUILDINGS (N)

The pedestrian crossing allows employees who live in the Government Area (see below) who're on foot or riding a bicycle to cross from the housing area to the commercial areas. The speed limit here is 25, and you're required to stop if the crosswalk is occupied. This is also used as an access road for fire trucks and other emergency vehicles, so keep a sharp eye out when you're passing through.

Immediately adjacent to the crosswalk, on the north side of the road, are a couple of old, abandoned buildings. The larger building was the **Haynes Studio**, the second such building to be completed at Old Faithful (1897). The other building is a storage building used by Haynes.

In the early days of the park, Haynes employed motorcycle riders to drive to the various photo shops he owned picking up customers' film. They would transport the film to this building (which at the time was located in the main commercial area), whereupon the film would be developed and photographs produced. The motorcyclists would then transport the photographs back to the shops in time for the customers to pick them up the next day. The building has been abandoned for several years now, having been relocated to this site from a spot in front of the Old Faithful Inn (across the existing road from the parking lot) in 1933 and not used since.

17.0 / 0.6 GPS: 44.45569, -110.83556
OLD FAITHFUL GOVERNMENT AREA ACCESS ROAD (S)

The **Old Faithful Government Area** was originally the site of the Civilian Conservation Corps work camp in the 1930s. It later became the bus and maintenance yard for the Yellowstone Park Company, and in the 1960s grew into its present use as a housing and maintenance area tucked away from the main commercial complex. The Emergency Services Building, Employee Pub, Generator Building/Substation, Transportation Barn, and several other maintenance facilities, as well as housing for NPS and concession employees and contractors is located in this complex.

17.6 / 0.0 GPS: 44.46118, -110.84492 ELEVATION: 7333 FEET
OLD FAITHFUL INTERCHANGE

The **Old Faithful Interchange** was completed and opened in 1972, along with the associated entry roads, in an effort to route through traffic away from the main geyser basin. Prior to this, you could actually drive your vehicle right alongside Old Faithful herself, between the geyser and the Old Faithful Inn. You can see remnants of that old road in the foot and bicycle path that takes you out to Morning Glory Pool from the area near the new Old Faithful Visitor Education Center.

The runoff field you pass on the north side of the road just before you enter the interchange apron is from the Three Sisters Group (a group of thermal features) on the road leading to the Lower General Store, Lower Service Station, and the front parking lot of the Old Faithful Inn.

From this point, you can travel 15.9 miles (25.6 km) north to Madison Junction, return 17.6 miles (28.3 km) south and east to West Thumb, or you can take the exit ramp into the Old Faithful Commercial Area. See the Old Faithful Development section for details about the history, buildings, features, and trails in this area.

Old Faithful Interchange
to
Madison Junction
————————————— ⊰o⟨⟩o⊱ —————————————

The road from the Old Faithful Interchange to Madison Junction is 15.9 miles (25.6 km) long, and affords access to most of the well-known thermal features in the park. This stretch of road is one of the busiest on the Grand Loop circuit, especially in the aftermath of an eruption of Old Faithful when many are leaving the area. And traffic can back up for miles if a herd of bison decide they wish to make use of the pavement during a mass exodus from the area.

Three of Yellowstone's major visitor-accessible thermal fields can be found along this road, and the Firehole River is known for some of the best fishing in the park. The Lower Geyser Basin is home to some 1,800 thermal features, 125 of which are named. These include those found at Fountain Paint Pots and a variety of features found along Firehole Lake Drive.

Midway Geyser Basin is home to about 170 features, only a dozen of which have official names. The Excelsior Geyser crater can be found here, as can the largest hot spring in the park (and third largest in the world), Grand Prismatic.

The Upper Geyser Basin encompasses roughly 800 known features, including more than half the geysers found in the park (and 30% of those in the world). Some of the most predictable, most popular and most photographed geysers can be found here, including Grand, Giantess, Beehive, Riverside, Castle, Grotto, and of course, the world's most famous geyser, Old Faithful. Black Sand Basin and Biscuit Basin are also located in the Upper Geyser Basin. The Upper Geyser Basin is one of the most intensely studied thermal areas on the planet, and approximately 200 of its features have official names.[1]

The road between Madison Junction and the Upper Geyser Basin has existed since the early 1880s, but today's alignment looks little like the original path built by Superintendent Philetus Norris. It has been realigned several times to move traffic away from the sensitive thermal features. For example, the main road formerly passed right through the middle of both Fountain Paint Pots and the Upper Geyser Basin. The paved footpath from Old Faithful to Morning Glory Pool is a remnant of that old road.

As you drive along this road, you're likely to see several small herds of bison, especially along Fountain Flats and in the area between Old Faithful and the Fairy Falls trailhead. It's not uncommon to see grizzly bears along the route as well. Elk are fairly rare in this area, as are most other large mammals, however.

There are several picnic areas along this route, each with its own vault toilet. Toilets can also be found at the Midway Geyser Basin and Fountain Paint Pots parking areas. The road itself is in excellent condition, having been completely rebuilt in the 1990s, and there are a significant number of pullouts located on both sides of the highway.

0.0 / 15.9 GPS: 44.46118, -110.84492 Elevation: 7333 Feet
Old Faithful Interchange
Interchange Spring (W)

The **Old Faithful Interchange** and the roads into/out of the Old Faithful complex were constructed in the 1969-1972 time frame, opening to the public on September 21, 1972. Prior to that, you could drive right in between the Old Faithful Geyser and the Old Faithful Inn, pass right alongside Morning Glory Pool, Riverside Geyser, and several other thermal features. Now, the interchange, which cost $1,555,281 to build in 1970, allows through traffic to completely bypass the complex. But while it allows for more efficient traffic flow, many believe the interstate-like cloverleaf design of the interchange doesn't belong in a national park.

From here, you can travel south 17.6 miles (28.3 km) to West Thumb and Grant Village, 15.9 miles (25.6 km) north to Madison Junction, or you can take the access road into the Old Faithful commercial area.

The large pool you see on the west side of the road between the southbound entrance ramp and the bridge is known colloquially as **Interchange Spring,** specifically because its location. Many assume it just developed at this location, but the spring was actually uncovered by work crews as they were preparing the area for the building of the interchange.

0.4 / 15.5 GPS: 44.46359, -110.85215
BLACK SAND BASIN (W) [𝅺]
BLACK SAND POOL TRAIL (E) [𝅺]

Black Sand Basin is a small thermal area of about 20 mostly named features on the west side of the road. These include Cliff Geyser, Emerald Pool, and the gorgeous Sunset Lake. It gets its name from the tiny black obsidian particles that cover the bottom of Black Sand Pool within the basin and, to a lesser extent, the entire area.

In the park's early days, this area was known as Sunlight Basin, and the original Black Sand Basin was at Black Sand Pool, which is accessible via the trail on the east side of the road. Black Sand Pool is responsible for large outwash you see on the northeast side of the road just a few hundred feet ahead, in fact.

Handkerchief Pool, one of the park's most famous features in its early days lies within this basin, but is now inaccessible because of the persistent threat of vandalism. In its heyday, tourists would drop their handkerchiefs into the pool and watch as they were sucked under only to emerge a few moments later nice and clean.

Over time, vandalism would take its toll, however. Rangers pulled an ungodly amount of debris out of its vent over time, including a large log. The pool eventually stopped functioning and was roped off, and at some point the walkway was removed. The pool was also known as the Devil's Laundry for a brief period of time.

0.6 / 15.3 GPS: 44.46556, -110.85398
SILENT DOG/BOBBY SOX FOREST (E)

These dead, silicified trees have been standing since before the park was discovered. They were killed by subterranean heat, and then acted like straws, drawing up siliceous water into their trunks by means of capillary action. When the water evaporated, the silica was left in the wood, leaving them partially petrified.

There are several of these "forests" around the thermal basins; they're often referred to as "Silent Dog Forests" because the trees have no bark. The outwash here comes primarily from Black Sand Pool which, in the park's early days was the extent of what was then called Black Sand Basin (see entry above). Some old-timers may also remember these forests being called "Flapper Forests" because of their "bare limbs."

1.7 / 14.2 GPS: 44.48066, -110.85392
DAISY TRAIL TRAILHEAD (E) 🚲 🚶
MYSTIC FALLS TRAIL TRAILHEAD (W) 🚶

The **Daisy Trailhead** is a short trail that takes you to the Daisy Geyser via an old road (part of the original road system in the Upper Geyser Basin). Bicycles are permitted along this trail.

Across the highway is a short dirt path that leads to the **Mystic Falls Trail** west of Biscuit Basin. It is primarily intended for those who wish to use the trails with stock so they don't have to worry about negotiating around the Biscuit Basin parking lot with horse trailers or having to walk the animals through the geyser basin.

1.9 / 14.0 GPS: 44.48297, -110.85241
FIREHOLE RIVER (LOWER CROSSING)
SEISMIC GEYSER (SE)
ISLAND GEYSER (W)

The **Firehole River** crosses from the east side of the highway to the west side here. The bridge was built in 1967 as a part of the reconfiguration of the road system in the area and the construction of the Old Faithful Interchange. The confluence of the Little Firehole River and the Firehole River are off to your west.

Seismic Geyser is to the southeast, so named because it formed during the Hebgen Lake Earthquake in 1959. As of this writing, Seismic erupts for 4 to 8 minutes every 20-40 minutes, to heights measuring a few feet.[2]

Island Geyser can be seen erupting in the small island to the west. It, too, was formed during the 1959 earthquake, along with several others on the island. After the Borah Peak (ID) Earthquake in 1983, Island became the dominant geyser there. Currently, it remains in a near steady state of eruption, reaching about ten feet in height.[3]

2.0 / 13.9 GPS: 44.48421, -110.85139
ARTEMISIA TRAILHEAD (E) 🚶
BISCUIT BASIN/UNFAITHFUL FALLS (W)
MYSTIC FALLS/UPPER BASIN OVERLOOK TRAILHEAD (W) 🚶

The **Artemisia Trail** takes you to the Artemisia Geyser (located at 44.47832, -110.84855), which erupts to a height of about 30 feet for 15 to 30 minutes at a time. Its interval is rather unpredictable, however, ranging from nine hours to more than thirty hours. Note that this trail is closed from the park's spring opening until Memorial Day weekend for bear management purposes. The outwash you see alongside the road here comes largely from Cauliflower Geyser (erupts every 20-40 minutes to heights of 4 to 60 feet, located at 44.483483, -110.850434), Mirror Pool (44.483148, -110.850335), and several smaller (mostly unnamed) geysers located a short distance up the trail. The trail to Artemisia follows the old road that was used until 1972, when the current interchange opened.

Artemisia was named for the sagebrush-colored deposits around its cone, the word being Latin for a type of sagebrush. If you continue to follow the trail on past Artemisia, you'll make your way to the west end of the Upper Geyser Basin Trail at Morning Glory Pool.

Biscuit Basin is another small thermal area with several interesting features. The basin gets its name from biscuit-like knobs once found around Sapphire Pool and some of the other hot springs in this area. A large, explosive eruption of Sapphire in 1959 (after the earthquake) washed away many of these formations, but the area retains its name. Approximately 30 identified features are present in this area. These include Sapphire Pool, Black Opal Pool, and the quite active Jewel Geyser, which is known for its explosive thermal eruptions.

At the rear of the basin is the trailhead for the **Mystic Falls Trail** and the trail that takes you up onto the **Upper Geyser Basin Overlook**. Mystic Falls is a 70-foot tiered waterfall on the Little Firehole River. The trail to Mystic Falls is 1.1 miles (1.8 km) from the trailhead. If you choose to go further up to the Upper Geyser Basin Overlook, it's an additional 1.2 miles (1.9 km). If you make the full loop, it'll be 3.0 miles (4.8 km). You can also take the Summit Lake Trail, which is a 7.5-mile (12 km) trail that takes you to a small lake, and if you continue past the lake another half mile or so, you'll come across Smokejumper Hot Springs, a small thermal area of about 100 unnamed hot springs and pools.

If you pull into the Biscuit Basin parking lot, or if you're traveling southbound as you approach this area, in late June you'll often see a waterfall falling off the Madison Plateau to the south. It is called "**Unfaithful Falls**" because of its itinerant nature. The falls is also known as Phantom Falls by many of the long time residents of the area because of its tendency to appear and then disappear.

In their book, *The Guide to Waterfalls of Yellowstone and Their Discovery*, park historian Lee Whittlesey and his two co-writers state that this waterfall is on a seasonal, unnamed tributary of the Little Firehole River. They believe the creek is restricted by a temporary snow dam in the early part of the runoff season, and once that snow melts, the waterfall drains water from the creek until the water level goes down. Thus, its itinerant nature.[4]

The small red-stained thermal area you see on the hill below Unfaithful Falls is known as Hillside Springs. It is a collection of two dozen features, all of which are unnamed except for Asta Spring. The name is a shortened form of *astacin*, a red pigment found in many crustaceans (e.g., lobsters).[5]

2.1 / 13.8 GPS: 44.48629, -110.84993
Old Roadbed (E) [Southbound Only]

If you're headed southbound, you'll notice a path headed through the woods on the east side of the road – a path where the trees are smaller than those surrounding them. This is the north end of the old road bed that went through the geyser basin. The road connected to the paved walkway you see terminating at Morning Glory Pool today.

Prior to the opening of the Old Faithful Interchange in 1972, you could drive right between the Old Faithful Visitor Center and Old Faithful herself, parking in front of it to watch her eruptions. If you've visited Yellowstone during the height of the summer season, you can probably imagine what kind of traffic problem would exist in the area today if that were still allowed.

3.8 / 12.1 GPS: 44.50697, -110.83346
Mallard Creek Trailhead (E) 🚶

The **Mallard Creek Trail** is a four-mile (6.4 km) trail that terminates at Mallard Lake. From there, you can take the Mallard Lake Trail and follow it back to the employee cabin area near the Old Faithful Lodge.

This trail is closed from the park's spring opening until Memorial Day weekend for bear management. The trail generally follows Mallard Creek, a seasonal creek that has its headwater at the lake and drains into the Firehole River. Mallard Lake is the site of three backcountry campsites.

4.2 / 11.7 GPS: 44.51236, -110.83339
Fairy Falls RV Pullout (W)

This pullout is overflow parking and parking for RVs for the Fairy Falls Trailhead (see entry below).

4.4 / 11.5 GPS: 44.51420, -110.83174
Fairy Falls Trailhead (W) 🧍
Rabbit (Till) Geyser / Three Vent Spring (E)

The parking lot is the trailhead for the 1.6-mile (2.6 km) **Fairy Falls Trail**. The waterfall is a 197-foot plunge type waterfall located on Fairy Creek, and is one of the tallest waterfalls in the park. This trail, too, is closed until Memorial Day weekend for bear management, and when open is one of the busiest in the park. It is not uncommon to see traffic parked along the roadway outside the entrance to the parking lot at the height of the day. This waterfall is best seen in the early spring when the snow runoff is at its peak. Approximately ¾ mile into this hike is a small, unnamed hill that many people use as a vantage point for photographing Grand Prismatic.

A little further down the trail (an additional 9⁄10 mile) can be found Imperial Geyser and Spray Geyser. Superintendent Horace Albright allowed a pool of journalists in the park at the time to name Imperial in 1927.

An interesting feature at the trailhead is the iron bridge that facilitates crossing the Firehole River. This is one of only two remaining bridges in the park from the U.S. Army era. The bridge was constructed in 1911 and originally used to transport traffic over the Gibbon River further north; it was relocated to this site in 1925. The other surviving bridge is at the entrance to the Indian Creek Campground. It was built at the same time, but was rehabilitated in late 2012.

The large white field you see on the east side of the main road is the runoff field from what is today often referred to as **Till Geyser** (major eruptions every 5.5 to 11 hours to heights of 20 ft). According to both park historian Lee Whittlesey and Yellowstone geyser expert Scott Bryan, this geyser's legitimate name is Rabbit Geyser. However, Whittlesey states that a park geologist gave the geyser its newer name (Till) in 1971 being unaware of the history and original name.[6] This is a double vented geyser which is located just a few hundred feet off the road. If you hike back to it, watch your footing and take a wide path around it.

The small pool just off the east side of the road north of Till's runoff field is **Three Vent Spring**. The pool gets its name from the fact that there are three vents under the water, vents which are easily seen in the late part of the summer when the water levels decrease substantially. Behind (north of) Three Vent is an unnamed, tomato-soup looking pool (this is not the spring officially given the name Tomato Soup Spring/Pool, however). The reddish tint comes from iron oxides in the water.

Just to the south of Three Vent Spring is the vestigial remains of the old road that took trucks back to the old Rabbit Creek Landfill. This landfill was one of a small handful the park used to dispose of its garbage up until the early 1970s, when they were all closed as both a bear management tool and to prevent environmental degradation (this one was closed in 1969). This particular landfill was put into service when the garbage dump at the Old Faithful Auto Camp Bear Feeding Area was closed in the early 1930s. Grizzly Pool and the old Y-5 drill hole are also located back along this area as well.[7]

4.5 / 11.4 GPS: 44.51547, -110.82979
RABBIT CREEK

The multi-pronged creek you see flowing under the road at this point is **Rabbit Creek**, which drains an area to the east and is fed by several thermal springs in a grouping known as the Rabbit Creek Thermal Area. The stream was given its name in accordance with naming park features for the wildlife and flora of the area.

4.8 / 11.1 GPS: 44.51809, -110.82541
CATFISH GEYSER TURNOUT (W) 🏃

The large pool south of the river at its bend is **Catfish Geyser**. Catfish erupts to a height of just a couple of feet for about five minutes every fifteen minutes or so. A park visitor was badly burned here in 1978. If you want to walk out and get a better look, follow the little trail off to the south of the parking area. DO NOT walk straight out into the thermal area – you'll notice a sign on the ground indicating this area is dangerous and therefore closed to foot travel. According to park historian Lee Whittlesey, the specific reason Catfish was given its name is unknown, though he suspects a park naturalist may have named it because it is shaped like a catfish's mouth. There are several other thermal pools named for the catfish throughout the park as well.[8]

The thermal field you see off in the distance to the northwest is Midway Geyser Basin, which, if you continue traveling northward, you'll pass shortly.

5.1 / 10.8 GPS: 44.52199, -110.82782
FLOOD GEYSER/CIRCLE POOL TURNOUT (W) 🏃

The large, colorful pool just below the turnout is known as **Circle Pool**, the third largest hot spring in the park (8820 sq ft). Just south of that, on the Firehole River's eastern bank, is Flood Geyser which can often be seen erupting as high as 25 feet every one to 45 minutes. It is the largest active geyser in the Midway Geyser Basin. The open crater on the opposite bank is West Flood Geyser which can erupt as high as 12 feet, though eruptions are rare. The little geyser right next to Circle Pool is Tangent Geyser, which has infrequent, small eruptions.

The turnout is well designed, but there are no signs or interpretive displays to indicate what features are present. It is officially known as the Flood Geyser Turnout, though some sources list it as the Circle Pool Turnout.

5.5 / 10.4 GPS: 44.52598, -110.83392
MIDWAY BLUFF PULLOUT (E)

Midway Bluff is the large rock outcropping on the hill above you at this pullout. You can climb the steep trail to this area to get an excellent aerial view of Midway Geyser Basin, to include Grand Prismatic Spring, the largest hot spring in the park. Be very careful climbing and descending this trail.

In the 1910s-1920s, there was an NPS Road Camp on the east side of the existing road just south of the bluff. By 1930, however, it had been removed.

5.8 / 10.1 GPS: 44.53018, -110.83459
MIDWAY GEYSER BASIN (W) 🚹 🚻

Technically, **Midway Geyser Basin** is a part of the Lower Geyser Basin, but is given its own name since it is seen and managed as a separate set of features. And though there is a rather large parking lot here, during the busy part of the summer, vehicles will be parked out onto the main road and the area will be quite congested. Unfortunately, if you get here too early in the morning, the cold air will cause huge quantities of steam to emanate from all of the features, obscuring much of their beauty.

There are two major thermal features at this point of Midway Geyser Basin. The first is Excelsior Geyser. Today, with a width of 276 by 328 feet, it is little more than a large, gurgling pool of very hot water. Prior to 1890, however, it was one of the largest geysers in the park, erupting as high as 300 feet in incredibly explosive eruptions. Over time, the explosive eruptions blasted out its crater, which is now much wider than it was in the late 19th century.

It currently discharges some 4000+ gallons of hot water per minute into the Firehole River (that's over 2 billion gallons of water annually). The water discharge from Excelsior and Grand Prismatic (see below) raise the temperature of the Firehole River by 40°F, to approximately 110°F (43.3°C) shortly downstream.

The second feature is the world-renowned Grand Prismatic Spring, generating some six million gallons of water per day. At 370 feet (113 m) in diameter, it is the largest spring in the park and the third largest in the world (two in New Zealand are larger). The colorful rings around the pool are a variety of bacteria and algae that grow in the different temperature gradients, from hotter to cooler as one moves out from the center of the pool.

To get the best photos of Grand Prismatic, it is necessary to shoot it from an elevation, preferably when the sun is high in the sky. There are two good spots for this. One is Midway Bluff, just across the street and south of the parking lot (see above), and the other is a hill to the west of the basin along the Fairy Falls Trail (which is closed each spring until Memorial Day Weekend). The hill doesn't have an official name, but you'll see the foot trails leading up to its peak.

Turquoise Spring and Opal Pool are the only other thermal features of note here. The boardwalk is handicap-accessible, though the incline of the ramp might be a bit tough for someone without sufficient upper body strength (or a partner to push them).

6.2 / 9.7 GPS: 44.53289, -110.82750
Whiskey Flats Picnic Area (E) 🪧 🚻

The **Whiskey Flats Picnic Area** has 13 tables and a vault toilet. It is handicap accessible. This picnic area typically opens later each year than many others because maintenance crews have to go in and remove downed trees, branches, dirt, etc., and water pooled in the Whiskey Flats area often backs up into the picnic area, restricting access until early June. For the longest time, this picnic area had no signs because every time they posted one, someone stole it.

6.4 / 9.5 GPS: 44.53389, -110.82351
Whiskey Flats Overlook (E)

This pullout provides an overlook of **Whiskey Flats**, a marshy meadow sometimes referred to as Whiskey Lake during the early part of spring, as the flat meadow is entirely under water. Again, there are usually no signs for this area because people often steal them.

While no one knows for sure why this name was given to the area, the park's historian, Lee Whittlesey, speculates that the early stage coach drivers and perhaps Army personnel disposed of their whiskey bottles by tossing them out into the field as they passed through this area.[9]

6.8 / 9.1 GPS: 44.53536, -110.81770
FIREHOLE LAKE DRIVE ENTRANCE (E) 🚗
WHITE CREEK CROSSING

Firehole Lake Drive is a short scenic drive that takes you by a variety of interesting thermal features, including Great Fountain Geyser, whose eruptions can reach 250 feet. It is the largest predictable geyser in the Lower Geyser Basin.

White Dome can also be found along this road. This centuries-old geyser cone was once the symbol of the Yellowstone Association. This drive is closed for bear management until Memorial Day weekend. You can find a map and detailed descriptions of the Drive's thermal features in the Miscellaneous Roads section.

Because of weight restrictions on a couple of the small wooden bridges on this road, and some tight turn radii, larger vehicles such as RVs, buses, and vehicles pulling trailers are not permitted on this road.

Just north of the entrance road is **White Creek**, named for the white deposits found along its edges.

7.5 / 8.4 GPS: 44.54488, -110.80968
TANGLED CREEK CROSSING

Tangled Creek emanates from Hot Lake on the Firehole Lake Drive. This is the main artery of the creek, and the small creek just to the south of this one is a secondary artery. It gets its name from the interlaced channels of its path.

7.7 / 8.2 GPS: 44.54663, -110.80826
FOUNTAIN PAINT POTS SOUTH ENTRANCE (W) 🚹 🚻

The **Fountain Paint Pots** area contains examples of all four types of thermal features found in the park: geysers, hot springs, fumaroles, and mud pots. There are about 30 named and unnamed features here, including the larger namesake mud pot, Fountain Paint Pot, the largest mud pot in the park. During the early spring, this mud pot is rather soupy, but as the season progresses, and the water begins to dry up, it gets more and more muddy until, by the end of the season, it is largely a dry clay pit with gas vents. Fountain Paint Pots has had several names over the years, including Mud Puff, Chalk Vat, Devil's Paintbox, and Mammoth Paint Pot (for its size). Its current name was settled by a park naming committee in 1927.[10]

Fountain Geyser can also be found here. Fountain erupts every 3.5 to 11 hours with blasts that reach up to 100 feet.[11] This is one of the major geysers in the Lower Geyser Basin, and was considered attractive enough to have a hotel constructed nearby situated such that visitors could sit on its front porch and watch the geyser. See the entry for the site of the old Fountain Hotel below.

Another interesting feature is Clepsydra Geyser, named after a water clock of Ancient Greece. It was given its name because of the almost clock-like eruption pattern it exhibited when first surveyed in the early days of the park. Ever since the 1959 Hebgen Lake Earthquake, however, the geyser has been in what's referred to as a "wild phase," or a nearly constant state of eruption. It is one of the prettiest and most-often photographed features in the park. Pick up a trail leaflet for details on this and other features here.

One other thermal feature of note can be found here, Celestine Pool. With a temperature of around 200°F (93°C), it is quite hot. Park historian Lee Whittlesey, in his compelling book, *Death in Yellowstone*, opens Chapter One up with the heartbreaking story of a man who attempted to rescue a friend's dog that had jumped into the pool on July 20, 1981. The dog began yelping from the burns, and the man ran to the edge of the spring and began stripping.

Despite impassioned pleas from onlookers not to jump into the water, the man dove in an attempt to save his friend's pet. After a few seconds in the pool the man climbed out and made the comment, "That was a stupid thing I did." Suffering third degree burns over 100% of his body, he was taken to the clinic at Old Faithful and then flown to a burn center in Salt Lake City, where he died the next day. The dog died in the pool.[12]

7.8 / 8.1 GPS: 44.54842, -110.80675
FOUNTAIN PAINT POTS NORTH ENTRANCE (W) [图] [图]
EXIT FROM FIREHOLE LAKE DRIVE (E)
LEATHER POOL (W)

See notes above regarding Fountain Paint Pots. The exit for Firehole Lake Drive is on the east side of the road.

As you continue driving north and come around the bend, you'll notice **Leather Pool** on the west side of the road. If you're traveling northbound, you may also notice what appears to be a straight line going across the field in a northerly direction on the east side of the road. This hot pool was once used to supply hot water to the old Fountain Hotel, located on the hill off to the north (see below). The line (which is much easier to see in the spring) is the old pipeline used to transport that water to the hotel. It was wrapped in leather and the chemical disparity between the leather and the dirt cause a unique growth of grass along the old pipeline's length, making it somewhat easier to spot.

Leather Pool was once bright blue and had a brown algae lining, thus its name. It was known as White Sulphur Springs in the days of the Fountain Hotel. The Hebgen Lake Earthquake caused a change in the pool's temperature, however, causing its temperature to rise, thereby killing the algae.

8.4 / 7.5 GPS: 44.55613, -110.80774
SITE OF THE OLD FOUNTAIN HOTEL (E)

Behind the little grove of trees on the hill on the east side of the road is the site of the old **Fountain Hotel**. Fountain was one of the great hotels of the park's early days, built and operated by the Yellowstone Park Association (the forerunner of the Yellowstone Park Company, who's operation was inherited by Xanterra Parks and Resorts, the park's primary concessioner today). Construction began on the hotel in 1890, roughly around the same time as the Lake Hotel. The buildings looked very similar to one another because they used the same set of plans. The Lake Hotel, of course, would go on to be modified several times by architect Robert Reamer, and therefore looks much different than what the Fountain Hotel did in its day. The original cost of the hotel was $100,000 (1890$).

The hotel had 133 rooms capable of housing up to 250 guests, and was equipped with the latest amenities, including hot and cold running water, electricity (added in 1901), and a guest laundry. The rooms were painted in different colors using paint made from clays taken from the Mammoth Mud Pots (now the Fountain Paint Pots – see above). Cattle were raised on site to provide dairy products and fresh beef to guests, and there was a corral from which tourists could rent horses.

The hotel was originally designed as a stopover for tourists who were visiting the Upper Geyser Basin. They'd stop here after a day in the Norris and Lower Geyser Basins, get up the next morning to go see the wonders

Fountain Hotel, ca. 1917. Though long gone, parts of this old hotel live on in the Laurel Dorm at Old Faithful.

in the Old Faithful Area, and then return here for a good night's sleep before taking off early the next morning for the Canyon and Lake areas.

The construction of the Old Faithful Inn in 1904 dealt the first blow to the hotel's popularity. Guests preferred to stay at the Inn near the geyser basin to reduce the amount of time they spent on the road (and the Inn was considered more elegant). The advent of allowing automobiles into the park in 1916 sealed the grand lady's fate, however. Now that vehicles could transport people much further distances between the various points of interest, there was no longer a need for the layover in the Fountain area. So, in 1917, the hotel was abandoned. It sat unused until 1927, when it was torn down. Many of its parts were used to expand the women's dorm (now the Laurel Dorm) behind the Old Faithful Inn, and the remainder was burned.

Today, you can still see the foundation of the F-shaped structure in the trees on this hill, as well as the foundation for the building's laundry and a variety of other occupational debris lying around. If you walk to the northeast of the foundation, you'll find the old garbage dump for the hotel. Guests would assemble each evening to watch the big bruins feed on the food scraps left over from the evening's dinner. A chance photograph of a bear feeding on the refuse here was used to create the logo for the Yellowstone Park Company, a logo that is still in use today.

In his book, *Death in Yellowstone*, park historian Lee Whittlesey recounts the story of a gentleman named Leroy Piper, who on July 30, 1900, after purchasing a cigar at the hotel's gift shop, stepped out onto the front porch and was never seen again. Despite a massive search, no sign of the man was ever located. Whittlesey postulates that the man may have gone off walking and fallen into one of the many hot pools around the area. To this day, no one know for sure what happened to him, however.[13]

Keep in mind as you walk around the site that even the old fragments of glass and broken china are park artifacts and removing them is against the law. Help preserve the integrity of this site for future visitors to enjoy.

8.5 / 7.4 GPS: 44.55819, -110.80871
THUD GROUP (E)
PORCUPINE HILLS /ROCK POINT/QUAGMIRE GROUP (NE)
KALEIDOSCOPE GROUP/TWIN BUTTES (W)

On the east side of the road is a small group of about 18 mostly unnamed thermal features. The group is collectively known as the **Thud Group** because of the distinctive noises many used to make when the area was more active. During the time the Fountain Hotel was in use the group was known as the Hotel Group.

Many of these features were damaged during the time the hotel was in operation. People would throw trash and debris in them, do laundry in them, and bathe in those with lower temperatures. Kidney Spring is a small geyser in the Thud Group (directly east of the pullout) that demonstrates the extent of that damage. In the park's early days it had been documented as erupting to heights of 10 feet, but its eruptions now reach a meager four feet in height.[14]

Keep in mind you can only watch these from the pullout; the area is closed to hiking because the ground is unstable. Walking out into this area could result in serious burns.

The little pocket of land north of the Thud Group is where the two different parties of the Hayden Survey and other expedition teams would come together during their exploration of this area of the park. It was referred to during that time period as Camp Reunion.

If you look to the north and northeast from the Thud Group turnout, you'll notice a series of hills, one large one on the west, separated from another three hills to the east. These are the **Porcupine Hills**, a series of thermally-cemented moraines (gently rolling hills of glacial sediment deposits). The hills were named after another indigenous animal of the Yellowstone area.

You may notice a rock outcropping on the third hill from the west. This is known officially as **Rock Point**, but many locals refer to it as Lover's Leap, as it was a popular site for the Fountain Hotel savages to congregate for romantic purposes (known in the day as *rottenlogging* - wooing, courting, etc.) in their off hours. Another, although lesser used name for it was Suicide Point, though no known suicides have occurred there.[15]

On cold mornings you can often see steam rising from the base of the Porcupine Hills. This is from the **Quagmire Group**, an area of about 100 mostly unnamed thermal features. One of the more well-known features is Snort Geyser, which sits just below Lover's Leap. The group was originally known as the "Camp Group" because various Hayden/Peale Expeditions camped in the meadows between the turnout and the hills. The name was changed to Quagmire because of the murky nature of most of the springs.

In the distance to the west lie **Twin Buttes**, two moraines of roughly equal height. These twin hills are known by a variety of monikers (including the "Mae West Mountains"), mostly reflecting the female chest in some way. The legitimate names for the two hills are North Twin Butte (7875 ft/2400 m elevation) and South Twin Butte (7923 ft/2414 m).

The thermal field between the roadway and the twin buttes off in the distance is a small collection of thermal features known as the **Kaleidoscope Group**. Consisting of about two dozen identified features, most of these have names. Kaleidoscope Geyser is the largest geyser in this group, though it is tough to see except for its initial eruption, which has been known to reach heights of 120 feet. The area and its namesake feature were named for the colorful elemental deposits and algal growth around the edges of the pools. Several roads criss-crossed this area in the early 1900s but have since been removed and the area rehabilitated.

9.4 / 6.5 GPS: 44.56985, -110.81641
MARY MOUNTAIN WEST TRAILHEAD (E) 🚶

Sometimes referred to as the "Nez Perce Creek Trail," the **Mary Mountain Trail** leads through Nez Perce Valley to Mary Lake, and from there on to Hayden Valley, a total distance of some 20 miles (32.2 km). This used to be an old stagecoach route to the Canyon area for visitors who'd stayed in the Old Faithful or Fountain areas the night before, and indeed was the only route between west and east sides of the park until 1892.

The road was generally benign except for a steep section on the approach to Mary Lake that was difficult for loaded stagecoaches to climb. It came to be known as the Devil's Stairway. Passengers were often asked to get out of the coaches and help push it up this hill, and at least one person, a U.S. Congressman, died from a heart attack while doing so in 1890. The middle and eastern sections of the trail are rife with grizzly bears, and the trail is often closed during the late summer for public safety reasons.

The road was largely abandoned for visitor use in 1892 after the road between Old Faithful and West Thumb was completed, but was used for administrative purposes until World War II. Today, no vehicular traffic is permitted, generally speaking.

During the early days of the park prior to the road being closed, the road intersection that existed here was known as Prospect Point (and appears on maps of the day that way), because travelers from Mammoth would always wonder what "prospects" awaited them down the road in either direction.

It was in this valley in 1877 that Chief Joseph and the Nez Perce (pronounced *nez PURS*) captured and subsequently released a party of park visitors during their historic flight from General O.O. Howard's troops. The trail's east trailhead is ¼ mile north of Alum Creek in Hayden Valley. The west trailhead here lies nestled between two of the four Porcupine Hills.

This trail is closed from the park's spring opening until June 15 each year for bear management purposes. And, given the prevalence of the bears in this area, overnight travel/camping is prohibited. A hiker was killed by a grizzly bear on the Canyon side of Mary Mountain in 2011. If you hike the trail at any time of the year, be sure to follow all the rules regarding hiking in bear country, including carrying bear spray with you.

If you hike to the east, past Porcupine Hills, you'll pass through a couple of small thermal areas known as Morning Mist Springs (named by Hague for the appearance of steam rising from the woods in the early morning) and Culex Basin (also named by Hauge, after the genus of mosquitoes, perhaps for their prevalence in the area).[16]

9.7 / 6.2 GPS: 44.57294, -110.82067
Nez Perce Creek Crossing

The **Nez Perce Creek** is named after the Nez Perce Indian Tribe, not surprisingly. The bridge here was built in 1935, and rebuilt in 1997 as a part of the reconstruction of the road between Old Faithful and Madison Junction. The creek has its headwater at Mary Lake, some 10 miles to the east, and empties into the Firehole River just north of Fountain Flats Drive.

9.9 / 6.0 GPS: 44.57418, -110.82272
Chief Joseph Story Turnout (W) 🔭

This turnout has a storyboard that details the story of the Nez Perce War and the pursuit of the Nez Perce through the park in 1877 by the U.S. Army.

9.9 / 6.0 GPS: 44.57471, -110.82369
Nez Perce Patrol Cabin Access Service Road (E)

This ⁹⁄₁₀ of a mile long gravel road leads to the **Nez Perce Patrol Cabin**. The cabin is one of about three dozen such structures NPS rangers use to patrol the park's backcountry and to conduct research. The cabin sits on the site of one of the park's Civilian Conservation Corps camps in the 1930s. There is a new vault toilet next to the cabin as well as two old wooden outhouses (used before the new toilet was erected). The cabin has also been known as the Fountain Patrol Cabin (not to be confused with the old Fountain Solider Station which was located to the north of here near Fountain Flats).

10.3 / 5.6 GPS: 44.57806, -110.82906
Fountain Flats Drive (W) 🚶
Nez Perce Picnic Area (W) 🌲 🚻
Mattie Culver Gravesite (W) 🔭
Site of the Old Marshall & Firehole Hotels (W)
Site of the Old Fountain Soldier Station (E)

Fountain Flats Drive is part of an old service road between here and the Old Faithful area. Its original south terminus was located at what is now the RV and overflow parking pullout just south of the Fairy Falls trailhead. The old service road was known as the Fountain Freight Road, having gotten that name from the fact vehicles making deliveries to the Old Faithful area were required to use this bypass so as not to interfere with traffic on the main road. Constructed in 1884, it was originally known as the National Park Road, and later, during the years following the creation of the NPS, the Firehole Cutoff Road.

The name "Fountain Flats" itself refers to the large meadow that stretches from here south to the Fountain Paint Pots area. During summers in the late 1880s and early 1890s, there was a rather large Army encampment along the flat area just south of the road, to include even a shooting range. In his seminal manuscript on the place names of Yellowstone, park historian Lee Whittlesey states that there was a building that served as a park jail on the north end of the flats, circa 1885.[17]

Today, vehicles can only drive along the first mile or so of the road to the Ojo Caliente parking area. Until 1997, however, it was possible to drive an additional mile and a half or so further south to Goose and Feather Lakes. At the time there were six-table picnic areas at both sites, as well as a vault toilet at Goose Lake. All of that has since been removed and the area rehabilitated. Also, as an interesting point of trivia, the 1962 Disney movie *Yellowstone Cubs* was filmed in the area around Goose Lake.

You can still hike and ride bicycles along the old road. See the Miscellaneous Roads section for a road log of Fountain Flats Drive, including information about the Ojo Caliente Spring, Queen's Laundry, the Sentinel Meadows Trail, and other features associated with this area.

The **Nez Perce Picnic Area** has 12 tables, 3 grills, and a handicap-accessible vault toilet. The picnic area was the site of an old Shaw and Powell tent camp from 1913-1916. The creek itself is quite busy during the summer with visitors seeking a quick place to cool off and enjoy the water.

Behind the vault toilet at the picnic area is the grave of **Mattie Culver**. She was the wife of the caretaker of the Marshall Hotel, a Mr. E. C. Culver. She died in the early spring of 1889 of what was probably tuberculosis, but couldn't be buried until the spring thaw allowed for the digging of a grave.[18]

On the plot of land behind where the grave is located is the site of the old **Marshall and Firehole Hotels**, built in the 1880s. The Miscellaneous Roads section has further details about these two structures as well.

The **Fountain Soldier Station** was located just off the road to the east of the intersection here. The clearing in the woods to the east was the site of the station's barn and several smaller support buildings. The rocks in the woods behind the site were removed from the area by road crews clearing the space for the buildings.

11.4 / 4.5   GPS: 44.59336, -110.83056
FIREHOLE RIVER PICNIC AREA (W) 🪑 🚻

The **Firehole River Picnic Area** has 12 tables and a vault toilet, and is an excellent location on the river to enjoy an afternoon picnic. The picnic area is also a great place from which to fish.

This stretch of the Firehole (and the picnic area) is very popular with those who enjoy fishing along the river.

11.7 / 4.2 GPS: 44.59821, -110.83141
Firehole Gravel Pit Service Road (E)

The **Firehole Gravel Pit Service Road** leads to a gravel pit that is used to stage gravel and aggregate material for many of the roads built within the park. This area is also used as a construction material dumping area.

12.7 / 3.2 GPS: 44.60751, -110.84600
Christmas Tree Rock (W)

Here just south of the bend in the Firehole River you'll see three rocks in the middle of the river. **Christmas Tree Rock** is the center of these three – the one with the tree growing out of it.

The rock was given its name by concession employees in the 1960s, and is based around the annual celebration of "Christmas in Yellowstone," celebrated each August 25th in the park. This celebration itself revolves around a long-told mythological story of a supposed freak snowstorm in the park stranding tourists at some point in the past. They and the employees, having nothing better to do, decided to celebrate the Christmas-like atmosphere in the park. This included crossing into the river climbing up onto this rock, and decorating its tree as a Christmas Tree. Decorating the tree is not done so much these days, as the rangers tend to frown upon such activity.

Despite the continual recounting of the story, there is no evidence that such a snowstorm ever happened, however. Regardless, every August 25th, park employees decorate their dorms, stores, and the lodges for Christmas, hold parties, and some even exchange gifts.

This area up to Elk Island (see below) is a rather popular, if unsanctioned swimming area during the busy part of the summer season (especially if the Firehole Swimming Area on the Firehole Canyon Road is still closed).

13.4 / 2.5 GPS: 44.61486, -110.85431
Fly Fishing Turnout (W) 🎣 🏊
Elk Island (W)

This is another popular area from which fishermen access the Firehole River. The little island in the middle of the river is known by several different (colloquial) names, the most common of which is **Elk Island**. And indeed, elk can occasionally be seen foraging on the island. The island was used by expedition parties as a campsite in the early days of the park's history.

13.6 / 2.3 GPS: 44.61725, -110.85496
EXIT FROM FIREHOLE CANYON DRIVE (W)
UPPER FIREHOLE CASCADES (W)

This is the exit from **Firehole Canyon Drive**. Do not enter here. See the description below at 15.3/0.6 for more details about this road.

The 20-foot, tiered cascade you see just south of the intersection is the **Upper Firehole Cascade**. Once you drive to the end of the Firehole Canyon Drive, you can park and walk down the old abandoned roadbed to get good photos of the rushing water here.

13.7 / 2.2 GPS: 44.61831, -110.85560
MESA SERVICE ROAD (E)

The **Mesa Service Road** leads to a maintenance equipment and supplies staging area, a small NPS maintenance yard, the Madison Electrical Substation, and a carcass disposal area used by the NPS to dispose of carcasses from animals being hit by cars or dying too close to the roadway. You can hike back along this road, but cannot enter the disposal area for safety reasons. This is the south end of an old road segment that was once part of the original road that brought travelers here from the Gibbon Falls area.

14.1 / 1.8 GPS: 44.62405, -110.85932
MADISON HILL TURNOUT (W)

If you're going northbound here, you're starting to descend **Madison Hill,** which slowly lowers you from you present elevation of 7,092 feet down to that of the Madison River at 6,792 feet.

14.4 / 1.5 GPS: 44.62753, -110.85766
DIRT UTILITY SERVICE ROAD (E & W)

The dirt service roads you see to the east and west are roads used by Northwestern Energy utility crews to access the power lines.

14.5 / 1.4 GPS: 44.62946, -110.85607
NATURALLY RESEEDED AREA TURNOUT (W)

This is one of several examples around the park of an area damaged by the 1988 wildfires, and where subsequent natural "reseeding" of the area has taken place, resulting in new tree growth.

14.9 / 1.0 GPS: 44.63310, -110.85718
PURPLE MOUNTAIN OVERLOOK (W)

This turnout provides an excellent view of **Purple Mountain** to the north, the site of a former fire lookout for the park, and until 2011 the location of one of the park's radio repeaters. There's a trail that leads to the peak's summit; the trailhead is just north of Madison Junction.

This area was the site of the last of the park's five stagecoach robberies, and the last known stagecoach robbery in the United States. Approximately one mile south of Madison Junction, on July 9, 1915, five coaches were robbed, their passengers being relieved of around $200 worth of cash and material possessions. The U.S. Army made it to the scene before the bandit was able to waylay any more coaches, but he was never apprehended.

15.1 / 0.8 GPS: 44.63562, -110.85833
MADISON WATER TANK SERVICE ROAD (W)

This is a service road that leads to the top of the hill on the west side of the road. The water storage tank that serves the campground and the Madison Government Area is located near the summit.

15.3 / 0.6 GPS: 44.63888, -110.85860
FIREHOLE CANYON DRIVE ENTRANCE (ONE WAY) (W) 🏴

The **Firehole Canyon Drive** is a 2.2-mile scenic road that takes you through Firehole Canyon, alongside Firehole Falls, to the Firehole Swimming Area, and back out to the main road.

Prior to the Hebgen Lake Earthquake in 1959, Firehole Canyon Road was part of the main route from Madison to points south, having opened to traffic in 1928. The canyon sustained significant damage from the earthquake, however, and the traffic was rerouted around the canyon onto what is now the main road through this area.

Prior to the earthquake, plans had already been in the works to reroute traffic around the canyon anyway, however. The road was so narrow that only one vehicle could pass at a time in some places, and falling rocks and debris presented constant maintenance headaches for the NPS road crews.

The U.S. Army Corps of Engineers had originally begun building the road through the canyon in 1909, but abandoned it a year later due to difficulties with its construction (largely due to the instability of the walls). In 1925, the NPS decided to give it another shot, and spent three years finishing the road, opening it up to traffic in 1928. They considered it much more scenic than the old (which is now the existing) road. Even today it is often closed due to rock slides and trees sliding down onto the road surface.

Firehole Canyon was formed as the result of erosion by a stream (in this case, the Firehole River) starting to flow at the junction where one layer of lava flowed over and into another.[19]

As you drive through the canyon, you'll pass Rhinoceros Rock, the Lower and Middle Firehole Cascades, Firehole Falls, and the Firehole Swimming Area before you reach the main road again. See the Miscellaneous Roads section for a road log and more details on all of these points of interest.

15.5 / 0.4 GPS: 44.64058, -110.86120
GIBBON RIVER CROSSING 🛶

The **Gibbon River** crosses under the road here just before it joins the Firehole River to form the Madison River. This is where the term "Madison Junction" originates, not from the road intersection. There are pullouts on the north side of the bridge, complete with benches, to allow visitors to watch the bison herd that tends to congregate here from time to time.

The bridge was built in 1960 when the new road through this area was constructed, and was rehabilitated in 1997 when the road between Old Faithful and Madison Junction was rebuilt. During the hot part of the summer, it is not uncommon to see sunbathers and waders along the eastern side of the bridge.

You may notice a small building in the trees next to the river just below the bridge on the west side of the road. This is one of the gauging stations in the park that the U.S. Geological Survey uses to measure stream flow.

As you leave this area heading south you begin climbing Madison Hill, and to the west you'll see National Park Mountain (see below).

15.7 / 0.2 GPS: 44.64332, -110.85920
MADISON SERVICE AREA (W) ⑦ 🛉 🚻 ⛽
MADISON INFORMATION STATION/AMPHITHEATER (W)
MADISON JUNCTION PICNIC AREA/COMFORT STATION (W)

The **Madison Service Area** is home to a museum/information station, bookstore, amphitheater, comfort station, and a picnic area. It sits at the junction of the Firehole and Gibbon Rivers, and overlooks National Park Mountain and National Park Meadow.

The **Madison Museum** is one of four such structures built in 1929-1930 using funds provided by the Laura Spelman Rockefeller Foundation (the others being the museums at Norris and Fishing Bridge, and the one at Old Faithful that was razed in 1970 to make room for the 1972 Visitor Center). Today, the museum houses the Yellowstone's Junior Ranger Program, as well as a small Yellowstone Association bookstore. The amphitheater was built in 1934 by the Civilian Conservation Corps.

The museum faces National Park Mountain, and overlooks National Park Meadow. The mountain gets its name, of course, from the original "creation myth" of the men of the Washburn-Langford-Doane Expedition (1870) sitting around the campfire discussing the setting aside of the Yellowstone area to become the first national park. Today, it is widely believed that such a discussion did not take place during this camp (or, at least, there's no documentation that it did).

The **Madison Junction Picnic Area** has 14 tables, and a nearby comfort station (built in 1997) with flush toilets and vending machines. While the rest room facilities are handicap accessible, the picnic area itself is not easily accessible to wheelchairs. During the winter, the Madison Warming Hut is located in front of the comfort station.

At the time it was built, the primary road through this area passed in front of the museum and crossed the Gibbon River 400 feet west of the present crossing (and thus why the museum faces the mountain). From the river, the road continued southwestward into the Firehole Canyon, which was the main road through this area at the time. The large meadow in front (west) of the museum is known as National Park Meadow, named because it sits at the foot of the mountain of the same name.

The area that is now the paved parking lot was the original auto campground at Madison and, in fact, today's amphitheater sits on what was the campground's sewage system. As a part of the Mission 66 Program, the new campground was constructed, and the junction reconfigured, moving the road north to its present alignment. The old road bed and facilities that existed prior to this were removed and the area rehabilitated.

As an interesting bit of trivia, in 1932, all of the national parks that existed at the time had plaques honoring former NPS Director Stephen T. Mather (d. 1930) erected within them. Mather had been the founding director of the park service, and this was a way of honoring the work he'd done to protect America's natural and historical places. In Yellowstone, that plaque sits embedded in a boulder in front of the Madison Museum.

The Madison area was the location of the park's semi-centennial celebration on July 14, 1922.

15.9 / 0.0 GPS: 44.64542, -110.85845 Elevation: **6845 Feet** Madison Junction

From this point, you can drive 13.3 miles (21.4 km) north to Norris Junction and the Norris Geyser Basin, 13.9 miles (22.4 km) west to the West Entrance and the Town of West Yellowstone, or 15.9 miles (25.6 km) south to the Old Faithful area.

West
Entrance Road
————————— ⟶○⟨≈⟩○⟶ —————————

The West Entrance Road is 13.9 miles (22.4 km) long and generally parallels the Madison River, world famous for its outstanding fly-fishing opportunities. The road takes you through the lushly forested Christmas Tree Park on its west end, through the Madison Valley and the gorgeous Madison Canyon, and ends at Madison Junction at the foot of National Park Mountain.

A road into the west entrance has existed since the park's earliest days. In the 1870s, a man by the name of Gilman Sawtell, the owner of a hotel located at Henry's Lake in what is now Idaho, built the first road into the west side of the park. It traveled from Virginia City, then the capitol of the Montana Territory, to the Lower Geyser Basin by way of the Madison Canyon (not unlike today's existing road). This early road was generally in very poor condition, was dangerous, and remained waterlogged for much of the year, however. It was called the Virginia City and National Park Free Road, the "free" differentiating it from the toll road at the North Entrance.

After Philetus Norris was named Superintendent, he had a new road constructed from what is today West Yellowstone to the Fountain Flats area. It traveled inbound roughly four miles along the existing route, and then took a southward turn, passing through what we now call Marshall's Park and Buffalo Meadows before terminating at the confluence of the Nez Perce Creek and the Firehole River near today's Nez Perce Picnic Area.[1] The vestigial remains of this old road can be found at milepost 4.0/9.8 (see below).

In 1900, the U.S. Army Corps of Engineers (USACE) constructed a new road to replace the original Virginia City and National Park Free Road that roughly traversed the road we travel today. The Army's road was of much better construction than the one Sawtell had constructed, however.

Shortly after this road was constructed the Town of West Yellowstone was born (albeit by a different name), and stagecoaches began bringing visitors into the park. The Monida and Yellowstone Stagecoach Company began service and established a transportation complex along what is known today as Barn's Hole Road (see below). By 1924, an official entrance station had been established at the west boundary and is today easily the busiest portal into the park.

The existing West Entrance Road largely follows the road built through this area by the USACE, with just a few minor realignments. The only major deviation occurs at Riverside Drive. This scenic side road was part of the original highway, but the new section was built higher up on the hill to prevent the river from damaging or closing the main road.

You'll often encounter several herds of bison and elk as you travel along this road, along with a variety of smaller mammals, including coyote, fox, and perhaps the elusive bobcat. This road is very heavily traveled in the mornings as tourists enter the park, and in the evenings around dinner time as they head back to their hotels in West Yellowstone. Combine this with traffic stopping to watch the wildlife and travel via this stretch of highway can be quite trying at times.

The only bathroom located along this route is a vault toilet at the Madison River Picnic Area just west of Seven Mile Bridge (approximately halfway between the two end points). There are toilets at the West Entrance and the Madison Service Area just south of Madison Junction, however. The road is in very good condition, and there are a number of pullouts along the river side of the road

0.0 / 13.9 GPS: 44.65865, -111.09719 ELEVATION: 6682 FEET
YELLOWSTONE BOUNDARY

The west boundary of the park is adjacent to the town of West Yellowstone, which in its early days was known as Riverside or simply as Yellowstone.

Just outside the park's western boundary, the West Yellowstone Visitor Center includes staff from the town's Chamber of Commerce, the U.S. Forest Service, and the National Park Service. Interpretive Rangers from Yellowstone are usually present to answer questions about the park, to provide backcountry camping permits (during the peak summer season), and to provide information about services within the park. The town itself has a plethora of hotels, restaurants, stores, and a variety of other services for visitors.

0.1 / 13.7 GPS: 44.65803, -111.09502
ECHO CANYON (HAMILTON STORES) DRIVE (S)
WEST ENTRANCE GOVERNMENT AREA (S)
SITE OF WEST BOUNDARY (RIVERSIDE) CAMP (N)

On the south side of the road just inside the west boundary is an NPS and concession housing and maintenance area. The West District rangers are based here, and the Human Resources Office and Warehouse for Yellowstone General Stores, operated by Delaware North are here as well. The first building constructed in this complex was a bunkhouse for rangers who worked in the area, built in 1929 (and still in use as a bunkhouse).

The entrance road gets its name from Echo Canyon, which is located approximately ten miles southeast of this area. On some maps, the road is labeled at "Hamilton Stores Drive."

On the north side of the roadway (in the woods) is the site of the old West Boundary, or "Riverside" camps. Beginning in 1907, the Wylie Camping Company operated one of the tent camps here, and in 1917 it became an auto camp after Wylie and the Shaw and Powell Camping Company were merged into the Yellowstone Park Camping Company. It operated for another two seasons before it was shut down due to World War I, and never reopened.

0.4 / 13.5 GPS: 44.65686, -111.08984
WEST ENTRANCE STATION 🏠 🚻 ⑦

The current **West Entrance Station** was built in 2008, as was the Ranger Station immediately south of and adjacent to it. Here you'll pay your entrance fee, pick up the park's newspaper and other information, get updates on road conditions, and other information. There's also a campground and lodging information board here so you can see which facilities in the park are full. This is easily the park's most popular entrance, with over one million people entering the park here each summer. During the peak season, traffic can back up into the town.

0.4 / 13.5 GPS: 44.65674, -111.08884
WOLVERINE LANE (S)
CHRISTMAS TREE PARK

Wolverine Lane is another entrance into the housing and maintenance area and the YGS Warehouse complex, though it is normally closed off and accessible only to official vehicles.

As you enter/leave the park, you'll pass through a 3+ mile stand of lodgepole pine trees, the most common tree in the park. Early stagecoach drivers nicknamed this drive **"Christmas Tree Park"** because it resembled a Christmas tree farm. A wildfire in the area had destroyed older trees, and the regrowth consisted of uniform groves of trees.

Interestingly, in 1906, one of the park's original concession operators, Frank J. Haynes, who at the time was part owner of the Monida and Yellowstone Stagecoach Company bringing visitors in from the western side of the park, sought permission to construct and operate a hotel on the eastern edge of the Christmas Tree Park area, along the south bank of the Madison River. The Department of the Interior preferred to have the existing hotel concession operator run all the hotels in the park, though, so the new structure was never approved. Haynes would eventually divest himself of all but his photography operation, and go on to be one of the park's three most influential concession operators. Mount Haynes (ahead if you're traveling east) is named in his honor.[2]

0.8 / 13.1 GPS: 44.65550, -111.08113
Barn's Hole Road (N) 🚗 🪑

Departing from the north side of the highway, **"Barn's Hole Road"** is an old gravel road approximately one and a half miles in length. In 1907, the Monida and Yellowstone Stagecoach Company erected its offices, garages, and barns for its horses along this road, and thus its name. The railroad had just reached West Yellowstone and Monida and Yellowstone provided park tours for the visitors who arrived via this entrance.

When the park was opened to motor vehicles in 1916, the stagecoaches fell out of favor, to be replaced by multi-passenger touring vehicles. The barns and garages (some 25 buildings) were converted for use in servicing these vehicles, and ownership was transferred to the newly created Yellowstone Park Transportation Company. The diagram on the facing page shows how the complex was laid out when it was set up for stagecoaches, circa 1909. Most of the facilities along this road were demolished in the mid-1960s, with three or four remaining until 1974.[3]

Today the road serves as access for fly fishing along the "Cable Car Run" of the Madison River. This stretch of the river got its name from the old cable car system strung across the river to provide supplies to the barns in this area (the footings from the old cable car system are still visible on both shores). There are a couple of picnic tables and bear-proof trash receptacles at the end of the road.

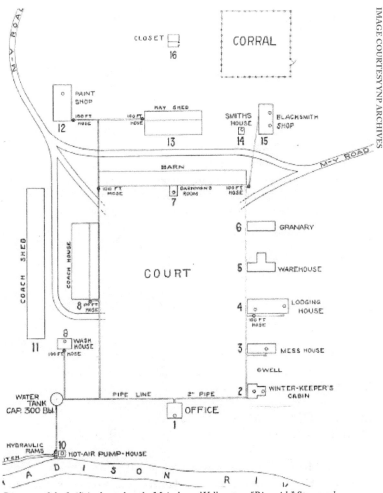

Diagram of the facilities located at the Moinda and Yellowstone "Riverside" Stagecoach Complex, located along what is today Barn's Hole Road near West Yellowstone, ca. 1909.

1.8 / 12.1 GPS: 44.65279, -111.06235
FISHERMAN'S ACCESS TURNOUT (N)

Fisherman's Access Turnout is a short, paved road that affords access to the Madison River. At one time, there was a single picnic table here, but it has since vanished.

As you head east from here, you're driving through the southern end of the Madison Valley, which is bounded on the south by the Madison Plateau. As you travel eastward, the plateau becomes more recognizable to the south of the highway.

2.1 / 11.7 GPS: 44.65146, -111.05529
Montana/Wyoming State Line

You'll cross the state boundaries here (the real line is several hundred feet west of the sign for it). The park's boundaries do not follow state borders because the park boundaries were laid out prior to the establishment of the states of Montana, Wyoming, and Idaho.

Originally, the park was a rectangular box, with its boundaries described in terms of set distances from specific features. For example, the park's western boundary was set as "15 miles west of the most western point of Madison Lake" (today known as Shoshone Lake). This put Yellowstone's western border two miles inside the state of Montana after the state boundaries were demarcated.

2.3 / 11.5 GPS: 44.65194, -111.05181
Turnout @ Wyoming State Line (N) 🛶

This turnout provides an access to the Madison River. Directly across from the easternmost access point is where the service road to the old West Yellowstone Fire Lookout intersected with the main road. You can only barely make it out, and have to get off the road and into the trees to see it, however. The road was obliterated in the late 1960s. See the next entry down for information about the lookout.

3.0 / 10.8 GPS: 44.65184, -111.03799
West Turnout for Two Ribbons Trail (N) 🚶 ♿

The **Two Ribbons Trail** is a ¾ mile long, mostly boardwalked trail that highlights the effects of fire on the lodgepole pine trees common in the area. This area was heavily damaged by the North Fork Fire in 1988; an interpretive sign at the trailhead explains how the fires impacted this area, with the emphasis being on how the fire burned some trees and not others (thus the "two ribbons" in the trail name). The trail is handicap accessible and can be accessed via this trailhead or one at the next turnout to the east of this one.

Directly across the highway from the turnout is a small, unnamed hill upon which was located the old West Yellowstone Fire Lookout Tower (also known as the Madison River Fire Lookout Tower). Built in 1934 by the Civilian Conservation Corps (along with several others throughout the park), it was used intermittently through the 1960s and was finally removed in 1969.

3.4 / 10.5 GPS: 44.65119, -111.03070
EAST TURNOUT FOR TWO RIBBONS TRAIL (N) 🚹 ♿

This is the eastern turnout and parking area for the **Two Ribbons Trail**. See notes above.

4.0 / 9.8 GPS: 44.64974, -111.01830
OLD FOUNTAIN TRAIL (S)
SITE OF THE RIVERSIDE MAIL STATION/SOLDIER STATION (S)

If you blink as you pass by you might miss this, and it's much easier to see when you're traveling eastbound. On the south side of the road, appearing to head into the forest to the southeast, you'll notice the scar from an old road built by the park's second superintendent, Philetus W. Norris. The road was used from 1880 up until around 1900, and afterwards was used as a patrol trail (known for a time as the "Madison Trail," and today as the **"Old Fountain Trail"**).

This old road followed the south face of Mt. Haynes, passed through Marshall's Park and Buffalo Meadows, and ended near the intersection of what is today known as Fountain Flats Drive and the Grand Loop Road near the location (at that time) of the Marshall and Firehole Hotels near today's Nez Perce Picnic Area.[4] The road was built to bypass the first road constructed through this area, one which generally followed the path of today's road. This original road followed the river through Madison River Canyon and stayed marshy or flooded much of the season. The stagecoaches were constantly having to stop and cut up fallen trees, move rock debris, and were getting bogged down in the wet sand and dirt. This new road alleviated those problems by traversing flat meadows and the Madison Plateau.

In 1900, the U.S. Army Corps of Engineers built a new road along the Madison River, which, with some minor exceptions, followed today's road alignment, and Norris' Road was abandoned. Today, the trail is occasionally used by skiers during the winter, but otherwise sees little, if any foot traffic.

Just to the south of the intersection was the site of the old **Riverside Mail Station** and the **Riverside Soldier Station**. The soldier station, built in 1892, was one of a number of such stations the U.S. Army constructed as posts for protecting the resources of the park when they assumed control of Yellowstone in 1886. A small contingent of troops was stationed here to protect the area around and along the west entrance roads. This series of outposts formed the basis for the ranger stations and patrol cabins still in use today. The rangers would relocate to a new building in the Riverside Transportation Complex at Barn's Hole (See 0.8/13.1 above) in 1945.

The mail station was established by Superintendent P. W. Norris in 1879 to facilitate mail movement from Virginia City to Mammoth. It was abandoned in 1920 and razed in 1945 along with the old soldier station. If you hike along the road a few hundred feet and turn south, you can still see evidence of the old buildings and occupational debris here today. Keep in mind that removing artifacts from the park is a violation of federal law, and leave any items you find from this era lying where you locate them.

4.8 / 9.0 GPS: 44.65085, -111.00192
WEST ENTRANCE/EXIT FROM RIVERSIDE DRIVE (N)

Riverside Drive is a 1.1-mile (1.8 km) long scenic drive along the Madison River. When the West Entrance Road was originally constructed (1900), this was part of the main road. When the existing roadway was realigned, this section was left intact as a scenic side trip. The pavement along this side road is almost always very rutted and scarred, so expect a bumpy ride.

5.6 / 8.3 GPS: 44.65712, -110.99047
MADISON RANGE TURNOUT (W) 🛉

From this turnout, you have an excellent view of both the **Madison Range**, outside the park to the northwest, and the southern end of the Gallatin Range to the north. The Gallatin Range includes peaks inside and outside the park, stretching toward the Bozeman area. There is no interpretive signage here.

5.7 / 8.1 GPS: 44.65899, -110.99049
SOLDIER'S PIT SERVICE ROAD (S)

The **Soldier's Pit Service Road** leads to a gravel pit used by the park to stage road construction materials and supplies, as well as one of the park's three law enforcement shooting ranges (the other two are near Arnica Creek and at the Stephens Creek Administrative Area). The area's name comes from its proximity to the old soldier station at Riverside (see above). This area was one of their shooting ranges as well, in fact.

The road itself was part of an old stagecoach shortcut that existed before the main roadway was built. It exited at the Madison River just south of where today's Seven Mile Bridge exists (the previous bridge having been removed with the construction of the existing roadway).

5.9 / 7.9 GPS: 44.66202, -110.99152
EAST ENTRANCE/EXIT FROM RIVERSIDE DRIVE (N)

This is the east entrance or exit from **Riverside Drive**, described above. If you are traveling eastbound at this point, you'll be entering what is known colloquially as Eagle Curve, named because of its proximity to an eagle's nest (see next entry below)

6.3 / 7.6 GPS: 44.66614, -110.98825
BALD EAGLE'S NEST (S) 🔍

Immediately on the south side of the road, an American Bald Eagle family can often be found nesting in the nest at the crown of the tree. The park service posts a "no stopping" zone ¼ mile to either side of the nest during times when eggs or babies are present to ensure they're not disturbed.

If you're headed westbound, once you past the nest, you'll enter Eagle Curve (see note in the entry above).

6.8 / 7.1 GPS: 44.66868, -110.98083
FLYFISHING TURNOUT/GRASSHOPPER HILL (N) 🖼

This is one of the many pullouts and turnouts designed to afford access to the Madison River. **Grasshopper Hill**, located across the river, was given its name by local fishermen for the prevalence of the little insects during August.

7.5 / 6.4 GPS: 44.66461, -110.96731
MADISON RIVER PICNIC AREA (N) 🏕 🚻 🖼

The **Madison River Picnic Area** has seven tables and a vault toilet, and is handicap accessible. The picnic area is right along the river and is an excellent place from which to fish as well.

7.6 / 6.3 GPS: 44.66366, -110.96538
SEVEN MILE BRIDGE

Here you'll cross the Madison River Bridge, known colloquially as "**Seven Mile Bridge**" because it is approximately that distance from the West Entrance. The bridge was built in 1958 as part of the Mission 66 Program.

Note that there is a bridge that is officially known as the Seven Mile Bridge. It is found along the road between Norris and Mammoth at the crossing of the Gardner River. This can be an important distinction to make if you're giving someone directions.

This stretch of the river is popular with trumpeter swans, and they can occasionally be seen in the area. In fact, for many years, there was a nesting pair just south of the bridge.

7.7 / 6.2 GPS: 44.66327, -110.96436
GNEISS CREEK TRAILHEAD TURNOUT (N) 🚶

Immediately to the east of the Madison River Bridge, there is a small parking area for the eastern **Gneiss Creek Trailhead**. The Gneiss Creek Trail is a 14-mile (22.5 km) trail that parallels the Madison River, ending at its western trailhead on U.S. Highway 191 just outside the park's western boundary. The parking area is also a nice vantage point from which to watch the Trumpeter swan and other water fowl along the river.

7.8 / 6.1 GPS: 44.66207, -110.96235
AVENUE OF TRAVEL TURNOUT (S) 🚶 ❊

The "**Avenue of Travel**" turnout is an interpretive display about the historical use of the various paths and roads that have passed through this part of the park. There is also a sign about the Trumpeter Swan, which occasionally nests in this area.

As you drive eastward, you are entering the Madison Canyon. If you're driving to the west, you're leaving the Canyon.

7.9 / 5.9 GPS: 44.66047, -110.96077
MADISON CANYON WEST TURNOUT (S)

This turnout has a nice view of the western end of the **Madison Canyon**. The canyon is considered by many to be rivaled only by the Grand Canyon of the Yellowstone in terms of beauty inside the park. In the late evenings during the summer, the angle of the sun casts a purple haze on the mountains here, and it is simply stunning to see.

If you're westbound, you're entering the Madison Valley, which is bounded on the south by the Madison Plateau, and which extends several miles northward west of the Gneiss Creek Trail.

As you travel eastward, note the meandering Madison River. This area is known to local fishermen as the Oxbows.

9.0 / 4.9 GPS: 44.64950, -110.94903
Nine-Mile Turnout (N)
Nine-Mile Hole (S)

The small turnout on the north side of the north side of the road is known as **Nine-Mile Turnout** for it's distance from the west entrance. Not coincidentally, local fishermen know the area on the south side of the road (the small island in the river) as **Nine Mile Hole**.

9.2 / 4.7 GPS: 44.64918, -110.94649
Rockslide (N)

On the north side of the road, you'll notice the debris from an old rockslide. This is the remnants of a rockslide that blocked the West Entrance Road after the Hebgen Lake Earthquake in 1959.

9.9 / 4.0 GPS: 44.64753, -110.93170
Talus Turnout (S) ✳
Mount Jackson (N)

The large collection of rock at the base of the mountain across the river is known as "talus" (pronounced *tay luhs*), and is collapsed volcanic basalt. This turnout is officially known as the Talus Turnout, and there's a small interpretive sign that explains what talus is.

The turnout is also known as the "Mt. Jackson Turnout," as it affords a view of **Mt. Jackson** (8257 ft/2517 m) on the north side of the road. The mountain is named for William Henry Jackson, a photographer who accompanied the Hayden Survey into the area in 1871. His photographs, along with paintings by Thomas Moran, helped convince Congress to set aside Yellowstone as the world's first National Park.

This area along the river is known as the "Madison Notch" to local fishermen.

10.4 / 3.5 GPS: 44.64483, -110.92332
Mt. Haynes Turnout (S) 🕅 ◀ ♿

This turnout affords a view of **Mt. Haynes** (8235 ft/2510 m). Formerly known as Mt. Burley, Superintendent Horace Albright renamed the mountain in 1921 after the death of Frank J. Haynes, one of the park's early concessioners. For 40 years, Haynes operated a series of photo studios and shops throughout the park, and was one of the most influential people of the park's early years. Upon his death in 1921, his son, Jack E. Haynes, assumed control of his enterprise and continued to operate the studios until his death in 1962. Jack Haynes' wife continued to operate the shops until 1967, when she sold all of the company's assets to the park's General Stores operator, Charles A. Hamilton.

Mt. Haynes isn't really considered a true mountain, per se, but rather an outcropping of the rock that forms the Madison Plateau. The high cliffs on the south side of the road west of Mt. Haynes are known as Lookout Cliffs, so named by Superintendent P. W. Norris because he "could see for miles" when he stood atop them.[5]

The only wheelchair accessible fishing spot in the park is located here. A short boardwalk provides access to a 70-foot long fishing platform.

11.8 / 2.1 GPS: 44.64076, -110.89549
THREE BROTHERS TURNOUT (S) 🅟 🚶

The turnout affords an excellent view of the **Three Brothers Mountains**, a series of three outcroppings or pinnacles of the mountain face to the south of the river. No one is entirely sure how the mountains got their name, but park historian Lee Whittlesey believes it may have originated from NPS personnel who transferred into Yellowstone from Yosemite National Park, where there is a similar feature with the same name.[6]

This turnout is also an excellent place to watch a large colony of Uinta Ground Squirrels. These squirrels live underground in a very complex colony consisting of up to several dozen members. They're fun to watch as they pop up and out of their holes and scurry about. You'll have to catch them early in the season, though, as they go into hibernation in August, and don't come out until the following spring.

12.2 /1.7 GPS: 44.64039, -110.88885
HARLEQUIN LAKE TRAILHEAD TURNOUT (S) 🚶

This turnout provides access to the **Harlequin Lake Trailhead**, which is located across the road on the east side of the turnout. This trail is an easy, ½-mile (0.8 km) trail that leads to Harlequin Lake, a fishless, lily pad-covered lake nestled in a stand of pine trees. The large curving bend in the river here is known to local fishermen as Big Bend.

12.5 / 1.4 GPS: 44.64036, -110.88272
OUT OF THE ASHES TURNOUT (S) 🎋

There is an interpretive panel here about the 1988 fires that blew through this area, and how that event helped to regenerate a forest that had been decimated by beetles.

12.8 / 1.1 GPS: 44.64176, -110.87668
MADISON ELK HERD TURNOUT (S) 🛗

This turnout has a panel that explains how the Madison Elk Herd uses this area during the summer and the winter.

13.1 / 0.8 GPS: 44.64426, -110.87239
MADISON WASTEWATER TREATMENT PLANT SERVICE ROAD (N)

This service road leads to the **Madison Wastewater Treatment Plant**, which provides sewage treatment for the Madison Campground and the government housing and maintenance area located north of Madison Junction.

13.7 / 0.1 GPS: 44.64624, -110.86106
MADISON CAMPGROUND ENTRANCE (S) 🅰️ 🚌 🏕️ 🚹 🚻 🎣 🛗

The **Madison Campground** has 277 sites, including several that are wheelchair accessible. The campground, built in 1961 as part of the Mission 66 Program (though there'd been an "auto camp" just south of here for years prior), is one of the most popular in the park and is usually one of the first to fill up each day, sometimes as early as 10 or 11AM during the peak season. This campground is operated by park concessioner Xanterra, and you can reserve sites in advance by contacting them at 866-439-7375. The 2014 daily rate is $25.00.

The campground has an incredible view of National Park Mountain and the "junction" or confluence of the Firehole and Gibbon Rivers to form the Madison River (given its name in 1805 by Lewis and Clark, even though they never saw it this far south).

A short foot trail leads to the Madison Amphitheater where rangers present evening programs at 9:00 or 9:30PM during the summer season, as well as the Madison Information Station, a historic museum where the park's Junior Ranger Program is based. You'll also find one of Yellowstone Association's bookstores inside.

13.9 / 0.0 GPS: 44.64542, -110.85845 ELEVATION: 6845 FEET
MADISON JUNCTION

This is the end/beginning of the West Entrance Road. From here, it is 13.9 miles (22.4 km) back to West Yellowstone, 13.3 miles (21.4 km) north to Norris Junction, or 15.9 miles (25.6 km) south to the Old Faithful complex.

Madison Junction
to
Norris Junction

The road from Madison Junction to Norris Junction is 13.3 miles (21.4 km) long, and is widely regarded as one of the least interesting within the park. Even during its initial construction, Lt. Hiram Chittenden remarked that this was "...the worst, most tedious, and least interesting drives in the park."[1] However, it is one of the most heavily traveled because it provides access to the northern and eastern areas of the park from those entering from the West Entrance (through which over 1.4 million people pass each summer) or those headed north from the Old Faithful area. There are a number of secondary features along the road that have some appeal to visitors, however, including Terrace Spring, Beryl Spring, Gibbon Falls, and the trails to Monument Geyser Basin and Artist Paint Pots.

The original 1892 road between Norris and the Madison/Firehole Falls area passed through Norris Geyser Basin and traveled east of the Gibbon Canyon and Gibbon Falls area. The road as it currently exists was originally constructed by the U.S. Army Corps of Engineers (USACE) in 1905, and then completely rebuilt by the Bureau of Public Roads in the mid-1930s. The north end at Norris Geyser Basin was constructed in the mid-1960s to provide a bypass around the thermal features; prior to this, the road traveled right through the middle of the basin.

The southern half of this road was reconstructed in the early 2000s, while the new two-mile segment between Tanker Curve and Gibbon Falls was undertaken over a period of ten years, finally reaching completion in the fall of 2010. Prior to the construction of the realignment, visitors traveling south would negotiate Tanker Curve and then travel through Gibbon Canyon along the Gibbon River. It was a very scenic drive, but there were a number of problems that had plagued this short stretch of roadway for decades. The road itself was very close to the river, and during high water periods (runoff from the spring snow melt), the rushing water would eat away at the banks and occasionally the roadway itself. During heavy rains, loosening mud and rock from the canyon walls would slide down onto the roadway, shutting down the area and occasionally washing vehicles off into the river.

The curve at the north end of the segment was the scene of a major traffic accident in 1970 when a tanker truck carrying petroleum products failed to negotiate the curve, rolled over, and caught fire. The almost 180-degree hairpin turn recorded the highest number of automobile accidents each year for many years. And at the south end of the segment, the old pullout at Gibbon Falls ranked eighth highest on that list. So the construction of the bypass high up on the eastern canyon wall solved a great many headaches for the NPS if it did make for a somewhat less scenic drive.

The road itself is in excellent shape, having been the last on the Grand Loop to undergo reconstruction. There are vault toilets at three of the picnic areas, Tuff Cliff, Iron Spring, and Caldera Rim. The only significant animals you're likely to see through here are the occasional small herd of bison and perhaps a grizzly bear or two. During the late July and early August time frames, this road is often clogged with bison migrating eastward back to Hayden Valley for the annual rut. As much of the road passes through an area bounded on one side with steep canyon walls, and the other side with a river, the bison have little choice but to use the roadway, so bring your patience with you.

0.0 / 13.3 GPS: 44.64542, -110.85845 ELEVATION: 6845 FEET
MADISON JUNCTION

Madison Junction is named for the nearby confluence or junction of the Gibbon and Firehole Rivers to become the Madison River. From here you can travel west 13.9 miles (22.4 km) to the West Entrance, 15.9 miles (25.6 km) south to Old Faithful, or 13.3 miles (21.4 km) north to Norris Junction.

0.1 / 13.2 GPS: 44.64636, -110.85624
MADISON GOVERNMENT AREA (W)

The **Madison Government Area** here was completed during the Mission 66 building program in Yellowstone (1959-1962). Prior to that, it was a road camp. The area houses NPS and concession employee residences, maintenance facilities, and office space.

0.1 / 13.2 GPS: 44.64640, -110.85574
PURPLE MOUNTAIN TRAILHEAD (E) 🏃

There is a small parking area on the east side of the road for the **Purple Mountain Trailhead**. The six-mile (10.6 km, round trip) trail begins on the west side of the road and leads up to the summit of the mountain, which lies behind the government housing complex. The trail up and the summit itself offer excellent views of the Gibbon River and its valley. Purple Mountain was the site of a fire lookout tower from 1946 to 1969, and was the site of one of the park's radio repeaters until recently.

0.8 / 12.6 GPS: 44.64919, -110.84472
TERRACE SPRINGS (N) 🌊
TERRACE SPRINGS MEADOW (S)

There's a small parking lot here, and a short, handicap-accessible boardwalk that leads you to **Terrace Springs** and the dozen or so mostly unnamed springs in the area. The main spring (Terrace Spring) gets its name from the terraces in its runoff channels. Terrace is unique in that it deposits both limestone and geyserite, suggesting a complex underground plumbing system. The collection of springs here discharges roughly 1220 gallons of water per minute.[2] The large expanse of flat land on the south side of the road is known as **Terrace Spring Meadow** for its proximity to the spring.

Bath Spring (the small pool in the northern curve of the boardwalk) was at one time a popular place to swim and soak, and thus its (colloquial) name. During the Hebgen Lake Earthquake in 1959, two park employees were soaking in the spring as the water completely drained from it after the initial shocks of the quake. The average temperature of the spring is 107°F (41.7°C).[3]

1.4 / 11.9 GPS: 44.65018, -110.83144
UNNAMED FISHERMAN'S TURNOUT (S) 🎣

There are several unnamed pullouts and turnouts along the Gibbon River on this stretch of roadway to afford fishermen access to the river.

1.6 / 11.8 GPS: 44.65026, -110.82905
TUFF CLIFF TURNOUT/PICNIC AREA (N) 🏕 🚻 🌊

The **Tuff Cliff Picnic Area** is a small, handicap-accessible picnic area with three tables and a small vault toilet.

Tuff Cliff is on the eastern face of a foothill of Purple Mountain (see above), and is composed of very soft, burned rock known as *tuff*. A sizeable chunk of the cliff sloughed off the face of this mountain during the 1959 Hebgen Lake Earthquake. There's an interpretive sign here that explains the formation of this material.

4.4 / 8.9 GPS: 44.64930, -110.77431
GIBBON FALLS PICNIC AREA (S) 🏕

The **Gibbon Falls Picnic Area** currently (as of late 2013) has no tables and no facilities. This was a picnic area prior to the building of the new road segment between Gibbon Falls and Tanker Curve, but it was converted into a materials and equipment staging area for a couple of years as a part of the construction work. It was reconstructed in 2010 after the roadwork was completed, but funding limitations have prevented NPS from securing tables and a vault toilet for it.

Across the river from the picnic area is the site of one of Shaw and Powell's permanent camps from 1913-1917, and a Wylie Lunch Station from 1898 to 1917.[4] The area was known during that period as Sleepy Hollow. Canyon Creek empties into the Gibbon River just below the picnic area, and the hill immediately south of where the creek joins the river is known as Canyon Creek Hill. Tourists stopping here would often climb up onto the hill to take in the view of the valley.

The original road through here followed the power lines off to the east (generally not visible), and eventually came out at what is today the Mesa Service Road (see the Old Faithful to Madison Junction section for details).

The road was realigned from the east side of the canyon to the west side around 1900. This was done primarily because of the new Madison Junction that had just been constructed by the U.S. Army Corps of Engineers. Having the road on the west side made it easier to connect to the main circuit at Madison without having to build several bridges and span some hills that might otherwise make construction more difficult. Otherwise, there'd have been a two mile detour out of the way from Mesa Junction to visit the Madison area.

4.9 / 8.4 GPS: 44.65477, -110.77117
GIBBON FALLS PARKING AREA (E) 🅿

Gibbon Falls is an 84-foot (25.6 m) high waterfall located along the Gibbon River. The parking area here was constructed in 2010 in concert with the road realignment (see below), replacing the much smaller lot constructed in 1931. The new wall along the pedestrian sidewalk is built just high enough to obscure the view of the falls from the highway. The previous wall was low enough to allow people in automobiles to see the waterfall, and this often led to major traffic jams as people stopped in the middle of the road to take photographs.

5.0 / 8.3 GPS: 44.65753, -110.76944
GIBBON RIVER CROSSING/SOUTH END OF NEW ROAD SEGMENT

This is the south end of a new road segment completed in 2010. Prior to this opening up, traffic was routed along the west side of the river. There were numerous problems with this, including high water washing out portions of the road during the spring runoff, and rock/mud slides along the canyon walls closing the roadway (occasionally even washing vehicles into the Gibbon River). The new bridge here was built in 2009-2010 as part of this new segment.

5.3 / 8.0 GPS: 44.65965, -110.76618
IRON SPRINGS PICNIC AREA (W) 🎋 🚻

The **Iron Springs Picnic Area** was named for a series of cold springs that exist along the banks of the Gibbon River in this area. The spring was used as a watering stop for early park tourists according to park historian Lee Whittlesey.[5]

This picnic area was constructed in 2010 and, as is the case with the Gibbon Falls Picnic Area, the NPS has not installed any tables here (though it does have a handicap-accessible vault toilet).

6.2 / 7.1 GPS: 44.65957, -110.75075
CALDERA RIM PICNIC AREA (N) 🎋 🚻

The **Caldera Rim Picnic Area** sits just below the rim of the Yellowstone Caldera, easily visible on the hillside to the west. There is a vault toilet here, but no picnic tables or other facilities (as of late 2013).

6.8 / 6.5 GPS: 44.65935, -110.74449
TANKER HILL / NORTH END OF NEW ROAD SEGMENT

This is the north end of the new segment of highway completed in 2010 (the south end is at 5.0/8.3 – see above). Prior to the completion of this section of road, traffic would drive through a hairpin curve along the bank of the river, visible just off the west side of the bridge. In 1970, a tanker truck carrying fuel oil rolled over and burst into flames here, leading the curve to become known as "Tanker Curve." The name was so ingrained in local usage that many hated to see the moniker pass into oblivion with the advent of the new road, so they've attached the name "**Tanker Hill**" to the slight incline you drive up if you're headed south.

That accident is illustrative of why the curve consistently had the highest number of accidents of any location in the park. The need for someone to drive several miles to report the incident led to the installation of several roadside pay telephones throughout the park (remember, this was in the days prior to the existence of cell phones), including one just north of Tanker Curve, which has since been removed. Two of these still exist, however, one at the Cavalry at Yellowstone Turnout just north of Norris Junction, and one at the Cascade Picnic Area in Hayden Valley.

7.4 / 5.9 GPS: 44.66794, -110.74444
GIBBON RIVER CROSSING

The Gibbon River crosses under the road here over a bridge built in 2002 (which replaced one constructed in the 1930s).

8.2 / 5.1 GPS: 44.67866, -110.74635
BERYL SPRING (W) 🌋

Beryl Spring (pronounced like singer Burl Ives' first name) was named for the color of the spring's water and its resemblance to the gemstone. The bridge over the spring's runoff channels was constructed in 1962 and rebuilt in 2002. Like many other park features, this spring has had a plethora of names in the past, including Laundry Spring and Gibbon Boiling Spring.[6] The large bellowing fumarole behind the spring (that produces much of the steam on warmer days) is a separate feature, though it has no official name.

8.6 / 4.7 GPS: 44.68376, -110.74453
MONUMENT GEYSER BASIN TRAILHEAD (W) 🥾
GIBBON RIVER BRIDGE

The Gibbon River crosses under the road here over a bridge originally constructed in 1936 and then reconstructed in 2002-2003.

The **Monument Geyser Basin** is a small field of about 30 mostly dormant, unnamed thermal features. It was named by Superintendent P. W. Norris in

1878 for the gravestone-like appearance of many of the old cones, including one characteristically named Thermos Bottle. The trail is approximately one mile (1.5 km) long and climbs about 500 feet in elevation. It was also the first trail constructed in the park (in 1880).

9.4 / 4.0 GPS: 44.69414, -110.74591
GIBBON MEADOWS SOUTH PULLOUT (W)
SYLVAN SPRINGS THERMAL AREA (W)
PAINTPOT HILL/GIBBON HILL (E)

The large, expansive meadow to the west of the road here is known as **Gibbon Meadows** for the fact the Gibbon River flows through it. The river (and every other feature with the name) is named for General John Gibbon, who was the military commander of the Montana Territory in the 1870s.

The smaller hill to the east is **Paintpot Hill** (named for its hosting Artist Paint Pots, see below), and the large hill behind it slightly to the north is **Gibbon Hill**. Across the road from this pullout you may see a faint remnant of the old foot trail that once led to Artist Paint Pots. A few years ago the existing parking lot was constructed to replace the small turnout that was located here.

The thermal field visible on the hills to the far west of the meadow is known as **Sylvan Springs**, home to approximately 90 mostly unnamed thermal features. Dante's Inferno, which churns violently almost continuously, can be found here, as can Sylvan Spring, Coffin Spring, and Evening Primrose Spring. At one time there was a trail that led to this area, but it has long since been abandoned. If you walk out into this area, use extreme caution.

9.6 / 3.7 GPS: 44.69770, -110.74403
ARTIST PAINT POTS (E) ⁂
GEYSER CREEK CROSSING

Artist Paint Pots is a moderately-sized thermal area of about 60 features. Of these, only two have official names, Blood Geyser and Flash Spring. The hill upon which the paintpot field is located is known as Paintpot Hill, not surprisingly. The area got its name from the bright colors of the springs and the belief that the collection resembled an artist's palette. The trail through the area is about ½-mile long (0.8 km).

The small meadow just south of the entrance driveway to Artist Paint Pots was home to an NPS road camp in the 1910s-1930s. Note that some older trail guides still list the access to this area as a small pullout 3.9 miles south of Norris Junction. This old pullout was removed in the early 2000s and replaced by the existing parking area.

Geyser Creek passes under the road here (as well as under the entrance road into the paintpots parking area). It was given its name by Superintendent P. W. Norris, perhaps for the fact that it passes through a small thermal field (today known as the Geyser Springs Group) on the east side of Paintpot Hill. The creek that passes under the road just north of the entrance to the parking area has no official name.

10.0 / 3.3 GPS: 44.70386, -110.74552
GIBBON MEADOWS NORTH PULLOUT (W)
GIBBON MEADOWS PIT SERVICE ROAD (E)

This is the northern boundary of **Gibbon Meadows**, which was a popular place for visitors to set up informal campsites during the very early days of the park.

The **Gibbon Meadows Pit Service Road** leads back to a road and construction material staging and disposal area. The original road through this area was located about 300 yards east of here at this point (the old roadbed is still visible if you hike back behind the service area).

10.2 / 3.1 GPS: 44.70613, -110.74518
GIBBON MEADOWS PICNIC AREA (W) 🦖 🚻

The **Gibbon Meadows Picnic Area** it situated right along the river. It has nine tables as well as two handicap-accessible vault toilets.

10.5 / 2.8 GPS: 44.70956, -110.74202
CHOCOLATE POTS PULLOUT (W) ⛲

Chocolate Pots is a group of two large and another twenty or so smaller warm springs on the shores of the Gibbon River, most of which have a dark brown or dark red appearance (and thus the name). The color comes from iron sinter, a hydrous form of iron oxide that is not found at any other location in the park.

One of the larger cones is directly across the river at the middle of the pullout, while the second is on the bank closest to the road about 50 yards north of the north end of the paved parking area. If you go exploring in this area, watch your footing as there are hot springs hidden by the grass.

10.6 / 2.6 GPS: 44.71084, -110.73999
GIBBON RIVER RAPIDS PULLOUT (W) ⚐

Gibbon River Rapids is a gorgeous two-stage rapid along the Gibbon River. The pullout itself is a bit downstream from the rapids, so you'll have to park and walk up the edge of the river a bit if you wish to get a really good view of them. In the middle of the lower set of rapids is a well-weathered rock known as Duck Rock (see below).

10.7 / 2.5 GPS: 44.71133, -110.73859
DUCK ROCK (W)

Duck Rock gets its name from the fact that it is shaped like a duck's head. It sits in the middle of the Lower Gibbon River Rapids, hidden behind the trees on the west side of the road. You'll have to park in the pullout south of this point and hike back along the road and down into the woods to see it.

11.6 / 1.7 GPS: 44.71748, -110.72288
ELK PARK (W) 🏕

The large expanse of flat land on the west side of the road here is known as **Elk Park**. This was another area used as an unofficial camping site for visitors in the early days of the park (especially the 1880s), and was apparently named by early tourists for the prevalence of elk in the area. The area is drained by the Gibbon River which meanders through the meadow from north to south.

As you drive north out of Elk Park, the road begins to curve to the east as you start to head up Norris Hill. Note the darkened dirt/grass shadow that appears to continue straight from the roadway as the turn begins (much easier to see during the spring and winter). Prior to 1967, the main road went right through the middle of Norris Geyser Basin. It passed right by Black Growler – you can still see the old pavement just to the east of it, in fact. This shadow is the scar where the old road connected into the section you were just traveling on (if you're headed north).

Just off the pullout apron to the west is a small group of about ten hot springs, all of which are unnamed. They're part of a larger group of thermal features known collectively as Elk Park Springs; the balance of them are located to the north along the old rehabilitated road bed. If you venture off the pavement, be careful where you step, lest you end up with a badly burned foot.

11.9 / 1.4 GPS: 44.71745, -110.71711
PARK CREEK CROSSING

Park Creek flows from its source (runoff from Gibbon Hill) and then empties into the Gibbon River. It was named for the fact that it crosses Elk Park.

12.8 / 0.6 GPS: 44.72010, -110.70151
TANTALUS CREEK CROSSING

Tantalus Creek drains the basins at Norris, both the Back Basin (formerly called Tantalus Basin) and Porcelain Basin. It was apparently named for the son of the Greek god Zeus.[7]

13.3 / 0.0 GPS: 44.72734, -110.69657 ELEVATION: 7536 FEET
NORRIS JUNCTION 🚻 🏠 🥾 ⑦

Just before you arrive at Norris Junction (or after you depart, if you're traveling south), you may notice a couple of buildings just over the hill on the east side of the road. This is the Norris Wastewater Treatment Plant, which treats sewage generated by the facilities at Norris Geyser Basin and the Norris Government Area (located on the Norris to Canyon Road).

This bypass road around the Norris Geyser Basin was constructed in 1964-1966, opening to public traffic in the spring of 1967. The road cost $840,397.80 (1966 $) to build, and was designed to route traffic away from the thermal features in the basin. Prior to this, you drove right through the middle of the Porcelain Basin area, right behind Black Growler. This is why the thermal field now in "front" of the Norris Museum is referred to as the "Back Basin." When the museum was built, this area was indeed behind the building, making the name appropriate for the time.

The burned out area on the east side of the road is the result of a prescribed burn a few years ago. Prescribed burns are used to thin out vegetation, reducing the potential for a major wildfire (which could damage the wastewater plant and its related infrastructure in this case).

From this intersection, you can drive 13.3 miles (21.4 km) back to Madison Junction, 11.6 miles (18.7 km) east to Canyon Junction, 21.5 miles (34.6 km) north to Mammoth Hot Springs, or you can turn into the Norris Geyser Basin parking area. For further information on the facilities and features found in the Norris Basin, see the Norris Junction to Canyon Junction section.

Norris Junction
to
Canyon Junction

The road from Norris Junction to Canyon Junction is 11.6 miles (18.7 km) long and was originally known as the "Norris Cutoff." When the road was first completed, it was not intended for use by tourists, and little thought was given to providing a scenic drive. Even as the road has been realigned over time, there's little in the way of substantive points of interest for the average visitor and is lined for its entire route with pine trees. In fact, tour bus operators often refer to it as Lodgepole Alley because it carries you through twelve miles of lush, forested landscape.

The road began as a stagecoach path cut through the forest in 1884 by the Yellowstone Park Improvement Company. They were seeking a shorter path to get supplies to the new tent camp they'd established at Canyon the year before. Prior to this, they were forced to travel all the way down to the Mary Mountain Road, travel east to Hayden Valley, and then cut back north for several miles, taking them a considerable distance out of the way. This new "cutoff" would shave several miles and hours of travel time needed to resupply the camp.

The following year, construction of an official road began under the auspices of the U.S. Army Corps of Engineers (USACE) under the direction of Lt. Daniel Kingman. Kingman hired a civilian construction supervisor by the name of James Blanding to oversee construction of this segment of road, and would later name a rather steep hill along its length for him. Some fifteen years later, Lt. Hiram Chittenden would go on to remark that Blanding Hill was "...a long, difficult, and dangerous ascent which is impossible to maintain in good condition."[1] The road would eventually be relocated northward to help level out some of the grades, but the 8% incline is still the most significant grade on the park's public road network.

This 1885-1886 road followed the Gibbon River through the Virginia Canyon, a route that required negotiating "Devil's Elbow," an 80-degree bend in the road just west of the cascade itself. The turn was a blind one, and there were a great many stagecoach accidents there. In 1903, Chittenden would carve a new road into the face of the canyon wall above the elbow to help alleviate the problem. This is the path the scenic road takes now. It not only made travel through the area safer, but also had the added benefit of being more visually appealing because it afforded a better view of the cascade and the small canyon through which it passes. In the 1960s, the existing main road was constructed to the north, and the 1903 segment became the Virginia Cascade Drive, a scenic side road.

Much of the entire twelve miles of this route has been realigned from its original path, mostly during the 1950s-1960s. The west end was realigned from the Norris Meadow Picnic Area, and then again in 1967, when the bypass was built to prevent traffic from driving through Norris Geyser Basin. On the east end, the current Canyon Junction is the fourth iteration of the intersection of the Norris Cutoff Road and the Grand Loop Road in the canyon area. The existing intersection was built in the late 1950s with the advent of the new Canyon Village, constructed as part of the Mission 66 Program. Prior to this, the previous junctions were located further southward near the site of today's Brink of the Upper Falls Road and the site of the old Canyon Hotel (presently the Canyon Corrals).

The road itself is in excellent condition, and has several stretches where it is possible to pass slower vehicles. This makes it possible to exceed the speed limit rather easily, however, and the rangers spend a considerable amount of time making traffic stops along this road. Given its high elevation and the fact that Blanding Hill is shielded from the sun for much of the day, sections of this road ice over frequently during the early and latter parts of the season. This often results in periodic closures until the park's road crews can get out and plow it, and quite a few "slide off" accidents by drivers who're either caught off-guard by the ice or who're unfamiliar with the hazards associated with the hill.

There are no bathroom facilities along the route so you may wish to consider using the toilets at Norris Junction or Canyon Village prior to setting out. You're not likely to encounter many animals along this road during much of the year, save for the occasional wandering bull bison. During the late July-early August time frame, however, many of the bison herds from the west side of the park will use this route to get back to Hayden Valley for the annual rut (mating season). You may also see the occasional bear in the area as well, especially near the junctions.

0.0 / 11.6 GPS: 44.72734, -110.69657 ELEVATION: 7536 FEET
NORRIS JUNCTION
NORRIS GEYSER BASIN (W) 🚻 ⓘ 🏕 🚶

From here, you can drive 13.3 miles (21.4 km) south to Madison Junction, 11.6 miles (18.7 km) east to Canyon Junction, 21 miles (33.8 km) north to Mammoth Hot Springs, or you can turn into the basin parking lot.

Norris Geyser Basin is the hottest and most seismically-active thermal field in the park, primarily because it is located just outside the northwest aspect of the Yellowstone Caldera and along a series of faults. Much of the area is completely devoid of plant life and has a stark appearance. Many compare it to a moonscape, in fact. The heat and acidity of the soil here are largely responsible for the lack of plant life (save for the algae that can be found in the runoff channels of many of the springs).

The basin is divided into three major areas, Porcelain Basin, Back Basin, and One Hundred Spring Plain. There are trails that will take you through the first two, but One Hundred Spring Plain is not accessible to hikers.

Porcelain Basin is the large flat expanse in front (north) of the Norris Museum. It consists of about 50 mostly named thermal features, including Crackling Lake, Congress Pool, Whirligig Geyser and its smaller brother, Little Whirligig, Ledge Geyser, and the noisy steam vent known as Black Growler. Growler is perhaps the hottest steam vent in the park, averaging well over 250°F (121°C). It is believed to have been a rather robust geyser at one point. Over the course of the past 140 years, the vent has shifted position many times, moving further and further away from the museum.

There are two boardwalk loops to take you through this area. The eastern loop carries you out onto the Porcelain Terrace overlook, and is approximately ⁴⁄₁₀-mile long. The western loop takes you through the basin itself and is about ½-mile long. If you stop and look to the west as you approach Crackling Lake, you'll see another small thermal field on the hills in the distance. This is the Ragged Hills Thermal Area, home to about 60 unnamed thermal features. It, too, is inaccessible to the public.

Back Basin (also known as Tantalus Basin) is the large thermal area "behind" or to the south and southwest of the Museum. Though it appears to be in front of the building today and thus misnamed, when the building was originally constructed, the primary road through the area passed between the museum and Porcelain Basin (the asphalt along the shelf above Black Growler is a remnant of this old road). Until 1967 when the new bypass opened, visitors entered the museum on the other side and so the side that appears as the "front" of the museum today was at that time its rear. Consequently, the area behind the museum was given the moniker "Back Basin." Even though the entrance has been reversed, the name was left intact due to historical deference.

The basin is home to some 70 thermal features, all but a few of which have been given names. Some of the more popular features include Echinus Geyser, Porkchop Geyser (which blew itself out in 1989 and is now just a hot spring), Tantalus Geyser (named after the creek that drains the area), Puff and Stuff Geyser, Veteran Geyser, and Black Hermit's Caldron.

Back Basin is also home to the world's largest geyser, Steamboat. This huge geyser erupts to heights of almost 400 feet when it is active. Throughout the recorded history of the park, however, its eruptions have been wildly varied and completely unpredictable. It has gone as long as 50 years without erupting, but has also had periods of multiple eruptions over the course of several weeks. It erupted in August of 2013 for the first time since 2005.

One Hundred Spring Plain is a huge thermal field located northwest of Porcelain Basin. It is home to over 270 individual thermal features, less than a dozen of which have official names. There are no trails or boardwalks that lead to this area because it is simply too volatile and dangerous to build them. That is a shame because there are some rather unique features located in that area. There is a pullout that affords an overlook out onto the plain, however, along the Norris to Mammoth Road (see the entry at 1.6/19.3 in that section).

There are trail guides available at the museum and in the bookstore that provide detailed explanations of why Norris is a volatile as it is, as well as descriptions of many of the more popular features found in the area. T. Scott Bryan's book, *The Geysers of Yellowstone*, also has a wealth of information about the geysers and other thermal features in this area.

The Norris Museum was constructed in 1930 using a grant from the Laura Spelman Rockefeller Foundation, the same fund that paid for the museums at Madison, Fishing Bridge, and the original one at Old Faithful (torn down in 1972). The open air exhibit provides information about Yellowstone's geothermal geology and the microscopic life that can be found in the park's thermal pools. During the summer, an interpretive ranger is usually stationed in the area to assist visitors and answer questions. The far eastern side of the building houses an office used by the rangers who work at the museum.

There is a small Yellowstone Association Bookstore here as well. This building was originally a comfort station (bathroom) for the area, built in 1982. It was used until the late 1990s, when the old wastewater treatment system for this complex collapsed, requiring the NPS to close all the bathrooms. Vault toilets were used until the new wastewater treatment plant was completed in 2006. At that time, the 1930s-era comfort station was restored to service and the 1982 building was converted into the bookstore.

Steam Valve Spring can be found behind (south) of this building. Interestingly, the NPS has tried to plug this spring at least twice with asphalt (it sits in the middle of an old parking lot). It keeps springing back to life, however.

0.2 / 11.4 GPS: 44.72679, -110.69245
NORRIS WASTEWATER TREATMENT PLANT SERVICE ROAD (S)
NORRIS GOVERNMENT AREA (N)

The **Norris Government Area** dates to the 1920s when a road camp was constructed here. It served as a road camp until the 1960s, when it was converted to a service and maintenance area. Today it houses NPS employees and maintenance facilities.

The **Norris Wastewater Treatment Plant** was built in 2006, replacing several smaller disposal systems in use at the time, many of which had failed or were on the verge of failing. The plant processes waste generated by the comfort station and small office at the museum, as well as the Norris Government Area and the Norris Campground. The large patch of land you see to the east of the service road is the plant's subsurface disposal field. The small shed at the south end of the field houses monitoring equipment.

0.4 / 11.2 GPS: 44.72670, -110.68850
GIBBON RIVER CROSSING

The Gibbon River crosses from the south side to the north side of the road here. The bridge (culvert, really) was constructed in 1966 with the re-engineering of the road system in this area.

0.5 / 11.0 GPS: 44.72698, -110.68598
NORRIS MEADOWS PICNIC AREA (N) 🎑 👫 👪

The **Norris Meadows Picnic Area** has 16 tables and 4 grills, as well as a handicap-accessible vault toilet. The meadow itself is a great place to observe wildlife, including the sandhill crane.

This picnic area used to be known as the Gibbon River Picnic Area, and was once the site of a camp operated by a short-lived camping company called the Old Faithful Camping Company. When all of the camping companies were consolidated into the Yellowstone Park Camping Company in 1917, they continued the "Norris Auto Camp" (with a capacity of about 60 cars in 1923) for a number of years afterward. The road through here was part of the original Norris Junction complex until 1967.

0.8 / 10.8 GPS: 44.72503, -110.68073
NORRIS PIT/ASPHALT PLANT SERVICE ROAD (S)

The **Norris Pit** on the south side of the road is used to stage and stockpile construction and road materials. NPS and various contractors often operate an asphalt hot mix plant here as well during major road construction projects on the west side of the park.

1.3 / 10.2 GPS: 44.72148, -110.67199
ELECTRICAL SUBSTATION SERVICE ROAD (S)

The **Norris Electrical Substation** is the primary distribution point for electricity to the southern half of the park. A distribution line comes from Mammoth to this substation, and then splits out into two branches. One of these transmits electricity to Canyon, Fishing Bridge, Lake, Bridge Bay, West Thumb and Grant Village, while the other transmits electricity to Madison and then on to the Old Faithful area. As there is no connector between Old Faithful and Grant Village (and thus, no loop), a cut at any place along any of these lines shuts off everything downstream.

1.6 / 9.9 GPS: 44.71913, -110.66621
VIRGINIA CASCADE DRIVE (S) 🄿 👬 🌲

This two mile scenic side trip takes you along the Gibbon River to view the 60-foot Virginia Cascade. The cascade is named after the wife of Charles Gibson, president of the Yellowstone Park Association, which owned and operated many of the park's hotels from the mid-1880s on (and would later morph into the Yellowstone Park Company, the park's primary concessioner).[2]

Virginia Cascade Drive was (largely) part of the original road between Norris and Canyon. In 1962, however, the new bypass (the existing main road) was constructed as part of the Mission 66 Program, and the old road was left intact as a scenic road. See the Miscellaneous Roads section for a road log and more details about this road.

3.1 / 8.5 GPS: 44.71728, -110.63959
FIRES OF 1988 BOARDWALK TRAIL (S) 🚶

The boardwalk takes you through an area burned intensely in the 1988 fires. Downed trees from a microburst that occurred in July of 1984 contributed to the intensity of the fires.[3] The area was heavily scorched, but the fire opened the serotinous cones of the lodgepole pines, resulting in the very robust forest growth you see here now.

There are parking pullouts on both side of the road, but use caution if you're crossing over to/from the north. The road between Norris and Canyon has some of the highest speeding rates in the park.

3.2 / 8.4 GPS: 44.71644, -110.63724
ICE LAKE QUARRY SERVICE ROAD (N)

The **Ice Lake Quarry Service Road**, usually closed by three or four large boulders, leads to an area the NPS once used to quarry large rocks for road construction projects around the park. The quarry is a large depression where a hilltop was removed through the quarrying of gravel. Much of this material was used to build the bypass roads around Norris Junction and Virginia Cascades. The area is now used as a dumping ground for construction debris.

3.4 / 8.2 GPS: 44.71668, -110.63384
ICE LAKE TRAILHEAD (N) 🚶 ♿

The **Ice Lake Trail** is an easy ½-mile hike north to Ice Lake, and is one of the few trails easily accessible to those in wheelchairs. Ice Lake gets its name from the fact that it served as a source for blocks of ice for the hotels and lunch stations in the Norris area in the park's early days.

There are three backcountry campsites adjacent to the lake, including 4D3, which is one of only two handicap-accessible sites in the park (the other is OD5 located at Goose Lake - see the Miscellaneous Roads section for more details).

3.5 / 8.0 GPS: 44.71499, -110.63150
EXIT FROM VIRGINIA CASCADES DRIVE (S)

This is the exit from Virginia Cascade Drive. The large meadow to the southeast of the intersection is known as Virginia Meadow; it was the site of an NPS Road Camp in the 1910s-1930s.

3.7 / 7.8 GPS: 44.71314, -110.62813
WOLF LAKE CUTOFF TRAILHEAD (LITTLE GIBBON FALLS) 🏃
BLANDING HILL

The **Wolf Lake Cutoff Trail** (also known simply as the Wolf Lake Trail) will take you to Wolf Lake approximately two miles north via the Howard Eaton/Chain of Lakes Trail. A few yards in from the trailhead is a ¾-mile spur that leads to Little Gibbon Falls, a 25-foot waterfall on the Gibbon River. There is no sign or board notifying you of the trailhead here. Park on the south side of the road and look for the little orange trail marker on one of the trees on the north side of the road. Be careful crossing the road.

As you leave the turnout heading east, you'll cross the Gibbon River once again, and then begin climbing **Blanding Hill**, the steepest grade (8%) of any part of the Grand Loop Road. As you do so, you're climbing out of the Yellowstone Caldera onto the Solfatara Plateau. As part of the Mission 66 Program, the road up Blanding Hill was relocated northward during the late 1950s as to alleviate the need to climb an even steeper grade. The hill was named for James Blanding, the construction supervisor who oversaw the building of this section of the road in 1885.

5.5 / 6.1 GPS: 44.70352, -110.59640
NATURALLY-RESEEDED AREA TURNOUT (N)

Another area where the 1988 fires burned through, destroying many of the old growth trees. The trees here now are approaching 25 years old and are natural regrowth from the cones opened during those 1988 fires.

6.7 / 4.9 GPS: 44.70593, -110.57313
CYGNET LAKES TRAILHEAD (S) 🏃

Cygnet Lakes are a series of five small lakes on the Central Plateau south of the trailhead. They were given the name because a park naturalist observed trumpeter swans nesting on one of the lakes (cygnets are baby swans). The trail itself is almost five miles (8.0 km, one way) long, and is for day-use only.

7.5 /4.1 GPS: 44.71244, -110.55803
OLD ROADBED (S) [EASTBOUND ONLY]

On the south side of the road, you'll notice a berm and a path where the trees are smaller than those surrounding them. This is an old roadbed that used to take travelers from Norris to the Canyon area. It comes out at the Electrical Substation Road on the Canyon to Fishing Bridge Road 1.6 miles (2.6 km) south of today's Canyon Junction. The road was rerouted northward and then eastward to align it with the new Canyon Junction built as part of the Canyon Village development in the late 1950s.

You can hike along the old roadway for a distance of about two miles. You'll pass behind the Grebe Lake Service Pit (see below) and come up to the west side of a carcass disposal area. From this point eastward to the junction at the Grand Loop Road south of Canyon, the road is closed to public travel due to bear safety issues.

It was on this now closed section of road, approximately three miles west of the Grand Loop Road, the park's second stagecoach robbery took place on August 14, 1897. Two robbers waylaid six stagecoaches and a U. S. Army ambulance. They managed to get away with about $630 in cash and valuables, but were later apprehended and sentenced to two years in federal prison.

7.7 / 3.9 GPS: 44.71387, -110.55564
SOLFATARA PLATEAU THERMAL AREA (N & S)
OLD SERVICE ROADBED (S)

The main road here passes through a largely extinct concentration of old thermal features that has no official name, but it usually referred to as the **Solfatara Plateau Thermal Area**. The field contains mostly old fumaroles and dried hot springs, and you can often catch a strong smell of hydrogen sulfide as you drive through it. There are approximately 250 unnamed thermal features on both sides of the road, though most tend to be concentrated on the south side.

Also on the south side of the road you can make out the faint remains of an old road that used to be part of the Canyon area road system. This old road used to go from the original highway (the roadbed of which parallels the existing road to the south) up to Grebe Lake where a major fish hatchery operation was located from 1931 until the mid-1950s (see below). The road was obliterated when the current bypass was built in the late 1950s.

8.1 / 3.5 GPS: 44.71714, -110.54955
GREBE LAKE TRAILHEAD (N) 🚶

The **Grebe Lake Trail** is a three-mile (5 km) trail to Grebe Lake, named for a duck. This lake and Wolf Lake are considered the headwaters for the Gibbon River, and are popular spots for summer waterfowl.

From 1941 until the mid-1960s, Grebe Lake was the site of a fish hatchery operated by the U.S. Fish and Wildlife Service. It was a field hatchery to the main one near the Lake Hotel and sought primarily grayling eggs. Operations ceased in 1958, but the structure wasn't removed until the mid-1960s. Today no sign of the hatchery operation remains.

If you continue around to the north side of the lake, the trail connects into a section of the old Howard Eaton Trail. From that point, if you head east you'll make it to Cascade Lake, or can take the trail to Observation Peak, one of the old fire lookout towers for the park. If you head west, you'll find yourself at Wolf Lake, Ice Lake, and if you continue on to its end, the Solfatara Creek Trail just north of the Norris Campground.

8.4 / 3.2 GPS: 44.71728, -110.54404
Grebe Lake Pit Service Road (S)

Also known as the Crystal Falls Pit or Crystal Falls Service Road Pit, the **Grebe Lake Pit** is a large construction equipment and material staging and storage area. Hiking or bicycling along the front entrance road is prohibited for safety reasons (lots of heavy equipment moving around).

8.9 / 2.6 GPS: 44.72004, -110.53286
Old Service Road (N)
Canyon Hill

There's an old service road running north out of the pullout here. If you're traveling eastbound, you'll shortly begin descending **Canyon Hill** into the Canyon Village area.

11.1 / 0.5 GPS: 44.73517, -110.50361
Cascade Creek Trailhead (N) [🥾]

The **Cascade Creek Trail** is a 2.5-mile (4 km) trail to Cascade Lake. The lake is the headwater for Cascade Creek, which was at one time the source of potable water for the Canyon area. You can also access the Observation Peak Trail from this trailhead, as well as the Howard Eaton Trail that leads in a westerly direction and will take you to Grebe, Wolf, and Ice Lakes, and then on to the Solfatara Creek Trail north of the Norris Campground. This stretch of the Howard Eaton Trail is often referred to as the Chain of Lakes Trails because it connects the four lakes.

If you're heading west, you'll shortly begin climbing Canyon Hill and head up onto the Solfatara Plateau.

11.2 / 0.4 GPS: 44.73578, -110.50099
CASCADE CREEK CROSSING
CASCADE MEADOW (S)

Cascade Creek crosses under the road here, flowing southward through the meadow, across the Canyon to Fishing Bridge Road, and then falling over the edge of the Grand Canyon of the Yellowstone as Crystal Falls (visible from just off the Uncle Tom Trailhead parking lot).

Cascade Meadows was site of a road camp prior to the camp being moved north of the highway to the site of present day government area (see below). Just south of here on the creek was an impoundment that siphoned water off for the old Canyon Hotel.

1.3 / 0.2 GPS: 44.73608, -110.49834
CANYON GOVERNMENT AREA SERVICE ROAD (N)

The **Canyon Government Area** is a maintenance and housing area for NPS and concession employees. The complex began its life in 1939 as a road camp for the Bureau of Public Roads, built in anticipation of the development of the new Canyon Village, originally slated to begin in the mid-1940s. This new camp replaced the one that had been located south of the old Canyon Hotel (see 2.1/13.2 in the Canyon to Fishing Bridge section).

11.5 / 0.0 GPS: 44.73591 -110.49325 ELEVATION: 7924 FEET
CANYON JUNCTION 🏕 ⚕ ♨ ⛺ 🍴 ⑦ 🅿 🛏 ✉ ⛽ ♻ 🍴 📷 🎣 🧺

Canyon Village, though constructed during the Mission 66 program in the 1957-1959 time frame, was proposed as far back as the late 1930s.

From the junction, you can drive through into Canyon Village, head north for 18.3 miles (29.5 km) to Tower Junction, south for 15.4 miles (24.8 km) to Fishing Bridge, or west 11.5 miles (18.5 km) to Norris Junction.

Norris Junction
to
Mammoth Hot Springs
————————⊳o⌒⌒⌒o⊲————————

The road from Norris Junction to Mammoth Hot Springs is 21 miles (33.8 km) long and is perhaps the least driver-friendly stretch of highway in Yellowstone at the present time. The section from Norris Campground to Golden Gate is scheduled to be completely rebuilt between 2014 and 2020, however. If you visit the park during this time period, be prepared for the occasional delays during the summer, and periodic road closures during the latter parts of the season.

The northern end of this road was originally constructed in 1878 as part of a road to connect Mammoth and the North Entrance with the only other entrance to the park at the time, that coming from Virginia City to near what is today's Madison Junction. The original road ran up Clematis Gulch, through Snow Pass and up onto Swan Lake Flat, then southward to today's Solfatara Creek Trail Trailhead, where it proceeded southeasterly past Lake of the Woods and along the Solfatara Creek to the site of the present Norris Campground. Most of these old roadbeds exist as trails today.

In 1885, the U.S. Army Corps of Engineers (USACE), under the direction of Lt. Dan Kingman, rebuilt the road and realigned it from Beaver Lake south to Norris along what is basically the existing route, primarily because the land was much more suitable for use as a roadbed. And while the road has been resurfaced and repaired over the years, it has not been rebuilt to current road standards. As a result, there are no shoulders and very few pullouts for use by slower moving vehicles. The lack of any shoulder has contributed to a great many rollover accidents as drivers will occasionally lose control of their vehicles when one or more wheels drops off the pavement and overcorrect as they attempt to regain control. These wrecks often lead to serious injuried or even fatalities, and close the road for hours.

You likely won't see too many bison or elk along this stretch of road, but it is quite popular with grizzly bears and the occasional black bear, especially the northern 10 miles (16 km) or so. At one time it was also rather common to see moose in the bogs of Willow Park, but in the aftermath of the fires of 1988, they've all but abandoned this area. Given the relative dearth of pullouts and the narrowness of the road surface, the traffic jams caused by any sighting can be rather lengthy.

The road itself is in very poor condition, marked with potholes and frost heaves, especially during the first half of the summer before the road crews can get out and patch it up. There are vault toilets located at the Beaver Lake and Apollinaris Spring Picnic Areas, the Sheepeater Cliff area, at one of the Willow Park turnouts about 10 miles (16 km) south of Mammoth, and at the Indian Creek Campground.

0.0 / 21.0 GPS: 44.72734, -110.69657 ELEVATION: 7536 FEET
NORRIS JUNCTION ⊞ ⑦ 大 ⛺

From here, you can drive 13.3 miles (21.4 km) south to Madison Junction, 11.6 miles (18.7 km) east to Canyon Junction, or 21 miles (33.8 km) north to Mammoth Hot Springs.

0.7 / 20.3 GPS: 44.73659, -110.69766
CAVALRY AT YELLOWSTONE TURNOUT (E) ※ (
NORRIS MEADOWS (E)
SITE OF OLD NORRIS HOTELS/LUNCH STATION (W)

This turnout has an interpretive display that discusses the role of the Cavalry in protecting Yellowstone National Park. The building you see to the northeast across the river is now the Museum of the National Park Ranger, but was originally one of the soldier stations the U.S. Army erected to house soldiers who patrolled the park (see below). The large expanse of open grassland to the east of this turnout is known as **Norris Meadows**, and was the home to an encampment of soldiers each summer until 1915.

Across the highway from this turnout, on the slight hill, was the location of the first two structures known as the **Norris Hotels**. The first was constructed in 1886, and then burned to the ground on July 14, 1887, when someone started a fire in a fireplace for which the chimney hadn't been extended through the roof. That three-story structure could host approximately 300 guests. Subsequent to the fire, a small ramshackle building and a tent camp were constructed on the site occupied by the parking area now (which, at the time, was still part of the hill on the west side of today's road). This second "hotel" would remain the only accommodation in the area until 1892 when, it, too, would burn.

On the site immediately adjacent to the latest structural casualty, a new lunch station was constructed. The **Norris Lunch Station** had a few rooms (tents) for guests and was open from 1892 until 1901, when a third Norris Hotel was opened in the Porcelain Basin. This new structure had 25 rooms and remained operational until 1917 when it closed for the same reason the Fountain Hotel in the Lower Geyser Basin closed – automobiles had rendered these hotels obsolete. The third hotel would remain as an abandoned hulk until it was razed in 1927.

Some occupational debris from the first hotel remains on the hill here, but the site of the third hotel is not visible from the road and lies in a closed area inaccessible to non-NPS personnel.

Approximately 1000 feet south of the south end of this turnout was where the original (1902) road through this area forked. If you were traveling south and wished to head east to the Canyon area, you took the east fork (a segment of this old road is the entrance driveway for today's Norris Meadow Picnic Area). If you wanted to continue on to the Norris Basin, or further south to Gibbon Falls or the geyser basins, you took the west fork. At that time, and up until 1967, the road ran right through the middle of the Norris Geyser Basin. See the chapter on the Norris Junction to Canyon Junction for more details. In 1966-1967, as part of the construction of the bypass around the geyser basin, this hill was cut out, and the existing road was built through the area.

As you continue to head north from here, you pass over the Gibbon River once again on a bridge constructed as part of the Mission 66 Program in 1960.

0.8 / 20.1 GPS: 44.73857, -110.69942
NORRIS CAMPGROUND (E) △ ⛺ ⌂ ▨ 🚶
MUSEUM OF THE NATIONAL PARK RANGER (E)
NORRIS HILL (E)

Norris Campground is one of the seven campgrounds operated by the National Park Service within Yellowstone (the other five are operated by park concessioner Xanterra). It has 116 campsites which are available on a first-come, first-served basis (reservations not accepted). The daily rate for 2014 is $20. The campground has comfort stations with flush toilets, but no showers.

The small ranger station located here was originally one of the barns for the Solider Station (now the Ranger Museum). It was remodeled into a house/ranger station in 1963 when the campground was built.

The **Solfatara Creek South Trailhead** is located at the dead end of the entrance road, just as the drive for Loop C departs to the north (the north end is at 7.1/13.9 on this road; see below).

The **Museum of the National Park Ranger** is an old Soldier Station constructed by the U.S. Army in 1908, the third building at this site.[1] It was one of 14 original outposts used by the military to protect the park's resources when it assumed control of Yellowstone from the Department of Interior in 1886. The original building here was constructed on this site in 1884 as a mail station. It was replaced in 1897 by a two-story structure that housed soldiers, and then in 1908 by this facility.

The building housed a contingent of five soldiers until the army left in 1916. From that point, it was used to house seasonal rangers in the Norris area until the Hebgen Lake Earthquake damaged the structure in 1959. In 1976, it was taken down and rebuilt using as much of the original materials as possible. From then until a complete renovation in 1990-1991, the building remained vacant. Today, it houses exhibits related to the rangers that serve and protect our national parks, and is well worth a visit. It is staffed by retired NPS rangers.

The hill immediately to the north of the junction here is known as **Norris Hill**.

1.2 / 19.8 GPS: 44.74125, -110.70540
OLD ROAD BED - SOUTH END (E) [NORTHBOUND ONLY]

You'll have to look quickly, and may only see a faint hint of it, but look for a slot in the taller trees that runs to the north here. This is the south end of an old segment of road used by early autos in the 1920s.

1.5 / 19.4 GPS: 44.74177, -110.71195
PORCELAIN BASIN OVERLOOK (W) 👤

This unimproved turnout affords an overlook of the **Porcelain Basin** area (to the south). The basin (with over 200 identified features, 40 of which have official names) gets its name from the milky-white geyserite that covers the ground throughout much of the area.[2]

1.6 / 19.3 GPS: 44.74311, -110.71309
ONE HUNDRED SPRING PLAIN OVERLOOK (W) 🏛

This unimproved (and usually very potholed) turnout affords an overlook of the **One Hundred Spring Plain** area of the Norris Geyser Basin. The area was given its name in the late 1880s by the U.S. Geological Survey for an estimate of the number of hot springs that could be found here (the number actually approaches 250, about 10 of which have official names).[3]

1.7 / 19.2 GPS: 44.74433, -110.71340
OLD ROAD BED - NORTH END (E)

On the east side of the road, running off to the southeast, you can see the north end of the old road bed referenced at 1.2/19.8 above.

2.2 / 18.8 GPS: 44.75064, -110.71633
HAZLE LAKE (W)

According to park historian Lee Whittlesey, **Hazle Lake** was given its name for its color in 1888 by tour guide George L. Henderson, who misspelled the word "hazel." Some tour guides call it Copper Lake, and for a time it was known as "Coelitus Lake" [sic] as the result of some poor gentleman losing his lunch here.[4]

2.6 / 18.4 GPS: 44.75240, -110.72231
FRYING PAN SPRING (E) 🔥

Frying Pan Spring is named for its appearance – the sizzling, bubbling water mimics hot grease in a frying pan. The water is not boiling, however. Escaping hydrogen sulfide gas is responsible for those little bubbles (and the smell!). Originally called Devil's Frying Pan, the pH of this spring is around 2.5 according to the park's thermal features database.[5] The entire area here is composed of about 10 springs, all of which are unnamed except for Frying Pan (which, officially at least, is the spring on the east side of the road). Frying Pan Creek drains this area into Nymph Lake (see below).

2.7 / 18.3 GPS: 44.75367, -110.72473
NYMPH LAKE (W)
ROADSIDE SPRINGS (W)

Nymph Lake is named for a genus of water lily found within the park (*Nymphaea*, which itself is named for a mythical Greek water fairy).[6] The lake's water is very acidic (pH < 5.0). It is believed to have been formed by a thermal explosion, and many consider it a large thermal pool rather than a true lake. The creek that flows out of the north end of the lake is known as Flood Creek, and the little collection of hot springs around the northeast end of the lake between it and the road is known as **Roadside Springs**.

3.3 / 17.6 GPS: 44.76129, -110.73041
BIJAH SPRING (W)

Bijah Spring is a small, slightly alkaline (pH= 7.5) spring off the west side of the road. Historians do not know how or why this spring was given its name (perhaps a modification or distortion of the word *bijou*, which means jewel or trinket in French). There is not yet a pullout here, so you'll have to sneak a quick peek at it as you drive by.

4.1 / 16.9 GPS: 44.77216, -110.73346
SOUTH TWIN LAKE (W)

The Twin Lakes were once one lake, but are now separated by an old beaver dam upon which trees and other foliage are growing. Interestingly, **South Twin Lake** freezes over in the winter while the North Twin Lake often does not. This is because the northern lake is fed by thermal springs.

4.4 / 16.6 GPS: 44.77581, -110.73685
NORTH TWIN LAKE (W)

North Twin Lake sits several feet higher in elevation than its southern twin. This lake drains via a small stream known as Flood Creek through its smaller twin to the south, and then through Bijah Spring and Nymph Lake before emptying into the Gibbon River west of Porcelain Basin.

4.9 / 16.1 GPS: 44.78107, -110.74092
ROARING MOUNTAIN (E) ⛟
LEMONADE LAKE (E)

Roaring Mountain was given its name in 1885 by the U.S. Geological Survey. In the park's early days, steam escaping from the fumaroles located on its 400-ft western face produced a loud "roar" that could be heard for miles. Many visitors today often wonder why the name exists since there's little, if any, noise emanating from its features.

The usually dry lake bed at the foot of the mountain is known as **Lemonade Lake** for the yellowish color of the water that can occasionally be found pooled there.

5.3 / 15.7 GPS: 44.78658, -110.73936
Obsidian Creek Pullout (W)
Semi-Centennial Geyser (W)

Semi-Centennial Geyser is the northernmost geyser in the park, and was given its name because its first large eruption occurred during the celebration of the park's 50th anniversary in 1922. Eruptions as high as 300 feet washed out the road and killed trees for hundreds of feet in all directions. Though it continued to erupt for a couple of months afterward, it has been largely dormant since late 1922. The geyser is hard to pick out if you don't know what you're looking for (it's the large dark pool through which Obsidian Creek flows).

Obsidian Creek gets its name from its proximity to Obsidian Cliff (see below). In the early days of the park's history, it was known as Willow Creek for the presence of the willow in the meadows (esp. Willow Park) through which it runs. The creek was originally planned to host the first fish hatchery in the park, but the decision was made to locate it in the West Thumb area instead.

5.4 / 15.6 GPS: 44.78784, -110.738674
Clearwater Springs (W)

This small pullout affords access to the small **Clearwater Springs** area, which consists of about 16 unnamed hot springs along Obsidian Creek. They were given their name for the fact that they do not deposit any kind of mineral material, unlike most other springs. They range in pH from 5.5 to well over 8.0.

If you walk out into this area, be sure you stay on the existing trails. Several people have been burned by stepping into one of the springs hidden by the grass.

6.0 / 15.0 GPS: 44.79586, -110.74086
Brickyard Hill (W)

The hill on the west side of the road here, just before you enter the almost 90-degree bend to the west (or behind you as you come out of the bend and head south if you're driving toward Norris) is known as **Brickyard Hill**. The hill's name was derived from colloquial use as a result of it being the source for clay for bricks used to construct buildings in the Mammoth area in the late 1890s (most notably fireplaces in many of the Fort Yellowstone buildings).

6.3 / 14.7 GPS: 44.79886, -110.74514
GRIZZLY LAKE TRAILHEAD (W) 🚶

The **Grizzly Lake Trail** is an almost two-mile (3 km) trail to Grizzly Lake, a gorgeous mountain lake named for one of the most feared and most revered creatures in the park. There is an overnight camp located near the lake if you wish to make an overnight stay of it (located about ½ mile north along Straight Creek). You can also connect into the Mt. Holmes Trail if you hike out an additional 1.5 miles (2.4 km).

7.1 / 13.9 GPS: 44.80661, -110.73549
SOLFATARA CREEK TRAIL - NORTH TRAILHEAD (E) 🚶

The **Solfatara Creek Trail** (or Solfatara Trail) is a 6.5-mile (10.5 km) trail with its south trailhead at the Norris Campground. This trail takes you up a steep hill known as Green Creek Hill (Lemonade Creek, which runs alongside this trail, was originally known as Green Creek for the color of its water), by Lake of the Woods and the small Amphitheater Springs and Whiterock Springs Thermal Areas, and through Norris Valley before continuing along Solfatara Creek to the campground (exiting at Loop C). Much of the southern half of this trail is unmaintained.

The trail generally follows what was the first road through this area, one that departed from the current road at Lemonade Creek a few feet up the road (see below). Built in 1878, the road (bridle path, really) immediately ascended Hibbard's Pass (named for a mountaineer friend of Superintendent P. W. Norris), took visitors along what has come to be known as Lake of the Woods Road, and then came back out at the east end of the present day Norris Campground. The entire road from Mammoth to Norris was known, not surprisingly, as the "Norris Road."

In 1885, a newer road suitable for stagecoach use was built approximately halfway between this road and today's road. This road was used until the current alignment was constructed by the U.S. Army Corps of Engineers in 1902. This latest route was selected primarily because the soil was more favorable for road development, and it got more sun in the early part of the season allowing the snowfall to melt off before traffic needed to use it.

7.2 / 13.7 GPS: 44.80796, -110.73379
LEMONADE CREEK CROSSING

Lemonade Creek originates in Amphitheater Springs, a small thermal area of about 40 unnamed springs southeast of this location. The water is very sour and acidic, and not suitable for drinking. It was given its name for the light green color of the water (likely due to the presence of sulfur). The creek drains into Obsidian Creek.

This was also the site of one of the emergency public phones for some time (west side of the road). Following the 1970 accident of a fuel oil truck in the curve known as "Tanker Curve," emergency phones were installed at several locations around the park to allow visitors to report emergencies without having to drive several miles to find a phone.

7.5 / 13.5 GPS: 44.81087, -110.73142
BEAVER LAKE PICNIC AREA (W) 🌲 🚻

The **Beaver Lake Picnic Area** has nine tables and a vault toilet, and is handicap-accessible. It gets its name from the lake just to its north. The lake was formed when a series of beaver dams was constructed on it, and it is the most acidic lake in the park (pH=5.1) to contain fish (brook trout).

A half dozen or so hot springs of the Amphitheater Springs Thermal Area are located on the hill across the road from the entry to the picnic area. These are perhaps the source of the lake's acidity. This area was home to a road camp during the U.S. Army days, as this was at the junction of the current road and the original Lake of the Woods Road.

8.2 / 12.8 GPS: 44.82174, -110.72832
OBSIDIAN CLIFF (E)

Obsidian is a natural glass that was formed when volcanic lava was cooled instantly, allowing few crystals to form in it. This particular mountain was used by a variety of different Native American tribes to provide materials for arrowheads and other tools. In fact, material from this cliff has been found as far away as Ohio and Georgia.[7] At one time the mountain was a distinct black color. Today, however, lichens growing on its surface have dulled its finish. **Obsidian Cliff** is 200 feet (61 m) high.

8.4 / 12.5 GPS: 44.82418, -110.72899
OBSIDIAN CLIFF TURNOUT (W) ⬚
OBSIDIAN CREEK CROSSING

This interpretive kiosk, which itself is on the National Register of Historic Places, tells the story of Obsidian Cliff. The exhibit structure was added in 1931, though it has been rehabilitated a couple of times. **Obsidian Creek** crosses under the roadway just south of the turnout.

8.9 / 12.1 GPS: 44.83110, -110.72811
OBSIDIAN CANYON
CRYSTAL SPRINGS (E)

You are traveling through the small **Obsidian Canyon** named for the creek which flows through it.

There's a series of small cold springs on the east side of the road here known collectively as **Crystal Springs**. The name was given because it was used as a watering hole for thirsty travelers in the early days of the park ("crystal clear water...").[8]

In the 1890s, a U.S. Army Patrol Cabin was constructed in this area. It was replaced with a newer cabin in 1927, but that structure was later relocated to Three Rivers Junction in the southwest corner of the park, where it is still used today as one of the backcountry patrol cabins.[9]

9.2 / 11.7 GPS: 44.83554, -110.73046
LILYPAD POND (E)

This small, seasonal body of water is known as **Lilypad Pond**, so named for the presence of lilypads during much of the time it contains water.

9.5 / 11.6 GPS: 44.83827, -110.73231
MT. HOLMES TRAILHEAD (W) 🚶 🐎

The **Mount Holmes Trail** is a 19-mile (30 km) round-trip trail that takes you to the summit of the tallest mountain in the Gallatin Range (10336 ft/3150 m), and one of the taller mountains in this part of the park. The reward is an incredible view from the top of the peak. While it is possible to make a day hike of this, many people elect to overnight at one of the campsites along the way (remember to check in with one of the Backcountry Offices to reserve a campsite before beginning the hike).

Mt. Holmes is home to one of the park's three primary fire lookouts. The tower was constructed in 1931, and is no longer staffed during the summer, its lookouts having been replaced by remote-controlled, wireless video cameras. The other two lookouts are on Mt. Sheridan (also typically unstaffed), and Mt. Washburn. One of the NPS' primary radio repeater sites is also located at the summit.

You can also reach Trilobite Lake on the northeastern flank of Mt. Holmes. This is a 14.5-mile (23 km) round trip.

9.8 / 11.2 GPS: 44.84250, -110.73353
APOLLINARIS SPRING (E) ⬏⁕

You might miss **Apollinaris Spring** as you drive by it, and there's no place to stop for it on the road except for a tiny, one-vehicle gravel pullout across the street from it. Your best bet is to stop at the picnic area just to the north and walk across the street.

Apollinaris Spring was believed by early visitors to the park to provide health benefits, since the water contains a variety of chemicals and minerals (calcium, silica, sodium bicarbonate, potassium chloride, etc.). Current park historian Lee Whittlesey states the name comes from a German spring which produced waters with similar mineral content, but former park historian Aubrey Haines believed the name came from the Middle Ages and had nothing to do with the German water. The steps and sitting area were constructed in 1925 using limestone from the Hoodoos just south of Mammoth Hot Springs.[10]

9.9 / 11.1 GPS: 44.84412, -110.73436
APOLLINARIS SPRING PICNIC AREA (W) 🍽 🚻

The **Apollinaris Spring Picnic Area** (named for its proximity to the spring across the highway) has six tables and a handicap-accessible vault toilet. There's also an old "comfort station" here that had running water, though it may be shut down and/or removed from the area soon. The station was constructed in 1931, and it was used as the model for all of the remaining (wooden) comfort stations built in the years that followed, many of which are still in service.[11] The water for the comfort station and spigots comes from an underground pipe run across the road from the spring itself. If you choose to visit the spring across the highway, use caution as you cross the road.

Just to the north of the picnic area, across the large meadow along the west side of the road, the Wylie Camping Company opened a tent camp from 1898 to 1906 (with a capacity of 60 people). In 1907, they relocated the camp further north to near Swan Lake due to the heavy mosquito population here during the summer. From 1910 to 1916, the area housed an encampment of U.S. Army soldiers during the summers.

In later years, from 1925 through 1935, the Yellowstone Park Camps Company operated a small auto camp here (with a capacity of about 40 cars). In 1936, the area was converted to a picnic area, a purpose it has served ever since.

10.4 / 10.6 GPS: 44.85088, -110.73587
Moose Bogs Turnout (W) 🏕

This turnout provides an interpretive display about the moose often found grazing in the Willow Park area.

This used to be the site of the old Winter Creek Picnic Area, which had six tables; it was removed in the late 1970s. Winter Creek drains into Obsidian Creek in the meadow west of the turnout.

10.5 / 10.5 GPS: 44.85331, -110.73591
Willow Park (W)

Willow Park was named for the prevalence of the willow bushes in the area and is a favorite hangout for moose. It extends for about a mile to the north from this area.

The large expanse of flat land was used as an "unofficial" camping site during the park's early days and then from 1913 to 1916 as a site for the Shaw and Powell Camping Company camp. It was closed in 1916 subsequent to the automobiles being allowed into the park, but many of the buildings remained until 1946.[12] The moose love this area for the willows and the moss in Obsidian Creek that drains the area.

11.1 / 9.9 GPS: 44.86150, -110.73647
Mid Willow Park Turnout (W) 🚻

This pullout is remarkable for the presence of a random vault toilet if for no other reason (it's roughly half way between Mammoth and Norris). If you're heading south, this pullout comes up without warning. The large flat meadow to the west of the pullout is Willow Park.

12.5 / 8.5 GPS: 44.88078, -110.73400
Indian Creek Campground (W) △ 🚻
Bighorn Pass East Trailhead (W) 🥾

The **Indian Creek Campground** is located at the south end of Swan Lake Flat (see description below), and is named for its proximity to Indian Creek, which in turn was named because the Bannock Indian Trail generally followed its banks. Many visitors assume the creek that runs in front of (on the east side) the campground is Indian Creek, but it is actually Obsidian Creek. The Gardner River passes by to the north, and Indian Creek itself is located a half mile to the northwest of the campground.

The campground has 75 sites available on a first-come, first-serve basis (no reservations), along with seven vault toilets. Generators are not permitted in this campground, and the daily rate for 2014 is $15. During the winter, the NPS operates a Warming Hut here.

From 1906 to 1916, this area was home to a campground operated by one of the park's early concessioners, the Wylie Permanent Camping Company (having relocated to this site from a previous site at Apollinaris Spring). The camp was abandoned in 1917 with the consolidation of all of the camping companies into a single entity.[13] This camp had been the first in the park to feature flush toilets.

There was also a small, special use campground to the west of the old Wylie Camp known as the "Superintendent's Campground." It was reserved for special occasions and use by VIPs with the permission of the park superintendent.

The tent camp was no longer needed once automobiles were allowed into the park and these kinds of facilities were replaced by the likes of the Mammoth Lodge, which would be built some four years later near the present day Mammoth Corrals. The campground was abandoned for a period of time and its facilities razed (though one building did survive into the 1960s). The NPS would later convert this area into the campground you see today.

The small one-lane bridge on the entry road is one of only two bridges remaining in the park that were originally built by the U.S. Army in 1911 (the other is the footbridge crossing the Firehole River at the Fairy Falls Trailhead). It was reconstructed in late 2012.

The **Bighorn Pass Trailhead** is located just across the bridge at the entrance to the campground. This is the east side of the trail, and the 19-mile (30 km) trail will take you over the Gallatin Range via Bighorn Pass to its west trailhead on U.S. Highway 191.

Further up Indian Creek from the campground, a slaughterhouse and dairy operation existed from ca. 1902 until 1907 (having replaced the previous dairy that existed on Clematis Creek at Mammoth). It served to provide fresh meat and milk to the hotels in the Mammoth area, as well as the camps in the area. The operation was discontinued in 1907 to prevent contamination of the creeks and the river which by this time were being used to provide potable water to the Mammoth area.

12.9 / 8.1 GPS: 44.88597, -110.73147
GARDNER RIVER/SEVEN MILE BRIDGE
GARDNER'S HOLE

The **Gardner River** crosses under the road here from west to east, and then travels through Sheepeater Canyon to the north before emptying into the Yellowstone River at the Town of Gardiner. The bridge here is officially called **Seven Mile Bridge**, because it is approximately seven miles south of Mammoth (though not the intersection from which the measurements in this book derive). The bridge was built in 1932.

Gardner's Hole is the large valley here, named for an early fur trapper in the area from the 1830s, Johnson Gardner (as was the Gardner River). The hole extends from the base of the Gallatin Range on the west to the hills on the east. The river's name differs from the town's name (Gardiner) because of a speech dialect. When explorer Jim Bridger was describing the layout of the area to a mapmaker, his southern accent caused him to pronounce Mr. Gardner's name incorrectly, adding an additional syllable. Thus, Gardner became Gardiner.

13.0 / 7.9 GPS: 44.88803, -110.73269
SHEEPEATER CLIFF TURNOUT/PICNIC AREA (E) 🚹 🎪 🚻

Sheepeater Cliff was given its name for the Sheepeater Indians, a sub-band of the Shoshone, so-named because sheep constituted a significant portion of their diet. The cliffs are composed of basalt lava that cooled quickly when it was extruded some 500,000 years ago.

The **Sheepeater Cliff Picnic Area** at the base of the cliff has five tables, and there's a handicap-accessible vault toilet located here as well. There is little room at the parking area, so large vehicles (buses, RVs, etc.) are prohibited.

13.5 / 7.5 GPS: 44.89402, -110.73406
MAMMOTH AQUEDUCT SERVICE ROAD (W) 🚶 🚲

The **Mammoth Aqueduct Service Road** takes you back to a construction material and equipment staging and stockpiling area, as well as the Mammoth South Electrical Substation. At the west end of the gravel road, there is a series of water impoundments that divert water from Indian Creek, Panther Creek, and the Gardner River for use in Mammoth. The water is captured and transported via an underground pipeline to a storage reservoir just north of Golden Gate Canyon, where it is held until treated and pumped to an underground tank in Mammoth.

You may hike or ride a bicycle along this road, but the only vehicles allowed past the gate are official NPS maintenance and utility service trucks. The road is also known as Swan Lake Flat Pit Service Road or the Mammoth Water Intake Service Road, depending on which map or source you're using.

15.3 / 5.7 GPS: 44.92055, -110.73154
GALLATIN RANGE/SWAN LAKE TURNOUT (W) 🅟

Swan Lake Flat (formerly Swan Lake Basin) used to be the bottom of a large glacial lake and all that remains is Swan Lake, which can be seen a few hundred feet west of the road. The lake gets its name from a history of trumpeter swans being seen on the lake. It's somewhat rare to see them here today, but the area around the body of water is usually quite rich with waterfowl of various other types.

At this turnout, you'll find an interpretive exhibit showing the names of the various mountains of the Gallatin Range you see to the west. The mountains, from south to north, are:

- **Trilobite Point** (10010 ft/3051 m)
- **Mount Holmes** (10336 ft/3150 m) You may be able to see the fire lookout atop its peak on clear days
- **Dome Mountain** It has two peaks (9903 ft/3018 m and 9826 ft/2995 m)
- **Antler Peak** standing on its own (10063 ft/3067 m)
- **Bannock Peak** (10332 ft/3149 m)
- **Quadrant Mountain** (10216 ft/3134 m) and its smaller brother, **Little Quadrant** (9915 ft/3022 m)
- **Electric Peak** (10961 ft/3341 m)
- **Sepulcher Mountain** (9652 ft/2942 m)
- **Terrace Mountain** (8002 ft/2439 m)
- **Bunsen Peak** across the highway from Terrace is also considered a part of the Gallatin Range (8527 ft/2599 m)

If you turn around and look to the east, you'll see some of the peaks of the Washburn Mountain Range, from north to south:

- **Prospect Peak** (9525 ft/2903 m)
- **Folsom Peak** (9236 ft/2815 m)
- **Cook Peak** (9724 ft/2964 m)

In 1917, at the south end of the flat, a large pit was dug, and almost all of the park's stagecoaches, buggies, wagons, and horse tack were pushed into it and buried. There was no longer any need for all of this equipment after automobiles were allowed to use the roads, so it was all disposed of.

16.1 / 4.9 GPS: 44.93123, -110.72938
GLEN CREEK STOCK TRAILHEAD (W) 🚶

The **Glen Creek Trail** follows Glen Creek for some two miles before veering off into other trails. This small parking area is restricted to use by stock trailers. A new, larger parking area is slated to be constructed just north of this when this section of road is rebuilt in the late 2010s.

16.2 / 4.8 GPS: 44.93228, -110.72827
BUNSEN PEAK TRAILHEAD (E) 🚶 🚲
GLEN CREEK TRAILHEAD (W) 🚶
GLEN CREEK CROSSING

The **Bunsen Peak Trailhead** is the starting point for the trails to the summit of Bunsen Peak and Osprey Falls. The trail follows an old administrative road around the base of the mountain until you break off to head to the summit or the waterfall. If you continue along the old roadbed, you'll end up at the south end of the YACC Camp 1.5 miles south of Mammoth (see description below at 19.7/1.3). This road was built as a scenic road in 1879 by Superintendent P. W. Norris. It was the first "secondary" road in the park, and was designed to give visitors a scenic view into Gardner Canyon. It was eventually closed to public travel and was used for a time for administrative purposes, but that, too, has ceased.

The trail to the summit of the peak is a four-mile (6 km) round trip if you return to this trailhead. The trail to Osprey Falls includes three miles (4.8 km) along the road, then another 1.5 miles (2.4 km) to the 150-foot waterfall. You can walk or bicycle along the paved/gravel section of the trails.

Bunsen Peak (8570 ft/2612 m) is believed to be the remnant of an old volcano, or perhaps a volcano that only partially formed, but cooled before it could erupt. The peak is named for Robert Bunsen, who, although he's much more widely associated with the Bunsen Burner (which he had little, if anything to do with), also did a lot of research on geysers, especially in Iceland. Even though he never visited Yellowstone, Ferdinand Hayden named the peak in 1872 in his honor. There was a fire lookout atop this peak from 1934 (built by the Civilian Conservation Corps) until the mid-2000s when it was removed.

The **Glen Creek Trailhead** is across the road and leads off to the west, connecting into several other trails such as the Fawn Pass, Snow Pass, Bighorn Pass Cutoff, Fan Creek, and Sepulcher Mountain trails.

Glen Creek passes under the road from the west to the east just north of these trailheads.

16.3 / 4.7   GPS: 44.93377, -110.72645
RUSTIC FALLS OVERLOOK (E) 🚻
KINGMAN PASS

Rustic Falls is a 47-foot waterfall located at the south end of Golden Gate Canyon where Glen Creek falls over the edge of the canyon's wall. At one time, the amount of water flowing over the edge here was "enhanced" by water diverted from the Indian/Panther Creek area to provide water for Mammoth (the water flowed via Glen Creek into the reservoir). In the late 1970s, however, the water system was re-engineered and a new pipeline laid directly to the reservoir from the diversion dams. The pipeline runs under the viaduct today, and the water flowing over the edge of the falls is the natural flow of Glen Creek.

There is a sign here that explains the construction of the road through this area by the U.S. Army Corps of Engineers. At this point, you are at **Kingman Pass,** named for Lt. Daniel Kingman, the engineer who built the first road through this canyon, and who is responsible for the basic configuration of the Figure-8 road system that connects the main features of the park today.

16.4 / 4.5   GPS: 44.93479, -110.72451
GOLDEN GATE VIADUCT
GOLDEN GATE CANYON/RUSTIC FALLS TURNOUT (E) 🚻
PILLAR OF HERCULES (E)

The **Golden Gate Canyon/Rustic Falls Turnout** affords a view of Golden Gate Canyon to the north, as well as Rustic Falls to the south. Golden Gate Canyon is named for the golden-yellowish color of its walls (which are composed of welded rhyolite tuff). The yellow hues come not from the natural color of the rock, but rather a species of lichen that lives on the rocks. It's not uncommon to find osprey or golden eagles nesting in the canyon.

The existing viaduct along the roadway, often referred to as the "**Golden Gate Bridge**," was constructed in 1977, and is the third such structure built to carry traffic through this area. It replaced a viaduct that had been built in 1901-1902, and widened in 1932-1933. The original viaduct had been constructed of wood in 1885, and was designed to carry stagecoaches in one direction at a time.

Prior to the existence of this route up to Swan Lake Flat, travelers had to utilize a road built through Snow Pass to the west of here. This involved climbing some steep grades (which was hard to do with a loaded stagecoach), and added an extra 1.3 miles (2.1 km) and often several hours of travel time to every trip. Lt. Dan Kingman engineered the original route through the canyon in 1885, and Capt. Hiram Chittenden, who would go on to engineer several other major road projects within Yellowstone, oversaw construction of its replacement in 1902. Upon completion of the project, Chittenden stated that this had been the most difficult project he'd undertaken within the park up to that point.[14]

In 1933, work began on a project to widen the roadway to accommodate automobiles going in both directions simultaneously. The plan devised at the time called for a tunnel to be dug/blasted through the canyon wall to add the second lane. On May 23rd of that year, however, just before the tunnel was to have been completed, the entire thing collapsed in on itself. As a result, engineers simply removed all of the rock and widened/reinforced the viaduct that existed at the time.

In 1974, the Federal Highway Administration inspected the old bridge and found it to be structurally unsafe for use by the public. As a result, the 1933-era bridge was destroyed, and the existing one was built in its place.

The thumb-shaped rock sticking up at the north end of the viaduct is known as the **Pillar of Hercules**. The rock was in place when the first viaduct was constructed, and it has been physically picked up and moved out from the walls with each subsequent widening or rebuilding of the bridge. This gives the entrance (if you're traveling south) to the bridge and the canyon a "gate-like" feel to it, and thus the name "Golden Gate" was born.

16.7 / 4.3 GPS: 44.93686, -110.72120
GLEN CREEK SERVICE ROAD (E)

The gated grass/dirt road running down the hill to the east here is a steep (21% grade in some places) service road that goes down to the Mammoth Reservoir. It is known to locals as the **Glen Creek Service Road** because it travels along the creek down to its terminus. It is a rarely used back entrance to the reservoir area and provides access to the aquaduct that transports water to the reservoir.

This is the remnant of the original road (1885) that was built to carry traffic from Mammoth up to the (at that time) newly built Golden Gate Viaduct. It was built primarily to prevent early engineers from having to build a road through the Hoodoos, which was considered to be too difficult because of all of the blasting that would need to be done to cut through the rock.[15] In 1900, in concert with the construction of the new viaduct by Capt. Hiram Chittenden, the road through the Hoodoos was built, and this road was abandoned for public use.

17.3 / 3.7 GPS: 44.94429, -110.71660
THE HOODOOS 🛐
SILVER GATE (W)
TERRACE MOUNTAIN (W)

The short section of roadway here through the huge travertine boulders is known as **The Hoodoos**. Hoodoos are rock formations that remind a person of goblins or spirits related to witchcraft, and the name is given to this area for the huge, uniquely shaped rocks that line the road (the road was literally cut through the debris field). This area is sometimes referred to as the "Limestone Hoodoos" to distinguish it from another area known as the Hoodoos on the park's eastern boundary.

The little U-shaped drive through the rockfall was once part of the original stagecoach road through this area, and is often referred to as **"Silver Gate"** because of the sharp turn required to pass through it. The road was realigned at some point, and the short diversion through the rock formation was retained to give future visitors an idea of what travel through this area used to be like.[16]

All of these rocks were once part of **Terrace Mountain** above you and to the west. At some point in the not too distant past (ca. 100-1000 years ago), these rocks crumbled from the edge of the travertine formations that form the crest of Terrace Mountain (and for which that mountain is named).

17.5 / 3.5 GPS: 44.94664, -110.71433
CATHEDRAL ROCK PULLOUT (W)

Though this is isn't a formal pullout and it isn't paved, it affords an excellent view of **Cathedral Rock** on the north face of Bunsen Peak, especially in the evening when the sun is shining on it from the west. The rock was apparently given its name during the construction of the original road through Golden Gate Canyon in 1885.[17]

Since you're in a blind curve on the southbound side of the road, exercise caution when merging back into traffic in either direction. People often come flying around that curve, and it can be difficult to get into traffic safely.

17.9 / 3.1   GPS: 44.95174, -110.71332
Burn Mosaic Pullout (E) 🏕
Mammoth Reservoir / Joffe Lake (E)
Africa Lake (S)

At this pullout, you'll find an interpretive display describing the burn mosaic left behind on and below Bunsen Peak by the wildfires of 1988.

If you look down into the valley below you to the east, you'll see the **Mammoth Water Reservoir.** The water piped in from the diversion dams on Panther Creek and the Gardner River pools here. It is pumped to a treatment plant hidden in the woods to the north, and then on to an underground tank behind the Mammoth Hotel, where it is then gravity fed to the various offices, restaurants, stores, residences, and the hotel. The reservoir was constructed in the 1930s to replace the old, much smaller pond located just below the terraces in Mammoth (see note below at 20.2/0.8).

There's also a small hydroelectric generating plant at the outlet of the reservoir that generates as much as 230KW of power. It was installed in 2012 and is expected to save the park as much as $80,000 per year in electrical costs (vs. using commercial power).

The body of water southeast of the reservoir is **Joffe Lake**, accessible via a dirt road at the south end of the YACC Camp area (see 19.7/1.3 below). The lake is named after Joe Joffe, a long-time assistant superintendent (and former acting superintendent) of the park. This lake was created at the same time as the reservoir (as an overflow catch basin), and is an excellent spot for families to take young children to fish.

If you look to the south from the pullout, you'll see **Africa Lake**, so-named because its shape resembles that of the continent. The lake is known to some old-timers as Beatty Lake after an NPS employee who drove a brand new pickup into the lake in 1933. It has also been known as Kidney Lake (again, for its shape).

18.8 / 2.1   GPS: 44.96374, -110.70850
Mammoth Snowmobile Rental Hut Turnout (E) 🚻 🛥

This facility is where park concessioner Xanterra rents snowmobiles and initiates park tours during the winter. Xanterra offers free shuttle service to/from the Mammoth Hotel to transport patrons back and forth. The facility opened in 1989, the site being selected because it is at a high enough elevation to ensure sufficient snow pack on which to operate the snowcoaches and snowmobiles. The facility is closed during the non-winter months (though they do use it for training sessions). The vault toilet located on the site is generally open year round.

18.9 / 2.0 GPS: 44.96533, -110.70775
UPPER TERRACE DRIVE (W) 🚻 🚹🚺

This one-way loop takes you above the terraces at Mammoth Hot Springs, and alongside several other thermal features. You may see some maps refer to this as Mammoth Loop Drive. There is a vault toilet at the south end of the pullout. See the Miscellaneous Roads section for a road log of this feature-laden drive.

As you depart the area heading to the north, you start your descent of Formation Hill (some refer to it as Mammoth Hill) and enter the Mammoth Hot Springs area.

19.7 / 1.3 GPS: 44.95929, -110.70353
YACC CAMP DRIVE (S) 🚶 🚵 🚲

This service road leads to the **Young Adult Conservation Corps (YACC) Camp** area. This area was the site of the original Civilian Conservation Corps work camp at Mammoth in 1933, and today serves as a base of operations for the park's summer wildland firefighting force, trail maintenance crews, and other seasonal maintenance work groups, as well as a youth conservation program run by the NPS each summer.

The huge Fleet Maintenance Garage where work is performed on the larger vehicles in the park's fleet (i.e., fire trucks, snow plows, and road construction equipment) is located back here, as is an NPS and concession employee residential area.

At the south end of the camp, the road from Bunsen Peak terminates (see above at 16.2/4.8 for the south end). There's also a dirt service road that takes you back to Joffe Lake and the Mammoth Water Reservoir and Water Treatment Plant.

Between this road and the Mammoth Corrals ahead, from 1909 until 1929, there was a bison "show corral" on the east side of the road where the park kept a small herd of bison to ensure tourists could see the magnificent animals. Remember, this was in the day when there were less than 200 in the park altogether, so visitors didn't see them wandering all over the park as we do today.

Behind this corral (to the east) was the "Yellowstone National Park Zoo," which housed a small herd of elk, a badger, an antelope, some coyote, several more bison, and a bear named Juno.[18] There was a zookeeper's (buffalo keeper) residence in the small valley as well from 1903 to 1936.

20.2 / 0.8 GPS: 44.96623, -110.70132
Mammoth Corrals (E) 🐎 ☗
Fort Yellowstone Cemetery (E) ⛒
Site of the Old Mammoth Lodge / Mammoth Plunge (E)
Old Mammoth Reservoir (W)

The **Mammoth Corrals** are on the east side of the road. Park concession operator Xanterra conducts horse ride excursions several times a day during the summer (using about 40 horses) from this location. The short road to the corrals terminates in a small parking area, so if you have an RV, bus, or are pulling a trailer, you'll need to park in the large turnout and walk down. The corrals have been in business since 1917, when it was opened in concert with the (then new) Mammoth Lodge.

Behind the corrals (to the west) is the **Fort Yellowstone Cemetery**, established while Camp Sheridan was still the park's headquarters. Soldiers and their relatives, along with several civilians who died in the park between 1888 and 1916 were buried here. When the U.S. Army left the park in 1916, they had the remains of 19-22 soldiers (sources differ on the exact total) disinterred and relocated to Custer National Cemetery at the Little Bighorn Battlefield. The last burial here was a civilian female. She was buried in 1957 next to her husband, who'd committed suicide following the death of their infant daughter. Both had been buried here in 1906. The fence around the cemetery was installed by the U.S. Army in 1915.

The large open plot of land to the north of the corral is the site of the old **Mammoth Lodge and Cabins**, as well as the **Mammoth Plunge**, a huge swimming pool. The original lodge building was constructed in 1917-1918 as a replacement for the various tent camps located around the area, and was similar in design to the lodges still standing at Old Faithful, Lake, and Roosevelt. After an expansion in 1923, it had a dining room, a dance hall, and a recreation hall. At its peak, there were around 100 guest cabins here.

In 1920, the swimming pool was added at the north end of the lodge complex. The pool would use water supplied via Bluff Creek which ran along the north side of the facility (and maintained a stable 90°F/32°C). The concrete pool basin was 3.5 feet deep on the shallow end and 7.5 feet deep on the diving end. Only one drowning is known to have occurred

A portion of Camp Sheridan, ca. 1900. Residence in the foreground was known as the "Beehive Residence" (for the amount of activity always going on around it) and initially served as quarters for the park's acting superintendent (military commander). It was torn down in 1925.

during the time it was open. The pool was closed in 1950 due to impending changes in public health regulations rather than a lack of use.

Many visitors to the park often ask about the gravel "sidewalk" that runs from the area of the corrals north to the developed area. This was installed in the latter days of the Mammoth Lodge's existence to afford those staying here easy access to the stores and shops in the village itself.

In 1934, a transition away from the lodge operation began with the transfer of several cabins to the Fishing Bridge, West Thumb, and Roosevelt areas (some of the old cabins still exist at Roosevelt even today). The decision had been made to re-brand the Mammoth market as being oriented toward the motor tourist. Much of the gargantuan Mammoth Hotel was destroyed, except for the north wing added in 1913, and a new facade was built onto the front of it. It remains standing as the Mammoth Hot Springs Hotel today.

As a part of this process, new cabins ("cottages" as they are known) were added to the hotel, and the Mammoth Lodge and its remaining cabins, along with the swimming pool were abandoned altogether in 1940. The buildings were razed from 1949 into the 1960s. You can still see remnants of the foundation of the lodge and the swimming pool building in the field today.

Further north still, the large hill is known as **Capitol Hill**. It was upon this hill that Superintendent P. W. Norris built the first governmental administrative building in a national park, the Blockhouse (see the

Mammoth Hot Springs Development section for more details on this structure). The large meadow southeast of the hill is known as Little Meadows, given this name by Norris for unknown reasons.

Across the main road from the corral, at the foot of the terraces, you'll notice a small mound. This is the old (original) **Mammoth Reservoir,** or what's left of it. The 1.8 million gallon open-air reservoir was constructed by Capt. Hiram Chittenden of the U.S. Army Corps of Engineers in 1901 to provide potable water to the area, as well as water for irrigation of the parade ground and for use in operating the hydroelectric generators at the old Mammoth Powerhouse.

The concrete dam and other appurtenances were removed from the reservoir in 1937 after a newer water system was constructed, but the water impoundment remains. It drains via Bluff Creek (Lost Creek). Prior to 1901, water for the Mammoth area was drawn from Clematis Creek and stored in a 100,000 gallon concrete tank that sat just above the location of the old McCartney Hotel.

The original road from the Mammoth area up to the upper terraces and the Golden Gate Canyon ran behind this dam (between the dam and the terraces). The road was obliterated in 1938.

20.4 / 0.6 GPS: 44.96955, -110.70186
LOWER MAMMOTH TERRACE PARKING LOT - SOUTH (W) 🚶
CAMP SHERIDAN SITE

The area on both sides of the road where this parking lot is located was the site of the original encampment of the U.S. Army known as **Camp Sheridan.** Most of the structures once located here, all built between 1886 and the mid-1890s, were razed in 1915, though a small number remained until 1965.

From 1916 to 1919, this flat area was the site of the first formal "auto campground" at Mammoth. After just four seasons, the campground was moved to the site of the current Lower Mammoth Housing Area, since there was already an informal campground there and it was proving to be more popular with visitors than this one (and was less threatening to park resources).[19] See the North Entrance Road section for more details on the campgrounds in that area.

The terraces above you are, from south to north, Canary Spring, Marble Terrace, Pulpit Terrace, Jupiter Terrace, and Mound Terrace.

Commandant's House, ca. 1917.

20.5 / 0.4 GPS: 44.97144, -110.70311
LOWER MAMMOTH TERRACE PARKING LOT - MIDDLE (W) [🚶]

Another parking area with access to the terraces. You're parked below Minerva Terrace here. On the slight hill across the street from the parking lot sat the last post Commandant's House from the Camp Sheridan era. Constructed in 1904, it housed a variety of park employees over the years, including the first principal of the Yellowstone Park School in the early 1960s.[20] The building was removed in 1963 or 1964.

20.6 / 0.3 GPS: 44.97283, -110.70377
LOWER MAMMOTH TERRACE PARKING LOT - NORTH (W) [🚶]
LIBERTY CAP (W)
CLEMATIS GULCH / SEPULCHER MOUNTAIN TRAIL (W) [🚶]
OPAL TERRACE (E)

This is the north parking lot for the Mammoth Terraces. The large, cone-shaped feature before you is **Liberty Cap**, a 37-foot tall extinct hot spring. Its unique shape is believed to have come about from a slow build-up of travertine over hundreds of years. At some point, the deposits finally sealed the spring off, leaving it standing much as you see it here today. The larger terrace behind Liberty Cap is Palette Spring.

To the immediate right of Liberty Cap (looking to the west) is **Clematis Gulch**, the small gully running up between the terraces and the residential structure (the Commissioner or Magistrate's Residence). The name "gulch" is synonymous with creek.

The small mound at the back of the gulch was the site of the first "hotel" built in the park by James McCartney and Henry Horr in 1871. It was little more than a 25' x 35' empty pair of rooms where visitors could rent space and throw down their own sleeping gear, but it was the only place one could find respite from the elements until 1880.

McCartney was evicted in 1881, and the building went on to be used for several other purposes, including a dormitory for employees who worked at the Cottage Hotel. It also served as a residence for park employees, and then in 1902 became a laundry operated by a Chinese gentleman named Sam Toy. Mr. Toy operated the laundry until it burned down in December of 1913 as the result of a hot iron being left in the wrong place.

A little further up Clematis Creek was the original Mammoth Dairy, which provide milk and other dairy products to the area's hotels until 1897 when the new dairy was built on Swan Lake Flat (it was relocated because Clematis Creek was being used as the source of potable water for the Mammoth area at this point). The first road out of the Mammoth area toward the south ran up the gulch as well. It passed up the gulch, around the west side of Hymen and Cleopatra Terraces, south to Orange Spring Mound, and then followed the ski trail, then south ascending Pinyon Terrace to a point where one can find Jewelled Cave. From the cave, the road proceeded west until it met the (today's) Snow Pass Trail, then followed that trail south up onto Swan Lake Flats, connecting into the same road used today south of the Glen Creek Trailhead (see 16.2/4.8 above).

Clematis Creek passes under the roadway here and drains through the field in front of the comfort station and service station before dropping into a sinkhole in front of the general store. It probably empties into the Gardner River at some point. The creek was named for the genus of wildflower prevalent throughout the park.

The **Sepulcher Mountain Trail** parallels Clematis Creek for a short distance (the creek has its headwater on the mountain). It branches off into the Howard Eaton-Mammoth Trail (which takes you down to the Glen Creek Trailhead at Bunsen Peak), the Beaver Ponds Trail (a five-mile loop that exits at the rear of the Mammoth Hotel), and up through Snow Pass to the Glen Creek Trail, the Clagett Butte Trail, and the Fawn Pass Trail.

Across the street from this parking area is **Opal Terrace**, which has sprung up next door to the old Executive House, currently used as the residence for the Executive VP for Yellowstone Operations for Xanterra. The site of the terrace was once home to a tennis court, but it was removed in 1947 due to encroachment of the new thermal feature. Several other steps have been taken to prevent the thermal feature from damaging the house, which was constructed in 1908.

20.7 / 0.2 GPS: 44.97399, -110.70395
OVERFLOW LOT FOR LOWER MAMMOTH TERRACE PARKING (E)
MAMMOTH PICNIC AREA (E) 🛆
COMFORT STATION PARKING (W) 🚻

The **Mammoth Picnic Area** on the east side of the highway has four tables, and access to the restrooms is at the comfort station on the other side of the road. The area is not easily accessible by those in wheelchairs.

On the west side of the road you'll find the **Mammoth Comfort Station**, a large bathroom facility constructed in 2006. The comfort station is located on site of the old Cottage Hotel, which was removed in 1964. The two houses located adjacent to the parking lot are park employee residences, so please do not disturb them. See the Mammoth Hot Springs Development section for information about these and the other structures in this area.

20.9 / 0.1 GPS: 44.97552, -110.70283
MAMMOTH YPSS SERVICE STATION (W) ⛽ 🚗
MAMMOTH GENERAL STORE (W) 🛒 🚗
TERRACE GRILL/MAMMOTH HOTEL DINING ROOM (W) 🍴 🚻

The **Mammoth Service Station**, operated by the Yellowstone Park Service Stations, provides gasoline and diesel fuel, but no repair services. You can also buy light snacks and travel essentials here as well.

The **Mammoth General Store** dates back to the early days of the park, and is currently the only concession-operated facility within the park that is open year-round. You can buy basic food and travel essentials, souvenirs, fishing supplies, and a variety of other odds and ends here. The store also has a small ice cream stand.

The **Terrace Grill** is a fast-food restaurant, and serves small salads, soups, sandwiches (including burgers and hot dogs), and a variety of other meals. It also has a small ice cream stand. The **Mammoth Dining Room**, on the opposite end of the building from the Grill, is a sit-down restaurant that offers full breakfast, lunch, and dinner service.

For more information on the history of all of these structures, see the Mammoth Hot Springs Development section.

Across the road is the old drill field used by the U.S. Army to practice maneuvers during their tenure here from 1886 to 1916. After the Army left, the field has been used for a variety of other purposes; there was once an amphitheater located in the middle of it. Today, the Mammoth elk herd can often be seen grazing here.

Immediately across from the general store is a fenced off sinkhole (from an extinct thermal pool, most likely) where Clematis Creek drops into the ground. In the early 1880s, there were two bath houses (operated by the Yellowstone Park Improvement Company, then owner of the National Hotel) located on the northwest corner of this sinkhole. Hot water was piped over from a nearby hot spring, while cold water from Clematis Creek could be used by the bather to regulate the temperature of the water s/he was bathing in. The structures were two of many bath houses in service around the Mammoth area during this time period (both were removed in the late 1880s).

21.0 / 0.0 GPS: 44.97634, -110.70094 Elevation: 6250 feet
Junction with Grand Loop Road to Tower (E)
Mammoth Hot Springs Hotel (W) 🛏️ 🍽️ 🚻
Gardiner High Road / Kite Hill (W)

From here, you can drive 21.0 miles (33.8 km) to Norris Junction, 5.1 miles (8.2 km) to the North Entrance, or 18.1 miles (29.1 km) to Tower Junction.

The **Mammoth Hot Springs Hotel** is located on the west side of the road here. The existing structure was completed in 1936, and includes the 1913 "north wing" of the original hotel that occupied the site. The hotel has 95 rooms and 97 cabins, with (2013) prices ranging from $86 for a simple room with no bath to $459 for a suite. More information about the history of the hotel can be found in the Mammoth Hot Springs Development section.

Behind the hotel is the entrance to the **Gardiner High Road**, a one-way dirt road that was at one time the primary route between Mammoth and the Town of Gardiner. You can find more information about it and a road log in the Miscellaneous Roads section.

The hill behind the hotel is known as **Kite Hill** (named for the proclivity of park employees to fly kites from it). It is the site of a handful of graves from the early days of the park (1883-1897). The easiest way to get to the top of the hill is via the Gardiner High Road. The hill is also known to some as Boot Hill, for unknown reasons.[21]

21.3 GPS: 44.97659, -110.69998
JUNCTION WITH OFFICER'S ROW (E)
ALBRIGHT VISITOR CENTER (E) ⑦ 🏠 👥

(*NOTE: Although the road ends at the junction for the purposes of this book, we continue north to cover the buildings/facilities located here.*)

The one way road to the east is known as **Officer's Row** (or Avenue C) for the series of large officers' quarters that line it to the east of the Visitor Center.

The **Albright Visitor Center** was originally the Bachelor Officer's Quarters, constructed in 1909 as a part of Fort Yellowstone. After the departure of the Army, Superintendent Horace Albright converted the building into an Information Center and small museum, and it has served that purpose (albeit under different names) ever since. Prior to the construction of the Heritage and Research Center in 2004, it also housed the park's archives. The building is undergoing a major renovation that is expected to take two years to complete.

21.4 GPS: 44.97748, -110.69890
MAMMOTH POST OFFICE/MAMMOTH CLINIC (E) ✉ ➕
ASPEN DORMITORY/YELLOWSTONE JUSTICE CENTER (W)

On the east side of the road, you'll find the **Mammoth Clinic**, opened in 1963 just prior to the razing of the hospital located next to the chapel. This is a minor emergency facility. Next door to it is the Mammoth Post Office, constructed in 1936. This facility is open year round and is the main post office for the park. The top floor of the building consists of apartments for those who work here.

On the west side of the road, you'll see the Aspen Dormitory (and behind it, the Spruce Dormitory), used to house employees of the park's primary concessioner, Xanterra, as well as the new Yellowstone Justice Center, built in 2007-2008. This building houses a courtroom, judge's chambers and office space, interview rooms, a holding area, and offices for NPS criminal investigators and the U.S. Marshal's Service.

This area was the site of the original Yellowstone Park Transportation Company (YPTC) complex, which housed several buildings, including a large facility for their offices, barns, and workshops for the stagecoaches. When the park moved to automotive transportation in 1917, the facilities were converted to service mechanical vehicles.

At 2:15 in the afternoon on March 30, 1925, a leaking oil burner spurted oil onto a hot forge in one of the shops, starting a fire that consumed the large building as well as 93 vehicles contained therein. Fortunately, the new YPTC facilities in Gardiner were pretty far along, and the company transferred its operations there. The original building had been constructed in 1904, and had been designed by none other than Robert Reamer, the architect who'd designed the Old Faithful Inn.

More information on all of these buildings and the history of this complex can be found in the Mammoth Hot Springs Development section.

21.5 / 0.0 GPS: 44.97813, -110.69731
JUNCTION WITH NORTH ENTRANCE ROAD

From this point, it is five miles (8 km) to the Roosevelt Arch and the Town of Gardiner, Montana.

U.S. Highway 191

U.S. Highway 191 is the primary route of travel between the Bozeman and Big Sky, Montana, areas and the park's entrance at West Yellowstone. The entire road is 82 miles (132 km) long from Four Corners in Bozeman, but only 20.2 miles (32.6 km) of it is inside Yellowstone National Park.

The road originally opened to vehicular traffic in 1911 and represented a compromise. Several had advocated for a "fifth entrance" into the park, this one from the northwest (at the time the Northeast Entrance was not considered an "entrance" per se into the park because it dead ended at Cooke City). U.S. Army Engineer Capt. Hiram Chittenden and others disapproved of that idea because of the cost associated with building the road and significant maintenance costs for a road that would only be usable for 2-3 months out of the year. They also didn't want to see undisturbed portions of the park destroyed by having a road built through them. The original plan for the road was to have it enter the park on the west where the Gallatin River enters the park, cross over Bighorn Pass, and exit onto the Grand Loop Road approximately seven miles south of Mammoth near today's Seven Mile Bridge.

The road was therefore completed to the town of Yellowstone (later to become West Yellowstone), with 14 miles (22.5 km) of it inside the park at the time (this was before the addition on the northwest corner of the park in 1929). It would be two years before the Department of the Interior would allow automobiles to use the segment of road within the park. The road remained in substandard condition until the mid-1930s, when it was rehabilitated in concert with other work being done on park roads at the time.

While much of the road follows the original alignment, significant portions of it were relocated eastward to reduce the curves and the number of bridges required to carry traffic over the waterways. You can still see hints of the old roadway on the west side of the river in several spots.

While speed limits along much of the highway outside the park are in the 60-70 mph range, drivers are restricted to 55 mph along that portion inside the park. The NPS has rangers who are dedicated to patrolling this stretch of highway, so speeders are often caught. The road itself is in excellent condition and is well-maintained. There are no public toilets along the highway inside the park.

0.0 / 20.3 GPS: 45.05420, -111.15531 ELEVATION: 6708 FEET
NORTHERN BOUNDARY

The Yellowstone sign marks the northern boundary of the park. In fact, you are literally almost on top of the northwest corner of the park, as the actual boundary is in the middle of the Gallatin River just off the roadway. The park's western boundary follows the river southward for some distance.

You'll see several different markers/benchmarks in this area that have been used over the years to delineate the park's boundaries. The red-tipped, white posts with the "Boundary Line" signs attached to them are the latest and (believed to be) most accurate. As you travel south, you'll see these occasionally along the west side of the road on the opposite side of the Gallatin River. On the side of the road opposite the sign, there are two other markers, one of which is a small concrete block with a tiny brass plug in it, while the other is a thick solid white post with several notations carved into it. You'll also see white concrete posts along the west side of the road. These were placed by the Montana Highway Commission as mile markers for the highway.

This northwest corner of the park was added in March 1, 1929, specifically to protect the fossilized forests on the hills above Specimen Creek (not to be confused with Specimen Ridge in the northeast portion of the park). This added several additional miles of U.S. Highway 191 into the park's jurisdiction.

0.9 / 19.4 GPS: 45.04812, -111.14003
DAILEY CREEK TRAILHEAD (E) [🚶]
DAILEY CREEK CROSSING

Dailey Creek and the **Dailey Creek Trail** are named for Andrew J. Dailey, an early settler of the area. On some maps, the name is misspelled as "Daly." The trail provides access to Dailey Pass and the quickest access to the Sky Rim Trail (6 mi/9.6 km) from this side of the park. Dailey Creek itself passes under the road immediately south of the entrance road into the parking area.

2.5 / 17.7 GPS: 45.03432, -111.11345
Black Butte Trailhead Parking Area (W) 🚶

This is the parking area for the **Black Butte Trail**. The trailhead itself is across the street and to the north about 50 yards. Once on the trail, it is seven miles (11 km) to the summit of Bighorn Peak, at one point winding through the Gallatin Petrified Forest.

Black Butte Creek crosses the road between the parking lot and the trailhead itself. The large hill to the southeast of the trailhead is Black Butte (8396 ft/2559 m), the creek's namesake.

2.9 / 17.4 GPS: 45.02973, -111.10946
Black Butte Ranch (W)

Black Butte Ranch is a private ranch that has its entrance inside the park. The park's boundary here continues to follow the river.

4.0 / 16.2 GPS: 45.01990, -111.09134
Wickiup Creek Crossing
Site of the old Gallatin Ranger Station (W)

Wickiup Creek crosses here and drains into the Gallatin River. The creek was named for the presence of wickiups nearby.

Just to the north of the creek crossing, you may be able to see the vestigial remains of an old driveway running off the road to the west. This driveway led to the old **Gallatin Ranger Station** that used to sit next to the tree line to the west (and was just inside the original park boundary when built).

4.7 / 15.5 GPS: 45.01230, -111.08168
Specimen Creek Trailhead (E) 🚶
Lightning Hill (E)

The **Specimen Creek Trail** is an 8.5-mile (14 km) trail that takes you to Shelf Lake and then on to the Sky Rim Trail. This trail is often confused with the Specimen Ridge Trail found in the northeastern section of the park.

The area around the trailhead was at one time a campground, originally known as the Gallatin Campground. Its name was changed in later years to the Specimen Creek Campground, and was apparently removed in the 1970s.

The hill to the immediate east of this trailhead is known as **Lightning Hill**. Labeled as "Specimen 8975" on many USGS topographic maps, the hill has an elevation of 8975 feet (2736 m). It was given its name because it was used by rangers based at the nearby Gallatin Ranger Station to check for fires caused by lightning following thunderstorms in the area.[1]

6.3 / 13.9 GPS: 44.98967, -111.07965
OLD GALLATIN ROADBED (W)

If you look across the river to the west, you'll see remnants of the original road that carried traffic through this area, including several road cuts in the small foothills along the base of the mountain.

6.9 / 13.2 GPS: 44.98110, -111.07923
TERMINAL MONUMENT CREEK CROSSING

Terminal Monument Creek crosses under the road here and empties into the Gallatin River. The creek gets its name from the fact that it begins near the very northwest corner of the state of Wyoming, a spot which is marked with a benchmark (or monument, as they're often called).

7.5 / 12.7 GPS: 44.97123, -111.07878
GALLATIN RIVER CROSSING

The **Gallatin River** crosses the road here, flowing westward. It's headwater is Gallatin Lake located in the Gallatin Range inside the park just south of Bighorn Pass, and its mouth is at the Missouri River.

8.7 / 11.6 GPS: 44.95835, -111.06713
BACON RIND CREEK TRAILHEAD (W) 🚶
BACON RIND CREEK CROSSING

The short drive to the west takes you to the **Bacon Rind Creek Trailhead**. The trail is a two-mile (3.2 km, each way) hike that takes you along the creek to the park's western boundary. At the park's boundary, the trail takes you into the high mountain areas of the Lee Metcalf Wilderness. Check with the USFS Ranger Station in West Yellowstone for maps/details.

Bacon Rind Creek crosses under the road here immediately south of the drive. According to park historian Lee Whittlesey, the creek gets its name from breakfast that was served to the Army scouts who camped in the area in the late 1880s.[2] The trailhead was the site of an NPS Road Camp in the 1910s-1930s.

9.4 / 10.9 GPS: 44.95050, -111.05947
FAWN PASS WEST TRAILHEAD (E) 🚶

The **Fawn Pass Trail** has its western terminus here. The 21-mile (34 km) trail has its other end at the Glen Creek Trailhead near Bunsen Peak on the road between Norris Junction and Mammoth Hot Springs. You can also access the Fan Creek Trail, which is 1.5 miles (3 km) from this end.

10.9 / 9.3 GPS: 44.92858, -111.05395
BIGHORN PASS WEST TRAILHEAD (E) 🚶

This is the west end of the 19-mile (30 km) **Bighorn Pass Trail**, which has its eastern terminus at the Indian Creek Campground on the road between Norris Junction and Mammoth Hot Springs. The trail takes you through Bighorn Pass (elev 9088 ft/2770 m) in the Gallatin Mountain Range.

The Montana/Wyoming State Line crosses the highway 1,500 feet north of the entrance to the trailhead, though it isn't marked. From here southward for about the next three miles, the boundary runs generally along the road, moving back and forth across the road as it meanders from east to west.

The Gallatin River moves away from the highway at this point, moving eastward, further up into the Gallatin Mountain Range.

12.0 / 8.2 GPS: 44.91249, -111.05316
DIVIDE LAKE (E) 🎣

Divide Lake gets its name from the fact that it lies on the divide between the drainage area for the Gallatin River to the east and the Madison River to the west (via Grayling Creek). The lake tends to dry up in the latter part of the summer.

14.6 / 5.6 GPS: 44.87603, -111.04674
OLD ROADBED - NORTH END (W)

If you're headed southbound, this is easier to see. Off from the west side of the highway is an old roadbed that was part of the original road through this section of the park. If you follow it southward approximately ½ mile, you'll come across a curve known as "Horseshoe Bend" where the road originally crossed an unnamed tributary of Grayling Creek.

The road remained entirely on the west side of the creek for about two miles south of here. The other end can be found at 16.6/3.6 below.

266 Yellowstone Mileposts

14.9 / 5.3 GPS: 44.87221, -111.04505
GRAYLING CREEK CROSSING

This is the first crossing of **Grayling Creek** if you're heading south (or last if you're heading north). The creek gets its name from the fish.

16.1 / 4.1 GPS: 44.85743, -111.05392
GRAYLING CREEK CROSSING

Grayling Creek crosses under the road.

16.3 / 3.9 GPS: 44.85544, -111.05752
GRAYLING CREEK CROSSING

Grayling Creek crosses under the road again here. The Montana/Wyoming State Line crosses the road approximately 100 feet north of the bridge, though it is unmarked.

16.6 / 3.6 GPS: 44.85264, -111.06250
GRAYLING CREEK CROSSING
OLD ROADBED - SOUTH END (W)

Grayling Creek crosses here once again.

Off to the west in the woods behind the pullout, though it's hard to tell at this point, the original road headed north from here (see the note above at 14.6/5.6).

20.0 / 0.2 GPS: 44.81059, -111.09463
TEPEE CREEK CROSSING

Tepee Creek crosses under the road here, and eventually empties into Grayling Creek a few hundred feet south of the bridge.

20.2 / 0.0 GPS: 44.80813, -111.09719 ELEVATION: 6757 FEET
PARK BOUNDARY

The park boundary here is marked by a small sign and is exactly 11 miles (17.7 km) north of the junction of Canyon Street and Yellowstone Avenue in West Yellowstone. The speed limit within the park is 55 miles per hour (88 kph), so if you're headed north and have been used to driving 65-70, it may catch you off-guard. The NPS is fairly aggressive about enforcing the speed limit through this area. No hazardous materials are allowed through the park, either, so if you're a commercial vehicle hauling these kinds of materials, you'll need to detour around via U.S. 287.

If you're heading south, there are a couple of locations of interest related to the park. The Gneiss Creek West Trailhead is located off the cemetery road 1.4 miles (2.2 km) south of the park boundary. This trail takes you across to its east trailhead at the Seven Mile Bridge on the West Entrance Road. At 3.5 miles (5.6 km) south of the boundary, Cougar Creek Road follows Maple Creek eastward toward the park's west boundary. This road does not take you into the park, though it does skirt the boundary line for a few hundred feet.

And at 6.5 miles (10.5 km) south of the boundary, running east off the main highway, is Ecology Lane. At the end of this road, you'll find the West Yellowstone Compost Facility, which is where much of the garbage generated in the park ends up.

Miscellaneous Roads

There are a variety of side roads, scenic roads, and other stretches of roadway throughout Yellowstone that are not routinely traveled by the average visitor. Many of these were at one time part of the main road but were transformed into scenic side roads by virtue of new road alignments. Each provides the visitor with unique opportunities to see the park in a way missed by most others and are well worth the time you'd take to explore them.

The roads are organized in the order you come across them as you travel around the park on the Figure-8 Grand Loop Road, just as the balance of the road logs were. The roads, in order, include:

- Old Yellowstone Trail
- Gardiner High Road
- Blacktail Plateau Drive
- North Rim Drive
- South Rim Drive
- Gull Point Drive
- Firehole Lake Drive
- Fountain Flats Drive
- Firehole Canyon Drive
- Virginia Cascade Drive
- Upper Terrace Drive

OLD YELLOWSTONE TRAIL

Though this road is known by a variety of different names (in particular Reese Creek Road and Stephens Creek Road), its official name is **Old Yellowstone Trail**.

This road takes you into the area known as the "Game Ranch Addition" or "Boundary Lands Addition," a section of land added onto the park in 1932 to provide for additional protected lands where pronghorn and other animals foraged and spent their summers. Prior to the annexation, hunters would use this area to hunt for animals as soon as they left the park, and park superintendent Horace Albright believed there was a real threat of the hunters and harsh winters decimating their populations. Thus, the proposal was made to add this land, which was accomplished in 1932 via an Executive Order signed by President Franklin D. Roosevelt.

During the 1940s and 1950s, the area was used to grow hay for the park's elk and bison; there were even irrigation ditches constructed to facilitate watering of the grasslands (water came from the nearby Wilson Springs). This ceased in the early 1960s, however, with the changing management philosophies of the National Park Service.

The lands along this road is used today primarily for administrative and research purposes. While the area itself is not overly popular with visitors, it offers wide, expansive views of the Yellowstone River Valley and the surrounding mountains.

0.0 / 4.6 GPS: 45.03085, -110.71267
JUNCTION WITH MAIN STREET IN GARDINER
ARCH PARK/PICNIC AREA (N) 🏕 🖼

Old Yellowstone Trail departs from Gardiner to the west, just north of the Roosevelt Arch.

Arch Park was initially created at the time of the arch's construction in 1903. It was designed to "beautify" the entrance to the park. Over time, it fell into disuse and disrepair, but several years ago was restored to something approaching its original appearance. Today, there are seven picnic tables (two of which are under a shelter) and a grill here.

0.1 / 4.5 GPS: 45.03086, -110.71266
ENTRANCE ROAD TO GARDINER PUBLIC SCHOOL (N)

The first two turns west of the junction take you into the Gardiner Public School complex. The school holds grades PreK-12 and has a student body of approximately 250 students. Part of the school building itself is inside Yellowstone National Park, and the children of many park employees based in Mammoth attend classes here.

Bison from the park like to hang out on the school's football field during the early part of the spring, making the field conditions, shall we say, less than optimal for most sports. The small building south of the field houses local and county offices (Sewer & Water Department, Sheriff, and a library).

0.2 / 4.4 GPS: 45.03156, -110.71401
HERITAGE AND RESEARCH CENTER (N) ✴

Completed in 2004, the **Heritage and Research Center** (HRC) is the park's museum, archive and research library. The facility now holds over 5.5 million items related to the park and its history and is the only NPS site to have "affiliate" status with the National Archives and Records Administration (NARA). The agreement with NARA means that all of the park's vital records are stored in the park, allowing researchers to have direct access to them while in the park itself.

Tours of the facility are available on Tuesdays and Thursdays during the summer. Contact the staff at 307-344-2662 for details.

The creek that runs under the road just west of the HRC is unnamed.

0.8 / 3.7 GPS: 45.03446, -110.72547
TINKER'S HILL (GARDINER) CEMETERY (N) ✴

This cemetery is known as **Tinker's Hill Cemetery**, or the Gardiner Cemetery. It was given its name from the fact that the first person buried there was a tinker, or tin worker. Many of the graves are unmarked.

There are several colorful figures from early park history buried here, including "Uncle" John Yancey (d. 1903) and the park's first chief ranger, James McBride (d. 1942). The cemetery is owned by a private organization out of Gardiner, but they have abandoned it.[1]

2.1 / 2.4 GPS: 45.04405, -110.74733
LANDSLIDE CREEK CROSSING

Landslide Creek crosses under the road here. It originates on Sepulcher Mountain (9652 ft/2942 m) to the south, and gets its name from the numerous landslides that occur on the peak's north face. The small airstrip across the river is the Gardiner Airport.

2.5 / 2.0 GPS: 45.04754, -110.75407
STEPHENS CREEK CROSSING

Stephens Creek is named after Clarence Stephens, who was an assistant superintendent of the park. From 1879-1882, he owned the ranchland where the Stephens Creek Administrative Area is located (see next item below).

2.6 / 2.0 GPS: 45.04775, -110.75427
STEPHENS CREEK ROAD (S)
STEPHENS CREEK ADMINISTRATIVE AREA (S)

The **Stephens Creek Administrative Area** is used by the park for a variety of activities. It houses a law enforcement shooting range, bison capture facilities, winter corrals for the park's 100+ horses, and provides feed storage and supply services for the park's stock operations. NPS staff also receive their training in horse operations at this location. Finally, there's a nursery where indigenous plants are raised and used to revegetate areas where roads or buildings are removed. This area is named after Clarence Stephens as well.

The house sitting approximately 500 yards south of the main facility is known as the Rife House, named after Ernest Rife, the man who owned it in 1923. It was originally built in 1917, and moved to its present location and remodeled in 1934. Today it is used to house park staff.

This entire area was taken by the government in an eminent domain action when the land was annexed by the park in 1932. This facility is not open to the general public.

3.0 / 1.6 GPS: 45.05164, -110.75848
VEGETATION STUDY AREA (S)
SITE OF THE FORMER TOWN OF CINNABAR

The fenced in area on the south side of the road here is a vegetation study area, one of several spread throughout the park. This particular one and two others nearby are being used to study the potential for restoring native vegetation to the Gardiner Basin.

On the north side of the road, you'll note the raised ground that was the old railroad bed that ran through here to the Town of Gardiner.

This area was the site of Cinnabar, the town created by the Northern Pacific Railroad in 1883 specifically to serve as a terminus for its line to Yellowstone. At the time, a mining claim on lands between here and Gardiner prevented the railroad from laying track all the way to that city, so the line was ended here. There was a hotel, at least one saloon, a blacksmith shop, and several other structures in this area. In 1903, the railroad was finally able to get its track to Gardiner, and much of the town of Cinnabar was literally picked up and moved. Today, hardly a trace remains of the old town.

Passenger rail service continued to Gardiner until 1948, and freight service until 1975. The railroad tracks were removed in 1976.

4.4 / 0.1 GPS: 45.06494, -110.77536
REESE CREEK/PARK BOUNDARY

Reese Creek is named after George J. Reese, who owned land and ranched along the northern end of the segment of this road located in the park. This is the lowest point inside the boundary of the park (5282 ft/1610 m).

The road continues on from here to Corwin Springs. Off to the northwest, you can see Devil's Slide down the face of Cinnabar Mountain. This interesting feature was created by layers of different types of rock that have been tilted vertically and have eroded at different rates. It was given its moniker by the Washburn Expedition in 1870.[2]

GARDINER HIGH ROAD

The **Gardiner High Road** is a one-way, scenic side road which originates behind the Mammoth Hot Springs Hotel. Constructed in 1879 by the park's second superintendent, Philetus W. Norris, it was the second road between the park's headquarters and the town of Gardiner. It was used until 1884 when the U.S. Army Corps of Engineers completed a new road through Gardner Canyon (at a cost of $7,750).[3]

The new road was easier to travel and more scenic but prone to washouts and avalanches. Consideration had been given to moving main route back to this road, but the better scenery kept the road in the canyon where it remains to this day (albeit with a slightly different alignment than it originally had).

This road has also been referred to in some documents as "Slide Lake Road," since it passes near Slide Lake just before it exits at the North Entrance.

Mileage figures for this road are provided in one direction only since the road is one-way from Mammoth to Gardiner.

0.0 GPS: 44.97741, -110.70137
ENTRY BEHIND MAMMOTH HOT SPRINGS HOTEL

The entry to this road is located behind the Mammoth Hot Springs Hotel at the north junction of the road into the cottage area. If the gate is open, the road is open.

0.2 GPS: 44.97906, -110.69973
FORT YELLOWSTONE/MAMMOTH VILLAGE OVERLOOK(E) 🏛

This spot on the road affords an excellent overlook of the Mammoth development in general and Fort Yellowstone in particular. Since there's no pullout here, be cognizant of any vehicles behind you and don't block the road. There's a small pullout around the curve ahead. You can park and walk up onto the hill to get some good photos if you prefer.

0.2 GPS: 44.97947, -110.69931
MAMMOTH RESERVOIR/ELK PLAZA SERVICE ROAD (S)
BEAVER PONDS NORTH TRAILHEAD (S) 🚶

This service road takes you back to the first cemetery at Mammoth on Kite Hill. This hill was given its name because park employees can often be seen flying kites here during the summer. The cemetery has 14 graves, but only a handful of those interred here have been identified. Park historian Lee Whittlesey's book, *Death in Yellowstone*, has information on the history of these grave sites.

The road also leads back to the huge underground reservoir for the Mammoth area, and to the area known as Elk Plaza, a large open space where a cellular/radio tower is located. Elk Plaza was used as a shooting range for the U.S. Army during its first couple of years in the park (until a new range was built near Gardiner - see the North Entrance Road section for details).

The **Beaver Ponds North Trailhead** intersects with the road as well. This is a two-mile (3.2 km) trail to a series of ponds dammed by beavers (oddly enough). You can return to this trailhead or make the loop and end up at its south trailhead which is located at Clematis Creek next to the Mammoth Terraces.

1.2 GPS: 44.99232, -110.70256
WYOMING/MONTANA STATE LINE

At this point, you're crossing into Montana from Wyoming. There is no sign here, however.

1.9 GPS: 45.00251, -110.70487
UNNAMED CREEK CROSSING

An unnamed tributary of the Gardner River crosses under the road here on its way down the hill to Slide Lake. The creek drains Beaver Ponds. Slide Lake was given its name because it was formed when mudslides dammed up a low spot in the creek, creating the lake.

3.7 GPS: 45.02186, -110.70170
Valve Vaults (W)

Off in the distance to the west on a slight hill, you'll notice a valve access for waterworks. There's a pipeline running through this area, and the vault affords access to the pipeline for maintenance work.

4.0 GPS: 45.02521, -110.70082
Junction with the North Entrance Road

The road terminates here right at the North Entrance kiosks. Once you ensure there's no oncoming traffic, you do not need to stop at the kiosk to show entrance permits unless requested to do so by the ranger.

Blacktail Plateau Drive

The **Blacktail Plateau Drive** is part of the original stagecoach road through this area of the park. The U.S. Army Corps of Engineers referred to this as the "Crescent Hill Canyon Road."

Mileage figures for this road are provided for one direction only since this is a one-way road. This road is usually closed until mid- to late-July, and will often close without notice due to poor road conditions (especially after heavy rains) or public safety issues (e.g., an animal carcass near the roadway). Sections of the road have a grade of about 10%. Recreational vehicles, vehicles pulling trailers, buses, and low-clearance vehicles are not allowed.

0.0 GPS: 44.95812, -110.54179
West Junction with the Mammoth-to-Tower Road (S)

The entrance to this road is kind of hidden, and you come up on it pretty quickly with no warning, so be prepared for it.

0.2 GPS: 44.95612, -110.54042
Frog Rock Service Road (W)

A vestigial dirt road from the Frog Rock Pit intersects at this point. Do not enter this road. In the winter, the old road is part of a ski trail.

1.0 GPS: 44.95128, -110.52657
Dirt Service Road (S)

An old dirt service road runs south off the main roadway here.

1.5 GPS: 44.94895, -110.51912
Grizzly Bear Rock (S) ⛾

A rock formation that reminds visitors of a grizzly bear can be seen on the hill to the southeast from this point.

1.7 GPS: 44.94903, -110.51462
Utility Box (N)

You'll notice an electrical service box off the north side of the road here. Electrical service is provided to the Roosevelt, Tower, and Mount Washburn areas from Mammoth via an underground cable laid in 1987. These boxes can be seen along the road every so often, and provide a means to splice and service those cables. In this part of the park, those cables generally follow this old roadway.

2.7 GPS: 44.94441, -110.49727
Oxbow Creek Crossing

Oxbow Creek crosses under the road here, flowing through Phantom Lake on to the Yellowstone River. It gets its name from the fact it's mouth is at an oxbow bend in the Yellowstone River.

3.6 GPS: 44.94043, -110.48206
Garnet Creek Crossing
The Cut
Crescent Hill (E)

Garnet Creek crosses the road here. The creek is named after its proximity to Garnet Hill, which is interesting given that it runs along the west side of Crescent Hill here (in front of you).

As you pass the creek, you're heading into an area known as **The Cut**, which is basically the deep gorge the creek passes through as you head east. It was originally called The Devil's Cut, but the name was later changed because it was felt there were too many features in the park named after the Devil. **Crescent Hill** (7851 ft/2393 m) got its name because it appeared as a crescent on early park maps.

5.3 GPS: 44.92069, -110.47128
ELK CREEK CROSSING
YANCEY HILL

Elk Creek crosses under the road right here in this hairpin curve. You begin descending Yancey Hill at this point.

5.4 GPS: 44.92143, -110.46913
ELK CREEK VALLEY PULLOUT (N)

This small overlook affords you a view down into the small valley formed by Elk Creek.

6.9 GPS: 44.92200, -110.44410
EASTERN TERMINUS OF BLACKTAIL PLATEAU DRIVE

The road ends here. However, when the road was initially constructed, it continued on across what you see as the Grand Loop Road today, and into Pleasant Valley below. The valley was the site of John Yancey's hotel and saloon from 1884 until 1906. Today, this old trail is used as a horse trail by the concession operator at Roosevelt.

NORTH RIM DRIVE

The North Rim Drive takes you along the northern rim of the Grand Canyon of the Yellowstone. It was originally constructed in the 1895-1896 time frame by the U.S. Army Corps of Engineers.

Traffic on this road used to flow south *from* the Canyon Village complex, but several years ago the traffic pattern was reversed, so you now start from the south end. This is a one way road, so the mileage figures are only provided from south to north.

During the peak summer season, traffic often backs up along this road, even out onto the Grand Loop Road in some instances. If you encounter that, be patient. It doesn't take long for it to clear out in most cases.

0.0 GPS: 44.72059, -110.49962
SOUTH JUNCTION WITH THE GRAND LOOP ROAD

This is the south junction of the North Rim Drive and the Grand Loop Road.

0.1 GPS: 44.71968, -110.49796
BRINK OF THE LOWER FALLS PARKING AREA 🚶 🚻 🚹🚺

The trail from this parking area takes you down to the brink of the Lower Falls of the Yellowstone. The trail is ⁴⁄₁₀ of a mile long each way and is mostly packed dirt/gravel. It does get pretty steep in a couple of places, but there are benches placed at many spots along the way for you to rest. There's a comfort station on the west side of the road that opens in late June, and vault toilets a little further north on the east side of the parking lot.

0.5 GPS: 44.72157, -110.49042
CANYON WASTEWATER TREATMENT PLANT (N)

You might notice a fairly large building on the hill above you as you drive through here. This is part of the **Wastewater Treatment Plant** for the Canyon Village area.

0.7 GPS: 44.72152, -110.48756
BIG SPRING CREEK CROSSING

Big Spring Creek crosses the road here and falls down the wall of the canyon to empty into the Yellowstone River. It gets its name because it originates from a large cold spring in the F-J cabin area in Canyon Village.

0.8 GPS: 44.72230, -110.48519
LOOKOUT POINT/RED ROCK POINT (E) 🚻

Lookout Point is perhaps the best vantage point of the Lower Falls from the North Rim. There's an interpretive sign here that provides information about the osprey, which you can often see nesting on spires in the canyon.

Red Rock Point offers a slightly better view of the falls, but requires a very steep one mile hike (some of it boardwalk) to the observation platform. The "red rock" in the name refers to a reddish-colored spire below the Lower Falls, its color resulting from iron oxide in the rock.

0.9 GPS: 44.72335, -110.48459
GRAND VIEW POINT (E) 🚻

Grand View Point provides an excellent view of the canyon, but you can't see either of the waterfalls from this vantage point. Historians are unsure how this vantage point got its name.[4] On the west side of the road is a trail that leads into the P-Loop of the Canyon Lodge cabin complex.

1.3 GPS: 44.72913, -110.48143
INSPIRATION POINT ROAD (E) 🏃
GLACIAL BOULDER/GLACIAL BOULDER TRAIL 🏃

Inspiration Point was given its name by an early park guide based on the intensity of the color in the canyon walls.[5] There is a viewing platform from which you can see a long view down the canyon with the Lower Falls off in the distance. The original platform here fell off into the canyon during an earthquake in 1975 (no one was on it at the time).

The **Glacial Boulder** is a huge, house-sized glacial erratic, or rock deposited by a retreating glacier. In this case, geologists believe this rock was transported some 40 miles (64 km) or more, and was left here in the Precambrian era.[6]

The **Glacial Boulder Trail** takes you to the Seven Mile Hole Trail (3 mi/5 km), Washburn Hot Springs (4.8 mi/7.7 km), and ultimately to the summit of Mt. Washburn (8.5 mi/13.5 km). The hike to Mt. Washburn from here is the most difficult and least used of the three routes to its summit. The Seven Mile Hole Trail is an 11-mile (18 km) round trip to the bottom of the Grand Canyon.

This trail was known in the park's early days as the Rowland Pass Trail; it was the first horse trail into the area from Tower Fall via the eastern face of Mt. Washburn. Originally, plans had called for the first road between Canyon and Tower to be constructed along this trail, but the route over Dunraven Pass was selected instead, largely because it afforded easier access to Washburn's summit. Rowland Pass was named for George Rowland, a man who was a traveling companion of park Superintendent Philetus Norris during an exploration of the area in 1878.

1.9 GPS: 44.73443, -110.48743
EXIT FROM CAMPER SERVICES PARKING LOT (N)

The driveway at the north intersection of the roadway here is an exit from the Canyon Village Camper Services parking lot. The Camper Services Building has showers and laundry for visitor use (whether you are a guest at the campground or not).

2.0 GPS: 44.73546, -110.48945
CANYON CAMPGROUND THREE-WAY 🔺🏕🍴📷♨

This is a three-way intersection. If you turn south you'll enter Canyon

Village. Turning north takes you into the Canyon Village Campground, and going straight takes you toward Canyon Junction.

The Canyon Campground was constructed in 1956-1957 as part of the Mission 66 project to create the village. It has 272 sites (which are reservable), each renting for $25 per night in 2013.

2.1 GPS: 44.73581, -110.49051
ENTRANCE INTO CANYON RANGER STATION PARKING LOT (N)

The building at the end of the driveway on the north side of the road is the Canyon Emergency Services Building, which houses the law enforcement rangers, a fire truck and an ambulance.

2.1 GPS: 44.73587, -110.49133
WEST ENTRANCE TO CANYON VILLAGE ⊪ ⊨ ⊠ ⋒ ♲ ⫫ ⊒ ⫝

Turning left (south) here takes you into the main entrance for Canyon Village. There's a post office, Visitor Center, the Canyon Lodge (which contains a dining room, cafeteria, and a deli, as well as a lounge), two General Stores, and the Canyon Visitor Education Center.

2.2 GPS: 44.73591 -110.49325
CANYON JUNCTION ⊞ ⫽

From here, you can drive 18.3 miles (29.4 km) north to Tower Junction, 11.6 miles (18.7 km) west to Norris Junction, or 15.4 miles (24.8 km) south to Fishing Bridge Junction. On the northeast corner of the intersection is the Canyon YPSS Service Station, which provides fuel and limited vehicle/RV repair services.

SOUTH RIM DRIVE

The **South Rim Drive** was originally built immediately after the Melan Arch Bridge was constructed across the river by the U.S. Army Corps of Engineers in 1903. The road affords access to Artist Point as well as several other trails along and around the South Rim of the Grand Canyon of the Yellowstone.

0.0 GPS: 44.70814, -110.50376
JUNCTION WITH THE GRAND LOOP ROAD

This is the junction of the South Rim Drive and Grand Loop Road.

Melan Arch Bridge, n.d.

0.0 GPS: 44.70818, -110.50303
CANYON SERVICE ROAD (N)
CHITTENDEN BRIDGE

The **Canyon Service Road** (also known as the Crystal Falls Road) that runs north immediately west of the bridge was part of the original road complex through the Canyon area up until the late 1950s. The road affords access to the water intake for the Canyon area and the old Canyon Bridge over Jay Creek, and terminates at the Brink of the Upper Falls parking lot. Along this road was the old housekeeping cabin complex, a ranger station, general stores, and several other structures, all of which were removed once the new development up the road was completed.

The current **Chittenden Bridge** was constructed in 1962 to replace the 1903-era Melan Arch originally constructed by Army Engineer Capt. Hiram Chittenden. The new bridge was given the engineer's name in honor of the work he did on the road system throughout the park. Despite there being locations further upstream where a shorter span would have worked, this location was chosen specifically so the bridge would not be seen from the vantage points for the Upper or Lower Falls in the canyon.

The original Melan Arch Bridge (see image above) was named after the man who developed the engineering techniques used to build it, Josef Melan. His company typically received royalties for every bridge built using his design, but he waived the royalty fees in this case because of the bridge's importance to the park and its visibility.[7]

0.2 GPS: 44.70858, -110.50125
WAPITI LAKE TRAILHEAD (E) 🥾 🚻
CHITTENDEN BRIDGE PICNIC AREA (E) 🪑

This turnout is the trailhead for the **Wapiti Lake Trail**, as well as several others, including the Clear Lake/Ribbon Lake Loop and Wrangler Lake. This area was the site of a group camp for a number of years.

The **Chittenden Bridge Picnic Area**, located on the south side of the parking lot, has four tables and a handicap-accessible vault toilet.

0.6 GPS: 44.71350, -110.49513
Uncle Tom's Trail/Upper Falls View (W) 👟 🚻 🚻
Haircut Rock
Woodchopper Hill (E)

This is the trailhead for **Uncle Tom's Trail**, and you can also connect into the South Rim Trail here as well. The Uncle Tom's Trailhead is a short walk to the north from the parking lot, and then you'll have a 500 foot descent into the canyon down a series of 328 steps. It doesn't take very long to get to the bottom, but coming back up is quite strenuous. In fact, there's an old saying that the trail is 328 steps down, and over 5,000 coming back up, due to the difficulty many people have with making it back to the top. Take lots of water with you and rest frequently on the provided benches coming back up. Climbing on the rocks off trail is prohibited in this area. If you knock rocks off into the crowd below they can injure or kill those below. At least two people (both children) have been killed on this trail as a result of rocks being dislodged or thrown from above.[8]

Herbert F. "Uncle Tom" Richardson had originally petitioned the government to allow him to build an elevator to take tourists down into the canyon. When that was rejected in 1890, he constructed a rope ladder that people could descend to get an in-canyon view of the lower falls. This rope ladder was later (1905) replaced with a wooden stair structure and then in the 1950s replaced with today's steel structure.

Just a few steps to the west from the parking lot will put you at an overlook of the 109-foot Upper Falls of the Yellowstone. You'll also be able to see Crystal Falls, which is Cascade Creek falling 129 feet over the edge of the canyon.

As you enter the driveway into the parking lot, you'll notice on the immediate right what appears to be an old roadbed blocked off by a series of boulders. This old road led to a meadow that became the site of the first Canyon Corral when the first tent camp was located on the site of the current parking lot. Tourists could take horseback and buggy rides from here.

From 1903 to 1913, this area (the present day parking lot and the area in the woods around the existing comfort station) was the site of a periodic tent camp of the Shaw and Powell Camping Company (SPCC). In 1913, the SPCC received permission to build a permanent tent camp here, which they did (known from 1913 to 1917 as the "Twixt Falls Camp").[9] These facilities were taken over by the Yellowstone Park Camping Company in 1917, and operated until the first Canyon Lodge was constructed on the same site in 1921-1925. The new and improved lodge and cabin facilities could accommodate over 700 guests.

In 1957, following the opening of the new Canyon Village, the Lodge and its related structures were abandoned. Over the next couple of years, many of the cabins and support buildings would be relocated to other areas of the park (especially the Lake and Fishing Bridge areas). The old Lodge building itself (which was the original dining hall for the tent camp, constructed in 1912) was sold off and relocated to Nevada City, Montana.[10] What was left would eventually be razed and replaced with this parking lot and the comfort station.

There remains one relic from this period here. If you walk over to the northeastern apex of the curve of the parking lot (opposite the side you drive in on), and walk down into the wooded area, you'll notice a small clearing with an interestingly shaped rock formation. This small formation is known as "**Haircut Rock**," (44.71563, -110.49591) because it was just the right size for Lodge employees to sit on while someone cut their hair; it was located right behind the main lodge building, which was facing south.

The hill across the road from the entrance to the parking lot is known as **Woodchopper Hill**. It gets this name from a log cutting operation that operated here from 1923 to 1932, preparing logs for all of the new lodges and their related structures being built during this time period.

1.5 GPS: 44.71889, -110.48202
Artist Point Parking Lot 🚻 🚻

Artist Point was given its name because it was erroneously believed that artist Thomas Moran painted his famous "Grand Canyon of the Yellowstone" from here. In reality, the inspiration for it came from Moran Point on the other side of the canyon (it wasn't painted until he returned east). However, this is the vantage point from which the second most-photographed feature in the park is commonly made. Many consider the view here to be one of the most majestic in the country. The South Rim Trail continues west from here to Point Sublime.

GULL POINT DRIVE

Gull Point was named for the California seagull, in accordance with the practice of naming park features after local fauna. **Gull Point Drive** is a remnant of the original road through this area.

When the Bridge Bay development was constructed in the early 1960s, a new (existing) bridge was constructed over the entrance to the bay and the road relocated westward a few hundred yards. This section of road then became a scenic side road. The original bridge, which sat lower to the water just east of the current bridge was destroyed when the new one was completed.

This is a two-way road, and mileage figures are given for both southbound and northbound travel. The road is often closed during the early part of the season because high water swamps the road.

0.0 / 2.0 GPS: 44.53055, -110.43596
NORTH JUNCTION

The north junction is directly across the road from the entrance to the Natural Bridge Service Road/Trailhead.

0.1 / 1.9 GPS: 44.53124, -110.43385
BEND IN THE ROAD ⛱

Even though this is not an official picnic area, there are two picnic tables at this roughly 100 degree bend in the road. It is an excellent place to watch the boats coming and going to/from Bridge Bay Marina.

0.2 / 1.8 GPS: 44.53028, -110.43397
BRIDGE CREEK LAGOON

As you round the bend, the small pool of water on the west side of the road is **Bridge Creek Lagoon**, so named because Bridge Creek empties into it.

0.5 / 1.5 GPS: 44.52620, -110.43371
GULL POINT LAGOON (W)

The large body of water on the west side of the road here is known as **Gull Point Lagoon**.

1.0 / 1.0 GPS: 44.52509, -110.42514
LAKE HOTEL VIEW PULLOUT (N) 🏨

This is a small pullout with an excellent view of the Lake Hotel.

1.2 / 0.8 GPS: 44.52552, -110.41975
GULL POINT PICNIC AREA (N) 🛉 🛉

The **Gull Point Picnic Area** is the second largest and one of the more scenic picnic areas in the park, with 21 tables and a handicap-accessible vault toilet. It is restricted to smaller vehicles only - no RVs or vehicles pulling trailers are allowed due to the small spaces and the tight turning radii.

1.8 / 0.2 GPS: 44.51891, -110.41845
BEACH PULLOUT (E)

This is a small turnout that affords access to a relatively secluded black sand beach, just a short walk to the east.

2.0 / 0.0 GPS: 44.51536, -110.41904
SOUTH JUNCTION

This is the south junction of Gull Point Drive and the Grand Loop Road.

FIREHOLE LAKE DRIVE

Firehole Lake Drive is a short scenic road that takes you past an interesting collection of thermal features, including one of the park's most notable geysers, Great Fountain. This road typically opens in early to mid-June each season.

Recreational vehicles and buses are not permitted on the road due to weight restrictions on a couple of wooden bridges (there have been several RVs that have sunk through these bridges, each time requiring the NPS to close the road to all traffic for several days until the bridges can be repaired). Firehole Lake Drive is a one way road, so only the northbound mileage is provided.

0.0 GPS: 44.53536, -110.81770
SOUTH JUNCTION

This is the south junction of Firehole Lake Drive and the Grand Loop Road.

0.5 GPS: 44.53563, -110.80826
SERENDIPITY MEADOW (S)

Serendipity Meadow is named for an area of thermal features located in the southern end of the meadow known as Serendipity Springs. The area contains about 30 unnamed thermal features and was discovered by researchers through serendipitous circumstances, thus the name.

0.6 GPS: 44.53562, -110.80491
BROKEN EGG SPRING (N)

The small spring on the north side of the road here is known as **Broken Egg Spring**. It was given its name in 1895 by U.S. Army Engineer Lt. Hiram Chittenden, who stated, "it is shaped like an egg set endwise in the ground with the upper part of the shell broken off."[11]

0.8 GPS: 44.53499, -110.80194
FIREHOLE SPRING (N)

Firehole Spring is the small pool just below the eastern edge of the pullout. It is not named for its proximity to Firehole Lake or any other feature with the "Firehole" name, but rather because of the flickering of the light that occurs as the steam bubbles enter the pool from the bottom of its basin.

Though it is named as a spring, most geologists consider it a perpetual spouter, given its almost continual spurting of water (up to six feet high in some instances).

0.9 GPS: 44.53518, -110.80096
WHITE CREEK CROSSING

White Creek crosses under the road here. It is named for the white deposits through which it travels as it drains through the area. The creek, which empties into the Firehole River west of the main road, has as its source a series of hot springs in the hills to the southeast. Researchers recently discovered that not a drop of cold water enter its stream for its entire length (with the obvious exception of rain).[12]

0.9 GPS: 44.53565, -110.80024
SURPRISE POOL (W)

Surprise Pool gets its name from the fact that the spring's superheated water erupts into a boil when its surface is disturbed. Keep in mind that throwing things into the park's thermal features is not only destructive to them but is illegal as well.

1.0 GPS: 44.53631, -110.79949
GREAT FOUNTAIN GEYSER (W) ⊻⁕

Great Fountain Geyser is the only predicted geyser outside the Upper Geyser Basin and is considered by many to be one of the "must see" geysers in the park. It erupts to heights of around 100 feet every 12 hours on average (with a range of 8-17 hours). The geyser is surrounded by decorated concentric circles of geyserite deposits and has a 16-foot vent. Predictions for the geyser, when available, can usually be obtained from the Old Faithful Visitor Education Center or the little prediction board at the entrance to the boardwalk around the geyser.

1.2 GPS: 44.53919, -110.80239
WHITE DOME GEYSER (W) ⊻⁕

White Dome Geyser gets its name characteristically. Based on the size of its cone, the third largest in the park, it is probably one of the oldest thermal features in the Yellowstone.[13] White Dome erupts every 15-90 minutes (range of 9 minutes to 3 hours) on average to heights of about 30 feet.[14]

About 250 yards to the east of here is Mushroom Spring, where the *Thermus aquaticus* organism was discovered in 1969. This organism was used to develop the DNA coding technology used today to identify criminals and perform genome mapping operations.

1.3 GPS: 44.54032, -110.80175
TANGLED CREEK CROSSING

Tangled Creek crosses under the road here, one of several places, on a bridge that was built in 1935. The creek is named for the complex interweaving of its channels as it passes through the fields. The creek has its origins in the hills east of this area, and drains through Firehole Lake and Hot Lake before weaving its way across the field, under the main road and emptying into the Firehole River west of Fountain Paint Pots.

1.6 GPS: 44.54283, -110.79619
PINK CONE (GEYSER) (N)

Located right off the side of the road here is **Pink Cone**, a small geyser named because of the rose color (caused by manganese oxide) of its cone.

The word "geyser" is not in its official name because, when it was given its name in the park's early days, no one had seen it erupt and thus it was not identified as a geyser. Pink Cone erupts to heights of 15-20 feet for about 15 minutes every 18-23 hours.[15]

1.7 GPS: 44.54317, -110.79406
Ranger Pool/Old Bath Lake (S)
Bead Geyser (N)

Just past Pink Cone on the southeast side of the road is **Old Bath Lake**, known commonly by two other names, Ranger Pool, and Tank Spring (as well as a host of additional monikers from the park's early days). There was a bathhouse here from 1908 until the 1930s. The pool gets its "Ranger Pool" name from the fact that law enforcement rangers have had to dedicate so much of their time to preventing people from bathing in the lake. Because of its history, it is considered one of the park's most historic archaeological sites.[16]

Directly across the road from this lake is Bead Geyser, believed to be the most regular geyser in the park. It erupts every 30 minutes (on average) for 2.5 minutes. Geyser was named for egg-shaped "beads" that surrounded it until tourists pilfered them all.

1.9 GPS: 44.54318, -110.79140
Tangled Creek Crossing

Tangled Creek once again passes under the road here, as it leaves the south end of Hot Lake. The original bridge here was built in 1935, but has been rebuilt many times because of heavy RVs and buses that occasionally come through this area (even though they're not supposed to). The bridge often collapses under their weight.

2.0 GPS: 44.54271, -110.78840
Unnamed Creek Crossing

An unnamed creek crosses under the road here, draining from the southeast end of Hot Lake.

2.2 GPS: 44.54419, -110.78540
Firehole Lake/Black Warrior Lake ⁑

This is a large parking area for Firehole Lake and its associated thermal features. The lake (which is on the east side of the road) gets its name from the flickering light effects generated through the bubbling of steam from its basin floor. There is a short boardwalk around the south edge of the lake that take you along the 20 or so smaller thermal features adjacent to the lake.

2.3 GPS: 44.54458, -110.78662
BLACK WARRIOR LAKE (S)
STEADY GEYSER (S)

The source of the name of **Black Warrior Lake** (west side of the parking lot) is believed to have some connection to black manganese oxide deposits in the basins and Tangled Creek which drains through this area.

Steady Geyser, located on the east side of Black Warrior Lake, was given its name because of its nearly steady spouting of water (and thus, many consider it a perpetual spouter rather than a true geyser). Its activity and height have decreased over the past few years.

2.8 GPS: 44.54702, -110.79641
OLD FIREHOLE LAKE SERVICE ROAD (N)

You'll have to look closely, but there's an old roadbed heading northwest off the existing road here. This was part of the original "side road" that passed through the Firehole Lake area and later led to an old quarry and construction material staging area/disposal areas. In fact, if you walk out into the area you can still find remnants of old construction debris. Aggregate material from this area was used to build the bypass road around Fountain Paint Pots in the late 1920s (the road originally ran right through the middle of the paint pots - you can still see evidence of the foundation on the northwest side of the main paint pot there today).

3.3 GPS: 44.54842, -110.80675
NORTH JUNCTION

This is the north junction of the Firehole Lake Drive. Right across from it is the entrance into the Fountain Paint Pot parking lot (though it's illegal to cross and enter). If you turn south, you'll head back to the Old Faithful area, or you can turn north and continue on to Madison Junction.

FOUNTAIN FLATS DRIVE

Fountain Flats Drive is named for the fact it crosses over the large flat meadow named for its proximity to Fountain Geyser and its namesake paint pots. Today, the road ends at a parking area just north of the Ojo Caliente Spring, but up until the mid-1990s, you could drive all the way south to picnic areas at Goose Lake and Feather Lake some one and a half miles hence.

0.0 GPS: 44.57806, -110.82906
North Junction
Nez Perce Creek Crossing

As soon as you turn into the road, you'll cross over the **Nez Perce Creek** on a bridge built in 1997 as part of the reconstruction of the roads in the Old Faithful to Madison Junction area.

0.0 GPS: 44.57735, -110.83025
Nez Perce Picnic Area (N) 🏕 👫
Grave of Mattie Culver (N) 🪦

The **Nez Perce Picnic Area** has 12 tables, three grills, and a handicap accessible vault toilet. This picnic area is pretty popular during the summer, largely because it is so close to the creek. You'll often see people lounging and wading in the creek on hot days. Located behind the vault toilet at the picnic area is the grave of **Mattie Culver**, the wife of the winter caretaker at the Marshall (later the Firehole) Hotel located adjacent to this site. Mrs. Culver passed away on March 2, 1889, from what was probably tuberculosis (she was approximately 30 years old).

When she died, the ground was so hard from being frozen it was impossible to dig a grave for her. With the assistance of soldiers from the U.S. Army post near here, her husband, E.C. Culver, formed a temporary casket made from two barrels to hold her remains until the spring thaw came about and they could dig an appropriate grave for her. Today, the grave is fenced in, and you will occasionally see fresh flowers laid at its headstone. Author Nan Weber wrote an interesting book about Mattie's life entitled, *Mattie: A Woman's Journey West*.

0.2 GPS: 44.57659, -110.83153
Hygeia Spring (S)
Site of the Marshall Hotel/Firehole Hotels (N)

Along the south side of the road here is **Hygeia Spring**, named after Greek goddess of health. The spring was used to heat water for the Marshall and Firehole Hotels, and had a small bath house installed on its east side (complete with a small "tub" dug into the formation itself).

The flat space to the north between the current road and the river was the site of the **Marshall Hotel**, built in 1880 by George Marshall. This was the first hotel in the deep interior of the park, and also served as Marshall's house and the mail station. In 1885, a second structure was built on the south side of the creek here across from Hygeia Spring. It was known as the **Firehole Hotel**. It served guests until 1891 when the new Fountain Hotel was opened further south.

All of the buildings associated with these hotels, with the exception of two cottages, were burned in 1891. The cottages were used for a variety of purposes, including housing park employees and Army personnel. They, too, were later razed.

0.5 GPS: 44.57122, -110.83268
MAIDEN'S GRAVE SPRING (W) 🔭 👤

A short trail leads to **Maiden's Grave Spring** at the edge of the river. The spring was named by an early guidebook writer for its proximity to the grave of Mattie Culver (see above).

0.8 GPS: 44.56768, -110.83485
OJO CALIENTE PARKING AREA
FREIGHT ROAD TRAILHEAD 🚶
SENTINEL MEADOWS/QUEEN'S LAUNDRY 🚶
IMPERIAL MEADOWS TRAIL/FAIRY FALLS 🚶
GOOSE LAKE/FEATHER LAKE 🚶 🚴

At the end of the road is a circular turnaround and a parking area. At the south end of the turnaround is the trailhead for the Sentinel Meadows, Imperial Meadows and Fairy Falls Trails. These trails take you back to a variety of interesting features. This trailhead is often referred to as the Fountain Freight Road Trailhead, or simply the Freight Road Trailhead. The old road was once known as the Fountain Freight Road because it was used as a bypass for vehicles making deliveries to the Upper Geyser Basin area.

Approximately 1800 feet down the trail, you'll come upon a hot pool on the west side of the road, right on the north shore of the Firehole River. This is **Ojo Caliente Spring**. Ojo Caliente means "warm eye" in Spanish, and this pool of water lives up to its name; the water here measures over 201°F (94°C). On June 13, 1958, a six-year old boy out fishing with his father lost his footing and fell into the pool. He died two days later from the burns he sustained.[17]

Immediately after you cross over the bridge (built in 1984), the **Sentinel Meadows Trail** is on the west side of the road. This is a two-mile (3.2 km) trail to Sentinel Meadows, a small thermal area of about 30 features, including the infamous **Queen's Laundry**, or as it is officially known, Red Terrace Spring. There is a small building here known as The Queen's Laundry, which was the first building constructed by the government in a national park purely for tourist use, and is the only building remaining from the first era of civilian administration (1872-1886). The 8' x 19' building was started by Supt. P.W. Norris, but never completed (he left office before it was completed, and his successor wasn't interested in finishing it). The now decrepit building was designated as a National Historic Site in 2001.

If you continue south down the Freight Road Trail, approximately 2500 feet further you'll come to a bend in the trail. Just off the west side of the trail here is another small thermal field known as Fairy Springs. This area consists of approximately 100 features, all but one of which are unnamed (the named one is Boulder Spring, so-named because its waters emanate from a group of small boulders at the edge of the pool). Continuing around this bend and then entering the next one, you'll pass a small, unnamed lake.

Approximately one mile down the trail from the parking lot, you'll find the **Imperial Meadows Trail**. This trail takes you through a small area of about 60 mostly unnamed thermal features, and then curves southward to Spray Geyser and Imperial Geyser before heading back toward Fairy Falls. The Sentinel Meadows Trail also connects into the Imperial Meadows Trail just as it makes that southward curve, so you'll want to bear left if you wish to go to Fairy Falls (a distance of just over 2.5 miles from this point).

If you stay on the Freight Road Trail and continue on southward, you'll arrive at a group of three lakes. The larger and most southerly of the three is **Goose Lake**. The small lake in the foreground is **Gosling Lake**, and the one to the east of both of them is **Feather Lake**. Up until 1995, there were picnic areas at Feather and Goose Lake, but they were removed and the road from the trailhead was made into a hiking/bicycle only trail.

On the north side of Goose Lake is backcountry campsite OD5, one of only two handicap accessible campsites in the park (the other is at Ice Lake, the trail to which runs north off the Norris to Canyon Road). Before camping there, be sure you check with one of the Backcountry Offices first. Goose Lake was also the site of one of the park's road camps in the 1930s. If you continue past the three lakes, you'll end up at the **Fairy Falls Trail**. This entire trail is an approved bicycle route, though the loose gravel surface makes bicycling difficult in many places.

FIREHOLE CANYON DRIVE

Firehole Canyon Drive is a scenic side road that was part of the main road from Madison to Old Faithful for a period of time. The U.S. Army Corps of Engineers began construction on the road through the canyon in the 1900s, but it was abandoned in 1910 because of its narrowness and the difficulty of building the road. It was used as a side road until 1926 when it was reconfigured to be a part of the main road. The road was plagued with rock and debris fall, requiring constant vigilance by the park's road maintenance crews, however, and was heavily damaged in the Hebgen Lake Earthquake of 1959. Therefore, in 1960, the NPS completed reconstruction of the bypass you now travel as part of the main road, and the Firehole Canyon Road became a scenic detour once again.

This is a one-way road, so mileage figures are supplied for southbound travel only. No RVs or large buses are permitted due to the narrowness of the road and traffic/pedestrian congestion, especially at the swimming hole area during August and September.

0.0 GPS: 44.63888, -110.85860
JUNCTION WITH GRAND LOOP ROAD

The Firehole Canyon Road is usually closed until late May or even early June until the NPS can get a road crew into the area to remove all of the trees and rocks that have fallen into the roadway during the winter. Unless posted, you can hike or ride a bicycle past the gate, but if conditions warrant, the NPS does close this road to all travel at times.

0.3 GPS: 44.63754, -110.86364
MADISON WATER PUMPING STATION (S)

The small building you see in the woods on the hill above you is the water source for the Madison area. Water is taken from a spring on the hill, treated in this building, and pumped up to the large water tank on the hill (visible from the Madison Campground). Just ahead of this, along the shoreline as it approaches from the right, is where the original road joined the canyon road during the time when this was the main road between Madison Junction and Old Faithful (may not be visible during the height of the summer season).

The large mountain you see before you as you head into the curve is National Park Mountain.

0.6 GPS: 44.63366, -110.86514
RHINOCEROS ROCK (W)

In the river below the road here is a rock that has been dubbed "**Rhinoceros Rock**." If you look closely at the south end, the rock protrusion looks like the horn on a rhino's head. Thus, the name. There is a very small pullout here; if you elect to stop, ensure you're not blocking the roadway.

0.8 GPS: 44.63230, -110.86389
LOWER FIREHOLE CASCADE (W)

These cascades are colloquially referred to as the **Lower Firehole Cascade**.

1.0 GPS: 44.62956, -110.86294
FIREHOLE FALLS 🛝

Firehole Falls is a 40-foot waterfall on the Firehole River. There is a decent sized turnout here, but after you've parked you have to walk across the traffic pattern to see the falls, so be mindful of oncoming vehicles.

1.1 GPS: 44.62813, -110.86263
MIDDLE FIREHOLE CASCADE (W)

This cascade is known colloquially as **Middle Firehole Cascade**. There is no turnout here, so you'll need to admire them as you pass by.

1.9 GPS: 44.61834, -110.86037
FIREHOLE SWIMMING AREA (S) 🏊 🚻

The **Firehole Swimming Area** is one of the two sanctioned swimming areas in the park (the other is the Boiling River north of Mammoth). There are two vault toilets here. This area typically doesn't open until very late in the season due to high water (late July or August, usually), and there are no lifeguards on duty. And while swimming itself is permitted, climbing on or diving from the cliffs or the trees is illegal and dangerous. In July of 2010, a Taiwanese visitor drowned while swimming here, so be careful.

2.1 GPS: 44.61818, -110.85750
PARKING AREA (N)

This is an unpaved overflow parking area for the swimming hole. During late August and through much of September, this area gets very congested, so pay attention to what the drivers are doing.

2.2 GPS: 44.61721, -110.85548
UPPER FIREHOLE CASCADE TRAIL (S) 🚶

The path running south here is part of the old roadbed, and now serves as a trail along the river to the **Upper Firehole Cascade**, as it is colloquially known.

2.2 GPS: 44.61725, -110.85496
SOUTH JUNCTION

This is the south junction with the Grand Loop Road. Turn right to head toward Old Faithful, or left to return to the Madison Junction area.

VIRGINIA CASCADE DRIVE

The **Virginia Cascade Drive** takes you to Virginia Cascade along the Gibbon River (via Virginia Canyon). This was part of the second iteration of the original road through this area. In the 1960s, the main road was relocated to its present alignment north of this old road, and this original section was kept as a "scenic" side road (see the Norris Junction to Canyon Junction section for further details on its history).

The road is one way, so mileage figures are only provided for west to east travel. It typically does not open to public travel until mid- to late June.

0.0 GPS: 44.71913, -110.66621
JUNCTION WITH THE NORRIS CUTOFF ROAD

This is the west junction with the Norris to Canyon Road.

0.5 GPS: 44.71456, -110.65845
VIRGINIA CANYON OVERLOOK (S) 📷

This small turnout provides an overlook into Virginia Canyon.

0.8 GPS: 44.71511, -110.65254
DEVIL'S ELBOW VIEW (S) 📷

If you look down into the canyon at this point, toward the east, you'll see a sharp bend in the river. When the original road was constructed between Norris and Canyon, the road ran along the river down in this canyon. The sharp bend around the rock on the north side of the river here was known the "Bend in the Road," initially, but became known as "**Devil's Elbow**."

It was given its name because of the sharp, 90-degree turn required here, and the prevalence of accidents as a result of stagecoach drivers not slowing down enough, or encountering an oncoming coach as they rounded the corner. U. S. Army Engineer Capt. Hiram Chittenden relocated the road to the top of the canyon wall (the road you're on now) in 1905.

0.9 GPS: 44.71398, -110.64997
Damaged Road/Cascade View (S) 📷

The side of the road is unstable here, so the NPS has placed parapet retainers along the side to keep cars from driving off the side. Unfortunately, this is one of the best places to see the Cascade as well. If you stop here to take photos, be mindful of traffic behind you.

1.1 GPS: 44.71319, -110.64742
Virginia Cascade Brink (S) 🏞

The road widens here a bit at the brink of the **Virginia Cascade**. The cascade is named after the wife of Charles Gibson, president of the Yellowstone Park Association, which owned and operated many of the park's hotels from the mid-1880s on (and would later morph into the Yellowstone Park Company, the park's primary concessioner up until the mid-1960s).

1.5 GPS: 44.71281, -110.63905
Virginia Meadow Pullout (S)

The small pullout here affords an excellent view of **Virginia Meadow**, the vast open space along the Gibbon River to the east.

1.8 GPS: 44.71455, -110.63468
Virginia Meadow Picnic Area (E) 🪑 🚻

The **Virginia Meadow Picnic Area** has six tables and a vault toilet. When this was the original road, it also served as the trailhead for the Ice Lake Trail.

2.0 GPS: 44.71499, -110.63150
East Junction

This is the east junction of the Virginia Cascade Drive and the Norris Cutoff Road. You can head east from here to get to Canyon Village, or turn west to head back toward Norris Junction.

UPPER TERRACE DRIVE

The **Upper Terrace Drive** affords an up-close view of many of the thermal features at the top of the hot springs terraces at Mammoth Hot Springs. The road is one-way and very narrow, however, and thus RVs, buses, and trailers are not permitted. The road is a mile and a half long, though it is flat for the most part and easily walkable if you wish to park your vehicle at the entrance. There is a vault toilet at the parking lot.

This road typically doesn't open until mid-June after trail crews clear the area of downed trees and other hazards left over from the winter. It is a popular ski trail in the winter.

0.0 GPS: 44.96533, -110.70775
ENTRANCE/EXIT

This is the entrance AND the exit for the drive, so be alert for vehicles coming through from the other direction as only one vehicle at a time can pass through the gate. If you're entering, you'll take an immediate right into the one-way drive and continue northward.

0.0 GPS: 44.96612, -110.70794
MAIN TERRACE PARKING AREA (W) 🚶 🚻

Just a few hundred feet north of the entrance is a small parking area. You can park here and take one of the boardwalks along the top of the Main Terrace.

0.2 GPS: 44.96833, -110.707646
CUPID SPRING PARKING AREA 🚶

This parking area is located at **Cupid Spring**. Boardwalks afford access to the spring, Fissure Ridge, and Trail Springs, and boardwalks down to the lower Terraces, including New Blue Spring, Mound Terrace, Minerva Terrace, Cleopatra Terrace, and Palette Spring.

0.3 GPS: 44.96925, -110.70840
ESPLANADE PARKING AREA (N) 🚶 🚻

This parking area is located on top of a dry spring known as **The Esplanade**, some 330 feet above the parking areas below. This is an excellent overlook of the Mammoth development. An esplanade is an open level space separating a town from a fortress, and this feature appears to have been named because of the semblance of being on such a fortress while viewing the town from this vantage point. If you turn and look to the west while standing here, you'll see Narrow Gauge Terrace and Cheops Mound directly south of it. Narrow Gauge got its name from its appearance as a grade railroad bed, and Cheops Mound was given its name because of its pyramidal appearance. Cheops (pronounced *kee-ops*) was the builder of the first pyramid in Egypt.

0.4 GPS: 44.96822, -110.70919
PROSPECT SPRING PARKING AREA (W)

This parking area is located on the east side of **Prospect Spring**, named for its proximity to Prospect Terrace. Across the road from the parking area to the south is Highland Terrace, an extinct hot spring. The end closest to you is known as The Buttress, ostensibly named for its shape.

0.6 GPS: 44.96752, -110.71289
NEW HIGHLAND TERRACE (S) 🏞

Up until 1951, this was a forested area. That year, however, a spring broke out and quickly formed **New Highland Terrace**. The terrace engulfed the (now dead) trees you see still standing.

0.7 GPS: 44.96616, -110.71513
ORANGE SPRING MOUND (N) 🏞
LITTLE BURPER (S)

After you come around the sharp curve, there's a small parking area on the south side of **Orange Spring Mound**, characteristically named for the orange appearance it gets from the algae growing in its water runoff. Tangerine Spring is on the east end of the mound.

Across the street from the parking area is a small mound with two springs on top of it. The one in front is known as **Little Burper**, while the rear one is unnamed (officially). Little Burper gets its name from the fact that it "belches" bubbles from time to time.

0.9 GPS: 44.96574, -110.71297
BATH LAKE (SW) 🏞
APHRODITE TERRACE (N) 🏞

There's a small parking area here at **Bath Lake**, so named because it was used as a bathing pool by visitors in the park's early years, up until 1926, in fact. In 1919, a bath house was constructed here, though it was torn down in 1928, a few years after the Mammoth Swimming Pool was constructed (which has also since been razed). The lake dried up in 1926, and remained so until the Hebgen Lake Earthquake in 1959, whereupon it once again filled with water. However, it returned to a dry state in 1984 and has remained little more than a shallow, empty crater since. The metal covered concrete access port next to the lake covers an old borehole drilled into the ground in 1929 as part of a survey of underground temperatures throughout the thermal areas in the park.

Aphrodite Terrace is across the road from the lake. Park historian Lee Whittlesey named this one himself after it broke out in 1978, naming it after the Greek goddess of love.[18]

As you leave this area and go around the first bend in the road, to the north you'll see an unmarked, fenced-in feature known historically as the Devil's Kitchen. Devil's Kitchen was a large cave just to the east of the identically named spring. For years, it was possible to descend a ladder down into the hot cave. The cave was closed to human entry in 1939 because NPS officials were concerned the high levels of carbon dioxide in the air within the cave might pose a threat to humans.

1.1 GPS: 44.96301, -110.71390
WHITE ELEPHANT BACK SPRING (N)

White Elephant Back Spring was given its name because someone thought it looked like the vertebral column in the back of an elephant. The spring itself has been dry for some time, though there are some occasional springs that pop up in various places around the mound. On the northwest face of the mound are The Grottoes, a series of small caves, and the Sulphur Pits, a series of small sulfur pits.

1.5 GPS: 44.96511, -110.70844
ANGEL TERRACE (W)

Angel Terrace was given its name for the purity of its whiteness. The terrace is fed by three different springs (Angel Springs 1, 2, and 3), and the shelves have each gone through several cycles of being active and inactive.

1.6 GPS: 44.96533, -110.70775
EXIT/ENTRANCE

As you get ready to head out, keep an eye out for any vehicles that may be trying to enter through the same gate.

BECHLER ROAD/CAVE FALLS ROAD

This is the "forgotten road" of the park and is very lightly used. It's also very much out of the way. One must drive to Ashton, Idaho, located some 55 miles west and south of West Yellowstone on Highway 20.

It is also possible to get there via the Grassy Lake Road between Flagg Ranch and Ashton, the eastern entrance to which is in the Flagg Ranch complex. Most of that road is dirt/gravel, very potholed, and not recommended for anything other than high-clearance vehicles, however. The distance is around 11 miles using that route, but it typically doesn't open until late in the season.

To reach Bechler easily, you turn east on Highway 47 from Highway 20 in Ashton, and drive six miles (9.6 km) to Cave Falls Highway, and then east an additional 16.4 miles (26.4 km). Bechler Road runs north from here (the intersection is at 44.13057, -111.04687). The 1.5 mile (2.4 km) gravel road leads back to the Bechler Ranger Station and the trailheads for many of the trails in the southwestern corner of the park. 🚶 🥾

The Bechler Ranger Station is a small building that was originally constructed at West Thumb in 1904, and relocated here in 1946. The Ranger Quarters was the original Solider Station built here in 1911. The horse barn is also a 1911 structure, though it has been rehabilitated a couple of times.

If you continue driving an additional three miles (4.8 km) on the Cave Falls Road, you'll come to the parking area for Cave Falls itself (44.14456, -110.99780), where you'll find a picnic area with four tables and a vault toilet. 🏕 🚻

Developments:
Introduction

When Yellowstone was first created, there was a natural tendency for both those who were responsible for operating and protecting the park and those who were visiting the park to congregate in and around the areas where its thermal features, waterfalls, and other attractions existed. As time progressed, a variety of individuals and companies would come forth to provide those visitors with a variety of goods and services - everything from curios to food to tours to a place to lay their heads for the night. Indeed, this began before the park officially existed.

The Department of Interior (DOI) early on recognized that it was necessary to ensure these "concessioners" didn't overrun the park and that they operated in a safe and legitimate manner.[1] DOI didn't want to see Yellowstone become overwhelmed with cheesy, unregulated souvenir salesmen like what had become popular at Niagara Falls. Indeed, one of the justifications for creating the park was to prevent that from happening. So Interior (and then Congress) set about developing rules and regulations about where concessioners could build their stores, how close they could be to the park's sensitive areas, and so forth.[2] These rules would change over time, but the same basic process is in place today.

This book is not about the history of the concession process or even the concessioners themselves, however, but rather the places where they helped develop little communities. Most, though certainly not all, of those developments still exist today, many replete with structures that were built to accommodate visitors to the park in its earliest days.

This section of the book takes you through each of the major park developments and provides a short history of the significant buildings at each location. Details about old structures that are no longer present are also provided for historical context.

CONCESSION OPERATORS

While the National Park Service is responsible for the park and the protection of its resources, they do not operate concession services such as hotels, stores, service stations, and so forth. These operations are handled by concessioners awarded exclusive, long-term contracts to provide these services to the public. These contracts are typically for 10- to 20-year terms.[3] This is done to allow those who run the concessions to recoup their investments in the structures and other infrastructure they're required to build and maintain to provide those services.

Today, there are four primary concession operators and two cooperating organizations in Yellowstone. They include:

Xanterra Parks and Resorts: Xanterra operates the vast majority of non-NPS visitor contact services, with the exception of the general stores, medical clinics and service stations. All of the lodges, restaurants, gift shops, marine-related services, tour operations (including horse rides), and the five larger campgrounds are run by this company. Xanterra provides concession services at a number of state and national parks throughout the United States; their Yellowstone operation is based out of the Gardiner Complex at the North Entrance to the park.

Xanterra originally came to Yellowstone as Amfac in 1995 as part of their acquisition of TW Recreation Services who, at the time, held the primary concession contract in the park. In 2002, the company changed its name to Xanterra. The company held the concessions contract from that point forward, and in 2013, they were awarded a new 20-year contract to operate the lodges and other facilities and services described above. They have a permanent staff of about 120 employees, and hire roughly 3000 additional seasonal employees during the summer, broken down as follows:

- Gardiner: 110 Employees
- Mammoth: 250 Employees
- Roosevelt:: 125 Employees
- Canyon: 390 Employees
- Lake Village/Bridge Bay/Fishing Bridge: 450 Employees
- Grant Village: 230 Employees
- Old Faithful: 700 Employees

Delaware North Corporation: The Delaware North Corporation operates the park's 11 General Stores, those formerly operated by the Hamilton Stores until 2002. They have a regional office in Bozeman, plus a support office and warehouse at the park's West Entrance complex.

The contract to operate the Yellowstone General Stores will be up for renewal in 2015. DNC has a permanent staff of about 30, and hires roughly 700 employees over the course of the summer:

- Mammoth: 40 Employees (including some year-round)
- Roosevelt/Tower: 45 Employees
- Canyon (2 stores): 90 Employees
- Fishing Bridge/Lake/Bridge Bay: 130 Employees
- Grant Village (2 stores): 60 Employees
- Old Faithful (2 stores): 120 Employees
- West Entrance: 50 Employees

Yellowstone Park Service Stations (YPSS): YPSS operates the park's seven service and repair stations. They have four full time employees and hire roughly 80 employees each summer. YPSS was founded as a joint operation between various store owners throughout the park and the Yellowstone Park Company, a predecessor to Xanterra. The service station operation would be sold off in 2003 subsequent to the transfer of the Hamilton Stores franchise to Delaware North, and now operates independently.

Medcor: Medcor has been the park's medical contractor since 2003. They operate the three clinics, including the two seasonal clinics at Lake and Old Faithful and the year round clinic at Mammoth. Combined, the three offices see more than 10,000 patients over the course of a typical year. The main clinic is staffed with physicians and nurses, while the two satellite clinics are staffed with a physician's assistant and three nurses each. They have four permanent staff and hire roughly two dozen employees each summer.

The clinics are primarily designed for outpatient and emergent care. In the event of a serious injury or life-threatening illness, they will stabilize the patient and call in a helicopter to airlift him/her to a hospital in either Idaho Falls, ID, or Jackson, WY.

Yellowstone Association (YA): The Yellowstone Association is the park's educational partner and operates the bookstores found throughout the park (generally in the visitor centers, but there are standalone stores at Norris and West Thumb, plus their headquarters at Gardiner). They also operate the Yellowstone Institute, which provides a wealth of educational courses and training opportunities throughout the summer and the winter. They have a permanent staff of about 25, and hire roughly 50 seasonal workers to staff their stores during the summer. YA began as the Yellowstone Museum and Library Association in the mid-1930s. Money raised through memberships (which get you discounts around the park, among other benefits) is used to support educational and interpretive programs throughout the park.

The Concessioners. From left to right, William Nichols (Yellowstone Park Company), NPS Director Conrad Wirth, Charles A. Hamilton (Hamilton Stores), and Jack Haynes (Haynes Photo Shops) at the groundbreaking for Canyon Village, June 25, 1956.

Yellowstone Park Foundation (YPF): The Yellowstone Park Foundation is Yellowstone's primary fundraising partner. Formed in 1995, they've raised millions of dollars to help fund projects throughout the park that might not otherwise have been completed. These include funding half the cost of the new Old Faithful Visitor Education Center, funding trail improvements, funding a project to restore and rehabilitate the park's patrol cabins, etc. They also funded the rehabilitation and restoration of the old Haynes Photo Shop at Old Faithful into a museum dedicated to the Haynes legacy in the park. They have a permanent staff of about 10 people and hire a small handful during the summer.

Time Line of Concession Companies

Understanding the history of the developments necessarily requires an understanding of the various companies that have operated concessions within the park. Because of the similar names, reading through some of the following chapters may be difficult to follow. The following chart provides a condensed summary of the various machinations these organizations went through as time passed from just before the park's establishment up through 2013. There are many dozens of other concession operators who've operated at one time or another within the park and who are not included in this chart. The reader is encouraged to avail themselves of Mary Culpin's history of the concession operations for a detailed summary of those operations.

Timeline of Major Yellowstone Concession Operators [4]

Camps, Hotel, Lodges, Tours & Related Services

- **YPIC:** Yellowstone Park Improvement Company[5] (1883-1885)
- **WCC:** Wylie Camping Company (1883-1905)
- **YPA:** Yellowstone Park Association (1886-1909)
- **YTC:** Yellowstone Transportation Company (1883-1891)
- **YNPTC:** Yellowstone National Park Transportation Company (1892-1898)
- **YPTC:** Yellowstone Park Transportation Company (1898-1936)
- **SPCC:** Shaw & Powell Camping Company (1898-1917)
- **WPCC:** Wylie Permanent Camping Company (1905-1917)
- **YPHC:** Yellowstone Park Hotel Company (1909-1936)
- **YPBC:** Yellowstone Park Boat Company (1911-1936)
- **YPCC:** Yellowstone Park Camping Company (1917-1919)
- **YPCC:** Yellowstone Park Camps Company (1919-1924)
- **VGC:** Vernon Goodwin Company (1924-1928)
- **YPLCC:** Yellowstone Park Lodge & Camps Company (1928-1936)
- **YPC:** Yellowstone Park Company (1936-1979)
- **TWAS:** TWA Services (1979-1983)
- **TWS:** TW Services (1983-1988)
- **TWRS:** TW Recreation Services (1988-1995)
- **Amfac:** Amfac Parks and Resorts (1995-2002)
- **Xanterra:** Xanterra Parks and Resorts (2002-   )

Shops & Stores

- **Haynes:** Haynes Photo Shops (1884-1967)
- **Ham:** Hamilton Stores (1915-2002)
- **YPSS:** Yellowstone Park Service Stations (2002-   )
- **DNC:** Delaware North Corporation (2002-   )

These abbreviations are used in the following timeline tables to conserve space. The exact relationships between these different entities is described briefly in the tables as the changes occurred.

There are two critical turning points that should be noted, however. First, in 1936 all of the non-store concessions were consolidated into the Yellowstone Park Company. You can see that in the outline to the left. Second, the Haynes Photo Shops were sold to the Hamilton Stores enterprise in 1967, so that entity ceased to exist at that point, and all of their shops were either morphed into general stores or were abandoned altogether.

Year	Hotels	Camps & Lodges	General Stores	Photo Shops	Other
1871	James McCartney & Henry Horr open the McCartney Hotel @ Clematis Gulch.				
1872			Yellowstone National Park established March 1, 1872		
1880	George Marshall & John Goff open 6-room Marshall Hotel at site west of present day Nez Perce Picnic Area				
1881	McCartney Hotel closes				
1883	YPIC organized; builds tent hotel at Old Faithful on site of present day Inn (west lot). YPIC builds tent hotels at Norris, Lake, and Canyon on site near present day Brink of the Upper Falls parking lot. 141-room National Hotel opens at Mammoth (YPIC)	William Wylie begins conducting tours of the park using portable tent camps.			Yellowstone Transportation Company (YTC) formed. Offers tours of the park via subcontracts with other stage coach operators.
1884	John Yancey opens hotel in Pleasant Valley. It has capacity of 20 guests. George Marshall & G.L. Henderson construct second hotel near curret Nez Perce Picnic Area.			Frank J. Haynes establishes first studio on Mammoth Parade Ground.	

Year	Hotels	Camps & Lodges	General Stores	Photo Shops	Other
1885	Charles Hobart & former YNP Supt. Robert Carpenter open "shack" hotel @ Old Faithful on site of present day Inn (capacity of 70). YPIC tent hotel (1883) converted to lunch station.				
	Marshall & Henderson build new 75-guest hotel to the southeast of Marshall Hotel. George Marshall retires & sells hotel to George Henderson. Henderson & Henry Klamer partner up and add cottages & store to hotel; rename it to the Firehole Hotel.				
	YPIC goes bankrupt.				
	Cottage Hotel opens @ Mammoth, under ownership of Walter & Helen Henderson.				
1886	Northern Pacific Railroad buys YPIC assets, and reorganizes into the Yellowstone Park Association (YPA)				
	YPA takes over YPIC. Opens new hotel building at Canyon (tents remain in service). Acquires & operates Shack Hotel (1885) at Old Faithful.				

Year	Hotels	Camps & Lodges	General Stores	Photo Shops	Other
1886 (cont)	YPA builds first hotel at Norris on the hill across the highway from today's Museum of the National Park Ranger.				
	Cottage Hotel Assn formed. Operates Cottage Hotel and acquires & operates Firehole Hotel.				
1887	Norris Hotel (YPA) burns on July 14.				
	YPA builds temporary hotel near Lake Outlet (Fishing Bridge).				
	Addition added to Cottage Hotel; now has 75 rooms				
1888	Tent hotel & lunch station erected at Norris to replace Norris Hotel.				Larry Matthews opens Trout Creek Lunch Station.
1889	Cottage Hotel Assn sold to YPA; YPA takes over operation of their hotels.				Yellowstone Lake Boat Co. formed by E.C. Waters.
1890	2nd Canyon Hotel (250 rooms) opens on side of present day Canyon Corrals (YPA)				

Year	Hotels	Camps & Lodges	General Stores	Photo Shops	Other
1891	Firehole Hotel at Nez Perce abandoned; razed. First Canyon Hotel closes & is abandoned. Lake Hotel opens (YPA) w/ 80 rooms. Fountain Hotel opens near Fountain Paint Pots (YPA); Shack Hotel at Old Faithful converted into lunch station.				Trout Creek Lunch Station closed. Matthews opens new lunch station at West Thumb (YPA) YPTC formed/assumes control of YTC assets/operations. Larry Matthews establishes Norris Lunch Station near site where old facility burned year before (YPA)
1892	Norris Tent Hotel/Lunch Station burns.				
1893			The Specimen House established at Mammoth by Ole Anderson (sells curios coated by minerals from the hot springs of the terraces)		
1894	Hobart's "Shack" Hotel/lunch station at Old Faithful burns. It is replaced with a temporary hotel with tents for guests.				
1895		WCC authorized to establish permanent camp operations throughout the park.	Jennie Ash establishes store & post office at Mammoth (today's General Store)		

Year	Hotels	Camps & Lodges	General Stores	Photo Shops	Other
1897			Henry & Mary Klamer establish store at Old Faithful (today's Lower Store).	Haynes establishes studio at Old Faithful.	Calamity Jane authorized to sell postcards of herself inside the park.
1898		WCC establishes camps at Canyon (near site of current Brink of Upper Falls parking lot), Lake (site of the current lodge), Old Faithful (near Daisy Geyser), and Apollinaris Spring. Lunch stations established at Gibbon Falls & West Thumb. Shaw & Powell authorized to travel with portable tent camps.			Yellowstone Park Transportation Company (YPTC) is formed and assumes control of YNPTC assets and oeprations.
1901	Third Norris Hotel/Lunch Station (25 rooms) opens at Porcelain Basin (YPA). Additions completed to Mammoth Hot Springs Hotel (27 rooms), Lake Hotel (17 rooms), & 2nd Canyon Hotel (24 rooms) (YPA) Tent cabins added to Old Faithful Lunch Station.				Matthews Lunch Station at Norris closed.
1903	123-room addition added to Lake Hotel (YPA)			Haynes house/studio at Mammoth relocated to base of Capitol Hill.	Sam Toy operates laundry service out of old McCartney Hotel bldg.

Year	Hotels	Camps & Lodges	General Stores	Photo Shops	Other
1904	Old Faithful Inn opens (YPA) w/ 140 rooms 80-room North Wing, columns added to Lake Hotel (YPA) Name of National Hotel changed to Mammoth Hot Springs Hotel (YPA)	Lunch station (tent) at West Thumb replaced with new building (w/ small number of rooms for guests) (YPA)			
1905		WCC sold to new owner, and becomes Wylie Permanent Camp Company (WPCC)	Jennie Ash renews lease for store for 10 more years.		
1906	Yancey's Pleasant Valley Hotel in Paradise Valley burns and is not rebuilt or replaced.	WPCC builds tent camps on site of present day Roosevelt Lodge and at Swan Lake (relocated from Apollinaris Spring)			
1907		WPCC establishes permanent camp at Riverside (along Barn's Hole Road)			
1908			Jennie Ash transfers ownership of store to Walter Henderson & Alexander Lyall. Anna & George Pryor buy Ole Anderson's Specimen House (built in 1896), modify it to include coffee shop, bakery, etc., and renames it the Park Curio & Coffee Shop.		

Year	Hotels	Camps & Lodges	General Stores	Photo Shops	Other
1909	YPA sells its assets and leases to newly created Yellowstone Park Hotel Company (YPHC)				
1910	Cottage Hotel closes and is temporarily abandoned.	Old Faithful Camping Company begins operating portable tent camps in the park.		Addition added to Mammoth Studio.	
1911	Third Canyon Hotel is completed; incorporated the 2nd hotel (YPHC). 124-room North Wing added to Mammoth Hot Springs Hotel (YPHC)			Rear wing added to studio at Old Faithful.	
1912		WPCC authorized to establish permanent camp/lunch station at Sylvan Lake. Tex Holm constructs lodge building @ Sylvan Lake.	George Pryor sells his interest in the curio store to Elizabeth Trischman. Trischman & Anna Pryor become partners in store operation that lasts until 1953.		
1913	100-room East Wing added to the Old Faithful Inn (YPHC). Mammoth Hot Springs Hotel renovated (YPHC). Top floor of original structure removed; North Wing added w/ 124 rooms; capacity now 600 guests.	WPCC relocates Sylvan Lake camp to East Entrance. SPCC establishes permanent camps at Gibbon Falls, Nez Perce Creek (site of current patrol cabin), Old Faithful (current site of lodge), West Thumb, Tower, Willow Park, and Canyon (site that became original Canyon Lodge)	George Whittaker buys the Henderson–Lyall Store at Mammoth; renames business as Yellowstone Park Store.		

Year	Hotels	Camps & Lodges	General Stores	Photo Shops	Other
1914		Lodge constructed by Tex Holm at Sylvan Lake is abandoned and razed.			Henry Brothers establishes bathhouse & plunge at Old Faithful.
1915			Charles A. Hamilton buys Klamer Store at Old Faithful.		
1916				Jack E. Haynes takes over Haynes Photo Shops from his father.	First NPS auto camps are opened at Old Faithful, Mammoth, (old Camp Sheridan site) Fishing Bridge, and Canyon.
1917	Norris Hotel and Fountain Hotel are closed and abandoned (YPHC) YPHC given exclusive rights to manage all hotels in the park.	Mammoth Lodge is opened by YPCC on site north of current Mammoth Corrals. WPCC & SPCC are merged into Yellowstone Park Camps Company (YPCC). All camps closed except OF, Canyon, Lake, Riverside, and Tower Fall. Old Faithful Camping Company opens Norris Auto Camp on site of picnic area.	Hamilton opens filling station next door to his store at Old Faithful. Also opens new store (in the abandoned Lunch Station Bldg) and filling station at West Thumb. Opens store at Lake in old E.C. Waters building in front of hotel. Pryor & Trischman receive 10 year lease to operate their store @ Mammoth.	Haynes converts abandoned stage stop at Tower to Photo Shop & adds general store to it.	West Thumb Lunch Station closed (YPHC); building used by Charles A. Hamilton for temporary general store. YPTC converts from horse-drawn carriages to motorized transportation.
1918		Dining Hall and Recreation Hall added to Mammoth Lodge (YPCC)	George Whittaker establishes store at Canyon (on site near current parking lot for Upper Falls overlook).		

Year	Hotels	Camps & Lodges	General Stores	Photo Shops	Other
1919		Yellowstone Park Camping Company changes ownership and name to Yellowstone Park Camps Company. Roosevelt Lodge opens (as "Camp Roosevelt," operated by YPCC). YPCC permanently closes Riverside Camp.	Hamilton builds new store near present location at Lake Village. Opens filling station next door (closes in 1989, now the Rescue Cache building).		NPS established 2nd Mammoth Campground on site of current lower housing complex.
1920		Lake Lodge opens on site of old WPCC Camp (YPCC). Mammoth Plunge (pool), laundry, and dance hall opened at Mammoth Lodge (YPCC)	Hamilton & YPTC jointly open and operate filling station next door to the Lower Store.	Haynes builds new photo shop at Mammoth at base of Capitol Hill. Haynes awarded concession at Tower Fall to operate shop, store, contingent upon him selling brake shoes.	Second, larger auto camp built by NPS at Old Faithful (site of today's east parking lot.
1921	Old Cottage Hotel remodeled into dorm for employees who work at Mammoth Hotel (YPHC)	Original Old Faithful Lodge building (dance pavilion) opened (YPCC) Swimming pool opened at Camp Roosevelt (YPCC)		Frank J. Haynes dies on March 10.	YPTC opens filling station at Canyon near Whittaker's store. Fishing Bridge Campground created east of Yell. River.
1922	Dining Room expanded at Old Faithful Inn (YPHC)	Canyon Lodge opens on old SPCC site (present day Uncle Tom's Trail parking lot) (YPCC)		Picture shops opened in lobby of Old Faithful Inn & Lake Hotel. Old Faithful studio remodeled.	Auto campgrounds opened at Madison Junction (site of the current parking lot behind the museum), Tower Falls (near site of the old Soldier Station), and West Thumb.

Year	Hotels	Camps & Lodges	General Stores	Photo Shops	Other
1923	113-room East Wing addition added to Lake Hotel (YPHC). Modifications made to dining room, kitchen, lobby (incl addition of fireplace & mantle).	Lobby, Dining Room, Kitchen, and Recreation Hall added to Mammoth Lodge (YPCC). YPCC awarded 20-year contract for camp operations.	Hamilton awarded 10 year lease for stores & authorized to operate stores in park campgrounds. Enlarges (lower) store at Old Faithful, and constructs new store in campground at Old Faithful. Whittaker receives 10 year lease to operate stores at Canyon & Mammoth.		Brothers bathhouse & plunge at Old Faithful expanded.
1924		Dining room, lobby, added to dance pavilion at Old Faithful Lodge (YPCC). Sylvan Pass Lodge (operated as Cody Lunch Station initially) opens at East Entrance. Uses tents to house guests (YPCC). Vernon Goodwin buys YPCC & operates it as the Vernon Goodwin Company. Housekeeping cabin complexes opened at Canyon and Old Faithful (VGC)	Hamilton builds new store at West Thumb & vacates old Lunch Station building. Constructs new store at Fishing Bridge; expands original store at Old Faithful. Whittaker & Pryor and Trischman jointly establish & operate store & deli at Mammoth Auto Camp.	Photo shop opens at Canyon (near site of present day Brink of the Upper Falls parking lot).	

Year	Hotels	Camps & Lodges	General Stores	Photo Shops	Other
1925		Original Canyon Lodge building constructed on site of current Uncle Tom's Trailhead parking lot (VGC). Recreation Hall and Dining Room wings added to Lake Lodge (VGC)			New, larger auto campground built by NPS at West Thumb.
1926	Lake Hotel lobby remodeled; new porte-cochere, sunroom added (YPHC)	Recreation Hall, Dining Hall, and lobby additions added to Lake Lodge (VGC) Old Faithful Camper Cabins complex w/ 300 cabins built on site of today's Snow Lodge. Cafeterias built at Canyon & Lake (VGC)	Charles Hamilton & George Whittaker form Yellowstone Park Service Stations (YPSS) and operate all filling stations in the park.		
1927	150-room West Wing & east expansion to the dining room added (now the Bear Pit) added to Old Faithful Inn. Lobby enlarged & new porte-cochere added (YPHC). 5 rooms removed to create gift shop. Old Fountain Hotel and Norris Hotel razed	Recreation Hall & dining room added, lobby expanded, gift shop added at Old Faithful Lodge (VGC) Cafeteria constructed at Mammoth Auto Camp (VGC) Gratiot Camp Company operates cabins at Lewis Lake for one season and folds.	YPSS builds new filling stations at Old Faithful (current Upper Service Station), Lake, and Mammoth.	Haynes Photo Shop opens at old Mammoth Campground (at the time located where current lower housing area is today). Shop at Tower expanded. New shops constructed at Fishing Bridge & at Old Faithful.	

Year	Hotels	Camps & Lodges	General Stores	Photo Shops	Other
1928		Yellowstone Park Lodge and Camps Company (YPLCC) formed when a partner buys out Vernon Goodwin. Cabins from Gratiot Camp at Lewis Lake transferred to West Thumb (YPLCC)		Existing studio & residence at Mammoth razed and replaced with new studio and dorm (existing building) at base of Capitol Hill. Old shop building is converted into residence (still in use today as Xanterra housing).	Cafeterias constructed at Old Faithful and West Thumb (YPLCC)
1929			Hamilton constructs new store near Old Faithful Campground (current Upper General Store).	Canyon store is remodeled and finishing lab added. Haynes adds deli & lunch services to Tower Store.	
1930		Swimming pool at Roosevelt razed Housekeeping cabins added to Old Faithful, Canyon, Mammoth, Fishing Bridge, West Thumb, and Roosevelt (YPLCC)	Hamilton receives 20-year contract to operate stores throughout the park. Hamilton constructs new store & filling station @ Fishing Bridge (current store & station, open in 1931).	Old 1897 studio at Old Faithful abandoned.	
1932			Pryor & Trischman buy out Whittaker's stores at Canyon and Mammoth, receive new 10-year lease.	Haynes builds new shop at West Thumb out of building moved from Fishing Bridge.	
1933				Abandoned 1897 studio building relocated to present site near government area.	

Year	Hotels	Camps & Lodges	General Stores	Photo Shops	Other
1934	Final expansion of 3rd Canyon Hotel completed. Now has capacity of over 900 guests & is nearly a mile in circumference (YPHC). Sylvan Pass Lodge abandoned (YPHC)	Mammoth Lodge closed. Cabins relocated to various other lodges & camper cabin complexes around the park (YPCC)	Hamilton assumes operation of Henry Brothers' geyser bath at Old Faithful. Renovates building & reopens as Old Faithful Geyser Baths.		New campground opened at Tower Fall. Old campground at Solider Station site closed.
1936	YPHC, YPLCC, YPTC, and YPBC merged into Yellowstone Park Company (YPC). Given 20-year lease to manage concessions. Older portion of Mammoth Hotel razed. Only North Wing remains. Front lobby and portico constructed. (YPC)	Cabins from Mammoth Lodge relocated to Roosevelt Lodge, Fishing Bridge, and West Thumb (YPC)		Haynes builds new Photo Shop at site of present Tower store due to road realignment. Old shop converted into dorm. New shop built at Camp Roosevelt.	Apollinaris Spring Picnic Area created from former auto camp operated by YPCC (1925-1935).
1937	Terrace Grill and Mammoth Dining Room constructed on southernmost portion of the original section of the Mammoth Hotel. New Recreation Hall and services building constructed (YPC). Cottage cabins added.				
1938				Canyon Photo Shop remodeled. West Thumb shop relocated to site near road junction.	Current Mammoth Campground constructed by the CCC.
1939			Hamilton builds new (existing) store at Fishing Bridge.		

Year	Hotels	Camps & Lodges	General Stores	Photo Shops	Other
1940	North Wing of Lake Hotel razed (YPC). Sylvan Pass Lodge razed (YPC)	Cottage cabins added. Mammoth Lodge building abandoned (YPC)	Filling station at Tower Fall closed & new "emergency" pump opened at Roosevelt Lodge.		First Fishing Bridge RV Campground created from western 1/3 of auto campground.
1941			Pryor & Trischman receive new 20-year lease.	West Thumb shop moved to final location at site of present day picnic area.	
1948			Hamilton constructs new filling station @ West Thumb		
1949		Abandoned Mammoth Lodge building razed.			Third auto campground opened at Old Faithful.
1950		Abandoned Mammoth Plunge (pool) razed. Mammoth Hot Springs Hotel renamed Mammoth Motor Inn; Terrace Grill renamed to Terrace Coffee Shop.	Last season of operation of Hamilton's Geyser Baths at Old Faithful.		
1953			Hamilton buys Pryor & Trischman Stores at Mammoth & Canyon. Now operates all stores in park.		
1955		Camper Cabins office building at Old Faithful burns to the ground (YPC)			
1956		Canyon Lodge abandoned at close of season (YPC). Cabins relocated to other sites, incl Lake Lodge. YPC awarded new 20-year lease; includes requirement for investment in Canyon Village, Grant Village, Bridge Bay.			

Year	Hotels	Camps & Lodges	General Stores	Photo Shops	Other
1957	New "Mission 66" Canyon Lodge and cabins constructed and open to the public (YPC) New Camper Cabins building opens at Old Faithful. Would become first Snow Lodge in 1972 (YPC)		Hamilton Store & new filling station open at the new Canyon Village. Hamilton dies of heart attack on May 28.		Fishing Bridge Campground opens.
1958					Montana States Telephone & Telegraph assumes responsibility for operating phone service in the park. Montana Power extends commercial power throughout the park.
1959	Third Canyon Hotel closed (YPC) Hebgen Lake Earthquake causes damage to Old Faithful Inn and other structures in the park. Third Canyon Hotel sold for scrap for $25.			Tower Photo Shop undergoes extensive remodeling.	Existing Tower Fall Campground constructed. Pelican Creek Campground constructed near Fishing Bridge
1960	Canyon Hotel burns on August 8. Cause never officially determined. (YPC)		Hamilton warehouse constructed at West Entrance government area		First phase of the Bridge Bay Campground opened.
1961					Madison Campground (existing) opens
1962	Original porte cochere removed from front of Lake Lodge (YPC)			Jack Haynes dies. His wife runs business until she sells it to Hamilton in 1967.	Grant Village & Norris campgrounds constructed by NPS. (YPC & NPS, resp). West Thumb campground closes.

Year	Hotels	Camps & Lodges	General Stores	Photo Shops	Other
1964	Old Cottage Hotel at Mammoth razed (YPC)				Fishing Bridge RV Park opens (YPC)
1965		Camper cabins removed from old Canyon development			
1966		In February, the YPC sells its assets and operating leases to the Goldfield Corporation, who continues to operate under the YPC name.			
		In September, Goldfield transfers YPC operations to a subsidiary, General Baking Company. They continue to operate in the park as YPC.			
1967		In April, the General Baking Company diversifies and is acquired by the General Host Corporation. It continues to operate in the park as the YPC.	Hamilton Stores buys assets of Haynes Photo Shops (incl 13 stores). All are now operated under the Hamilton name; many are closed & abandoned.		
1969					Eastern section of Bridge Bay Campground opened. Old Faithful Auto Campground closed.
1970			Mini store opened by Hamilton Stores at Grant Village.		Grant Village Service Station opens (YPSS), Old Faithful Cafeteria razed.
1972		NPS opens park to tourists for the first time in the winter. The Old Faithful Camper Cabins building is converted to house tourists & becomes Old Faithful Snow Lodge (YPC).			Pelican Creek Campground closed.
1979		In November, NPS terminates contract of YPC, buys assets of YPC, and issues emergency 2-year concession contract to TWA Services, owner of TWA Airlines.			

Year	Hotels	Camps & Lodges	General Stores	Photo Shops	Other
1980	Mammoth Motor Inn renamed back to Mammoth Hot Springs Hotel; Terrace Coffee Shop renamed to Terrace Grill.	Two lodge buildings constructed at Grant Village (NPS)			
1981	TWA Services awarded 5-year contract to operate lodging and other concessions.				
1982	TWA Services negotiates 30-year contract with NPS to operate park concessions. Mammoth Hot Springs Hotel opens permanently for winter use.		Grant Village Dining Room opens.		
1983	Trans World Corporation spins off airline; TWA Services becomes TW Services.		Lake House Restaurant opened at Grant Village.		
1984		Four lodge buildings & Registration Center constructed at Grant Village (TWS)	The old Specimen House at Mammoth is razed due to high radon levels.		
1988		TW Services changes its name to TW Recreation Services (TWRS). 1988 fires burn several cabins at the Old Faithful Snow Lodge (TWRS)	Grant Village General Store constructed by Hamilton Stores.		
1989			Old Haynes Photo Shop building (built in 1927) removed from Fishing Bridge.		Fishing Bridge Campground closed
1991	Renovations completed to Lake Hotel by TWRS in time for hotel's centennial celebration.				

Year	Hotels	Camps & Lodges	General Stores	Photo Shops	Other
1993	Cascade Lodge at Canyon opens (TWRS)				
1995	Amfac Parks and Resorts purchases TW Recreation Services, operates in Yellowstone as Amfac. They are awarded a 5-year contract to operate concessions.				
1998	Dunraven Lodge at Canyon opens (Amfac). First Old Faithful Snow Lodge is razed to make way for new building. First phase of new Old Faithful Snow Lodge opens (Amfac)				
1999	Second phase of new Old Faithful Snow Lodge opens (Amfac)				
2001	Amfac given 3-year extention of their contract.				
2002	Amfac changes its name to Xanterra Parks and Resorts; operates in Yellowstone as Xanterra.		New contract to operate Yellowstone General Stores awarded to Delaware North Corporation (DNC).		YPSS spun off from old Hamilton Stores group.
2005	Xanterra given 5-year contract with NPS to operate park concessions.				
2010			Abandoned Haynes Photo Shop at Old Faithful cut into two pieces and relocated to Old Faithful Government Area.		
2013	Xanterra awarded 20-year contract to operate park concessions.		Yellowstone Park Foundation establishes museum to honor Haynes' contributions to the park in a portion of the abandoned Haynes Photo Shop at Old Faithful. Main building is relocated to near its original site.		

Gardiner &
North Entrance
Development

The Town of Gardiner was officially founded in 1880, though the area had served as the main entrance to the park since before it was established. And while the development of the town began in earnest with the construction of the Northern Pacific Railroad Depot in 1902, it wasn't until the mid-1920s the park's north entrance development began to resemble what you see here today.

The Yellowstone Park Transportation Company (YPTC) had already begun building the warehouse and transportation maintenance facilities here in 1925 when a large fire burned their existing complex in Mammoth (See the Mammoth Hot Springs Development section for details). The fire accelerated the work, and the company transferred its headquarters to these facilities where its successor, Xanterra, operates today (along with Yellowstone Park Service Stations, YPSS, which operates the park's gas and repair stations). Most of the buildings in this complex were constructed during this period, and the complex has been designated as the Yellowstone Park Transportation Historic District.

At several points during the park's history there have been numerous discussions about relocating the park's headquarters from Mammoth to this area, though none of those has borne any fruit (for a variety of reasons). If you get the chance to visit the park's archives in the Heritage and Research Center, many of the master planning documents available from the 1930s and 1940s reflect designs that were considered with respect to these ideas.

The North Entrance's signature icon, the Roosevelt Arch, was constructed in 1903, and served as the primary gateway to the park for those arriving via rail, at the time by far the most popular way to get here. The advent of the automobile and the decision to allow people to drive into the park in 1915 would begin a gradual decrease in tourists using the railroad to get to Yellowstone, however, and passenger rail service ceased in 1948. Six years later, in the days before the preservation of historic structures received much attention, the old depot was razed, leaving a void in the historic fabric of this area. There are plans to build a reincarnated depot on the north end of Arch Park at some point.

Many visitors do not realize that Park Street, the road that runs along the fence line, is located within the park. In fact, the park's boundary literally exists at the entrance to the various buildings – you step out of the park and into the businesses. For over 100 years, the road itself was dirt and gravel and wasn't paved until 1965 as part of the Mission 66 Program.

Aside from relocation of the NPS entrance stations over the past 100 years, little has changed in this area. As park visitation has increased, traffic in this area has increased dramatically, and given the current road configurations with limited pullouts and photographic opportunities, congestion has become the norm during the busy July and August months. Plans have been developed to improve the traffic flow throughout the area to include a bypass that would allow those leaving the park to avoid having to go through the Arch. This project should begin very soon.

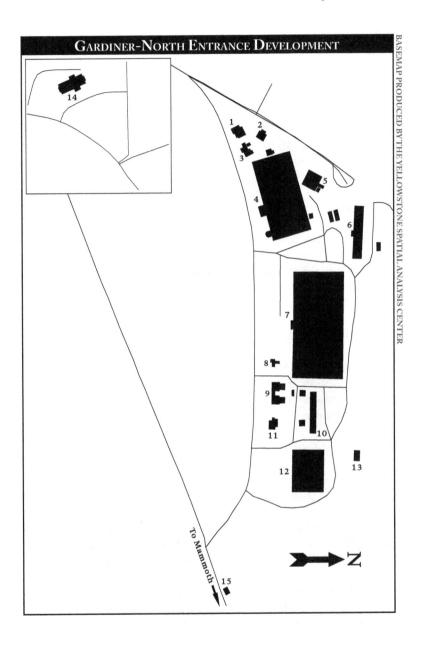

GARDINER-NORTH ENTRANCE DEVELOPMENT

BASEMAP PRODUCED BY THE YELLOWSTONE SPATIAL ANALYSIS CENTER

To Mammoth

1. NORTH ENTRANCE GATE HOUSE

The North Entrance Gate House sits at the northernmost point of the Gardiner complex. Designed by Robert Reamer and constructed in 1924, this structure was the first ranger station at the North Entrance. The building was constructed by the Yellowstone Park Transportation Company to replace the original soldier station that had been located on the site where the new warehouse complex was to sit in exchange for the land.[1] Today the building houses rangers who work at the North Entrance Station.

2. RESIDENCE G-1

This single-family residence (tucked in behind the Gate House & Residence G-2) was constructed in 1926. It was designed by Fred F. Willson, an architect out of Bozeman, Montana. The building is currently used as a residence for senior managers of Xanterra, the park's primary concession operator. Just east of the residence is a small garage, constructed in 1930.

3. RESIDENCE G-2

Known originally as the "Lockwood Residence," this structure was designed by Robert Reamer, the architect of the Old Faithful Inn and many other important structures in the park. It was constructed in 1926 and today houses senior managers for Xanterra.

4. YPC TRANSPORTATION BUILDING

Constructed in 1925 as the Yellowstone Park Transportation Company's (YPTC) repair shop, this building now houses administrative office space (including the Human Resources Office) and transportation support operations for Xanterra, as well as the company's bus dispatch operations center. The original bear logo for the old Yellowstone Park Company (YPTC's successor) is still emblazoned on the front of the building.

The small, single-story addition to the front center of this building is used by the Yellowstone Park Service Stations (YPSS) as its administrative office and storage space.

5. POWERHOUSE/BOILERHOUSE

The powerhouse was constructed in 1925 to provide power to the repair shop.[2] The structure now houses the boilers and related equipment used to heat and power the Transportation Building.

6. GARDINER BUNKHOUSE

This 1926 bunkhouse is now primarily for the employees based in the Gardiner area, but was originally built specifically for the concession bus drivers. The building has 32 apartment rooms and is capable of housing about 60 people. It was remodeled in 1968 to accommodate men and women. The small shed behind the bunkhouse was originally built as a garage in 1926.

7. SUPPORT SERVICES BUILDING

This building houses a variety of support functions for Xanterra, including the massive laundry that cleans all of the linens from the park's hotel and lodging operations, the employee uniform cache, the gift shop office and warehouse, etc. NPS also has some storage space inside this building. Built in 1925, it originally served as a storage building for the Yellowstone Park Transportation Company's bus and vehicle fleet.

8. RESIDENCE G-6

If this building looks like it's an out of place cabin from the Canyon area, there's a good reason for that. This was the prototype cabin constructed in 1956 to test the viability of the prefabricated structures that were going to be placed in the new Canyon Village lodge area. The building now houses YPSS staff based at Gardiner.

9. RESIDENCE G-3/G-4

This large duplex building was originally a bunk house and mess hall for employees of the YPTC.[3] Constructed in 1925, it was designed by architect Robert Reamer. Today it houses senior managers from Xanterra.

There's a small building behind the duplex that was originally a tool shed, but is now used as a spare "guest house" bedroom. There's also a small garage behind this guest house. It was built in 1930.

10. WAREHOUSE # 2

This building, constructed in 1938 as a materials storage shed and office space for the YPTC's construction superintendent, it now houses the Xanterra Purchasing Office along with the company's Food & Beverage maintenance shop.[4]

11. RESIDENCE G-5

Built in 1925, this house was originally known as the Kammermeyer Residence, for Fred Kammermeyer, who was the Transportation Superintendent of the Yellowstone Park Transportation Company at the time (his original residence at Mammoth burned in the 1925 fire). The building was designed by Robert Reamer, and today houses Xanterra senior staff. The small garage behind the building was constructed in 1930.

12. WAREHOUSE # 1

Constructed in 1937, this building is the 30,000 sq. ft. Xanterra Commissary Warehouse. It is used to warehouse food and supplies for the company's restaurant and hotel operations throughout the park.

13. GARDINER FIRE CACHE

This building houses firefighting equipment. It was constructed in 2008.

14. HERITAGE AND RESEARCH CENTER ⚹

This building is located on the west side of Gardiner, just west of the Gardiner School. Constructed in 2004, it houses the park's research library, archives, and museum. The library is open to the public, but the archive is open only by appointment. During the summer, tours are given of the facility. Check the park's website for information on dates and times.

15. NORTH ENTRANCE STATION 🏠

This small building sits just south of the junction of the North Entrance Road and Robert Reamer Avenue. Constructed in 1990, this structure is the latest in a series of facilities used to control entrance into the park here at the North Entrance dating back to the construction of the arch.

In 1903, a tent structure located just inside the Roosevelt Arch was used to check stages, and later vehicles, as they entered the park. This was replaced in 1921 with a new stone structure that included a small residence for the ranger. It burned in 1937 and was replaced by another similar structure. All of these stations suffered from being located on the "wrong" side of the road with respect to allowing the ranger to talk directly to the driver, however.

In the late 1940s, this problem was solved when a small clapboard structure was built in the middle of the road near the site of the present station. It

Stagecoach passengers leaving the Gardiner Train Depot enroute to Mammoth Hotel, ca. 1904. Hundreds of thousands of tourists (and park employees) passed through this facility.

was replaced in 1961 with a log and stone structure which later burned as well and was replaced by a small box-like structure resembling a highway toll booth. This small building was replaced by the existing station in 1991. During the height of the busy season today, an additional small box-shaped temporary building is deployed to facilitate two lanes of check ins.

Buildings No Longer Present

Gardiner Train Depot: The Northern Pacific Railroad built the Gardiner Depot in 1902-1903, when they finally obtained the rights to extend their line to the park's entrance. Prior to this, the railroad terminated at a town known as Cinnabar they'd built three miles up the road (mining rights between Cinnabar and Gardiner were the culprit). The Depot was designed by none other than Old Faithful Inn architect Robert Reamer and would see hundreds of thousands of passengers over its lifetime.

The automobile spelled the eventual doom for rail service to the area, however, and passenger service to Gardiner ceased in 1948 (freight service ceased in 1975, and the rails were removed the following year). The depot was razed in 1954, long before people became concerned about the historical value of such structures.

There are plans to reconstruct the depot on the north end of Arch Park as part of the revitalization of the Gardiner area in conjunction with the remodeling of the park's North Entrance traffic patterns.

First legitimate North Entrance Station, constructed just inside the Arch, ca. 1922.

North Entrance Station(s): There have been a half dozen buildings that have served as the entrance or checking stations at the park's north entrance. The first check station was a small tent facility set up just inside the Roosevelt Arch shortly after it was completed. In 1921, an official Entrance Station was constructed (pictured above) at the same location. That building would serve until it caught fire and burned on March 4, 1937. Its replacement would be built on the same site. Both of these were located on the right hand side of the road (as you face south), requiring a driver to lean across his passenger's lap to speak to the ranger upon entering.

Future stations would be built further up the road. In the late 1940s, a new station was erected in the center of the road at the intersection of what is today Robert Reamer Avenue and the North Entrance Road. This new building allowed rangers to contact vehicles entering and leaving the park simultaneously. This structure would be replaced by a newer one made out of logs in 1961. It, too, would burn and be replaced by a fifth building (that many said resembled a toll booth), and then it would be replaced by the current entrance kiosk in 1991.

In 2014, work is expected to begin on reconfiguring the traffic patterns in and around the North Entrance complex. A new, more modern entrance station will be constructed as part of this project, providing the rangers with more working room as well as the capability for dealing with multiple lanes of inbound traffic.

Mammoth Hot Springs Development

The Mammoth Hot Springs Development consists of four distinct areas. These include:

- Upper Mammoth, which includes Fort Yellowstone and the primary concession area
- Lower Mammoth, which includes the Mammoth Campground and the main NPS Housing Area
- The Young Adult Conservation Corps Camp, or YACC Camp Area, which includes the YACC camp itself, plus housing for NPS and concession employees as well as vehicle maintenance facilities
- The Upper Terrace Drive area

The Upper Terrace Drive has no facilities, and it is discussed at length in the Misceallaneous Roads section. The Lower Mammoth and YACC Camp areas are not generally open to the public, so they are not discussed in any great detail in this book.

The Upper Mammoth area is divided into two general sections. The first, Fort Yellowstone, is where the park's headquarters is based. The vast majority of the structures here were built in the 1890-1913 time frame during the U.S. Army's tenure as the park's custodian. All of these old facilities have been rehabilitated and re-purposed to serve as administrative or operational offices of the NPS, or in some cases as residences for senior NPS staff members. Its west border is the main entry road from Gardiner, and its south border is Officer's Row, so-named because many of the structures lining its north side were used to house U.S. Army officers.

The other section of the Upper Mammoth area is the concession area, which includes the General Store, the Service Station, the Mammoth Hot Springs Hotel and its cabins, support buildings for operations of the park's primary concessioners, the Yellowstone Justice Center, and a handful of dormitories and residences used by concession employees and NPS personnel.

The divided road that separates these two sections is known as the Esplanade. It was created in 1937-1938 during the first period of significant development in the Upper Mammoth Area following the departure of the Army. It was designed to give the area the feel of a civic center, and its construction coincided with the development of the Post Office and the new campground just below. Although additional buildings were contemplated for the civic center, none were constructed until some 25 years later. Over time, however, the clinic and the Justice Center have been added, as has a newer concession dormitory. The Esplanade is a popular spot for the Mammoth elk herd to gather during the day, especially in the latter parts of the summer as the annual rut (mating season) progresses.

To the immediate west of the Esplanade is the area that was once occupied by the old Yellowstone Park Transportation Company (YPTC) complex. Much of it burned in March of 1925, and though some smaller structures were rebuilt, the area was cleaned out in the mid-1960s during the Mission 66 Program's drive to "clean up" the park. Today, the concession dorms and some support buildings occupy the space.

Much of this complex is built on the remnants of an old travertine terrace not unlike those visible on the hills to the south. It is known as Hotel Terrace. Though there was some concern initially about the ground being able to support the weight of the buildings, time and experience have shown this to be a non-issue, generally speaking. There are several sinkholes in the area, however, many of which are visible in the drill field east of the hotel. You can see these as fenced-off areas today. One of the deeper ones, known as McCartney's Cave, is located directly across from the Superintendent's Residence.

Another enduring vestige of the reign of the U.S. Army Corps of Engineers (USACE) in the park is the grass you see covering the landscape in much of Mammoth. As this was an old terrace, it was largely barren and devoid of any vegetation (much like the surrounding landscape), so Capt. Hiram Chittenden had Kentucky Bluegrass shipped in and planted throughout the fort in 1903. If it were not for the grass, the area would be a dust bowl and largely unsuitable for use as the park's headquarters. In fact, the grass itself is a contributing component to the Fort Yellowstone Historic District's designation. The grass is a favorite of the Mammoth elk herd as well and, in all likelihood, the primary reason they stick around.

Note that, although the YACC Camp area itself is not a public facility, the access road to get to Joffe Lake, which is open to public access, and the north end of the foot/bicycle trail around Bunsen Peak can be found at the rear of this complex. If you're going to be using those trails or the lake, you're welcome to drive in and park somewhere out of the way. The road to Joffe Lake is unmarked, but if you follow the road around the north side of the housing area and then the dirt road behind the two medium-sized buildings across from the gargantuan maintenance facility, you'll find your way to the lake. The dirt road is only wide enough for one vehicle to pass in some places, so it may be kind of tight if another vehicle approaches from the opposite direction

In the other sections of Part II, the buildings are generally numbered from one upwards without skipping. However, most of the the buildings in the Fort Yellowstone area are known by the building numbers assigned to them in the park's facilities database (a practice begun in the 1930s as the NPS began building structures at Mammoth in the post-Army era). Since many who work in the Mammoth area know the buildings by their numbers, and since many historic records associated with the structures here refers to the buildings by their numbers, I've elected to keep them largely intact for this section. As some buildings have been demolished, there are holes in this numbering system, however. These missing numbers generally represent buildings that no longer exist or holes in the original assignment of numbers by park administrators.

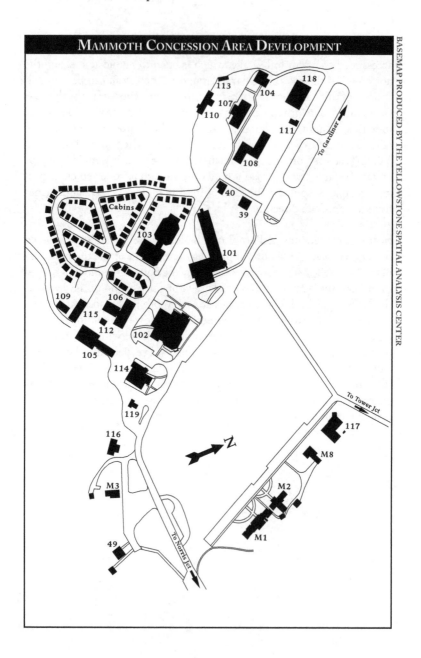

MAMMOTH CONCESSION AREA DEVELOPMENT

BASEMAP PRODUCED BY THE YELLOWSTONE SPATIAL ANALYSIS CENTER

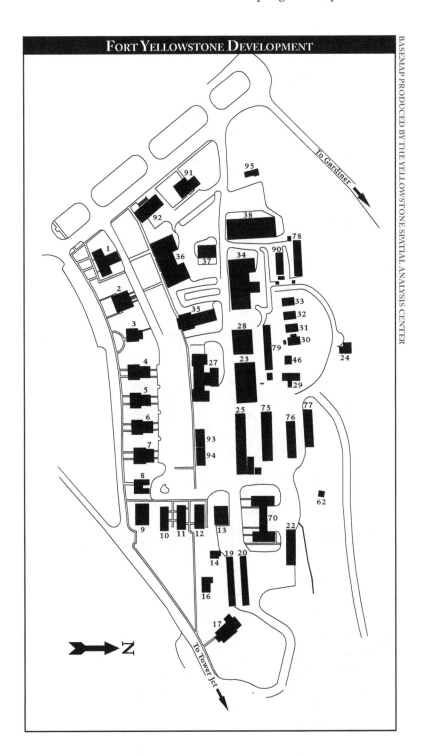

FORT YELLOWSTONE AREA

1. ALBRIGHT VISITOR CENTER 👤 ⑦ 🚻

Constructed in 1909 at a cost of $38021, this two-story rock-faced structure was originally the Bachelor Officer's Quarters for the post. The 8360 square foot building had six apartments for single officers and an Officer's Mess Hall, as well as room for housing visiting officers (transient quarters).[1] It was extensively remodeled and then named in honor of the park's former superintendent (and former direct of the NPS) Horace M. Albright in 1979.

Shortly after the Army left Yellowstone, Superintendent Albright had the building converted into an "Information Center," something akin to what we refer to as a Visitor's Center today, a purpose it has served ever since. Several offices of the Division of Interpretation are housed in the basement and on the second floor. Until the Heritage and Research Center opened in 2004, this facility also housed the park's library, archives, and a considerable amount of museum-worthy memorabilia. And, at least for a period of time up until the late 1970s renovation, some space on the second floor was used as winter residential space for NPS employees.[2]

The building itself remains largely intact as it was originally constructed, though the basement bathrooms were added in 1941. The interior of the Albright Visitor Center is undergoing renovation to improve its ability to withstand earthquakes, and to make the building more employee- and visitor-friendly. The project is expected to be completed in late 2015.

2. TRIPLEX EXECUTIVE RESIDENCE 2

This large, two and a half-story, rock-faced building was constructed in 1909 as the Double Captain's Quarters, originally housing the fort's doctor and one of the park's engineers. It cost $31936 to build. The structure has been remodeled on the inside, and today the 6908 square foot building houses three senior NPS officials.

3. SUPERINTENDENT'S RESIDENCE

This ornate, 4600 square foot building was constructed in 1909 to house the Commander of Forces (and therefore, acting superintendent) at the post. Today, it is the residence of the park's superintendent and is the only structure in the original fort that has retained its original use from day one. The structure cost $20,624 ($519,000 in 2012) to build and was designed to allow the Commander/Superintendent to host VIPs.[3]

The two and a half story residence is T-shaped and has three chimneys visible from the outside. The bottom floor has a kitchen, butler's pantry, dining room, living room, a bathroom, and a parlor. The second floor has four bedroom and two bathrooms, and the attic has four small bedrooms and a bathroom (probably used as servant's quarters originally). The basement is equipped with a laundry room, boiler, and a bathroom.

4. OFFICER'S ROW RESIDENCE 4

This duplex was constructed in 1897 to house married officers, usually captains or lieutenants. Today, it is used as a residence for the park's senior staff members. The building is based on a standard 3850 square foot plan in use by the Army during the time period (as were Residences 5-7). It cost $6838 to build in its day. These buildings also had servant's quarters.

5. OFFICER'S ROW RESIDENCE 5

This structure is identical to Residence 4 and was also constructed in 1897. It, too, cost $6838 to construct. Today it is used to house senior park staff. This particular building has the added distinction of having hosted President Theodore Roosevelt when he visited the Mammoth area during his trip to the park in 1903.

6. OFFICER'S ROW RESIDENCE 6

This structure is identical to Residences 4 and 5, but was built in 1891 at a cost of $6850. Today it houses senior park staff. From 1902 until at least the late 1950s, there was a tennis court in the open space across the street from this building.

7. OFFICER'S ROW RESIDENCE 7

This structure was also constructed in 1891, and is identical to its three siblings. It is also used to house senior park staff members.

8. OFFICER'S ROW RESIDENCE 8

Originally the Fort's Headquarters Building and then an electrical supply warehouse, it is now a residence for NPS senior staff. The building was constructed in 1891 at a cost of $1,550 ($39,000 in 2012).

As the park's headquarters, it housed offices for the park superintendent (normally the Post Commander), the post adjutant (the commanding officer's assistant), and the Sergeant Major, the senior enlisted man of the post, who served as a monitor of and an advocate for the enlisted personnel to the post commander.

As the park's compliment of soldiers grew to four troops (it was originally designed for the staff of one troop of approximately 50 men), the building became quite crowded. In 1913, a new hospital was built, and the headquarters functions were transferred to the old hospital. This building was then used as a warehouse for electrical supplies and equipment, and was later converted into a residence, a purpose it still serves today.[4]

9. OFFICER'S ROW RESIDENCE 9

This building was the Fort's original Guardhouse, and is situated next to where the road from Gardiner entered the Mammoth Development in 1891 when the structure was built (at a cost of $4950). It replaced the guardhouse at Camp Sheridan, which had been built in 1886.

Prior to the construction of this new facility, the only jail of any kind in the park was an old wooden building located on Fountain Flats near the old Marshall Hotel (near the confluence of the Nez Perce Creek and the Firehole River). It had been built by one of the park's assistant superintendents in 1884 (and wasn't razed until the 1920s).

The building consisted of four rooms. It had a capacity of 15 prisoners in three cells, supervised by a staff of ten guards.[5] After construction of a newer guardhouse (see the Mammoth Jail below), it was used to store ordnance, and then was remodeled in 1926 to serve as a residence. Today, it is used as a residence for senior NPS staff.

10. JAILHOUSE ROW RESIDENCE 10

This building was constructed in 1891 and was originally the Post Commissary, where soldiers were issued their equipment and uniforms. The original cost was $4198 and included 2460 square feet of floor space (plus another 1300 sq. ft. in a basement). In 1909, it was enlarged (due to the increasing size of the soldier compliment), and then in 1926 was remodeled for use as a residence. Today is it a duplex residence for NPS staff.

11. JAILHOUSE ROW RESIDENCE 11

This building was constructed in 1891 and was identical to Building 10, with the exception that this one did not have a basement. It was the

Quartermaster's Storehouse and was constructed at a cost of $3820. In 1898, 1909, and 1910 it was enlarged and in 1926, it, too, was remodeled for use as a residence. Today it is a duplex residence for NPS staff.

12. JAILHOUSE ROW RESIDENCE 12

This structure was constructed in 1891 as the Fort's Granary. The one and a half-story structure contained 12,000 cu. ft. of storage space, and cost $1560 to build. It was enlarged in 1910, and then remodeled in 1929 to serve as a residence. Today, it is used as a residence for NPS staff.

Buildings 10, 11, and 12 are referred to as "Jailhouse Row" residences because they're located on the same section of service road where the jail is located.

13. MAMMOTH JAIL

This 2000 square-foot concrete building was constructed in 1911 to replace the old Guard House (See Residence 9 above). Its original cost was $16348. The building has been extensively remodeled over the years and continues to serve as the park's jail. It has four cells, three for male prisoners and one for females. If the jail fills up, the NPS has agreements with local law enforcement agencies outside the park to temporarily house detainees. The Yellowstone Justice Center, constructed in 2008, was supposed to have included a new jail. For some reason, the U.S. Marshal's Service, which was to have funded the facility, decided not to pay for the jail, so this facility has remained in service as the park's detention center.

14. RESIDENCE 14

This small, 810 sq. ft. building was constructed in 1894 at a cost of $1945. It was originally the Hospital Steward's (later surgeon's) Quarters. Today, it serves as a residence for NPS staff. The building was known by locals as the "Joffe House" because former park assistant superintendent Joseph Joffe (for whom Joffe Lake is named) lived in it for a number of years.

16. RESIDENCE 16

Built in 1909, and originally known as the "Hospital Annex," this building housed 12 medical personnel (the hospital, razed in 1964, was located just behind this building), and then served as a storage warehouse.[6] It was 1375 square feet in size, and cost $2815 to build. Remodeled in the mid-1920s, the building is today used as a residence for NPS staff.

17. MAMMOTH CHAPEL

The post's Chapel was the last building to be erected by the U.S. Army in Mammoth. It was constructed in 1913 at a cost of just over $23,000 ($525,000 in 2012). The Gothic-style structure today hosts interdenominational services on Sundays (seating for around 400), as well as numerous weddings through the course of each year (see the park's web site for details about arranging for weddings inside the park). The bell tower was added in 1928.

In 1939, a private citizen fabricated and donated the two stained-glass windows found in the structure on opposite sides of the front vestibule. The north window is a depiction of the Old Faithful Geyser, while the south is a depiction of the Lower Falls of the Yellowstone.

19. MAMMOTH ELECTRICAL SHOP

This 22 foot by 160 foot building, which now serves as the Mammoth Electrical Shop, was constructed in 1903 and originally served as a coal shed capable of housing 1.2 million pounds (40,000 cubic feet) of coal.[7] The 3180 square foot building cost $4500 when first constructed.

20. CRAFT SHOP STORAGE BUILDING

The east end of this building was constructed in 1893 at a cost of $1275. Originally a 24 foot by 100 foot hay shed, it had a 79 foot extension added to it in 1910. It had a capacity of about 300,000 lbs of hay. Today, it is used as a storage shed for the park's Craft Shop.

22. MAMMOTH PLUMBING SHOP

The original portion of this building was constructed in 1898 and was the Quartermaster's Shop. An addition in 1901 added a carpenter and blacksmith's shop, and a 1902 addition added a plumbing shop and a sawmill. Today, it is the Mammoth Plumbing Shop.

23. MAMMOTH FIRE CACHE

This building was constructed in 1937 (using WPA funds) as a repair garage, and was not part of the original Fort Yellowstone complex. The building was used to perform maintenance on the NPS' larger equipment (fire trucks, plows, road construction equipment, etc.) until the new fleet maintenance garage was built at the YACC complex in 1992. It now serves as the Mammoth Fire Cache and houses both the structural fire department for Mammoth and the park's wildland fire operations headquarters.

24. Residence M-24

This single-story, L-shaped building was originally constructed in 1891 as the fort's bakery. The two-room, 300-square foot building was located near the Post Granary (Building 12) on the site currently occupied by the Building 70 Apartments. In 1934 it was moved to make room for that building and had a new wing added. When it was relocated it was remodeled into a residence, a purpose it still serves today (concession staff).

25. Mammoth Carpenter Shop

The original portion of this building was constructed in 1891 (at a cost of $5987), and had a 50-foot addition built onto the north end of it in 1902. It was a stable capable of housing 88 horses, and is the oldest existing stable in the park.[8] Today it is the Mammoth Carpenter Shop.

27. Yellowstone Center for Resources

This 8700 sq. ft. structure was originally constructed in 1897 as a troop barracks designed to hold 68 men. It cost $13187 to build at the time, and included dorm space, a kitchen and pantry, cook's room, an orderly room, a mess hall, and a bathroom. In 1909, a basement was added, and the kitchen and mess hall were relocated downstairs while the dorm above was expanded to accommodate a second troop (for a total of 100 men).

After the Army left, it was converted into a warehouse and served that purpose until the early 1990s when it was renovated to house the Yellowstone Center for Resources (YCR). YCR is the park's scientific and cultural affairs division. It was formed in 1993 to consolidate all of the park's scientific and historical personnel into a single functional organization.

28. Mammoth Maintenance Shop

This building was constructed in 1907, and replaced the original stable built on this site in 1897, which had burned a few months earlier. The structure was originally one of the Fort's cavalry stables, with a capacity of 84 horses. The replacement building cost $16729 to construct. It was shortened by 50 feet in 1935 to permit construction of the existing Fire Cache (Building 23).[9] It now houses the North District Maintenance Office.

29. VSO Storage Building

This T-shaped, one-story frame structure was erected in 1901 and originally served as a troop workshop, and later as a blacksmith's shop. The initial portion of the structure contained 1350 square feet and cost $1635 to build. The south wing was added in 1916. Today it is used as a storage building for the Visitor Services Office.

30. Soap Suds Row Residence 30

This series of small, 720 sq. ft. residences was originally constructed to house senior Non-Commissioned Officers (NCOs) and their families. Historically, these came to be known as "Soapsud" houses because the spouses of the NCOs would allegedly do laundry for the officers.

There is some question regarding the veracity of that story, however. As they were the wives of senior enlisted sergeants, and there were laundry facilities available in the immediate area (the old McCartney Hotel had been converted into a laundry), it is unlikely this was actually true to any great extent.[10] These buildings were located away from the Officer's quarters and, in fact, behind the stables for the troop's horses.

This particular structure was built in 1897 (at a cost of $1938) and today houses NPS staff. The first floor has a parlor, dining room, kitchen, pantry and a hallway, while the second floor has two bedrooms and a bathroom (total of 1090 sq. ft). Buildings 31-33 are structurally identical to this one, generally speaking, though 30 is a bit larger after a small addition was added at an unknown date.

31. Soap Suds Row Residence 31

This structure was built in 1891, and is today used to house NPS staff. Original cost to build it was $2040.

32. Soap Suds Row Residence 32

This structure was built in 1891, and is today used to house NPS staff. It, too, cost $2040 to build.

33. Soap Suds Row Residence 33

This structure was built in 1897, and is today used to house NPS staff. It cost $1938 to build.

34. Mammoth Supply Center

This building was constructed in 1909 (at a cost of $28962), and was originally a stable capable of housing 88 horses. A second floor loft was enlarged to increase its capacity in 1910. Today, it houses the Mammoth Supply Warehouse, which stores a huge variety of materials necessary for day-to-day park operations.

35. Canteen Building

Originally the Post Exchange, this building included a small grill/bar, billiard room, and a barber shop, as well as a gymnasium. The structure now houses a gymnasium (the rear wing of the T-shaped structure) and the Yellowstone Federal Credit Union. It was constructed in 1905 (at a cost of $20950), and is of Colonial-Revival style. It replaced a much smaller post exchange building which had existed on the same site. Children in Mammoth went to school here for many years prior to 1963.

36. NPS Administration Building

This huge, three-story stone structure was constructed in 1909 as a Double Calvary Barracks (with a capacity of 200 men), and remains the largest structure within the fort (24000 square feet). The building cost $95,469 to build ($2.5 million in 2012). It was extensively remodeled in 2006, and today houses many of the park's administrative offices, including that of the park superintendent.

A large fire on July 18, 1911, burned a portion of the roof and the top floor. Hundreds of soldiers and civilians fought the blaze for the better part of the day. No one was injured other than a single solider who fell through the three stories to the basement floor (he survived).

37. Blacksmith Shop

This 1944 square foot building was originally constructed in 1909 to serve as the Blacksmith's Shop and guard house for the men responsible for guarding the cavalry's horses in the various stables around the fort. It cost $7632 to build. For a period of time after the Army left Yellowstone, it was used as a storage shed by the Mammoth Fire Department. Today, however, it is once again used as a maintenance shop. Among the functions of its staff is the fabrication of components for buildings that still have their original cast iron fittings (e.g., the Old Faithful Inn).

38. Telecommunications Building

This building, constructed in 1909, was originally a stable capable of housing 88 horses, and had a second floor hay loft that ran the entire length of the building. It cost $28962 when constructed, and had 11,940 square feet of floor space.

Today it houses the park Communications Center (created in 1972), Telecommunications and Information Technology offices, and the Concessions Management Office. The building was at one time the Mammoth Fire Cache (prior to it moving to Building 23), and until 2002 was used to house the park's horse tack and equipment (now stored at the Stephens Creek barn). An extensive remodeling completed in 2004 reconfigured the building for use by the technology groups.

46. Soap Suds Row Garage/Storage

This small garage was constructed in the 1930s and was used as a garage for vehicles. Today it is used for storage.

47. Sign Shop Bake Room

The exact construction date of this building is unknown, but it was some time before 1949. It is used to cure the paint on signs built by the Sign Shop.

48. Mammoth Sign Shop

This building was constructed in 1903, and serves as the Mammoth Sign Shop. This shop creates all of the wooden signs you see throughout the park (except for the large park entrance signs).

62. Plumbing Storage Building

This small building was constructed in 1903 and was originally the Quartermaster Oil House, used to store petroleum products. Today it is used as storage space for the Mammoth Plumbing Shop.

70. Building 70 Apartments

This two-story English-Tudor style apartment building was erected in 1936 to provide housing for park employees, a function it retains to this day. It was the first government building built at Mammoth following the departure of the Army in 1918 and was funded by the Works Progress

Administration (WPA). The building is 80 feet by 160 feet, and has 20 apartments for NPS employees (six 4-room, eight 2-room, and six 1-room units). The building has a basement that houses storage cabinets and laundry facilities. Interestingly, the building sits on the site of an indoor shooting range (built in 1905) used by the U.S. Army during their tenure in the park.

75. MAMMOTH PAINT SHOP

This building was constructed in 1937 as a storage shed, but is now used as the Mammoth Paint Shop. Buildings 75-79 were all Works Progress Administration (WPA) projects.

76. GARAGE 76

This garage was constructed in 1937 and was not part of the Fort Yellowstone complex.

77. GARAGE 77

This garage was constructed in 1937 and was not part of the Fort Yellowstone complex.

78. GARAGE 78

This storage shed was constructed in 1936 and was not part of the Fort Yellowstone complex.

79. GARAGE 79

This 16-bay garage was constructed in 1936 and was not part of the original Fort Yellowstone complex.

90. POLE BARN - STORAGE SHED

This storage building was constructed in 1983.

91. MAMMOTH CLINIC ✚

The Mammoth Clinic opened in 1964. Prior to this, medical situations were treated at the Fort Yellowstone Hospital. The old hospital was deemed unsafe in the aftermath of the Hebgen Lake Earthquake (1959), however, and was razed in 1964 after the opening of this new clinic. The clinic is open year round and is staffed by a physician, nurses, and support personnel.

In the early 1960s, there was some political pressure on the park to relocate its headquarters from Mammoth to a "more centralized" location in the park. This resulted in a compromise to have a new hospital constructed at Lake (see the Lake Village Development section). As a result, a clinic was constructed at Mammoth rather than another hospital.

92. Mammoth Post Office ⊠

The Mammoth Post Office was constructed in 1936-1937. It is of French Renaissance Moderne style, the only building of that design located within Wyoming, and is listed on the National Register of Historic Places. It is open year-round. The bottom floor houses postal operations while the top floor is apartment and living space for post office employees. The bear statues at the front door are made from Indiana limestone, and were placed in 1941 using funds from the Federal Works Agency.

Postal service at Mammoth was originally handled via a small log structure located near the McCartney Hotel until 1895 (see below). When that building was torn down, the post office moved to the General Store and remained there until 1922, when it was transferred to what is now the Albright Visitor Center. It remained there until 1938 when this new structure opened.

93 & 94. Portable Office Buildings

These two portable buildings (known to employees as Buildings 1200 and 1202) were put in place in February of 2002 for the NPS Telecommunications Office so that their new building (38) could be renovated. The buildings were supposed to be on site no longer than four years, but 11 years later they're still present. They are currently used for temporary administrative office space when other offices are being renovated. They sit on a parking lot that was the site of the Building 26, an old Cavalry Barracks constructed in 1891. It was torn down to "consolidate parking" in the administrative area.

95. Old Mail Carrier's Cabin

This small, 512 sq. ft. building was constructed in 1895 by the mail carrier at the time. In 1903, a kitchen was added to it, and had a bathroom and entry foyer were added in 1933. It was one of several residences and buildings used by mail carriers to provide service between Livingston and Cooke City in the early days of the park. Today, it is the only remaining 19th Century log structure in the Mammoth area.[11]

This building has been used to house a variety of personnel who've worked in the park, including those from the NPS and concession companies. Lately, the building has been used for storage, and remains standing despite numerous attempts to have it torn down as an "eyesore" and "fire and safety hazard."[12] It is a component of the Fort Yellowstone Historic District and is individually listed on the National Register of Historic Places.

MAMMOTH CONCESSION AREA

39. "THE PAGODA"/NORTH DISTRICT RANGER OFFICE

Captain Hiram Chittenden, U.S. Army Corps of Engineers, had this 2760 sq. ft. building constructed in 1903 as work space for his engineering staff (first floor) and their quarters (second floor).[13] It gets its nickname, the "Pagoda," from its uniquely-shaped roof and the design of the outer walls. After the Army left the park for good in 1918, the building became the Superintendent's Office, and remained so until the office was relocated to the present Administration Building in 1960.

Today the building serves as the headquarters for the North District and Mammoth Subdistrict law enforcement rangers. From 1980 until 2008 when the new Yellowstone Justice Center was completed, the building also housed the park's courtroom.

40. CHITTENDEN HOUSE

U.S. Army Corps of Engineers Capt. Hiram Chittenden ostensibly had this house constructed as his personal residence in 1902, just prior to construction of the Pagoda (see above).[14] Since the departure of the Army, it has been used variously as a messhall, residence, and office space, and for a while was the office of the Yellowstone Association Institute. Today, it is being remodeled into a residence and will be used to host VIP visitors to the park. This building and the Pagoda (above) are included in the Fort Yellowstone Historic District.

49. COMMISSIONER'S RESIDENCE/GARAGE

The Commissioner's House, as it is commonly known, was the first stone structure to be erected at Mammoth (1894). It was not built by the military, but rather by the Department of the Interior. It was constructed after passage of the Lacey Act, which, among other things, provided for a full-time magistrate for the park. This building, too, is included in the Fort Yellowstone Historic District designation.

The original design of the structure included three jail cells, though they were rarely, if ever, used since the Fort had a guardhouse for that purpose. They were removed in 1926. The first floor also included a hearing room/office, kitchen, and living area, while the second floor had four bedrooms and a bathroom. Despite space limitations, the hearing room continued to serve as the park's courtroom until 1980, when that function was transferred to the Pagoda (see above). The house still serves as a residence for the judge assigned to the park.

The small building behind the residence was originally a barn for the judge's horse and buggy. Built in 1902 (some sources say 1912), it was used as a small garage for a time and is now used for storage.

101. MAMMOTH HOT SPRINGS HOTEL 🛏️ 🚻 🍸

The first hotel that occupied this location was originally known as the National Hotel. Construction began in late 1882 (part of it opened in 1883), and by the time it was completed in 1886 it had 151 rooms and had been renamed to the Mammoth Hot Springs Hotel.

The hotel was designed by architect Leroy Buffington of St. Paul, Minnesota. Not coincidentally, this was the headquarters of the Northern Pacific Railroad, which had a vested interest in the hotel. The structure was not well-built, however, and would often sway in the winds that raked the area from time to time. The completed hotel sat on a 414-foot by 54-foot foundation and was four stories high. It was situated such that hotel guests could look out upon the huge terraces (this also explains why there are no buildings between the hotel and a view of the terraces to this day).

In 1913, a new Colonial-Revival style "North Wing" was added, and modifications were made to the original structure. This included tearing off the top floor (reducing its instability). The changes brought the total room compliment to 275 rooms capable of hosting about 600 guests each night.

In 1936, a great many changes were made to the accommodations in the Mammoth Area. The Mammoth Lodge (see below) was slated for closure, and the large hotel was remodeled to appeal to the motor traveler. The original 1883-1886 portions of the hotel were razed, and a new lobby, gift shop, lounge, and porte cochere were added to the front of the remaining "North Wing," all designed by architect Robert Reamer. Ninety seven cabins, or "cottages," were added, primarily as replacements for the cabins that were being closed with the old Mammoth Lodge.

The final result was the structure you see before you today. The southernmost section of the original foundation remained intact, and the existing grill/dining room was constructed on top of it. The hotel retained the name Mammoth Hot Springs Hotel except for a brief period in the 1950s/1960s when it was renamed as the Mammoth Motor Inn in an attempt to appeal to those seeking lower-priced accommodations.

Due to funding limitations, very little expense was made on furnishings for the new lobby and lounge area of the remodeled hotel with the exception of the Map Room. The room is paneled from floor to ceiling in Philippine mahogany, and of course, the room's centerpiece, the large map composed of a variety of exotic wood veneers. The 17' x 10' map was also designed by Mr. Reamer.

Today, the hotel has 95 rooms and 97 cabins for use during the summer (only four of the cabins are used during the winter, each equipped with hot tubs). The 2014 rates ran from $91 for the low-end cabins to $482 for each of the two suites. Early plans had called for as many as 2,000 rooms in the Mammoth area, but with the advent of hotels and lodges in other areas of the park, and the automobile affording easy access to those areas, those plans never materialized.

Currently, the second floor above the lobby is used for administrative office space by Xanterra, the company that runs the hotels and lodges in the park. This is expected to change within the next five years as Xanterra renovates the old Haynes Photo Shop at the base of Capitol Hill (see below) and relocates their administrative and reservations operations to that space. The existing space in the hotel will then be remodeled into additional rooms for guests.

Throughout most of the hotel's history, it had been closed in the winter. This changed in the mid-1980s, but the facility still closes during the shoulder seasons. This, too, is expected to change soon, as plans call for the hotel, the dining room, and the grill to remain open on a year-round basis following the renovations referenced above.

The hotel sits on an extinct hot spring terrace known as Hotel Terrace, estimated to be 3200 years old. Behind the hotel is Kite Hill (families often fly their kites here during the summer), the site of the first cemetery in the park (used from 1883 to 1888). The cemetery has fourteen graves, only two of which contain identified persons. The hill has also been referred to as Boot Hill, though park historian Lee Whittlesey indicates there's no known source for that name.[15] The Mammoth Electrical Substation is located behind the hotel as is the large underground reservoir that stores potable water for the complex.

Hotel Cabins (Cottages)

Constructed in 1937-1938 with the remodeling of the hotel, these were of course designed by architect Robert Reamer as well. These little cabins have always been referred to as "cottages" because they're of a more "sophisticated" style and not like the rustic cabins found in other places throughout the park. Up until 1936, this area had been a marsh and was occupied by several concessions buildings, all of which were razed specifically to make room for the new cottages. Interestingly, the original plans called for relocating the cabins from the Mammoth Lodge to this area, but Reamer disliked them and felt they were inappropriate for the hotel.

It wasn't until 1958 that cabins got electrical heat (prior to this they were all wood-burning stoves). And, originally, most of the buildings had no bathrooms; guests used the three washhouses located on the perimeter of the complex. In the mid-1960s, however, bathrooms with showers were added to many of the cottages, while the bathhouses were retained for use by the others. One of the duplexes and two of the single cabins have hot tubs and are quite popular during the winter season. Today, there are six different styles/configurations of cabins: Duplex with bath; duplex without bath; single with bath; single without bath; duplex with shared bath; and single with bath and dressing room

The curved street around and through the cabin area was intentional so as to eliminate the feeling of being crowded in. A handful of these cabins house concession employees, but that will change within the next five years as the NPS has mandated that the concession operator return these to use as guest facilities.

102. Terrace Grill/Mammoth Dining Room

The Terrace Grill and the Mammoth Dining Room exist on part of the foundation of the original National Hotel. Interestingly, the south end of the old hotel housed a dining room and a small coffee shop (there's still an underground utility tunnel that connects this building with the hotel, in fact). The existing building was designed by architect Robert Reamer and was constructed in 1936-1937 along with the remodeling of the hotel.

The Grill is a fast food type establishment (with a small ice cream stand), with a dining area that seats 139 people. During the period when the hotel was known as the Mammoth Motor Inn, the grill was known as the "Terrace Coffee Shop." It had been designated as a "grill" to keep visitors from confusing it with the nearby Mrs. Pryor's Coffee Shop located just south of the hotel (no longer standing). The Mammoth Dining Room is a sit-down, full-service dining room that serves breakfast, lunch, and dinner, with seating for 166.

In the southwest corner of the building is the Employee Dining Room for Xanterra employees. It seats 100 people. The top floor of the structure is an 18-room dormitory, known as "The Terraces," that houses some 31 Xanterra employees.

103. CONCESSION ACCOUNTING OFFICE/EMPLOYEE REC HALL

Constructed in 1936-1938 alongside work being done on the hotel, this building originally housed a recreation hall, along with a newsstand, barber shop, beauty shop, gift shop, laundry, and a small clinic consisting of a single room and a dispensary. Today, the southern half of the building is used by park concessioner Xanterra as their accounting office. The north end is still a recreation center, but since 1986 it has been available only to park employees. There is also an employee apartment on the rec hall side of the structure.

The facility was originally built to replace the recreational and visitor support facilities that had been present at the old Mammoth Lodge (see below), which was abandoned with the construction of this building and the updates to the hotel. Like the hotel and the grill/dining hall, this building was designed by architect Robert Reamer.

104. CONCESSION ENGINEERING OFFICE/APARTMENTS

Originally built as a concession employee messhall in 1938, it now serves as the engineering office for Xanterra. The top floor consists of three apartments used as housing for senior Xanterra staff who oversee operations at Mammoth, including the Location, Food & Beverage, and Personnel Managers. After its tour of duty as a mess hall, it was used (1970s-early 1980s) as a print shop, and then converted into an office for the engineering staff of the concession companies in the mid-1980s.

105. LODGEPOLE DORMITORY

The Lodgepole Dormitory was built in two parts. The north end was constructed in 1924 as a men's dorm, while the south end was built in

1951 with the employee pub and public laundry on the first floor and more dorm space on the second. The laundry was later (1970s) converted to office space. Today the dorm has 34 rooms and houses 66 Xanterra employees, mostly those who're under legal drinking age.

106. JUNIPER DORMITORY

Built in 1913 (at same time as the north wing addition to the Mammoth Hotel) and expanded by 20 rooms in 1924, the Juniper Dormitory was originally a women's only dorm, but it now houses male and female residents. The dorm has 50 rooms and houses 99 Xanterra personnel, most of whom are over legal drinking age but in their first year as employees. It is the oldest dorm still in use in the park.

107. SPRUCE DORMITORY

Built in 1938 as a bunkhouse for Yellowstone Park Company tour bus drivers, this two-story, T-shaped dorm now has 22 rooms and houses 55 Xanterra employees. Its construction coincided with the remodeling of the Mammoth Hot Springs Hotel.

108. ASPEN DORMITORY

This is the newest of the Xanterra dormitory buildings at Mammoth. It was built in 1978 and underwent a major rehabilitation in 2010. The dorm houses 99 employees in 50 rooms that are either suites that share a bathroom or single rooms with their own baths. Older adults and those who've been with the company for some time are its primary residents.

109. YPSS DORMITORY

This small building was constructed sometime around 1924 as a small dormitory for employees of the Haynes Photo Studios. It was constructed by the Yellowstone Park Camps Company in exchange for a building Haynes operated near the old Mammoth Lodge. The building was later sold to store operator George Whittaker, who co-owned the service station constructed at Mammoth in 1920. It was relocated to its present site in 1965 and has been remodeled at least twice. Today it houses YPSS employees.

110. CENTURYTEL CENTRAL OFFICE

This building houses the CenturyTel Central Office for Mammoth, as well as work space for the company's technician. It was built in the early 1960s.

111. Ice Vending Kiosk

This small vending kiosk was built sometime prior to 1965.

112. Xanterra Security Office

This small structure was built in 1936 as a dry cleaning building to compliment the laundry that was located in the Lodgepole Dormitory to the west. It is now the Xanterra Security Office for Mammoth.

113. Bear Den Ski Hut

The Bear Den Ski Hut rents skis and snowshoes and sells skiing-related equipment and supplies during the winter.

114. Mammoth General Store 🏪

The Mammoth General Store is one of several stores operated throughout the park by the Delaware North Corporation. It was originally constructed in 1895 by a woman named Jennie Ash, and included the post office for Mammoth; it was known in the early days as The Post Office Store. In 1913, the store was bought out by another concessioner named George Whittaker, who had the 20 foot by 30 foot addition added to the front of the building (designed by Robert Reamer). In 1920, the post office functions were transferred to the new Visitor Center (see Building 1 above), and the store was modified to convert the space formerly occupied by the postal functions into additional residential space (where the store manager lives to this day).

The store was sold to Anna Pryor and Elizabeth Trischman in 1932, and they added a rear addition in 1938. These two ladies operated the store until 1953 when they were bought out by Charles A. Hamilton, who was the park's main general store concessioner by that point. Hamilton would add the front porch to the store in 1953, and then would enclose the rear porch in 1955, resulting in the structure you see before you today. This would complete Hamilton's consolidation of all of the general stores within the park under his control (not including the Haynes Photo Shops, which his family would later buy in 1967). The Hamilton family continued to operate the store until the contract was awarded to Delaware North in 2002.

Today, the Mammoth General Store is the only store in the park that is open year round. They sell basic food items, souvenirs, fishing and camping gear, and clothing. During the summer, they operate a small ice cream stand as well. At the height of the summer season, roughly 40 employees work here.

115. YGS WAREHOUSE BUILDING

Built in 1928, this structure was originally a stockroom for the Haynes Photo Shops. It now serves as a warehouse for Yellowstone General Stores.

116. MAMMOTH COMFORT STATION ▮▯

Constructed in 2006, this restroom facility sits on the north end of what was the site of the old Cottage Hotel (see below).

117. OLD HAYNES PHOTO SHOP

Located at the corner what is known as Avenue A and the Mammoth to Tower Road (Avenue B), this structure was built in 1928-1929. It was an "operations" building primarily (known locally as the "factory"), and contained facilities for photo finishing, an enlarging room, a copying room, a checking room, and an equipment repair room.[16] The second floor contained additional equipment and a lounge for the shop's employees, and in 1935 was modified to add more dorm rooms for the staff.

The building operated 24/7 to develop film and print photos for visitors, and remained in service for this purpose until Jack Haynes' wife sold the business to Charles Hamilton in 1967. Subsequently, it became a general store and then was a Christmas Store for a period of time. In 1999, the store closed. The building was transferred to the NPS, who used it as a storage building, a purpose it serves today.

Plans call for the rehabilitation of this structure and a transfer of administrative and reservations functions of Xanterra from the Mammoth Hot Springs Hotel to this building.

The original photo shop (where photographs, postcards, film, and other supplies were actually sold) was located just west of this building, next door to the Haynes Residence building (see Residence M8 below). It was razed following the completion of this new facility.

118. YELLOWSTONE JUSTICE CENTER

Completed in 2008, this structure houses the park's courtroom, judge's chamber, offices for prosecutors, witness rooms, etc., as well as office space for the NPS Criminal Investigations agents and the U.S. Marshal's Office. As originally designed, the building was also supposed to house a new jail, but the U.S. Marshal's Office pulled funding for it for some reason. The old jail (Building 13; see above) was renovated and continues to be used as the park's detention facility.

119. MAMMOTH SERVICE STATION 🅟

This Rustic-style building was constructed in 1920, and replaced an older station that had been converted into a service station following the introduction of automobiles into the park in 1916. It was the first "official" service station in the park (i.e., building constructed for the specific purpose of being used as a fuel station).

M1. CHILD'S RESIDENCE/EXECUTIVE HOUSE

Known as the Executive House, this large residence was built in 1908 for Harry W. Child, who was the founder and long time president of what would in 1936 become the Yellowstone Park Company, the primary park concession operator for much of its history. When Child passed away in 1931, William "Billie" Nichols, his brother-in-law, assumed control of the company and moved into the house, where he and his descendants lived until YPC was sold in 1966.

The Prairie-style structure was designed by Robert Reamer. Today, it is the home of Xanterra's Executive Vice President for Yellowstone. At one time (from 1926) there was a tennis court located between the building and the road, but it was removed in 1946 when Opal Terrace broke out.[17]

The small building behind the structure was originally the boilerhouse for the residence. It is now used for storage and a sauna.

M2. WAKEFIELD/HUNTLEY/NICHOLS RESIDENCE

The complete history of this house has only recently come to light, and as a result, it is now known that this building is the oldest in the Mammoth area.[18] It is believed the original structure was erected in 1885 or 1886 by James Clark, who at the time had a collection of tents and outbuildings in the area around this house, leasing overnight accommodations to tourists of the day (the collection was known as "Clark's Town").

In 1888, Clark sold his assets to the Yellowstone Park Association (YPA), who owned and operated the National Hotel and other hostels within the park. At that time, the residence was used by George Wakefield, a contract employee of the YPA. It was later occupied by Silas Huntley, one of the heads of the Yellowstone Park Transportation Company. In 1907, William "Billie" Nichols and his family would occupy the house. Nichols was the head of several concession companies within the park over time, and in 1936 would become the president of the Yellowstone Park Company until his death in 1957. All of the subsequent occupants of the house have been executives of the YPC, and it is today occupied by Xanterra's Director of Operations.

The structure itself was modified in 1926 to add three new rooms and a couple of bathrooms, and it underwent a major renovation in 2009. There are two smaller structures behind the house, an old gardiner's residence and a wood shed, both of which have unknown construction dates.

M3. HUNTLEY CHILD'S RESIDENCE

This Colonial-Revival style cottage was constructed in 1903 by the Yellowstone Park Association for its president, Harry W. Child. Child would later (1908) have the Executive House built and would relocate there (See M1 above). Harry's son, Huntley, would remain in this house until 1917. In the years since, the house has served as a residence for a number of different executive associated with the concession operations in the park, a purpose it serves to this day.

The small building behind it was originally one of the cabins at the old Mammoth Lodge and was relocated to this site in 1941. It is now used for storage. A small addition to the rear of the house was also added that year.

M8. HAYNES RESIDENCE

This residence, which is now used to house executive staff for Xanterra, was originally the second Haynes Photo Shop at Mammoth. It was built in 1920 and was remodeled into a residence in 1927 after the building next door was converted into the last shop used by Haynes. The little garage and darkroom were added in 1928.[19]

The vacant area to the immediate southwest of this building (between residences) was where the original Haynes Residence and Showroom was located from 1902 until ca. 1939. The building had originally been located just south of the hotel on the parade ground, but was relocated to the base of Capitol Hill (the hill behind these buildings) in 1902.

No Longer Existing Buildings

McCartney Hotel: Located in Clematis Gulch between the Commissioner's Residence and the terraces, this rustic, two-room log cabin was constructed in 1871 and was for several years the only place in the park where tourists could get out of the elements. Built by James McCartney and Henry Horr, it was little more than a 25 foot by 35 foot empty pair of rooms where visitors could rent space and throw down their own sleeping gear.

McCartney was evicted in 1881, and the hotel would live on until 1883 as the "Pioneer Hotel," operated by other people. The building went on to be used for several other purposes, including a dormitory for employees who worked at the Cottage Hotel. It also served as a residence for park employees, and then in 1902 became a laundry operated by a Chinese gentleman by the name of Sam Toy. Mr. Toy operated the laundry until it burned down in December of 1912 as the result of a hot iron being left in the wrong place.

National Hotel: Constructed in 1882-1886, this hotel was almost 420 feet long and had 250 rooms. The building had steam heat and electricity, as well as a host of amenities for the well-off traveler, including barber and beauty shops, a lounge, and a bar. The hotel even had a Steinway piano, a luxury in those days. The Dining Room on the hotel's south end could seat 200 guests at a time. Room rates were initially $4 per night ($109 in 2013), then increased to $5 per night in 1899 ($136).

The hotel remained largely unchanged until 1913, when architect Robert Reamer, designer of the Old Faithful Inn, designed and built a new "North Wing," which expanded the hotel's capacity by 124 rooms. In 1936, the original sections of the hotel were razed, leaving only the North Wing standing. Reamer then designed and built the front lobby and portico, which, when included with the old North Wing, comprise the Mammoth Hot Springs Hotel you see here today (see above).

Cottage Hotel: Constructed in 1885 on the site now occupied by the Mammoth Comfort Station (next door to the YPSS Service Station), and with an addition built in 1887, the hotel had 75 rooms with a capacity of 150 guests (at $2.50 per night, or $63 in 2013 funds). Its builder, G. L. Henderson, stated that he built the hotel because the Yellowstone Park Improvement Company (YPIC), at the time the owner of the National Hotel, was not providing suitable accommodations for all visitors all the time (they only catered to the more upscale visitors, if you will, and their hotel was closed in the winter). The hill behind the present day

Cottage Hotel, 1959.

comfort station is known as Clagett Butte (for the Montana delegate who introduced the bill that eventually led to the creation of Yellowstone), though Henderson named it "Temple Mountain," ostensibly in honor of the "temple" (hotel) he'd constructed.

The hotel was later purchased (1889) and closed (1910) by the owners of the National Hotel. The building was later remodeled and used as a dormitory for the hotel's male employees from 1921 until it was razed in 1964. The structure was three stories tall and occupied a footprint of about 36' x 40'.

Mammoth Lodge and Cabins: Constructed in 1917-1920 in concert with the lodges in other areas of the park, this building and its cabins were located on the land immediately north of the existing Mammoth Corral (from the driveway all the way up to where Bluff Creek passes under the road). You can still walk out into the flat field here and see the remnants of the foundations of some of the old buildings. The Lodge was abandoned in 1940 after the remodeling of the Mammoth Hot Springs Hotel and the addition of its cabins, and was razed in 1949.[20]

Mammoth "Plunge" (Swimming Pool): Located just north of where the old Mammoth Lodge and cabins were situated, along the south side of Bluff Creek, south of Capitol Hill, across from Jupiter Terrace. Constructed in 1920 as an adjunct to the Lodge, the "Mammoth Plunge" was one of two large swimming pools constructed in the park in the 1920s (the other was at Old Faithful). Water for the pool came from terrace runoff and from Bluff Creek, which drains the Reservoir Pool located just below the terraces. The building was razed in 1950 right after the Lodge itself was removed.

Norris Blockhouse, ca. 1903.

Yellowstone Park Transportation Company (YPTC) Complex: The site of the present day Justice Center, and the two concession dormitories was the site of the original YPTC Transportation Complex, a series of barns, stables, and support structures that originally housed the company's stagecoach operations. When the park converted to automobile travel in 1916, the structures were converted to serve the buses and automobiles used to transport tourists. The centerpiece was a huge barn/office structure designed by Robert Reamer, architect of the Old Faithful Inn.

On March 31, 1925, an accidental fire destroyed several of the buildings in this complex, including the massive Reamer-designed barn, as well as almost 100 of the company's buses and other vehicles. The total loss was estimated at over $700,000. Fortunately, the YPTC had begun building a new complex at Gardiner the year before, so the company was able to transfer its operations to that location (where its successor continues to operate to this day). It ordered new buses immediately and was able to begin providing tours right on schedule that summer.

Over time, additional buildings were constructed in this area, but all were later removed and replaced by the dorms (or converted into the dorms and other facilities still in place), and in 2008, the Yellowstone Justice Center.

Norris Blockhouse: Built atop Capitol Hill in 1879 by the park's second superintendent, Philetus W. Norris, this building was designed to afford a lookout for Indians. It was, in effect, the first headquarters for a national park.[21] Once the Army assumed control of the park, they used it for a

Cavern Terrace House and an outbuilding, ca. 1917.

variety of purposes, including as a residence. It was removed in 1909, and much of its wood was transported to the Lamar Valley where it was used in the construction of facilities at the Buffalo Ranch.

Building 26 (Cavalry Barracks): Built in 1891, this was the first enlisted men's barracks built at the new Fort Yellowstone. It was located south of what is today the Yellowstone Center for Resources. Designed to accommodate 60 men, it was 6520 square feet in size, and cost $13187 to build. It was torn down during the 1980s to consolidate parking in the area. Today, buildings 1200 and 1202 (the portables) are resting on part of the site, while the remainder is still used as a parking lot.

Weather Bureau Building: The U.S. Weather Bureau (at that time a part of the War Department) constructed an office and monitoring station on the vacant patch of land just north of the Pagoda in 1903. It served as a detachment of the forerunner of the National Weather Service from then until 1941 when they left the park. Following World War II, the building was converted into employee housing and it was used for that purpose until it was razed in the mid-1960s.[22]

Cavern Terrace House: This residential structure was located on the flat patch of land between Cavern Terrace and Reservoir Springs (just east of the boardwalk that runs south from the Middle Terraces Parking Lot at 20.5/0.4 on the Norris Junction to Mammoth Hot Springs Road Log). It was constructed by Superintendent Patrick Conger in 1884 to house one of his assistant superintendents. Conger's successor, David Wear, would go on to use the residence as his office, and the building would later house many important figures in Yellowstone's history, including the park's first chief ranger, James McBride. It housed NPS staff until it was razed in 1937.

First Fort Yellowstone Hospital, n.d. This was the second hospital built by the U.S. Army at Mammoth (the first was as Camp Sheridan). The building was replaced by a third hospital (1911) that was later damaged by the 1959 Hebgen Lake Earthquake, and was razed in 1964.

Fort Yellowstone Hospitals: There were two hospitals built within Fort Yellowstone (these were the second and third hospitals at Mammoth, since there'd been a first one in Camp Sheridan). The first of these new facilities, built in 1893, consisted of a two-story structure with nine rooms on the first floor and three rooms on the second (a total of 3000 sq. ft). It cost $11725.

With a capacity of only ten beds, it was deemed to be too small to serve the growing park (military personnel and civilians were treated here), and was replaced by the third hospital almost twenty years later. This building was then used as the post headquarters due to the staff outgrowing the original one (Building 8, listed above).

Second Fort Yellowstone Hospital (far right, south of the Chapel), 1952.

Pryor Curio Shop, ca. 1917. In 1953, Hamilton Stores owner Charles Hamilton purchased the store from Anny Pryor and Elizabth Trischman (sisters), and this became the Hamilton Coffee Shop until 1984.

The third hospital was built in 1911 in the open grassy area just east of the Chapel, at a cost of $49020. It had a capacity of 18 patients. The 7086 square foot facility was in service until 1964 when it was declared unsafe due in large part to damage it sustained during the 1959 earthquake. It was razed the following year along with the old annex building located behind it. A new park hospital was constructed at Lake, and a clinic was built next to the U.S. Post Office in Mammoth.

Specimen House/Pryor Curio Shop: Constructed in 1896 by park concessioner Ole Anderson as a place to sell trinkets and other items coated with the travertine from the runoff of the terraces, this building would later be sold to Anna Pryor and Elizabeth Trischman. They turned it into the Park Curio Shop, complete with a soda fountain, ice cream stand, and a small bakery. In 1953, store operator Charles Hamilton bought the shop and turned it into the Hamilton Coffee Shop, under which name it operated until it was razed (due to high radon levels) in 1984. The building sat on the vacant piece of land between the Huntley Child Residence (M3, above) and the Commissioner's House (49, above).

Tower Junction/ Roosevelt & Tower Fall Developments

The Roosevelt-Tower Junction complex is composed of four distinct areas:

- Roosevelt Lodge and Corrals and their related structures, along with the YPSS Service Station
- Tower Administrative Area, which includes the Tower Ranger Station
- Tower Fall Area, which includes the Tower General Store, the campground, and employee housing area
- Yancey's Hole, which was the site of a small hotel and saloon in the park's early days and is now used by the park's primary concessioner to host western-style cookouts.

The Tower Administrative Area is not discussed in any great detail in this book since it does not have any services available to the general public aside from the Tower Ranger Station (discussed at the end of this chapter).

Roosevelt Lodge Area

In 1919, Roosevelt Lodge became the first of many such lodge-type facilities constructed in the park. It replaced a series of tent camps that had been utilized on the same site for more than 20 years prior. The area was chosen for this use because of its isolation and the fact that it was located at a road junction. And although the camp was named for President Teddy Roosevelt, it is a myth that he stayed here during his vacation in the park in 1903.

President William McKinley had been assassinated some two years earlier, and the U.S. Secret Service was concerned for the safety of the new president. It was believed he'd be safer and could be afforded better protection if he stayed at the Tower Soldier Station, which, at the time, was located 1.5 miles up the road. So the president stayed at the soldier station while his entourage camped on the east side of Rainy Lake (see the Tower Junction to Canyon Junction section for more information on both of these sites).

Since its beginning, Roosevelt has been seen as a location providing minimal, rustic services. Therefore, you'll notice there are no large recreation or dining halls here. It is designed to have a rustic, "dude ranch" feel to it and is quite popular with tourists during its short but busy summer season. From here, you can take a horse ride or hop on one of the covered wagons and attend a western cookout each evening. The Lodge is also near the Lamar Valley, one of the more wildlife-rich areas of the park.

The corral operation has been a part of the camp since its construction (and, indeed, was present when there were tent camps here). Originally, they were located on the west side of the camp but were relocated to their present site in 1958 as part of the Mission 66 Program. This was done largely because they'd outgrown the old area, and Lost Creek, which runs through the camp, was being polluted by runoff from the horse operation.

The Roosevelt Lodge Historic District was designated in 1983; it includes the Lodge, many of the cabins, and several of the support buildings in the area. In the 1930s, there was discussion about closing the camp due to disrepair, lack of use, and unsanitary conditions (the U.S. Public Health Service even shut the lodge's kitchen down at one point). But cooler heads prevailed, and the area is extremely popular with park visitors today.

Tower Fall Area

The existing Tower General Store was originally constructed in 1936 after the road was relocated, and was extensively remodeled in 1959 (parts of the original store remain beneath the heavily remodeled exterior). This facility replaced a previous store built near what is today the employee recreation hall located adjacent to the Tower Fall Campground.

The first photo shop opened at Tower was originally a stage stop. In 1917, Jack Haynes remodeled the building following the demise of the stages in the park and turned it into one of his photo shops. The NPS agreed to allow him do this contingent upon him offering brake shoes for sale to motorists who'd just come down from Dunraven Pass or the summit of Mt. Washburn. The steep grades had a bad habit of wearing out brakes on the vehicles, and drivers would need to change them before moving on.

After the road was realigned in the mid-1930s, the new store was built on its present site, and the old store was remodeled into an employee dormitory. A new mess hall was constructed in 1941, and when the new (existing) dorm was constructed in 1985, it became an employee recreation hall.

The current Tower Fall Campground (32 sites) was established here in 1934, after having been located for some time near the site of the old Tower Soldier Station one mile to the west.

Yancey's Hole

Yancey's Hole began with the construction of a mail station and stage station in 1882. This was followed soon thereafter by small 20-guest "hotel" and saloon in 1884. These facilities were intended to serve those who were traveling to the Cooke City mines. In 1903, John Yancey died after a bout with pneumonia (acquired while he was attending the dedication of the Roosevelt Arch in Gardiner), and his nephew, Dan, inherited the operation. Dan had little interest in running them, however, and the place burned to the ground in 1906. Despite his early lack of interest in operating the hotel and saloon, Dan applied for permits to rebuild, but they were denied due to the pending construction of Camp Roosevelt nearby.[1]

Today, Xanterra operates an "Old West" cookout on the site of Yancey's old hotel. Visitors ride via horse-drawn wagons and are treated to grilled steaks and entertainment not unlike what they would have experienced in the Old West.

The facilities at Roosevelt Lodge (including the General Store) are generally the last to open and the first to close each summer. The lodge opens to tourists at the end of the first week in June and closes the day after Labor Day. The Yellowstone Association hosts a week-long educational program at the lodge the week after it closes to visitors, however.

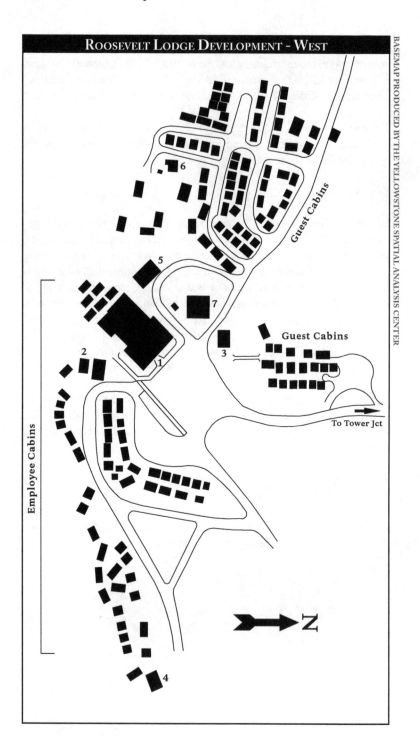

ROOSEVELT LODGE DEVELOPMENT - WEST

BASEMAP PRODUCED BY THE YELLOWSTONE SPATIAL ANALYSIS CENTER

Guest Cabins

Guest Cabins

To Tower Jct

Employee Cabins

N

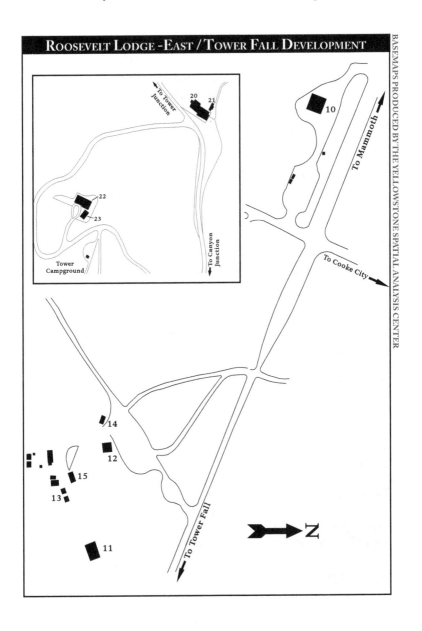

1. ROOSEVELT LODGE 🛏 🍴 🚻

Roosevelt Lodge was constructed in 1919-1920 to replace the original tent camp operation built here by the Wylie Permanent Camping Company in 1906. The area was given the name Camp Roosevelt in 1913, and then renamed to Roosevelt Lodge in 1950. This lodge was the first of the several lodge buildings constructed throughout the park and is the smallest.

Originally, the lodge utilized tents and tent cabins to house tourists. By 1929, however, the compliment was 37 wood cabins and 26 tent cabins. In 1936-1937, 70 cabins from the old Mammoth Lodge were relocated to Roosevelt, and over time, a variety of cabins from other areas of the park have been brought here to house guests and employees (see below).[2] Today, there are 80 cabins for tourists with a capacity of 264 guests. The 2014 rates ranged from $73 for the Roughrider Cabins to $121 per night for the Frontier Cabins.

The exterior of the structure remains largely as it was originally constructed. Some minor modifications to the building have been made over the years. In 1948, a new kitchen was built into the back of the lodge, complete with oil burners. Prior to this, all cooking was done on wood ranges. The kitchen was remodeled again in the mid-1980s. Adjacent to the kitchen is a 42-seat Employee Dining Room.

The building now includes an 82-seat dining room for guests, a small gift shop, the registration desk, rest rooms, a small lounge, and two small offices added in the late 1960s (one on each side of the fireplace).

The Roosevelt Lodge is one of only two front country locations where you can actually touch a petrified tree (the other is at the Albright Visitor Center). On the building's northwest front corner, you can see the end of a huge log embedded into the foundation. That is a petrified tree.

Guest Cabins

Guest cabins 77-78, 83-87, 90-96, and 99 are located to the northwest of the lodge building, near Lost Creek. These cabins are "Frontier" type cabins, and each has a sink, bathroom with a toilet and shower, and electric heat. These cabins were constructed in 1927, and later remodeled to add the running water and improved electrical service.

Guest cabins 1-18, and the balance of cabins 50-115 are known as "Roughrider" cabins. Each has a wood-burning stove and not much else (no toilet/bath facilities). There are two communal bath houses located in and around the cabin area (both constructed in 1938, though they, too, have been remodeled a couple of times since). These cabins are located to the north, west and northwest of the lodge building. Some of these cabins were constructed in 1927 to replace the original "tent" cabins erected on the site (though some have been replaced in later years). Many were relocated to Roosevelt in 1937 from their original posts at the old Mammoth Lodge. The communal bath houses located throughout the complex were constructed in 1937, though they have been remodeled several times.

Note that cabins 19-43 were removed at some point, and cabins 44-49 were the six removed to construct the Yellowstone General Store (see below).

Employee Cabins

The 55 employee cabins are located behind and to the east of the lodge building, and are almost identical to the "Roughrider" guest cabins in that each has a wood-burning stove, and no sink, toilet, or bathing facilities (with the exception of the nine managers' cabins). There are communal toilet and bath facilities in the center of the employee cabin complex. Most of these cabins were constructed in 1927, and 13 were relocated here from the Fishing Bridge area in 1982.

There are 142 employees who work in this area, including 110 lodge employees, 28 wranglers and stagecoach hands, and 4 YPSS employees.

2. Roosevelt Employee Laundry/Office

This building is one of the old employee cabins that has been converted into office space and a small employee laundry room. It was constructed in 1927.

3. Roosevelt Personnel Office

This cabin, constructed in 1924, is known historically as "Mrs. North's Cabin," as she was the house mistress in charge of the housekeepers and wait staff for several years in the early days of the lodge. Today, it serves as the personnel manger's office for the lodge concession operator.

4. Employee Recreation Building

This is a former employee cabin, constructed in 1927. It was converted into a Recreation Hall for employees in the 1980s.

5. ROOSEVELT HOUSEKEEPING OFFICE

This building was constructed in 1929 and houses the Housekeeping Office and the Linen Room.

6. ROOSEVELT MAINTENANCE BUILDING

This building was constructed in 1927 and was the original powerhouse for the lodge and the cabin area (equipped with a 12.5KW generator). Today, it serves as the Maintenance Office for the lodge.

7. YELLOWSTONE GENERAL STORE

This 1100 sq. ft. store was originally constructed as a Haynes Photo Shop in 1936. When Haynes died, the company continued to operate the store until 1967, when it was sold to Hamilton Stores. Today it is operated by Delaware North as one of its Yellowstone General Stores.

When it was constructed it dislocated six cabins, which are now located behind the lodge and are used as employee cabins (see above). The store sells basic supplies and light grocery items, and has a small food service with a limited amount of seating outside on the front porch. It is open from early June to early September and has six employees.

10. TOWER SERVICE STATION

The service station at the junction was constructed by Conoco in 1962 in conjunction with other improvements implemented during the NPS Mission 66 Program.[3]

The station replaced a single gasoline pump located near the lodge, which itself had been relocated to the area from Tower Fall in 1946, and was designed to serve as an "emergency" service to those who didn't have enough fuel to get to the next station.[4] Conoco had originally wanted to construct a station at the Tower Falls Store, but park superintendent Lon Garrison insisted it be located at the junction to better serve those traveling through the area. The station is open from early June until early September and has four employees.

11. ROOSEVELT CORRAL BARN & RELATED STRUCTURES

The barn complex includes a hay barn, saddling barn, two harness sheds, a tack shed, wrangler office, employee and guest restrooms, and a ticket sales building. The new hay barn was constructed in late 2011, and replaced an old structure that had been on site since 1976.

The facility offers six one- or two-hour horseback rides per day, and five or six stagecoach rides per day.

12. ROOSEVELT CORRAL TICKET BOOTH

Cookouts can accommodate 210 guests per day. They have 85 horses, three coaches and seven wagons.

The Yancey's Hole location includes six buildings, including a large dining shelter and serving shelter, two small storage sheds, and two vault toilets. Rides/cookouts are held seven days a week.

13. ROOSEVELT CORRAL TACK SHEDS

These small storage buildings house equipment for the horses.

14. ROOSEVELT CORRAL PUBLIC RESTROOM BUILDING

This is a public restroom building, constructed in 2001.

15. WRANGLER'S OFFICE

This is the head wrangler's office.

20. TOWER GENERAL STORE

The existing 8250 sq. ft. store was constructed in 1959 around the previous store which was built in 1936. It remained a Haynes Photo Shop until 1967 when Haynes' assets were purchased by Hamilton Stores, and all photo shops were converted to general stores or abandoned.

The original store opened near here as a stage station in the early 1900s; it was constructed by the Monida and Yellowstone Stage Company. In 1917, after stagecoaches were no longer allowed on the park roads, Jack Haynes converted it into a Photo Shop. It remained until it was replaced in 1936 by a store in the present location subsequent to the realignment of the roads in this area. The store is open from mid-May until mid-September and has roughly 40 employees. There have been discussions for years about relocating this store or tearing it down altogether and replacing it with another store and dormitory at Tower Junction.

21. Comfort Station 🚻

The comfort station was constructed by the NPS in 1975. The waste from this facility (and the store) is housed in a septic tank underground and periodically pumped over to a leach field at the Tower Campground.

22. YGS Dormitory

This 19-room dormitory was constructed in 1985, and houses roughly 38 employees who work at the Yellowstone General Stores located here at Tower Fall and at the lodge store. The dorm has an employee dining room (EDR) that seats 40. Just south of the dorm are six RV pads that are also used by employees of Delaware North.

23. YGS Recreation Hall

The building is a former mess hall/powerhouse constructed in 1947. When the new employee dorm was built, complete with its own EDR, this building was remodeled to serve as a rec hall for the employees.

Tower Ranger Station & Residence (Not Shown on Maps)

The existing Tower Ranger Station was constructed in 1971 and is staffed during the summer to provide backcountry camping permits and fishing licenses, as well as providing interpretive information for those with questions. If you need updated information about the status of the trails in the northeastern portion of the park, this is the place to stop in and ask.

The ranger residence is the first building you see alongside the driveway as you enter the Tower Administrative Area. This structure was built in 1916 to replace the 1907-era Soldier Station that had been relocated to this site from its original location a mile and a half east toward Tower Fall (see the Tower Junction to Canyon Junction road log entry at 1.4/16.9 for more details). It was felt that the soldiers would be able to better serve the park by being located at this crossroads rather than up the road since this area was open year round.

It was originally designed to accommodate up to five rangers, but now serves as the residence of rangers assigned to the Tower District. The ranger station, the residence in front of it, the station's corral, and Lost Creek are all part of the Tower Junction Ranger Station Historic District, designated in 1997.

Canyon Village
Development

The Canyon Village Development is the second youngest in the park, older only than Grant Village. Much of it was constructed in the late 1950s as part of the Mission 66 Program, replacing a haphazard collection of stores and visitor accommodations located further south in the area that exists today as the parking lot for the Brink of the Upper Falls. It was the first such project approved and implemented under the national program to improve facilities in the national park system in time for the 50th Anniversary of the National Park Service.

The village was designed by a San Francisco architectural firm, Becket and Associates, based on the Mid-Century Modern style that was prevalent in southern California at that point in time. The U-shaped arrangement of facilities was based in part on the early strip mall concept that was, at the time, considered to be the "in" thing in commercial development.

Many park purists, then and now, have decried the design of the development and the individual structures as inappropriate for the rustic setting of a national park, however. And while the original visitor center has since been replaced with a more modern structure that "fits in" with the architecture expected in a national park, the original stores and lodge buildings remain as testaments to the 1950s-1960s era. Perhaps ironically, the village is being evaluated for consideration to be designated as a historic district based on those exact qualities.

The development of the visitor accommodations at Canyon Village was troublesome from the outset as well. It took considerable effort for the park's concession operator, the Yellowstone Park Company (YPC), to secure the funding to build the pre-fabricated cabins that would be used to house visitors. Those same cabins exist to this day, though many have long since been condemned and destroyed. It is not uncommon at all for an arriving visitor to return to the registration desk refusing to stay in some of the older cabins. Interestingly, the cabins were never intended to become permanent housing - they were supposed to be "temporary," to be replaced by lodge-type buildings such as the two newer structures that were built in the 1990s.

The difficulty in obtaining the money needed to build the lodge and cabins was a harbinger of things to come. Shortly after the completion of the early parts of the village, the YPC would sell off its park operations to another company, setting the stage for a two-decade long battle over needed improvements and who would or should be responsible for paying for those improvements. These battles would doom any chances of completing the other major Mission 66 project in the park at the time, Grant Village. There was tremendous flux as the concession operation was sold to one company, who'd then be bought out by another, and then the arguments with the NPS would begin all over again. It would be 1979 before Congress would approve funding for the NPS to purchase the assets of the troubled operation and reassign the contract to operate them to a more stable company.

The first *Canyon Development Plan*, developed by the NPS in 1988, called for the demolition of these old cabins and the construction of six lodge buildings similar to what exists at Grant Village. Only two of these have been constructed, however, one in 1993 and the other in 1998. One of the requirements of the new concession contract awarded in 2013 was the commitment to construct additional lodge buildings and removal of the dilapidated cabins. At present, there is no specific time frame for that to be accomplished, however (though preliminary planning for the project is already underway).

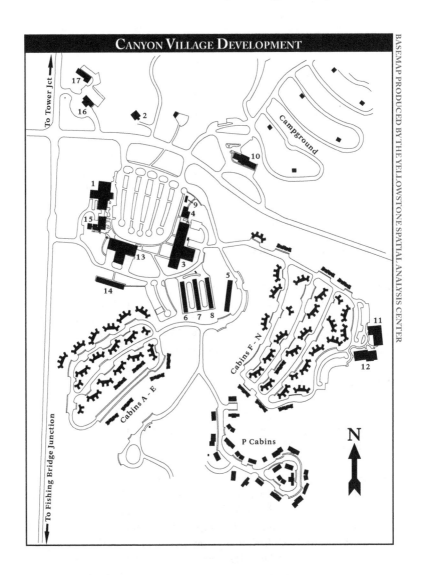

1. Canyon Visitor Education Center 🏠 👫

The Canyon Visitor Education Center (CVEC) opened in 2006, replacing the old Visitor Center, which had been built in 1957-1958 as part of the original development of Canyon Village under the Mission 66 Program.

The CVEC exhibits focus on the Yellowstone Supervolcano and what drives the park's geological processes. There's a large model of the caldera, as well as a Kugel globe (a large granite globe resting in a spherical, conclave base, supported by a thin film of water allowing it to be turned by hand). You'll also find restrooms, an information desk, a large Yellowstone Association Bookstore, and the Canyon Backcountry Office here.

2. Canyon Emergency Services Building 🏠

Completed in 2009, this facility houses the law enforcement rangers and emergency services equipment for the Canyon area. It is located in the woods across the road from the entrance to Canyon Village along a road that leads back to the water storage tanks for the village and what was the second Civilian Conservation Corps camp in the Canyon area.

3. Canyon Lodge 🛏 🍴 🍽

The Canyon Lodge opened in 1957, concurrently with 117 of the planned 500+ cabins in place (see below). The structure underwent a major rehabilitation in 2012.[1]

The first floor of the lodge is commercial space and has a cafeteria that seats 196, a dining room with seating for 180, and a deli/snack shop that seats 20. There's also a 62-seat lounge and a small gift shop. The basement has concession office space, a small employee pub, and a 94-seat Employee Dining Room (EDR). Originally, the basement housed a laundry for visitors' use, but those facilities were removed when the new Camper Services Building was constructed in 1968. The EDR and a small recreation area were added in its place. The building also has eight dorm rooms that house 15 employees (known locally as the "Moose Dorm").

4. Canyon Lodge Administration Building 🛏

Built in 1957, this small structure houses the check-in desk for the cabins and lodges, as well as the activities sales desk. See below for details on the cabins and the Dunraven and Cascade Lodge buildings.

A - N Series Cabins ("Aspen Hill" and "Cascade Loop")

These "Frontier" cabins were originally constructed in 1956-1957, and were designed to be "temporary." They consisted of prefabricated wooden panels fitted onto a foundation that rested on concrete blocks. The buildings originally had no insulation whatsoever, and were painted turquoise, green, and yellow, though they have been renovated a couple of times and are now painted the distinct brown color of other buildings within the park.

In 2002, 80 of the original cabins in this area were condemned and removed. The remainder are in pretty bad shape and are scheduled to be removed at some point in the near future (the fire department likes to burn one or two for training each season!). They are to be replaced by new lodge type buildings. Cabins in the Cascade Loop saw their last season in 2013.

Eight of the cabins are used for employee housing, and the remaining 323 rooms rented for $105 per night in 2013.

P-Series Cabins ("Beaver Meadows")

These "Western" cabins were constructed in 1969 and are much nicer (inside and out) than their predecessors. There are 100 rooms, each of which rented for $199 per night in 2013. If/When the new lodge buildings are constructed, these cabins may be repurposed as employee housing (though consideration is being given to keeping them as guest cabins).

5. BIGHORN DORMITORY

Bighorn Dormitory was constructed in 1968 and is the newest of the Canyon dorms. It has 59 rooms for 117 employees, and houses mostly staff members who're older and more mature (known as the "quiet" dorm).

6. BISON DORMITORY

Bison Dormitory houses mostly underage (under 21) employees. It has 50 rooms for 99 employees and was constructed in 1957 as part of the original development at Canyon Village.

7. GRIZZLY DORMITORY

Grizzly Dormitory is known locally as the "party" dorm as it houses the younger set (21-25). It has 50 rooms for 99 employees and was also constructed in 1957.

8. WAPITI DORMITORY

The Wapiti Dormitory has a mix of residents, including the younger set. It has 50 rooms for 99 employees and was built in 1957. All three of the 1957 dorms are basically mirror images of one another.

9. U. S. POST OFFICE ✉

The portable building that now houses the U.S. Post Office was at one time the Canyon Warming Hut, used during the winter to provide a respite from the cold and snow for those traveling through the area. The post office is usually open from early June to mid-September.

10. CAMPER SERVICES BUILDING 🚿 📷 ⛺

This building was completed in 1968 and houses the registration desk for the campground, along with showers and a laundry for use by campers or other visitors. The 2014 daily rate for the campground is $25.50.

11. CASCADE LODGE BUILDING

This two-story, 37-room lodge was constructed by the National Park Service in 1993. The rooms rented for $195 per night in 2013.

12. DUNRAVEN LODGE BUILDING

This two-story building was opened in 1999, having been constructed by the park's primary concession operator at the time, Amfac (now Xanterra). It has 44 rooms, and in contrast to its next door neighbor, this building also has an elevator. The reason this lodge has an elevator is the Americans with Disabilities Act, which took effect in the middle of 1992. The plans for the Cascade Lodge had already been approved and the contract let when the law took effect, so it wasn't required to have an elevator. These rooms also rented for $195 per night in 2013.

13. CANYON GENERAL STORE 🛍 🛒 🍴 🚻

The Canyon General Store opened on July 15, 1957, as part of the original Canyon Village development. The main floor has approximately 12000 sq. ft. of floor space, including a fountain which seats roughly 100 people. The basement has apartments for employees (managers) and an employee dining room, along with warehouse space. The store is open from mid-May until late September and has roughly 80 employees.

14. YGS DORMITORY

The YGS Dormitory was constructed concurrently with the main general store in 1957. It houses approximately 100 employees.

15. YELLOWSTONE ADVENTURE STORE 🛉 🍽 🕴

The Yellowstone Adventure Store opened as a Haynes Photo Shop in 1958. Upon the sale of Haynes' assets to Hamilton Stores in 1967, it became an outdoor "nature" store, offering fishing and camping supplies in addition to the usual store fare. It also has a small hot dog stand. The building has some limited residential space for store managers (the employees live in the YGS Dorm; see above). The store is open from mid-April until the park's closing day in early November and has 10 employees.

16. CANYON SERVICE STATION 🏠 🔧

This service station opened on July 1, 1957, with the original development at Canyon Village. The pumps are available 24/7, and the station offers minor automotive and RV repair services. It is open from early May through the middle of October.

17. YPSS DORMITORY

The dormitory for YPSS employees is located behind (north) of the service station. It was constructed in 1968.

NO LONGER STANDING BUILDINGS

Canyon Hotel 1: Constructed in 1886 in the general area of the current parking lot at the Brink of the Upper Falls, this wooden structure served as the primary hotel in the Canyon area until the second one was built in 1890. Guests stayed in tents.

Canyon Hotel 2: Constructed in 1889-1890 south of the present day Canyon Corrals, this structure could accommodate 250 guests. It was expanded in 1901 to add 24 more rooms, and was included in the construction of the third Canyon Hotel.

Canyon Hotel 3: The third Canyon Hotel was basically "added on" to the second structure. Designed by Robert Reamer, architect of the Old Faithful Inn, the new/improved hotel provided 375 rooms, and opened to visitors on June 20, 1911. Later additions would boost the capacity to 950

Canyon Housekeeping Cabins, ca. 1934. Note Upper Falls at lower left, and the old Canyon Bridge just above the falls. Just below the cabins you can see the cafeteria. The large open area in the lower right of the image is the location of today's Brink of the Upper Falls Parking Lot.

guests and would make the structure almost one mile in circumference. The structure occupied much of what is today the corral grounds at Canyon. In fact, if you park in the lot in front of the ticket booth and walk out into the grassy areas to the south and east of the pavement, you can still see traces of the old hotel's foundation.

A confluence of events would lead to the hotel's demise. Over the course of its existence, the hotel was plagued by structural and foundation problems caused by the natural instability of the ground in the Canyon area. This grew worse over time and by the late 1950s engineers were recommending the building be closed for public safety reasons.

On top of this, there was growing financial pressure to close the hotel. The new development at Canyon Village included hundreds of new cabins. The cost of staying in a cabin was higher than the room rate at the hotel, however, made necessary because of the large loan the Yellowstone Park Company (YPC) had taken out to pay for their new lodging facilities. However, guests seemed to prefer staying at the old hotel and many of the cabins remained empty each night. In fact, the hotel was now completely filling each evening, something it hadn't done in years.

Given these pressures, in 1959, YPC decided to close the hotel and sell it to a salvage company for $25. Much of the reclamation work had been completed when on August 8, 1960, the hotel burned to the ground.

Auto shelter located at the Canyon Auto Campground, ca. 1916. These were constructed at several of the new "auto campgrounds" established by the NPS around the park after the introduction of the autmobile to the park that year.

No official cause was ever determined, though there were many theories about how the fire started. These included concession employees accidentally starting the fire during a party in the abandoned structure, as well as the salvage company intentionally setting it on fire (unlikely, since the fire insurance had been canceled on the building). The author's personal favorite is that the grand old lady decided she wasn't going to go out with the indignity of being destroyed piece by piece, and decided she was going to go out in a blaze of glory.[2]

Brink of the Upper Falls Parking Lot: Site of much original development in the Canyon area prior to the current Canyon Village. This area, where a single comfort station (and its attendant lift station) exists now, was once home to the first Canyon Hotel, a general store and its warehouse, a tourist cabin complex, a ranger station, a gas station, a cafeteria and deli, a Haynes Photo Shop, and several support buildings. Today, it's almost impossible to tell that such a large development once existed in this area.

Fishing Bridge
Development

The Fishing Bridge area has historically been considered a "detachment" of the Lake Development and is still largely treated as such today (along with Bridge Bay) in park planning documents.[1] It is often referred to in earlier historical accounts as "Lake Outlet." The area had long been the site of a variety of camps and outposts prior to its development as a commercial center.

Development here began in earnest in the 1920s as visitors began to flock to the area for the fishing. The NPS deemed it desirable at the time to build an infrastructure to support those who wished to remain in this section of the park, to include the building of campgrounds complete with "comfort stations," and allowing the park's commercial vendors to construct restaurants, stores, and support facilities to provide goods and services.

Visitation and use of the area only became more intense as time passed. Boathouses were built north of the area's namesake bridge, and it was possible to rent boats and fish as far north as LeHardy Rapids. The bridge itself would be packed most of the day with anglers trying to catch the park's famous cutthroat trout.

Eventually, overnight accommodations in the form of a 305-unit "housekeeping cabin" complex arose, and the Fishing Bridge development would become one of the busiest in the park. Over time, concessioners built photo shops, stores, a cafeteria, service station and a repair garage. A 310-site campground and 346-site RV park (which itself replaced a smaller trailer camp) would eventually round out the development here.

By the 1960s, however, as a more robust understanding of how the park's ecosystems function took hold, park planners began to come to grips with the reality of how the Fishing Bridge development was impacting wildlife

Fishing Bridge Development, with the store left of center, 1960. Note the original RV campground in the upper left. After the new RV park was built in 1964, this was obliterated.

in the area, especially with respect to grizzly bears. The development here (and an "overflow" campground built in the late 1950s on the east side of Pelican Creek) was having a negative impact on many different aspects of the bears' survival. Indeed, Fishing Bridge occupies what scientists consider "pristine" environment for the grizzly. The vast number of people fishing off the bridge was also having a negative impact on the park's native trout population (which in turn also impacted the grizzlies as this was one of their primary food sources). There was genuine concern that all of the fishing was substantially reducing the trout population, and this was the primary reason fishing from Fishing Bridge itself was banned in 1973.

With that in mind, plans were developed to completely do away with all of the development at Fishing Bridge and return the area to its natural state. Pressure from the Wyoming Congressional delegation and other politicians, however, would prevent many of these plans from coming to fruition. Although the huge campground and cabin complex have gone away, most of the commercial development and the Mission 66-era RV Park still exist today.[2]

Much of the remaining development was designated as a National Historic District in 1987 primarily because it was the first commercial strip development in a national park. The Fishing Bridge Museum, one of four built in the 1929-1932 time frame, is also a National Historic Landmark.

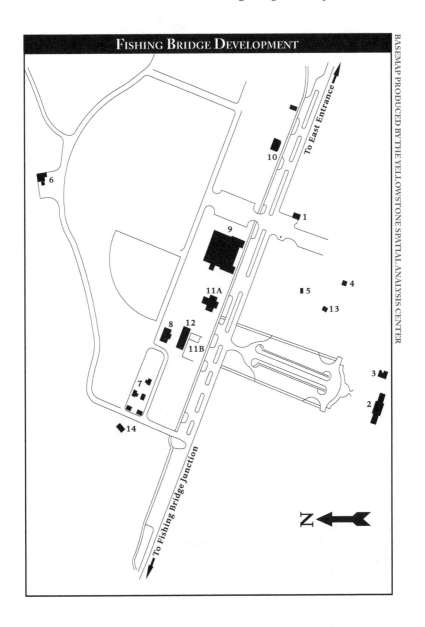

1. Fishing Bridge Warming Hut

Originally constructed as a ranger station in 1928, this building was moved to its present location and remodeled in 1934.[3] It is now used for storage during the summer and as a warming hut during the winter.

Across the parking area from the building is a new vault toilet installed in 2010. It replaced a couple of really old outhouses that were almost invariably in less than pristine condition.

2. Fishing Bridge Museum 🏠 ⍰

The Fishing Bridge Museum was the last of the four museums constructed in the park, opening in 1931. The building is sometimes erroneously referred to as the Fishing Bridge Visitor Center, but in reality it remains a museum. It became a National Historic Landmark in 1987 (along with the other two remaining museums at Madison and Norris).

Designed by Herbert Maier (American Association of Museums), and used as a model for many other museums in state and local parks around the country, the structure originally cost $118,000 to build and equip. The money came from the Laura Spelman Rockefeller Foundation.

By the late 1920s, tourists were no longer typically accompanied by tour guides, so they needed some mechanism to allow them to educate themselves about the wonders in the park. These museums were designed to fulfill that role. Today, the museum houses displays of various birds and other animals found within the park, as well as a visitor desk and a small Yellowstone Association bookstore.

The museum sits on what was from the early 1920s part of the original campground in this area. The land was taken specifically to construct the museum at the edge of the lake, and to add the parking lot and amphitheater. The amphitheater, located immediately adjacent to the museum, was also designed by Maier, and was constructed in 1932.

The parking lot was added in 1936 and had the effect of splitting the existing campground in half. In 1939, the western side of the complex was modified for use by campers arriving in recreational vehicles, a purpose it served until it was closed in 1964 when the new (existing) Fishing Bridge RV Park opened.[4]

3. Naturalist's Residence

This residence was originally designed for the interpretive ranger who was assigned to the museum, and was constructed in 1930 concurrently with the museum. It, too, was designed by Herbert Maier. It continues to house interpretive staff who work at Fishing Bridge.

4. Old Lift Station/Storage

Constructed in 1936, this little building was originally a lift station for sewage generated at the campground's comfort stations. Following the closure of the campground in 1989, it was used for a period of time as a physical sciences laboratory. Today it is used primarily for storage.

5. Comfort Station 🚻

This comfort station was constructed in 1936 along with several others to serve the campground that was present here at the time. With the removal of the campground in 1989, all of the others have been removed. This one was left standing to serve visitors to the museum, amphitheater, and picnic area.

6. Pump House/Generator

The larger of these two buildings is a lift station and pump house. Sewage lines from the Fishing Bridge, the Lake Village, Lake Government Area, and Bridge Bay terminate here and their sewage is pumped to the Wastewater Treatment Plant located approximately one mile to the north. The smaller building is a generator for the pumphouse.

7. YPSS Employee Cabins

These five cabins are all that's left of the huge guest cabin complex that existed at Fishing Bridge from the 1930s into the 1970s. The large barren area to the north and east of these structures was filled with cabins identical to these.

Today, four of the cabins house employees of the Yellowstone Park Service Stations, while the fifth (the easternmost) is a small office. Plans call for the expansion of the YPSS Dormitory (See #12 below), and the removal or repurposing of these cabins.

8. YGS Warehouse Building

Built in 1930, this was originally associated with the Haynes Photo Shop that was on the frontage west of the Repair Shop (see below) until 1990 when it was razed. When Hamilton Stores (now Yellowstone General Stores) assumed ownership of the Haynes assets in 1967, the building became a warehouse for their store located here.

9. Fishing Bridge General Store 🚻 ♿ 🚻

This 19881 sq. ft. store was constructed in 1931 to replace an older store (built in 1924) that had been located along the road much closer to the river (where today's eastern Fishing Bridge parking lot is located). It was remodeled in 1945, 1955, 1992, and again in 2006 to restore the interior to its original appearance. The main floor houses a store with a small grocery provision, while the top floor consists of apartments for managers and supervisors (originally used as employee housing for female staff when the store was first constructed). The bottom floor (basement) includes an employee dining room.

10. YGS Dormitory/ "Boys Dorm"

This building was originally constructed at Canyon in 1925 as a bath house for visitors. When Henry Brothers closed it down in 1933, Charles Hamilton bought it from him, and in 1950 relocated it to this spot. It was remodeled into a dorm for male employees, and is today a coed dorm.

11A. Fishing Bridge Service Station ⛽

The Fishing Bridge Service Station was constructed in 1930, along with the Repair Garage (see below). It is the oldest surviving gas station in the park. There is some speculation that Robert Reamer may have designed this building (and the repair garage), but there is little evidence to support this claim.[5] In addition to gasoline and diesel fuel, propane is available here.

11B. Fishing Bridge Repair Garage 🔧

Just to the west of the Service Station is what's left of the old Fishing Bridge Repair Garage (11B). It was heavily damaged when an accumulation of snow collapsed its roof in March of 2011. Plans are underway to design and reconstruct the facility, but since it was an historical structure, it requires a considerable amount of coordination with a variety of state and federal organizations. It was constructed in 1930 along with its neighbor.[6]

12. YPSS DORMITORY

Built in 1959, this is a dormitory for employees of the Yellowstone Park Service Stations (YPSS), which operates the service station and the repair garage. There are plans to expand this building by about 40% to allow YPSS to relocate those employees from the cabins to the dorm.

13. COVERED PICNIC AREA

Constructed in 1935, this was one of several covered picnic sites built in the old campground at Fishing Bridge, and the only one left standing. This is no longer used for picnicking, but for storage of lumber and other building materials.

14. HOSE REEL HOUSE/STORAGE BUILDING

This building was originally the "fire cache" for the Fishing Bridge development. It housed old carriages with reels of fire hose that were used to fight fires that broke out in the cabin complex and development. It's construction date is unknown, and today it is used as junk storage.

OLD FISHING BRIDGE INCINERATOR/BUNKHOUSE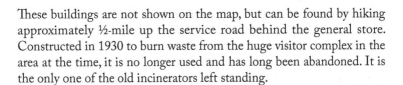

These buildings are not shown on the map, but can be found by hiking approximately ½-mile up the service road behind the general store. Constructed in 1930 to burn waste from the huge visitor complex in the area at the time, it is no longer used and has long been abandoned. It is the only one of the old incinerators left standing.

On the hill behind it can be found the old bunkhouse that was used as a residence by those who operated the incinerator. Today that building is used to store plumbing fixtures and other building materials.

OTHER NOTABLE FACILITIES IN THE AREA

Fishing Bridge Picnic Area 🏕

The Fishing Bridge Picnic Area is located on the west side of the parking lot of the Fishing Bridge Museum. There are 11 picnic tables here. The nearest toilet is the comfort station located in the woods northeast of the Museum.

Haynes Photo Shop at Fishing Bridge, ca. 1929.

Fishing Bridge RV Park/Camper Services Building 🚐 🚍 🍴 📷

The Fishing Bridge RV Park was constructed in 1964 as a part of the Mission 66 Program. It replaced the old RV campground that existed just west of the museum parking lot, along the south side of the highway. The park has 346 sites with complete hookups (50-amp electrical, water, sewer), and rented for $46.50 per night during 2014. The campground is open from roughly mid-May to mid-September each summer.

There's a camper services building on site with showers and a laundry, and there are comfort stations with toilets and running water located throughout the grounds. In addition to the sewer hookups, there's also a dump station on site. Note that only hard-sided campers are permitted due to the prevalence of grizzly bears in the area (no soft-sided or pop-up campers and no tents are allowed).

No Longer Standing Buildings/Facilities

Fishing Bridge Boathouses: There were two of these. The first one was built in 1920s, located on east side of the river just north of the bridge. It provided boats for rent to fishing parties. In 1935, a new boathouse was constructed on the west side of the river in anticipation of the new bridge being built. It was designed by architect Robert Reamer, the architect of the Old Faithful Inn and many other important structures within the park. This boathouse "floated" and was also used to rent small boats and canoes to those interested in fishing on the lake and river. The boathouse was removed in the 1970s in concert with modifications to other policies regarding the management of wildlife and visitors within the park (including the decision to ban fishing from the bridge itself).

Haynes Photo Shop: Originally located east of the existing Fishing Bridge General Store, the 60′ x 60′ building was constructed in 1928 and included a shop, an employee dining room, and a garage for employee vehicles. The building was removed in 1990.[7]

Pelican Creek Campground/Indian Pond Group Camp: In the late 1950s, in order to handle the ever-increasing overflows from the Fishing Bridge Campground, the NPS quietly opened a second campground along the east shore of Pelican Creek, north of the road. This 115-site campground wasn't used terribly often, but it, too, was situated in the heart of grizzly territory. It was closed in 1972, and the entire area was rehabilitated in the 1990s. The area is closed to the public today.

A small "group camp" existed on the east side of Indian Pond, used by the Boy Scouts, reunions, and other large gatherings. It, too, was closed in 1983. Little evidence of its existence remains.[8]

Lake Village
Development

The developments in the Lake Village vicinity consist of two distinct areas:

- The Lake Village Commercial Complex, which itself is composed of roughly three areas, the Lake Lodge and Cabins, the Lake Hotel and Cottages, and the Fish Hatchery area
- The Lake Administrative (Government) Area

The Lake Administrative Area is primarily an NPS housing and maintenance complex and has no public services. Therefore it is not discussed in any significant detail in this book.

The development at what is today Lake Village began in the park's early days with several boat concessioners who developed some small cabins and dock facilities in the area. These enterprising individuals would take visitors out for tours of the lake on small boats, setting the stage for tours that continue to this day from Bridge Bay.

Original tourist accommodations in this area took the form of a couple of itinerant tent camp operations, one owned by William Wylie and the other by the Yellowstone Park Association (YPA); both opened in 1887. The YPA camp was located in the open meadow in front of today's lodge, while the Wylie Camp was located on the site of the existing lodge itself. The Wylie camp would become a "permanent" camp in 1898, and would survive until 1919 when the current Lake Lodge was constructed.[1] The YPA camp would close down once the Lake Hotel opened for business in 1891.

In 1889, construction of the original Lake Hotel commenced. A nearly identical structure would be built near what is today known as Fountain Paint Pots on the opposite side of the park. The Fountain Hotel no longer exists, but the Lake Hotel would go on to be modified and expanded several times, the last handful of which were accomplished under the supervision of architect Robert Reamer. He transformed the building from a plain, clapboard structure into the grand old lady you see today. It is the second oldest operating hotel in the national park system (the Wawona Hotel in Yosemite, built in 1876, is the oldest).

Throughout the years there have been discussions about tearing the old hotel down. These became rather serious in the 1970s and early 1980s because the building, like many of the other lodging facilities in the park at that time, had become run down and decrepit and was considered an eyesore. It was rescued, however, when TW Recreation Services, then the lodging concession operator, agreed to rehabilitate the hotel in time for its centennial anniversary in 1991. Today, the structure is undergoing seismic retrofitting to ensure it survives an earthquake, and the interior is being remodeled to update the décor and guest amenities.

With the construction of the Lake Hotel, a gentleman named E. C. Waters constructed a boat dock and launch operation at the lake shore, roughly at the site where the little observation deck in front of the hotel is situated today. He brought a large steamer named the *Zillah* into the park in pieces, reassembled it on the lake, and used it to offer trips between the hotel and West Thumb. Visitors would have the option of traveling between the two locations via a bumpy, dusty stagecoach ride, or they could take a leisurely cruise across scenic Yellowstone Lake on Waters' steamboat.

In addition to the dock, he had several other buildings erected in the immediate vicinity of the hotel, including the area's first store and a residence for himself. Though all of those buildings have long since been razed, the dock itself remained in place until 1966, when it was removed as part of the "cleaning up" of the park initiated under the Mission 66 Program.

In 1896, Waters interred several animals in a corral placed on Dot Island (mainly bison, elk, and bighorn sheep). He used this "zoo" as a tourist attraction, and his boats would stop there as he ferried passengers from West Thumb to the hotel so the tourists could see the "wildlife."[2] The animals were malnourished and often mistreated, however, and the Department of the Interior finally ordered the zoo disbanded in 1907. Mr. Waters was subsequently banned from the park.

In 1905, Waters constructed another large steamer, this one named after himself; it was called the *E. C. Waters*. According to Waters, the boat was designed to carry as many as 600 passengers, but the U.S. Marine Service, responsible for certifying boats in passenger service at the time, would only license it to carry 250. Waters refused to operate this boat with so few passengers, however, and decided to beach the boat on Stevenson Island rather than lose money on its operation.

In 1924, the boat's boilers were removed through a hole cut into the side of the ship and relocated to the boiler house at the Lake Hotel, where they powered the structure and its related buildings for a number of years afterward.[3] Six years later, the old ship was burned by rangers in an attempt to rid the lake of its rotting hulk. Today, if you take one the SceniCruises out of Bridge Bay, you'll be taken to see the vestigial remnants of the old ship on the island.

Waters' boat operation was transferred to other concessioners a number of times and was eventually bought out by the Yellowstone Park Boat Company. This company was itself consolidated into the Yellowstone Park Company (YPC) in 1936. The YPC would remain the park's primary concession operators for almost three more decades until it sold its assets. Today, park concessioner Xanterra continues to operate boat tours and rentals on Yellowstone Lake.

The Lake Lodge building would be added in 1920 to complement the tent "housekeeping" cabins that had been located just northeast of the hotel. It, too, would be modified over time to morph into the structure you see today. There are plans to relocate some of the cabins behind the lodge due to their proximity to Lodge Creek, which the grizzlies use to fish during the early part of the season. Because of the bear activity, the cabins must remain closed, and the concessioner is unable to rent them for the first month and a half the lodge is open for business. After World War II, there was discussion about tearing the facility and its cabins down and consolidating lodging at the hotel. However, that was soon abandoned once concession operators saw how much park visitation increased after the war.

From 1901 to 1953, Yellowstone National Park was the largest source of wild cutthroat trout eggs in the country. The earliest fish hatchery operation in the park was conducted along what is today known as Little Thumb Creek (then "Fisheries Creek") near West Thumb, beginning in 1903. Over time, additional hatcheries would be constructed at Grebe Lake, Trout Lake, and a variety of other fish-related operations were undertaken at a great many lakes and stream throughout the park (Clear Creek and Cub Creek to name but two). The primary purposes of most of these hatcheries was to keep the cutthroat (and other fish) populations high enough to sustain the level of fishing that tourists were bringing to the park. However, the U.S. Bureau of Fisheries (a predecessor of today's U.S. Fish and Wildlife Service) began taking eggs to populate bodies of water in other parts of the country as well.

In 1913, the first large-scale fish hatchery was constructed near the Lake Hotel, just northwest of the existing Fish Hatchery building. Several additional structures were also added, including a messhall, residence, barn, bunkhouse, and a shop. These structures were not well-built, however, and a mere 15 years later they were already in need of replacement. The Bureau of Fisheries was given permission to construct a new hatchery and related buildings in 1928, and from 1928 through 1932, the new hatchery was constructed, along with a new messhall, bunkhouse, shop, several residences, etc. These are listed individually below.

Throughout the subsequent 20 years, National Park Service policy regarding stocking and harvesting of fish evolved to the point where they no longer supported manipulating fish populations. To that end, in 1957, the all of the park's hatcheries were closed, and the Lake complex was turned over to research. Today, the complex is used by the Aquatic Resources Branch of the Yellowstone Center for Resources, the scientific division of the park, as well as the U.S. Fish and Wildlife Service.[4]

The Lake Fish Hatchery Historic District was designated in 1985 for its contribution to the conservation practices within the park and throughout the western portion of the country as a result of its being used to supply cutthroat trout. The district includes the Fish Hatchery, built in 1932 and nine support buildings (identified below).

The Lake Historic District was designated in 1994. The District includes the Ranger Station, the Hotel, the Lodge, the General Store, and the old Lake Service Station (now used as a storage building). The Lake Hotel itself was individually listed in the National Register of Historic Places in 1991 for its unique architecture and historical contribution to the park.

In 1972, the Grand Loop Road, which up to that point had passed right in front of the hatchery, hotel, general store and the ranger station was rerouted, primarily to allow visitors to bypass the village. The new alignment allowed through traffic to pass to the west and those who wanted to enter the village to do so from the "rear." The old section of road was left largely intact between the hatchery and the ranger station, but the north and south ends were abandoned and consigned to foot and bicycle traffic.

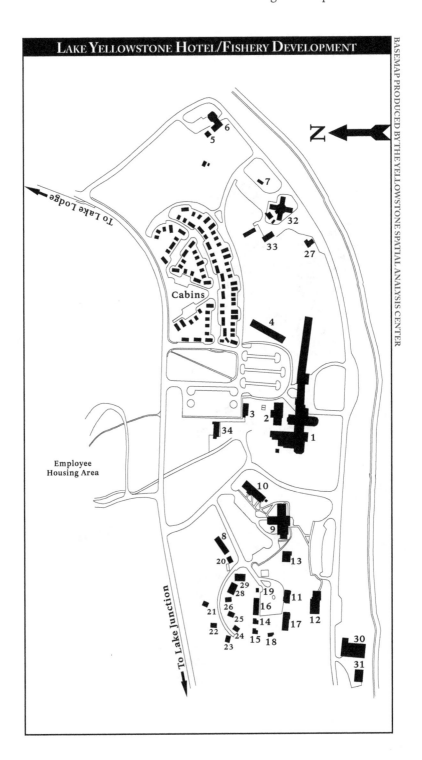

LAKE YELLOWSTONE LODGE DEVELOPMENT

BASEMAP PRODUCED BY THE YELLOWSTONE SPATIAL ANALYSIS CENTER

To Lake Hotel

N

1. Lake Hotel ⅋ 🛏 ❄ (⚥

Lake Hotel is the second oldest operating hotel in the U.S. National Park system. Construction began in 1889, and the hotel opened in 1891 with 63 rooms. Another 17 were added in 1901.[5] The original hotel was designed by architect N. L. Haller, using the same floor plan for both this structure and the Fountain Hotel, constructed along the same time line near Fountain Paint Pots (see the Old Faithful to Madison Road section for details about this hotel). Lake Hotel sits on the spot where President Chester A. Arthur and his entourage camped on their foray through the park in 1883.

In 1903-1904, the hotel underwent its first major modification under the supervision of architect Robert Reamer, who, at the time, was also busy overseeing the construction of the Old Faithful Inn. This new work included an extension of the east wing, addition of a north wing, and installation of the Ionic columns and transom windows you see in the original part of the structure today. The hotel began to take on the Colonial Revival appearance for which it has become famous. For a short period of time, the hotel was known as the Lake Colonial Hotel, in fact. After this work was completed, the building would have 210 rooms capable of hosting 446 guests.[6]

In 1922-1923, Reamer would once again design and build an extension onto the hotel. This time it would be the 122-room extension to the east wing. As crews were doing the groundwork for the foundation for the new section, they encountered a large boulder buried in the ground. The rock was so huge that it would be necessary to blow the thing up, and there was some concern that doing so might damage the existing hotel. Therefore, Reamer modified his design plans such that the new wing would be three degrees offset from parallel with the existing structure. Many who visit the hotel barely even notice this (from the inside or the outside), but if you examine an aerial or satellite image of the hotel you can easily see it.

Reamer would also add a new (existing) Dining Room to the west side of the original part of the hotel, redesign the lobby, and convert the old dining room into the Presidential Suite, a room later used by Presidents Calvin Coolidge and Franklin D. Roosevelt.

The final major structural change to the hotel came in 1928-1929, when Reamer enclosed the existing porte-cochere to create a larger lobby, and added a new porte-cochere to the east of the original's location (on the front of the first east wing expansion).[7] With the old porte-cochere removed

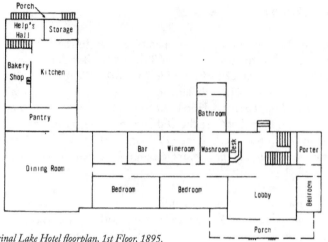

Original Lake Hotel floorplan, 1st Floor, 1895.

and the lobby expanded, Reamer created the magnificent "sunroom" that is quite popular with visitors today.

The north wing would be removed in 1940 (where the rear parking lot exists now) to facilitate the construction of a series of "cottages" (cabins) that are still in use today. By this time the owner of the hotel, the Yellowstone Park Company, wanted a more "modest" hotel to appeal to the average traveler (remember, the country was still in the midst of the Great Depression). The small cabins were completed that year, and used just one summer before the country entered World War II. For the next five seasons, the hotel and its new cottages would be closed and boarded up.

In the 1950s, serious consideration was given to razing the hotel, but the decision was made to keep it. Over time, inadequate attention to its upkeep allowed it to become run down and dilapidated, but in the mid-1980s the park's new concessioner, TW Recreation Services, began a multi-year project to rehabilitate and restore the hotel to its former glory. The renovations were completed in time for the hotel to celebrate its 100th birthday in 1991. In recent years, the hotel has undergone seismic rehabilitation to increase the likelihood it will survive a major earthquake, as well as an update to the interior decor in the lobby, dining room, and the guest rooms.

Today, the hotel has a 700-foot facade facing the lake and is three and a half stories tall. The hotel was listed on the National Register of Historic Places in 1991. The Hotel "Annex" building was originally the 56-room girl's dormitory. Other dorms, including the "H" Dorm and the "I" Dorm, were located in the general area of the rear parking lots and near the west end section of cabins, but were removed in the 1970s to facilitate the rerouting of traffic into the Lake Village area via the current entrance road. The rooms on the first floor of the old East Wing (constructed in 1903) have been converted into office space and public restrooms on one side, and into a Deli with a small seating area on the other side (this space was originally a lounge/conference area).

Perhaps one of the most unique facts about the hotel is that, until 1984, it supplied all of the other lodging operations in the park with ice. The northwest extension of the kitchen area had a huge ammonia refrigeration system that made large quantities of ice. It was removed in 1985.[8]

When the hotel first opened, a night's stay would cost $4.00 (equivalent to about $100 in 2013).[9] Today there are 158 rooms in the hotel proper, plus another 36 in the "Annex" (see below), as well as 110 cabins that were added in 1940-1941. The 2014 rates ranged from $149 per night for a cabin, $158 for a room in the Annex, $389-$399 for a lakeside hotel room, or $629 for the hotel's Presidential Suite. The Dining Room seats 254, and the small deli along the first floor hallway seats 24. There is an 88-seat Employee Dining Room located behind the kitchen at the rear.

The little creek on the west side of the hotel is known as Hotel Creek for its proximity to the hotel. In the early days of the hotel's existence, raw sewage was drained into the creek (and therefore into the lake).

Lake Hotel Cabins (500-600 Series)

These cabins were constructed in 1940-1941, and provide 110 guest rooms. Of these, 42 are single cabins, while the remainder are duplexes. Each cabin is a little over 300 sq. ft. in size and is equipped with a sink, shower and toilet. The cabins were extensively remodeled in 2003-2004. All are equipped with double beds.

2. Lake Hotel Boiler Building

This building houses the hotel's boilers and maintenance offices; it was constructed in conjunction with the 1922-1923 work on the hotel building. In 1924, the boilers from the beached *E. C. Waters* (see introductory section above) were removed from the vessel and relocated to this building to provide power for the hotel and its related buildings, a purpose they served until 1936 when they were swapped out for oil-fed boilers.[10] Today the boilers are fed by diesel fuel.

3. PERSONNEL OFFICE/WINTERKEEPER'S RESIDENCE

This structure, constructed in 1929 as the hotel maintenance manager's residence, now serves dual purposes. During the summer, it serves as Xanterra Personnel Office/Residence, while in the winter, the winterkeeper lives here. The winterkeeper is responsible for ensuring the general integrity of the hotel and its related structures during the winter, to include removing snow buildup that accumulates on the roof.

4. LAKE HOTEL ANNEX

This building, constructed in 1924, was originally a 56-room dormitory for the female housekeeping staff. It was known in its later years as the Sandpiper Dorm. In 1989, subsequent to the completion of the Goldeneye employee dormitory, it was converted to a lodge-type "annex" to the Hotel, with 43 rooms (36 now after some remodeling). The daily rates for these rooms are typically around half that of the "Lake View" rooms in the hotel.

5. LAKE FIRE CACHE

This small building houses firefighting equipment and supplies for the Lake area. The building was constructed by the CCC in 1934.

6. LAKE RANGER STATION 🏠

The Lake Ranger Station was constructed in 1923, replacing an aging Soldier Station located some distance away in the field in front of today's Lake Lodge. The building originally served as quarters for seasonal rangers as well, but today is mainly office space and a community room. The building was rehabilitated in 1985-1988 and interestingly can only be used during the summer. In the winter, the ranger staff has to use office space over in the Lake Administrative Area across and up the road to the north. Public parking is located on the station's south side, though the entry is now on the opposite side of the building.

7. COMFORT STATION 🚻

This comfort station (rest room) was built in 1931.

8. 4-PLEX MEDICAL RESIDENCE

Constructed in 1962 concurrently with the Hospital (now clinic), this four-unit residential building houses clinic staff.

9. Lake Clinic/Hospital ✚

The Lake Hospital, or Lake Clinic as it is now known, was constructed in 1962 as part of the Mission 66 Program. It was designed to replace the old Fort Yellowstone Hospital in Mammoth, which had become unusable due to a failing foundation and damage from the 1959 Hebgen Lake Earthquake.

The decision to locate the hospital at Lake vs. Mammoth was a political one rather than practical one. A Wyoming Congressman wanted the park's headquarters transferred to a "more central" location, meaning Lake, presumably to be closer to Cody and much deeper into Wyoming. The NPS was able to convince the politicians that relocating the park's entire administrative operation would be undesirable for several reasons, not the least of which were its distance from any semblance of civilization and the remainder of the park, the costs involved, and the fact that the Lake area is covered with deep snow during the winter. They did acquiesce to building the new hospital here, however.

The Hospital was originally equipped with 14 in-patient beds, six treatment rooms for itinerant/emergency care, its own laboratory, pharmacy, and radiology department. The original staff complement was two doctors, ten nurses, and several support staff. The crew even had their own cook.

In the early 2000s, however, it became too expensive for the NPS and their medical contractor (Yellowstone Park Medical Services) to maintain the level of equipment and training required to remain certified under Wyoming law, so the facility went from being one of the only hospitals in a national park to a seasonal clinic similar to that operated at Old Faithful. Today, it is staffed by a four-person team that includes a physician assistant (PA), two nurses (one of whom performs check-in and administrative functions) and a head nurse. There is a helipad behind (north) of the hospital used to land LifeFlight helicopters to transport patients out of the park for emergent and long-term treatment.

10. Trumpeter Dormitory

Built in 1962, this building was originally the nurse's dormitory for the hospital. When the hospital reduced its operation to a medical clinic, there was no longer a need for this much housing space, so the facility was transferred to Xanterra, the park's primary lodging and services concessioner. Today, they use the 16-room dorm to house management and supervisory staff.

11. South District Office

Built in 1930 as a messhouse for the Fisheries staff, this building now houses the South District Office for the park's Aquatic Resources staff.

12. Lake Fish Hatchery

This building was constructed from 1928 to 1930 by the Bureau of Fisheries (now the U.S. Fish and Wildlife Service) and is the oldest remaining log-structured fish hatchery in the United States. The new facility replaced an older hatchery constructed here in 1913.

Operated from 1930 to 1957, it served as the centerpiece of the major fishery operations within Yellowstone that had begun haphazardly in the late 1880s. Similar to most other buildings constructed within the park during this time period, it retains the "parkitecture" feel that took root in Yellowstone following the construction of the Old Faithful Inn. Its various support buildings were likewise designed to blend in with the surroundings (see below).[11]

Once the major fishery operations were closed down, the building was still used to support aquatic research activities. For a time in the late 1990s and early 2000s it sat largely abandoned or used for storage. Within the past couple of years NPS has renovated the building, and it is being evaluated for placement on the National Register of Historic Places. Additionally, consideration is being given to creating an interpretive exhibit for visitors about the history of fishery operations within the park. The hatchery and its related buildings comprise the Lake Fish Hatchery Historic District, designated in 1985.

The creek that passes just to the west of the hatchery building is known as Hatchery Creek. It was along this stream that much of the infrastructure required to harvest the eggs was located.

13. Residence/Office

Built in 1932 to house the Fisheries Director, this 2173 sq. ft. residence and office now houses the Aquatic Resources South District Manager.

14. Single-Family Residence

This small (465 sq. ft.) residence was built in 1931 to house Fisheries staff. Today it serves as a residence for staff of the Aquatic Resources Division.

15. SINGLE-FAMILY RESIDENCE

This residence is basically identical to the one listed above and is used for the same purpose.

16. YCR AQUATIC RESOURCES GARAGE/STORAGE

This building was originally constructed in 1930 as a six-bay garage for the storage of vehicles and equipment used by the Fisheries staff. Today it is used to store equipment used by the Aquatic Resources operation.

17. YCR AQUATIC RESOURCES OFFICE

Constructed in 1930 as a bunkhouse for the Fisheries staff, this building is now used as office space for the park's Aquatic Resources staff.

18. LAUNDRY/WASHHOUSE

This building was constructed in 1941 as a washhouse for the staff living in the Bunkhouse (see #17 above). Today it houses washing machines and dryers for use by staff living in the area.

19. FUEL/OIL STORAGE SHED

This small building was constructed in 1941 to house the generator used to provide power to the Fishery and its related buildings. Today it is used to store fuels and oils.

20-26. TRANSAHOME RESIDENCES

These small, transmobile residences (hence, the term "transahome") were added to the park to increase housing some time ago (specific dates are unknown, though many date to the 1950s-1960s), and are still used to this day. Many are in less than good condition, and some have been relegated to use as storage buildings. However, a significant number are still used to house NPS staff throughout the park, including those here.

27. RESCUE CACHE (OLD YPSS SERVICE STATION)

This building was originally a service station, constructed by Charles Hamilton in 1920 around the same time as his general store (see below).[12] At the time, and up through the early 1970s, the Grand Loop Road passed right along the front of this building. Following the construction of the bypass, however, traffic dropped off, and the station was less used. With the presence of the service station and repair center at Fishing Bridge (which is along a major traffic corridor), the service station here fell into disuse. Changes in environmental regulations on top of this led to the closing of the service station in 1989. Today, the NPS uses the building to store rescue equipment. The building is part of the Lake Historic District.

If you follow the dirt trail running northwest up the hill and into the woods behind this building, you'll find a couple of gravesites (take a right when you get to the top of the hill, and then a left). The one outlined in stone is the faux grave of Dave Edwards, a winter caretaker for E. C. Waters and his boat operation. In 1906, Edwards died in his boat while rowing to/from Stevenson Island, and was buried near this building.

When the decision to pave the parking lot and approach apron to the service station was made in the 1930s, Hamilton paid two men to dig up Edwards' grave and relocate it to a spot "east of the Lake Hotel." The two men, being a bit skeeved out at digging up the old grave, created a fake grave - the one that exists here today. Edwards' body remains buried under the asphalt in front of the old service station. The other grave contains a skull located on Stephenson Island in 1907, believed to be one of two men who drowned at West Thumb the year prior. See Lee Whittlesey's *Death in Yellowstone* for more details on these stories.

28-29. MedCor Employee Duplexes

These two duplexes house staff who work at the clinic.

30. 1926 Boathouse

This boathouse was constructed in 1926 by the Yellowstone Park Boat Company (later absorbed by the Yellowstone Park Company) to house its boats and other marine gear during the off season. The new facility replaced an older boathouse built on the same location, probably in the late 1890s. It is used today for the same purpose by the park's concession operator.

31. 1941 Boathouse

This boathouse was built sometime between 1930 and 1941 to support the operations of the Fish Hatchery (probably closer to the 1930 date as this is when the majority of the hatchery-related structures were built). It is used today by NPS to store boats and other marine equipment for the Aquatic Resources Branch.[13]

32. LAKE GENERAL STORE 🛈 ▤

This store was constructed by Charles A. Hamilton in 1919-1920 and has been remodeled several times since. Prior to this (1917), Hamilton had purchased and operated the original store near here built by E. C. Waters (no longer standing).

The store has a selection of souvenirs and some camping and fishing gear, as well as a small grocery area and a grill. The store has 5350 sq. ft. of floor space and is open from mid-May until late September. Approximately 40 employees work here during the peak season.

The two buildings behind the store are cold storage/warehouse buildings for supplies and stock.

33. YGS DORMITORY

This is the dormitory for employees of the Yellowstone General Store and, originally, the filling station, which was operated by the same owner at the time. It was constructed in 1919, and still houses store employees. The store manager lives in the mobile home directly behind the store.

34. LAKE VILLAGE POST OFFICE ✉

The Lake Village Post Office was constructed in 1972 and is open from roughly the end of May through the middle of September.

35. OSPREY DORMITORY

The Osprey Dormitory was constructed in 1983. It has 50 rooms and houses 99 employees of the Lake Hotel. Employees assigned to this dorm are usually the younger, but over-21 crowd.

36. PELICAN DORMITORY

Pelican Dormitory was built in 1986. It has 50 rooms for 99 employees, and is used to house the under-21 who work at the hotel.

37. GOLDENEYE DORMITORY

Goldeneye Dormitory was completed in 1988, and it, too, has 50 rooms for 99 employees. It is the newest dorm in the complex. It typically houses the more mature employees who've been working at the hotel for multiple years.

38. Teal Dormitory

The Teal Dormitory is a mobile "porta-dorm" with 16 rooms. This facility is used primarily to house transient employees and some junior supervisors. Plans call for the demolition of this building and construction of a larger dorm in its place.

39. Lake Lodge & Cabins 🛏️ 🍽️ 🚻 📷 ☕

The original portion of the Lake Lodge Building (the center section) was completed in 1919. Like the other lodges, it was an outcropping of the original "permanent" auto camp companies operated by various concessioners, in this case, the Wylie Permanent Camp Company (and then by the Yellowstone Park Camping Company). The original lodge included a series of canvas-top tents that had been used by the predecessor camp operation. In 1923, 50 additional such cabins were constructed. Over the next seven years, over 150 wooden cabins would be added to the lodge complex.

In 1926, the lodge building was renovated, the dining room and kitchen expanded, and the recreation hall was added, resulting in the building you see before you today. The recreation hall was originally used primarily to host dances, but today serves as a recreation space for employees only. It was also during this period that the remaining original canvas tent cabins were replaced by all wood cabins.[14] Most of these are still in use today, though they've been reconfigured into duplex and triplex units (the series A17-A30, B5-B20, and the C through E cabins).

Most of the renovations done since the building was finished in 1926 have been cosmetic and superficial, the last major physical change was the removal of the porte-cochere from the front of the lodge in the mid-1960s. In 1984, the dining room was converted to a cafeteria-style dining with seating for up to 209 people. The north end of the building behind the kitchen houses an Employee Dining Room with 38 seats.

In 1959, as part of the Mission 66 Program, twenty new quadriplex cabin structures were added (the F, G, H, and J series cabins). Fifteen years later, another five quad units (A1-A16 and B1-B4) were constructed to replace 64 condemned buildings that had been removed.

Several of the existing cabins are located close to Lodge Creek, which runs through the tree line located along the north side of the cabin complex. Since this creek is considered a prime bear feeding area, the cabins located closest to the creek remain closed and unrentable until well into the season each summer. As a result, plans call for the relocation of these cabins at some point in the not too distant future

In 2014, the cabin rates ranged from $80 for the 86 "Pioneer" (older) cabins to $199 per night for the 100 "Western" (newer) Cabins. The 20 "Frontier" (mid-range) cabins rented for $121 per night.

Across the road from the lodge is a small, rectangular granite block sitting alongside the road. Though it seems rather innocuous to those who pass by it, the block has particular significance to the way you get around the park today. In 1892, U.S. Army Corps of Engineers Lt. Hiram Chittenden had the block put in place to mark a reference point from which he designed the road system on the eastern side of the park. It would become the first permanent geodetic benchmark inside Yellowstone. For more on this marker and its significance, as well as a history of the other 500+ benchmarks located throughout the park, see my book, *Benchmark Hunting in Yellowstone National Park*.

40. MALLARD DORMITORY

Constructed in 1950, the Mallard Dormitory was originally the girl's dorm for the Lodge and its cabins. Today, the dorm is a co-ed dorm; it has 46 rooms that house around 89 employees, including managers and supervisors.

41. LAKE LODGE MANAGER'S RESIDENCE

Little is known about this structure, including its construction date, though it is believed to have been built in the early 1960s. The Lake Lodge location manager lives here during the summer, and the lodge's winterkeeper during the winter.

42. EMPLOYEE PUB

Constructed in 1926 as the laundry building for the Lodge (and other facilities located on the east side of the park), this building now houses the pub for the Lake area employees. It seats approximately 76 people.

43. LAKE LODGE BOILER HOUSE

Also constructed in 1926 concurrently with the major renovation and expansion of the Lodge, this was originally the powerhouse for the Lodge. Today it houses the boilers and maintenance offices.

44. Lake Lodge Personnel Office

This cabin was originally used at another location in the park, and was relocated here at some point (probably at the same time the seven employee cabins described below were moved here). The building itself was constructed in 1952, and now houses Xanterra's Personnel Office for the Lodge.

45. Linen Cabin

This building houses linen and housecleaning supplies for the Lake Lodge cabins. Little is known about the history of this building, though it likely dates to 1926 as well, given that it is the same style as the old laundry (now pub - see above) and is located immediately adjacent to it.

46. Lake Lodge Housekeeping Office & Storage Sheds

This small cabin was built in 1959 along with the Mission 66 guest cabins. It is the Housekeeping Office for the Lodge cabin complex. The two small storage sheds located to the cabin's southwest are old cabins that have been relocated to this area from other sites, probably concurrently with the seven employee cabins and the Personnel Office cabin referenced above. Both date to 1952.

47. Seagull Dormitory

The Seagull Dormitory was created in 1962 by bringing in two large wooden bunkhouse buildings from the old Canyon Lodge area and melding them together. If you look closely at the center of the structure, you can see where the two were joined together.

The dorm has 12 rooms for 24 employees and is used primarily when other dorms and housing space is full due to its poor condition.

48. Employee Cabins 01, 1, 2, 3, 4, 5 and 6

This series of seven cabins located in the woods behind Mallard Dorm (south of the guest cabin complex) houses lodge employees. The specific history of these buildings is largely unknown, but they were apparently relocated here from other locations in the park, perhaps Fishing Bridge or West Thumb. Cabins 1 and 4 date to 1952, while the other five were constructed in 1945.

49. OLD BARN/STORAGE BUILDING

Built in 1930, around the same time as the majority of the Fish Hatchery buildings, this old barn was used to house pack animals for the field crews. It is now used as a storage building for plumbing supplies and equipment.

50. LAKE LODGE LIFT STATION

This building houses a lift station to pump sewage from the Lodge to the Fishing Bridge Wastewater Treatment Plant.

OLD EMERGENCY PUMPHOUSE @ TOPPING POINT

This pumphouse, which is hidden in the trees at Topping Point directly in front of the Lodge (across the field), was constructed in 1941 to provide an emergency backup water supply for the Lodge and Hotel. The springs that have historically supplied the potable water for the area have a habit of drying up in the latter part of the summer. Prior to the interconnection of the Lake, Fishing Bridge, and Bridge Bay water systems in the late 1970s, this facility would draw water from the Lake to provide water for the area if the springs ran dry. The pumping system is no longer used, and the building has been abandoned for all intents and purposes.

OLD BUILDINGS NO LONGER PRESENT

Original Lake Soldier/Ranger Station: The original ranger (soldier) station for this area was constructed in 1898 on the flat meadow in front of the current Lake Lodge, between the Lodge and the small forested area at Topping Point directly in front of it (approximately where the old road bed crosses the creek). The building was torn down in 1923 when the existing Ranger Station was opened.

Lake Lodge Incinerator: This small incinerator was located north of lodge cabins between the north end of E cabins and Lodge Creek. It was constructed in 1928 and remained in service until 1943. The incinerator was removed and the area rehabilitated in 1993-94.

OTHER NOTABLE FACILITIES IN THE AREA

Lake Fish Hatchery Picnic Area ⊼

This small picnic area sits just east of the old boathouses, and south of the Fish Hatchery Building on the shore of Lake Yellowstone. There are a small number of tables here, (usually two, but sometimes three or four), though there are plans to expand and improve the facilities for this picnic area in the near future.

Underground Storage Tank

Buried in the hill north of the Lake Hotel cabin complex is a large underground storage tank that was used to hold potable water for the hotel and lodge complexes for a number of years. The tank is no longer used.

Lakeshore Trail 🚶 🚲

This trail is a remnant of the original Grand Loop Road that passed in front of the Lake Hotel. When the bypass was constructed around the Village in the 1970s, this old roadbed became a foot and bicycle trail. It runs from the pole gate in front of the Fish Hatchery back to the west for about one mile to a pullout located just north of the Lake Transfer Station.

Bridge Bay
Development

The Bridge Bay development, as it exists today, is the product of the Mission 66 program in the early 1960s. There had been an auto campground in this area for many years prior (and itinerant camping existed before that), but there were no significant facilities in this area before the construction of those present now.[1]

Prior to the opening of Bridge Bay, boat concession operators rented boats and fishing gear from two different locations, Fishing Bridge and West Thumb. All of those were discontinued in the years after the marina here was opened, and the buildings and docks at those locations were eventually demolished.

The 1960-1962 project included dredging out of the bay, realigning the approach road, building a new, higher bridge to allow boats safe passage, construction of the marina, store and ranger station, and the development of the western half of the campground (Loops A-D, with 191 sites). The 240-site eastern portion of the campground would be completed seven years later (Loops E-J). The amphitheater was also added in 1969.

The marina itself has 100 slips available for summer rental, as well as a fuel dock and a sanitary dock. The park's current concession operator, Xanterra, operates a variety of marine-oriented visitor concessions here. These include a SceniCruiser for providing tours of the lake (43-passenger capacity), seven guided fishing boats, twenty eight 18-foot rental motorboats, five rental canoes, and eight rental rowboats. The marina also has docks for the boats NPS uses to conduct patrols and research on the lake.

This development is under evaluation and consideration for inclusion in the National Register of Historic Places because it represents a unique situation where an east-coast style marina was built in a western national park.

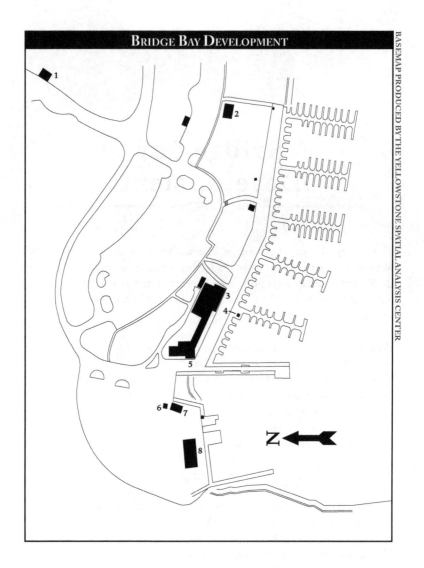

1. Campground Registration Building ⛺ 🚐

This building was constructed in 1964 and provides campground registration and support services. The 2014 rates are $25.00 per night. During the busy summer season, traffic can get quite congested and backed up here.

2. Picnic Area Comfort Station 🚻

This restroom building was built in 1969 along with those in the E-J Loops in the eastern half of the campground. The picnic area has 23 tables and is nestled in the trees along the bay.

3. Bridge Bay Marina Store 🛒

This small store is part of the larger, single structure that also houses the ranger station and the concession operator's activities and rental desk. It was constructed in 1963. The store has 8 employees and is typically open from late May to early September.

4. Clock House - Boat/Equipment Rental Shed

This small shed was constructed in 1964, and houses life preservers, oars and paddles, rope, and other materials that are necessary to support the concession operator's boat rental and scenic cruise operations.

5. Bridge Bay Ranger Station 🏠 🚻

The ranger station is part of the larger building housing the store and activities rental office (constructed in 1963). The ranger station occupies the bottom floor and has a top observation platform that allows the rangers to see out into the bay. There are restrooms in the rear on the bottom floor.

6. Marina Lift Station

Constructed in 2011 to bolster sewage capacity at the marina. This building pumps sewage down to the Bikini Beach Lift Station, which in turn pumps it on toward the Fishing Bridge Wastewater Treatment Plant.

7. Fish Cleaning Station

This small stand allows fishermen to clean their fish when they return to the docks. The exact date of the building's construction is unknown, but believed to be in the mid-1960s.

8. Boat Repair Center

The Boat Repair Shop, constructed in 1965, provides minor boat repairs for visitors.

Grant Village &
West Thumb Development

Though today many people find it hard to believe, up until the 1970s there was a large commercial development at West Thumb. Because of its significant number of thermal features, the area was among the first to be developed into a "hot spot" for tourists, and over time a substantial number of buildings and support structures were built to accommodate those visitors. All that is left today, however, is the small building that serves as the Yellowstone Association Bookstore during the summer and a warming hut during the winter. West Thumb's history is deeply intertwined with that of Grant Village, a story rich with political machinations and intrigue, discussions and debate that continue to this day.

The first "development" of any kind at West Thumb consisted of a boat dock built by E. C. Waters in 1891. At that point in time, the new road between West Thumb and the Lake Hotel was in poor condition, and the steamboat offered an alternative to a bumpy, dusty stagecoach ride. Waters operated his ferry service from West Thumb to the hotel for much of the 1890s. He would eventually lose his concession permits, but ferry and boat services (rentals, primarily) continued from and around West Thumb in one form or another until the early 1960s when Bridge Bay was completed. At that point, the old docks and the boathouse were removed and the area rehabilitated.

The first tourist facility to open at West Thumb was a lunch station that had been relocated here in 1892 from the Trout Creek area in Hayden Valley. The road from Old Faithful to West Thumb had been completed that year, and there was little traffic on the old Mary Mountain Road where the original station had been located, so its proprietor requested and received permission to move his operation here. In 1898, the Wylie Permanent Camping Company assumed responsibility for the lunch station, and added a small number of tents, turning it into one of their camps.[1]

In 1904, the tent-based lunch station would be replaced by a permanent building, complete with a small number of rooms for any visitors who might wish to stay in the area overnight. With the addition of more tents in 1911, the area became a "destination" stop for many tourists. The camp remained in use until 1917 when it was closed down as the result of the merger of the major camp companies into a single entity. Unlike other areas of the park where the tent camps tended to morph into lodge-based operations to cater to the automobile traveler, that did not happen here.

Major commercial development at West Thumb really got its start in 1917 when Charles A. Hamilton opened a store in the newly vacated lunch station building. The store would be the first he would establish himself after having bought out the Klamer Store at Old Faithful. Seven years later, in 1924, he would build his own store in the wooded area north of today's parking lot, and would use the old lunch station building to house his employees until 1927, when it was razed and replaced with a dormitory adjacent to the store.[2]

Hamilton also opened a filling station along with his first store, and it would operate until 1948, when it was replaced with a newer facility. The store and the filling station would survive until the 1980s, when they would be removed along with most of the other buildings in the area at the time.

The first auto camp was established by the NPS in 1922, around the same time as they'd constructed campgrounds in many other areas of the park. Because of the tremendous number of tourists wanting to camp in the area, a newer, more spacious campground was opened to the north of the old one just three years later. That campground operated until 1963, when it was closed with the opening of the new facilities at Grant Village.

The large cabin complex at West Thumb began its life in 1928 with a series of cabins relocated from Lewis Lake.[3] They'd been built there by the Gratiot Camp Company, about which little is known. Gratiot set up the camp and operated it for a single season, and for unknown reasons ceased operations. Its 76 cabins were acquired and moved here by the Yellowstone Park Lodge and Camps Company (YPLCC).

An additional 58 cabins were relocated to this area from the Mammoth Lodge after it closed in 1936. And, finally, in 1959, another 45 cabins were relocated here from the old Canyon Lodge, which had been closed subsequent to the opening of the new facilities at Canyon Village. In 1928, the YPC also built a cafeteria for tourists staying in the area (complete with a dorm for its employees).

In 1932, photographer Jack Haynes (Frank J. Haynes' son) opened a new photo shop at West Thumb (north of the Hamilton Store) using a building he'd had relocated from Fishing Bridge. It was moved in 1938 and then again in 1941, when it was relocated to its final resting place on the site of the present day West Thumb Picnic Area. The Haynes family would operate the shop until they sold all of their assets to Hamilton Stores in 1967. Hamilton would turn the shop into a mini-store and operate it until 1990, when it became the very last building to be removed from the development.[4]

Over the course of West Thumb's history, the area also served as a base for a Civilian Conservation Corps spike (temporary forward operating) camp in the 1930s, as well as a Blister Rust Camp in the early to mid-1960s. Little is known about these facilities, however.

With the commencement of the development of Grant Village in the early 1960s, the facilities and structures located in the West Thumb basin were gradually removed. Several cabins had been removed prior to 1970, but that year 126 of those that remained were bulldozed into the ground, furniture and all. The remaining 41 were used by employees for housing until they, too, were removed three years later. A small number of the old cabins were relocated to other places in the park and repurposed for storage.

In 1972, the highway around the West Thumb area was rerouted to take traffic away from the thermal basin. The new intersection was located to the southwest of the old development and basically resembled what you see here now, only with turn lanes and a bypass lane for through traffic. Those would later be removed resulting in today's T-shaped intersection. Once all of the buildings were removed, their foundation footprints were rehabilitated and today, unless you know what you're looking at, you can hardly tell this area was once home to a development half the size of what currently exists at Old Faithful.

Grant Village is the newest development in the park. Originally conceived by NPS landscape planner Frank Mattson in the mid-1930s, it didn't become an identifiable part of the park's master planning process until the late 1940s. And though there are many who suggest the village wasn't intended to be a "replacement" for West Thumb, the truth is much more complex. There had long been some concern about development encroaching upon the thermal features and other "sacred areas" throughout the park, not just at West Thumb. As a result of that, planners had begun looking for a place to relocate visitor services which, at the time, were based at West Thumb. Grant Village was the manifestation of that desire.

As the idea of Grant Village matured during the Mission 66 era, however, it was also sold as a "replacement" for facilities located at Fishing Bridge and, to a lesser extent, Old Faithful. Park planners had originally intended to remove everything at Fishing Bridge once Grant was fully fleshed out, largely due to concerns about the Fishing Bridge area being richly populated with grizzly bears. Human-bear encounters were becoming problematic in that area, and the NPS had decided the best way to deal with it was to remove the development and return the area to the bears. The removal of the stores, campground, and cabin complex at Fishing Bridge was to be offset by new facilities at Grant Village. A series of political gymnastics, however, prevented Fishing Bridge from being completely abandoned. This was quite the contentious issue during the 1970s-1980s, up until the fires of 1988 gave the public and the politicians another controversy to focus on.

Though surveying had been done for Grant Village as far back as the late 1940s, no overt action was taken toward building out the development until funding from the Mission 66 Program made it possible. Once the project got the initial go-ahead, NPS began carving out trees for the campground, utilities, a ranger station and a visitor center. Much of this work was completed in the 1961-1962 time frame, and the public campground opened in time for the 1963 summer season. Over the next five years, NPS would complete the visitor center, the ranger station, a maintenance complex, and employee housing facilities. The construction of visitor lodging was another issue altogether, however.

The Yellowstone Park Company (YPC), the park's lodging concessioner at the time, was unwilling to invest money in the building of new facilities here, believing that tourists would not want to stay here overnight, thus making it next to impossible for them to recoup their investment. And given that they'd gone deeply into debt to finance the construction of new lodging at Canyon Village a couple of years earlier, it is unlikely they'd have been able to secure funding regardless. YPC and its assets would be sold to another company in 1966, and the new owners also balked at forking out the millions of dollars that would be required to develop the level of housing the park service sought.

After 15 years of these battles, the NPS finally sought funding from Congress to build the lodging facilities themselves. The result was two of the six lodge buildings currently in use (Buildings B and C). These were completed in 1982. NPS was eventually able to convince TW Services, by this time the owner of YPCs holding and permits in the park, to build another four lodge buildings. These opened in 1984. Planners had originally envisioned as many as 700 motel-like lodge rooms and up to 350 cabins for visitor use in Grant Village. The 300 rooms in the six lodges were all that were ever constructed, though.

From that point forward, TW Services and Hamilton Stores began serious development of their support facilities. The large Hamilton General Store was constructed in 1984, as was large employee dormitories for both companies. Grayling Dorm, today Xanterra's primary housing facility, would be doubled in size in 2004, and 13 cabins from the Old Faithful area would be relocated to land adjacent to the dorm to provide for additional employee space. The two restaurants were constructed in 1982 and 1983. Today, over 350 concession employees work at Grant Village.

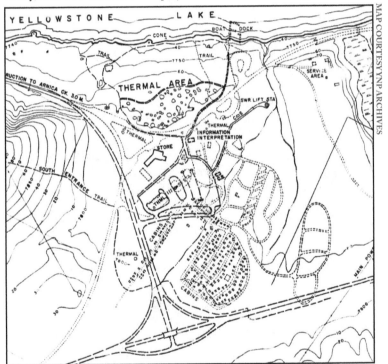

The map above shows the "old" West Thumb with the West Thumb of the mid-1980s. The lightly dotted lines indicate the old roads, buildings, and the cabin and campground areas. Notice in particular how the road ran right along the very edge of the thermal field. To the northeast of the cabin area was the 1925 auto campground, which replaced the original one located to the east of the cabins (southeast of the newer campground). The bolder dashed lines indicate the road system as it was constructed in the early 1970s. Today, the turn lanes and bypass lane are gone, and just the "T" intersection remains, but the basic road layout is roughly the same.

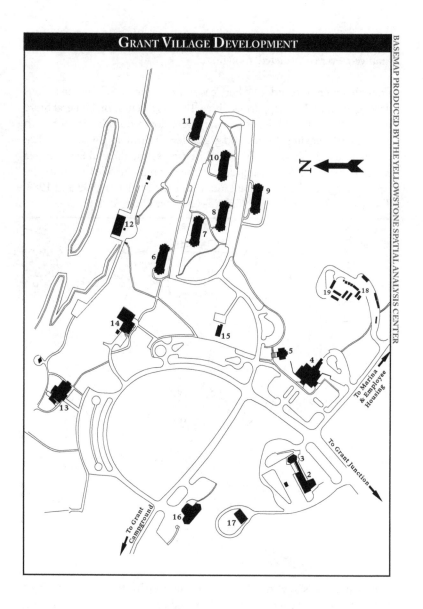

1. RANGER STATION/EMERGENCY SERVICES BUILDING

Not shown on the map, but located just inside the entrance to the village. This building was constructed in 1967 and houses the law enforcement ranger staff, as well as the village's fire truck and ambulance. The dirt service road just west of the ranger station leads back to a construction and maintenance materials storage and staging area.

2. GRANT VILLAGE SERVICE STATION

The Grant Village Service Station, operated by the Yellowstone Park Service Stations, was constructed in 1970. It provides a small retail store, gas, diesel fuel, and propane as well as towing/repair services. The station is generally open from the last week of May until the last week of September.

3. GRANT VILLAGE MINI-STORE

The Grant Village Mini Store is a satellite of the Grant Village General Store, located across the street. It, too, was built in 1970. It is generally open from late May until the last day of September and has a selection of light snacks and picnic items, basic camping and fishing supplies, and a few souvenir items. Approximately 10 employees work here.

4. GRANT VILLAGE GENERAL STORE

Open from early June to late September, the Yellowstone General Store was built in 1984. It is one of the larger stores in the park, with approximately 50 employees. The store has a small grocery, an extensive fishing and camping supplies section, a large range of souvenir items, and a grill and ice cream stand that seats approximately 80 people. The basement includes office space and an employee dining room.

5. LODGE REGISTRATION BUILDING/GIFT SHOP

The Lodge Registration Building was completed in 1984 concurrently with the last four lodge buildings. The building is the registration center for the six main lodges operated by Xanterra. It also includes a small gift shop and Xanterra's location manager.

6-11. GRANT LODGE BUILDINGS A THROUGH F

This series of six basically identical buildings provides 300 rooms for overnight guests (50 per building). The only differences among the buildings include the fact that the A Lodge has a small conference room on the second floor, and the lodge's Housekeeping Office is located in the D Lodge. Buildings B and C opened in 1982, and were constructed by NPS. The other four, constructed by TW Services, the park's lodging concessioner at the time, were completed in 1984.

All of the rooms are identical (two double beds) and in 2014 rented for $164 per night. The lodges are generally open from the last week of May through the last week of September.

12. Lake House Restaurant

The Lake House Restaurant serves a light fare, including breakfast and dinner (no lunch). It was constructed in 1983 and seats 180, and affords an excellent overlook of Yellowstone Lake (as well as the storms that move in over the lake during the summer).

The restaurant was originally intended to serve marina users, but with the closure of that facility, the Lake House gets most of its customers from overflow from the Dining Room or those seeking lighter meals.[5] It is generally open from the last week of May until the end of the third week in September.

Just east of the Lake House, along the drive from the marina parking lot, are the sewage lift station and a generator building for the lift station.

13. Grant Village Visitor Center & Museum

The Grant Village Visitor Center and Museum was constructed in 1966. Here you can ask questions of the rangers, obtain backcountry camping permits, and purchase books and other educational material from the small Yellowstone Association Bookstore. The museum has exhibits dedicated to the Yellowstone Fires of 1988, which heavily impacted the area in and around Grant Village. There are restrooms here as well. The facility is generally open from the last week of May to the end of September.

14. Grant Village Dining Room/EDR

The Grant Village Dining Room is the primary, full-service restaurant for the village, serving breakfast, lunch, and dinner. Reservations are highly recommended for dinner as the restaurant fills early and stays full until around 9PM each evening. Walk-ins are seated on a space available basis. The building was constructed in 1982, and seats 208 in the main dining room. There's a small, 14-seat lounge in the building, as well as a 66-seat Employee Dining Room (EDR). Unlike most of the other EDRs in the park, the entrance to this one is located at the front of the building. This often results in visitors mistaking it for the entrance to the Dining Room (much to the amusement of the employees who are in the EDR at the time).

15. GRANT VILLAGE POST OFFICE ⊠

The Post Office building was constructed in 1969 and is open from mid-May until mid-September each year.

16. CAMPER SERVICES BUILDING ⚥ ⚒ ▣

The Camper Services Building offers a laundry and shower facility for those camping in the Grant Village Campground, located approximately ¼ mile north of here. The campground and this building, constructed in 1962, were among the first facilities to open at Grant Village. The campground has 425 sites, including several group sites. The daily rate for 2014 is $25.50, which includes two showers per evening. Note that the campground registration building is located at the actual entrance to the campground and not in this facility as it is at Fishing Bridge and Canyon Village.

17. POWERHOUSE

Located adjacent to the village's electrical substation (behind the YPSS station and the Camper Services Building), the powerhouse contains generators capable of running the entire village in the event of a commercial power outage (which is a rather frequent occurrence).

18. XANTERRA MAINTENANCE OFFICES/OLD DORM

This series of old, repurposed 1929-era cabins (originally from Old Faithful) and portable buildings is used by Xanterra's maintenance and security staff. There's a maintenance office, along with electrical, plumbing, and carpentry shops, as well as two three-room portable dorm buildings that house maintenance and security personnel. They're known colloquially as the "old dorm", as opposed to the "new" Grayling Dorm (see below).

19. YPSS DORMITORIES

These three portable buildings are used to house YPSS employees who work at the Grant Village Service Station.

20. YGS Dormitory

Not shown on the map. This large dormitory for Yellowstone General Stores employees was constructed in 1984 concurrently with the large store. It houses approximately 60 employees.

21. Grayling Dormitory/Cabins

Not shown on the map. Grayling Dormitory has 76 rooms and 9 manager apartments to house 151 employees. The building consists of four wings. The original East and West wings were built in 1984 at the time of the completion of the last four lodge buildings and the restaurants. In 2004, the North and South wings were added. Adjacent to the dorm are 13 cabins that house another 98 employees. Each is a quad unit and was relocated to Grant Village from Old Faithful specifically to serve as employee housing.

22. Employee Pub

Not shown on the map. Located behind Grayling Dormitory, the Employee Pub is basically a metal pole building. It was constructed in 1994 and seats roughly 30 people. There's an asphalt basketball court outside the pub's east entrance.

West Thumb: Yellowstone Assn Bookstore/Warming Hut

This building was the ranger station at West Thumb until the development was removed. It had originally been located in the woods behind (north) of the old Hamilton Store complex (see below). Today, during the summer, the Yellowstone Association operates a bookstore out of this facility, and during the winter it serves as a warming hut.

Old Structures No Longer Present

As outlined in the introduction to this section, the West Thumb Area prior to the 1970s consisted of a development similar to that at Old Faithful, complete with stores, a post office, gas station, cafe, cabins and a campground. Some of the more important buildings included:

Hamilton Store: This 3872 sq. ft. store and its employee dorms were located in the wooded area north of the parking lot. If you look closely, you can see the smaller trees that have filled in the area since the buildings were removed in the early 1980s. The store was originally built in 1924, after Hamilton had been operating in an older building in the area.

West Thumb "Mini-Store", 1983. This was the last major building to be removed from the area.

Cafeteria: A small, 2400 sq. ft. cafe that served light snacks and coffee was located in the grass to the east across the sidewalk from the existing Yellowstone Association store. Built in 1928, it was operated by the Yellowstone Park Company primarily to provide meals to day visitors and guests in the cabins and the campground.[6] It, too, was removed in the early 1980s. A small recreation center for YPC employees was located just to the south of the cafeteria.

Haynes Photo Shop/Hamilton Mini-Store: Located along the sidewalk just to the southwest of the cafe, this small building sold postcards and photographic supplies. The photo shop building had been relocated from Fishing Bridge in 1932 (and expanded in 1936). It had originally been set up at a different location, was moved in 1938, and the moved once again to its final resting spot in 1941.

The building was taken over and converted into a "mini-store" by Hamilton Stores in 1967. It would the last building to be removed from West Thumb, having been razed in 1990. It was left in place until the road paving project between Old Faithful and West Thumb was completed.

Service Station: A small service station existed in the middle of today's parking lot. In fact, the section of parking spaces along that lot's center median used to be the pull-throughs in front of the pumps. When the underground fuel storage tanks were dug up, it is said that the temperature of the fuel was just a couple of degrees below gasoline's flash point. The original filling station had been built in 1927 by Charles Hamilton, owner of the Hamilton Stores, and was replaced with a newer one in 1948.

West Thumb Service Station, ca. 1983.

West Thumb Cabins: At the village's peak, there were 179 cabins (some of them duplexes) in the large expanse of vacant land to the south of the current parking lot (they expanded to the west across what is today the Grand Loop Road). If you walk off into the field south of the parking lot, you can still see hints of the old road system that afforded access to the cabin area.

The original cabins for this complex were relocated from a camp established in 1927 at Lewis Lake by the Gratiot Camp Company. The camp was unsuccessful and closed after that season, and all of its cabins were relocated to this site at West Thumb. A few years later, in 1937, several additional cabins were relocated from the abandoned Mammoth Lodge, and then in the late 1950s, more cabins from the old Canyon Lodge complex were moved here. When the decision was made to remove the cabins, a large pit was dug, and the cabins were bulldozed into the ground, complete with their furniture, fixtures, etc.

This cabin complex sat just north of an older tent cabin area consisting of approximately 30 tents. This small camp had been operated by the Shaw and Powell Camp Company from 1913 until all of the camping companies were consolidated in 1917. At that point, this camp was abandoned.[7]

Thumb Lunch Station: The original Thumb Lunch Station opened in 1892, and consisted primarily of tents. It was replaced by a permanent structure in 1904. The lunch station operated until 1917, when motorized vehicles made lunch stops obsolete. The building was torn down in 1927 following ten years of use as an employee dorm by Hamilton Store employees.

Old Faithful
Development

The development at Old Faithful includes four general areas:

- The Old Faithful Inn and Lower Concession Area
- The Old Faithful Lodge Area
- The Old Faithful Snow Lodge Area
- The Old Faithful Government Area

The government area is not generally accessible to the public and is therefore not discussed in much detail in this book. The complex houses primarily maintenance facilities and employee and contractor housing.

Development in the Old Faithful area began in 1879 with the construction of a log house in the oxbow bend of the Firehole River (directly north of the existing Lower Service Station). Superintendent Philetus W. Norris had the building constructed for one of his assistant superintendents. A few years later, the U.S. Army would construct a soldier station and several related buildings near this cabin in order to provide protection for the thermal features in this part of the park. Norris' building would be razed in 1908, and the soldier station would go on to become the first ranger station in the area. All of these buildings would be razed in 1923 after the completion of a new ranger station just west of the Old Faithful Lodge.

In 1883, one of the early park concession companies, the Yellowstone Park Improvement Company (YPIC), erected a "tent hotel" on the site of the present day Old Faithful Inn. It lasted just one year. In 1885, a "shack" hotel was constructed on the same site. Seven years later, the little hotel would be converted into a lunch station, as the new Fountain Hotel (opened in 1891) located up the road was a much more palatable place to spend the night for most visitors. In 1894, the lunch station would burn down and would be replaced with another tent lunch station (also with tents for guests). Some six years later, new "tent cabins" were added to the lunch station and once again tourists could spend the night in the Upper Geyser Basin in some semblance of luxury.

In 1903, park concessioner Harry Child brought in a previously unheard of architect, a man by the name of Robert Reamer, to design and build a grand new hotel in the basin. It would be built on the site of the previous tent and shack hotels, and would become one of the most widely recognized structures in the world, the Old Faithful Inn. You can read more about the Inn below. Reamer would go on to design several other buildings in the park, most of which remain in use today.

Two tent camps were erected in the Old Faithful area as well. In 1898, William Wylie constructed a permanent camp on the hill just to the west of Daisy Geyser. And though the camp is long gone, the hill is still known to the locals as Wylie Hill. The Shaw and Powell Camp Company would erect the second tent camp on the site of the present day Old Faithful Lodge in 1913. In 1916, the nascent National Park Service required the major camp companies to merge and form the Yellowstone Park Camps Company. At that time, the camp on Wylie Hill was removed and the old Shaw & Powell Camp was retained.

Five years later, a new "lodge" building would be constructed as a recreation and dining hall for the camp, and with a few renovations and modifications over subsequent years, would go on to become what we know today as the Old Faithful Lodge. Over the course of the 1920s and 1930s, the tents and tent cabins were replaced with canvas and wood cabins. These in turn would be replaced with all wood cabins in 1939, three years following the consolidation of the camp companies into the Yellowstone Park Company, which became the owner and operator of all of the lodging facilities within the park.

With the advent of the arrival of the automobile to the park, the area's first "auto camp" opened in 1916 next to the Shaw and Powell Tent Camp. In 1920, a second, larger campground would be built on what is today the East Parking Lot (the lot to the immediate east of the Upper YPSS Service Station and south of the Old Faithful Lodge). This campground was remodeled and enlarged in 1949, and remained in use until 1969 when it was closed and work began on reconfiguring the roads in and around the Old Faithful area.

At the south end of this campground was one of the park's infamous bear feeding areas (located where the current inbound road splits to go to either side of the east parking lot).[1] Each evening, hundreds of tourists would sit behind a fence and watch as dozens of the park's bears would comb through garbage from the Inn and the Lodge. This "show" was held from 1919 until 1936, when a pair of bears began fighting and crashed through the fence line. That marked the end of the bear feeding shows at Old Faithful (though they continued at the Otter Creek Bear Feeding Area until the outbreak of World War II).

Other concession operators also began building facilities in the area in the late-1890s. These included park photographer Frank J. Haynes, who built his first studio in the area in 1897, and Henry Klamer, who built the Lower General Store that same year, later to become the first store owned by long-time park concessioner Charles A. Hamilton (in 1915). In 1923, Hamilton would build a second, smaller store adjacent to the NPS campground, and would replace it in 1929 with the much larger Basin Auto Camp (BAC) Store (designed by Robert Reamer). This store still stands and is known today as the Upper General Store.

In 1914, a gentleman by the name of Henry Brothers built a large swimming pool on the flat piece of land across the Firehole River from the Inn.[2] He would also build several smaller swimming pools in and around the complex and the campgrounds that had been constructed south of the Lodge. In 1933, Charles Hamilton bought the pool facility from Brothers and remodeled it into a large swimming pool building, complete with hot tubs, locker rooms, and even sand porches for sunbathing. Hamilton operated the "Geyser Baths" until 1950 when the U.S. Public Health Service ordered it shut down. The building was razed the following year. Many of the smaller pools survived until the 1940s.

The Haynes family would build a new studio at Old Faithful in 1927. The old building would be abandoned (though it still stands). Over the succeeding years, the photo shop would be relocated and remodeled several times. Once the Haynes family sold its assets to Hamilton Stores in 1967, the building would be used as a satellite general store and eventually, it, too, would be abandoned. In 2013, however, a portion of the old store was rehabilitated as a museum to the Haynes legacy and restored to its original position just west of the Old Faithful Lodge.

Charles Hamilton and the Yellowstone Park Transportation Company entered an agreement to jointly build and operate filling stations in the Old Faithful area in 1920. That year they constructed a small station next door to the Lower General Store. Note that, at this particular point in time, the main road through the Upper Geyser Basin ran right in front of the Inn, the Lower General Store, and the Lower Service Station. This is why these two stores were built in their respective locations. In 1927, the joint venture constructed a second filling station and repair garage next door to the Upper General Store. It is still in use today as well. In 1947, Hamilton and the YPC, the Transportation Company's successor, would formalize their joint venture and form the Yellowstone Park Service Stations (YPSS) company.[3] YPSS continues to run the stations today, albeit as an independent entity.

In 1926, the Yellowstone Park Lodge and Camps Company (YPLCC; now the owner of the lodges and their related facilities) constructed a new housekeeping cabin complex in the area occupied today by the Old Faithful Snow Lodge and its cabins. The office of this complex would burn down in 1955 and would be replaced two years later by a new building located on the spot currently occupied by the Geyser Grill and the Bear Den Gift Shop of the Snow Lodge. This new building included office space, a dining room, and a lounge on the first floor, as well as dorm space for the housekeeping staff on the second floor. In the early 1970s, following the decision of the NPS to open up the park during the winter, these dorm rooms were converted into guest rooms, and this building became the first Old Faithful Snow Lodge. It was used until 1998, when it was razed and replaced by the existing Snow Lodge (constructed in 1997-1999).

In 1928, the YPLCC would also construct a sizeable visitor cafeteria on what is today the large tract of vacant land just southeast of the existing Old Faithful Visitor Education Center. It would remain in place until 1969 when it was razed to accommodate the new traffic pattern (see below).

In 1936, several of the different concession companies, including those that operated the hotels and lodges, were consolidated into a single entity known as the Yellowstone Park Company (YPC). The YPC would become the operator of all concessions other than the general stores and photo shops from this point forward.

In the area today known as the "West Parking Lot" (the lot north of the Ranger Station/Clinic), a large stagecoach compound had been constructed by the Monida and Yellowstone Stagecoach Company in the early 1900s. By 1920, this compound had been reconfigured for buses and new structures added (i.e., bus barn, drivers' dorms, messhalls, etc.) for the Yellowstone Park Transportation Company (YPTC). YPTC's successor, the YPC, would continue to operate from here until 1969 when all bus operations were relocated to the government utility area across the road. All of these old buildings were removed around this time to allow new roads to be built.

With the advent of the Mission 66 Program, three new villages had been proposed for construction. Two of these, Canyon Village and Grant Village, came to fruition (albeit on timelines not consistent with original plans). The third was to have been known as Firehole Village, and was to have included many of the facilities here at Old Faithful. The plan was to relocate many of the area's buildings to a large tract of land along the north end of Fountain Flats several miles up the road and reset the Upper Geyser Basin as a "day use" area. Fortunately, funding was never forthcoming to allow these plans to materialize (who would have wanted to have seen the Old Faithful Inn torn down?). At one point, another idea had apparently been floated to build the new village four miles northeast of Old Faithful at Mallard Lake as well. That never gained any traction, as it doesn't show up in any of the park's master planning documents.[4]

Regardless, there was still a need to address the ever increasing traffic and pedestrian congestion problems in the Old Faithful area. At this point in time, the main road through the area came down the hill from Kepler Cascade, passed immediately south of the Old Faithful Lodge and the Old Faithful Geyser, and ran along the north parking lot of the Inn, the Lower General Store and the Lower Service Station. If you've been in the Old Faithful area within the past two decades, you can imagine what kind of traffic nightmare that would engender today if the original road still existed. So plans were developed in the late 1960s to create a bypass for through traffic and to create a more manageable traffic pattern throughout the Old Faithful complex. The result included the large interstate-like interchange as the entrance to the complex, as well as the uniquely configured road system still in place today.

In addition to the construction of the new roads, the old roads were removed and rehabilitated for the most part. Some hints of the old road system still remain, however. The paved path from the Old Faithful boardwalk to Morning Glory Pool was once part of the original road system, for example. From there, the road continued on westward past Artemisia Geyser and reconnected into the existing Grand Loop Road approximately two miles north of the interchange (see the entry at 2.1/13.8 in the Old Faithful to Madison Junction Road section for more details). Much of the balance was reclaimed as sand and/or boardwalks.

The new inbound and outbound roads, however, have been confusing drivers since they opened in 1972, despite repeated attempts by the NPS to erect signage and make other improvements to better help drivers figure out where they're going. The creation of new traffic patterns within the complex resulted in dozens of older buildings being razed. And despite moving through traffic away from the thermal areas, many still consider the cloverleaf design of the interchange out of character for Yellowstone.

Today, the Old Faithful area is the busiest in the park at the height of the summer tourist season. Some 30,000 people visit the area daily during July and August, with 2,000 or more of those gathered on the boardwalk at any given time during the eruption of the area's namesake geyser. Anyone who's been caught in the "geyser flush" to get out of the parking lots following one of the eruptions knows just how bad traffic can get (especially if they've been caught up in one of the fairly common bison jams on the way out). Some 850 concession employees and 70 NPS employees work at Old Faithful during the summer.[5]

Many of the structures in this area are of historical significance. The Old Faithful Inn itself was designated a National Historic Landmark in 1987, and the Inn, Lodge, the stores, service stations, five of the old dorms, ten support buildings, and the guest cabins for the Lodge and the Snow Lodge are all part of the Old Faithful Historic District, designated in 1982.

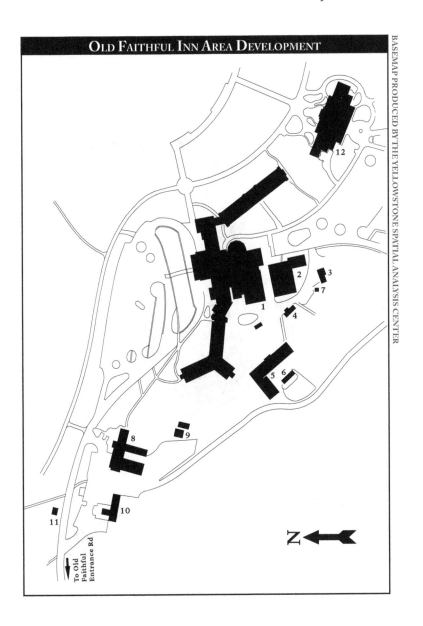

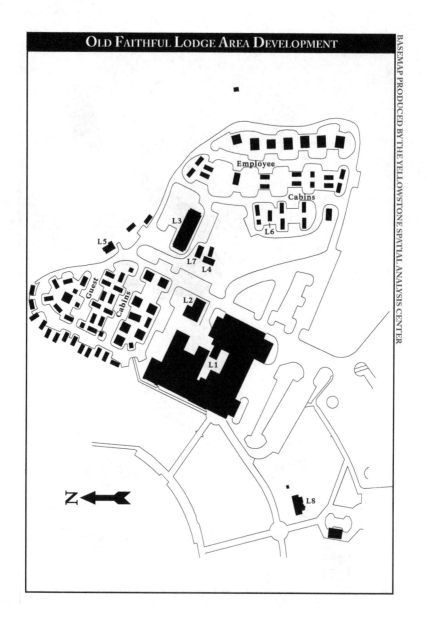

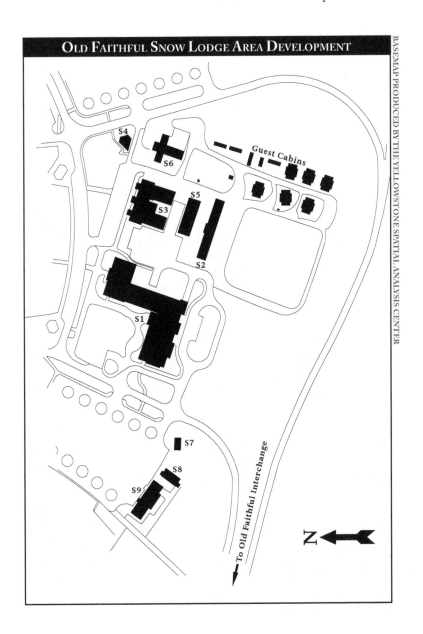

OLD FAITHFUL SNOW LODGE AREA DEVELOPMENT

BASEMAP PRODUCED BY THE YELLOWSTONE SPATIAL ANALYSIS CENTER

S4

S6

Guest Cabins

S5

S3

S2

S1

S7

S8

S9

To Old Faithful Interchange

N

Old Faithful Inn Area

1. Old Faithful Inn 🛏 🍴 ❄ 🍷 🚻

Constructed in 1903-1904, the Old Faithful Inn is recognized around the world as one of the iconic structures of the U.S. National Park system. It opened to guests on June 1, 1904, with 140 rooms and a capacity of 316 guests.

The Inn replaced a tent camp and a series of small buildings (details provided in the introduction) erected in the 1890s to provide accommodations to tourists. The tents were large cabins with canvas sheets extending approximately ¾ of the way down from the roof, and the interior divided into eight separate rooms by canvas sheet "walls." Meals were served at a central dining tent. Ironically, the Old Faithful area was from the outset the most heavily visited area of the park, but was the last to get a legitimate hotel.

In 1903, the Yellowstone Park Association hired a then little-known architect from San Diego named Robert Reamer to build their new hotel. Though Reamer would be best known for his design of the Inn and its subsequent additions, he would go on to design and build many other structures in Yellowstone as well (many of which remain standing).

The original structure, known as the "Old House," cost $139,972.01 to build and another $25,291.60 to furnish.[6] Much of the furniture in the lobby today is the same that existed when the hotel opened. Each piece is microchipped to ensure it can be traced if it is ever stolen.

In 1913, the 100-room East Wing was added at a cost of just over $100,000. The 1922 addition to the Dining Room expanded it past the fireplace that still sits in the middle of the cavernous room today. In 1927, the 150-room West Wing was added at a cost of $209,948.08. That same year the lobby and Porte-cochere were extended, the veranda added, and the multi-sided east extension to the Dining Room was added (now known as the Bear Pit lounge).

Over the past 110+ years, the Old House has been modified several times, mostly through the removal of rooms to make way for the updated or relocated services such as the registration desk (rooms 31 & 33), bell stand (rooms 26 & 28), and gift & Indian craft shop (odd numbered rooms 19 through 29). Additional rooms were removed to facilitate access to the new east (rooms 44 & 146) and west (room 202) wings when they were constructed.[7] The lobby area has also been redesigned several times, especially around the fireplace. Other modifications include the addition of plumbing and bathroom facilities to many of the Inn's rooms. Beginning in the mid-1990s, the entire Old House was renovated to its original glory in time for the structure's Centennial anniversary.

The Inn was significantly damaged during the 1959 Hebgen Lake Earthquake. The Dining Room chimney, made of stone at the time, collapsed, sending tons of rock through the roof. The sprinkler system was damaged, flooding parts of the building. The lobby fireplace was also seriously damaged, and it would be decades before it would be restored to its full functionality. Damage to the wooden structures of Crow's Nest and the Widow's Walk, though repaired, have closed those areas off to public access (you can, however, assist the bell staff with the raising and lowering of the flags on the Inn's roof – see the Bell Desk for details). The Crow's Nest was where small musical ensembles would serenade dancers each evening following dinner in the Inn's early days.

Perhaps the most impressive feature of this 188,000-square foot rustic structure is its 76-foot high lobby; it blends in seamlessly with the building's exterior. Designed by Reamer to blend in and "harmonize" with its surroundings, the asymmetrical and knurled wood-framed structure was built from materials quarried and harvested from the park itself. Its design is intended to make it appear as if it arises out of the very forested area in which it sits. This concept of blending rustic structures in with their environment is known as "parkitecture," and the Old Faithful Inn has come to represent the pre-eminent example of that building style.

The Inn was designed from the outset to be a space for wealthy travelers. It had electricity, plumbing, clawfoot bathtubs and marble counter tops. Dinner jackets for the men and fine dresses for the women were the expected attire at dinner. If you weren't a guest there, you couldn't even come in the front door to visit until after World War II.

Today, the Inn is valued at over $40 million.[8] It was added to the National Register of Historic Places in 1973, and is a National Historic Landmark. If you get the chance, the Xanterra offers daily tours of the Old House. These are very informative and quite worthwhile if you're interested in the history of this incredible building.

There are 89 Old House rooms, ranging in price (2014) from $109 per night for a single room without a bath to $254 for a 2-room suite with a bath. The East Wing has 74 rooms that rented for as much as $263 for a room with a view of the Old Faithful Geyser. The West Wing's 157 rooms rented for $174 to $234. There are also three semi-suites ($433 per night) and six suites ($539) available to guests. Many visitors have noted the small access door at the top of the stairs in the Inn's lobby. This leads to a small area known as Bat's Alley, eight rooms set aside specifically for the Inn's bell staff.

The Inn's Dining Room is open for breakfast, lunch, and dinner, and seats 304. The Bear Pit Lounge seats 70 and offers alcoholic drinks as well as light meal service. There's also a small deli and ice cream shop just off the lobby. A 100-seat Employee Dining Room is located at the rear of the Inn.

2. OFI Boiler House/Maintenance Office

Built in 1929 as a boiler room to supply steam and electricity to the Inn, this building houses both the boiler room and the Maintenance Office for the Inn's operator. The boilers now use diesel fuel from the tank farm located to the south.

3. OFI Electrical/Plumbing Shop

This four-room building was constructed in 1913 to serve as a small dormitory for the engineering staff at the Inn. It is now used as the electrical and plumbing shop.

4. OFI Maintenance Manager's Residence

Built in 1929, this four-room, 1.5 story building once served as the keeper's residence in the winter and the maintenance manager's residence during the summer. During the snow-laden winter months, the winterkeeper is responsible for ensuring the snow doesn't build up on the roof of the Inn and its ancillary buildings. The weight of the snow would collapse these structures if it wasn't removed periodically. Today it is used for storage.

5. Laurel Dormitory

Constructed in 1922, the dorm was originally known as the "Girl's Dorm" for the Inn. The building was modified in 1927 using materials left over from the destruction of the Fountain Hotel a few miles up the road. The dorm was known as the Windflower Dorm until 1988. It has 72 rooms for 140 employees and generally houses mostly younger, first-year Xanterra employees. The original "Boy's Dorm" next to it (southeast) was torn down in 2010 (see below).

6. Laurel Dorm Laundry/OFI Personnel Office

Built in 1929, this building houses the concession operator's Personnel Office as well as a laundry for those living in the Laurel Dorm.

7. OFI Pump House/Storage Building

Also built in 1929, this small building originally housed a pump that drew water from Myriad Creek (behind the house) and pumped it to the plumbing system for the Inn. Today, it is used as a storage building.

8. Yellowstone Lower General Store 🛉 ⛽ 🚻

The Lower General Store (known locally simply as the "Lower Store") was originally constructed in 1897 by Henry and Mary Klamer. The store was modified to add the "rustic" porch in 1904, and then a 16' addition was constructed in 1914. Henry Klamer would pass away in August of 1914, and his wife would sell the store to Charles A. Hamilton for $20,000 the following year. It would become the first of many stores throughout the park to bear the Hamilton name. Hamilton would remodel the store again in 1924, and it has been rehabilitated a couple of times since.

The store has two floors. The main floor consists of the store and its small grill, and storage space, while the second floor consists of the Manager's Office employee dorm roms and an employee dining room for store employees. It is generally open from mid-May to early October and has approximately 40 employees. The Manager's Office is known as the "Million Dollar Room" because Hamilton papered it with $1.8 million worth of canceled checks he'd used to pay off his debts.

9. Old Hay Barn

This large barn was constructed in 1921 and is used for storage today. Next to it is a root cellar.

10. YPSS Lower Service Station ⛽ 🔧

The "Lower" Service Station was constructed in 1920 by Charles Hamilton, and is basically a T-shaped structure. In 1947, Hamilton and the Yellowstone Park Company entered into a joint arrangement to operate the service stations throughout the park. This operation would eventually be sold off and is today operated by the Yellowstone Park Service Stations (YPSS). The station is open from early May to mid-October. Propane available.

11. Lift Station

Built in 1943, this is a sewage lift station that pumps raw sewage from the Old Faithful Inn, Lower General Store and the Lower Service Station to the Old Faithful Wastewater Treatment Plant located across the highway in the government area.

12. Old Faithful Visitor Education Center 🏠 ⑦ 🛉

Completed in 2010, the new Old Faithful Visitor Education Center (OFVEC) replaced an old, outdated visitor center constructed in 1972, which itself replaced the original Museum of Thermal Activity built in 1929. The new OFVEC incorporates many green and sustainable construction features and is designed to "sit upon" the land rather than being built upon a foundation embedded in it. This $27 million building was constructed partially using funds raised by the Yellowstone Park Foundation, the park's primary fundraising partner.

The OFVEC includes an information desk where you can talk to a ranger and obtain prediction times for many of the geysers in the area, as well as a large Yellowstone Association Bookstore. Additionally, there is a large exhibit hall with exhibits that focus on the geologic underpinnings of the park's hydrothermal processes. There's also a 200-seat auditorium where evening ranger programs are held during the summer and winter. The second floor is mostly office space for the staff, but there's also a small resource library available for researchers seeking information about the Old Faithful area. Check with the ranger desk for access. Public restrooms can be found just inside the front doors.

Old Faithful Lodge Area

L1. Old Faithful Lodge 🛏 🍴 🛉 🍸

The Old Faithful Lodge sits on the site of the original Shaw and Powell Permanent Camp erected here in 1913. The S&P camp mirrored a similar camp operated by the Wylie Permanent Camp Company located on what is today referred to as Wylie Hill just west of Daisy Geyser. In 1917, these two companies merged to form the Yellowstone Park Camping Company, and retained this site while closing the site on Wylie Hill. In 1920 that company, too, was sold and became the Yellowstone Park Camps Company, and began building lodges at different locations throughout the park. These lodge buildings were constructed in 1920-1926 to meet the needs of the new auto-based traveler.

The new building here at Old Faithful housed a dance pavilion and an amusement hall. In 1924, a kitchen and dining hall were added, followed by additional lobby space and the recreation hall in 1926. The new lobby included a curio shop, picture stand (operated by Haynes), soda fountain, barber shop, dispensary, and office space. Once the new rec hall and lobby were added, the original portion of the building (primarily the old dance hall) was torn down, leaving the building you see today (with some minor cosmetic and functional changes over the years).

In 1924, park concessioner Vernon Goodwin bought the Yellowstone Park Camps Company and operated as the Vernon Goodwin Company until 1928 when Harry W. Child bought him out and renamed it once again, this time to the Yellowstone Park Lodge and Camps Company. In 1936, the NPS required all of the non-store concession companies to merge into what became the Yellowstone Park Company (YPC). YPC operated most of the park's concessions until 1966 when the company was bought out by the Goldfield Corporation. The following year, Goldfield was sold to the General Host Corporation, which managed everything until 1979. Fed up with the lack of attention to the facilities, NPS bought out the company and all of its assets in the park, and let an emergency contract to TWA Services. TWA Services would change names a couple of times and would operate everything until they were bought out by Amfac in 1995, which later (2002) changed its name to Xanterra. Confused yet?

Today, the Lodge houses a small gift shop, a registration desk for the cabins (see below), a bake shop that sells coffee and pastries, and a 280-seat cafeteria-style dining room. The building originally had a 2nd floor dining room porch, but the 1959 Hebgen Lake Earthquake damaged the stairs leading to it, and it was removed in 1960. The Lodge also initially had a full service dining hall and lounge, but this was changed in the 1970s. The Lodge also has a spectacular lobby with huge windows affording an outstanding view of its namesake geyser. The Recreation Hall on the east side of the building is now used by employees and is off limits to the public.

Lodge accommodations include 60 Frontier style cabins and 36 Budget cabins (43 buildings). The primary difference is that the Frontier cabins have their own bathrooms while guests staying in the Budget cabins must use one of the communal wash houses situated throughout the complex. There is also a vending cabin in the complex where guests can obtain ice and drinks. The cabins are located along the scenic Firehole River. The 2014 rates range from $73 per night for the Budget cabins to $121 per night for the Frontier cabins. These cabins tend to fill up rather quickly each summer. Showers are available at the lodge's comfort station (or at the Inn).

Guest/Employee Cabins

From 1924-1927, approximately 200 new, all-wooden cabins were built for guests, replacing many of the old tent-cabins left over from the tent camp days. In 1939-1940, newer, all-wood cabins were constructed, giving the Lodge 414 cabins with 638 rooms at its peak. Shortly after the wooden cabins were constructed, many of the leftover half-tent cabins from the previous era were destroyed. The remaining cabins were dispersed to avoid having them exist in straight lines (which was deemed visually unpleasant). Bathrooms with showers were added to many of the units in 1954 (becoming the "Frontier" cabins of today).[9]

In 1983-1985, some 155 cabins were removed, many of them dispersed to other areas of the park.[10] This includes the 13 used for employee housing at Grayling Dormitory in Grant Village. In 1999, another 28 of the Lodge's cabins were converted for use as employee cabins (67 rooms) after the cabins and the old Snow Lodge were razed. The employee cabins are destined to be repurposed back to guest cabins within the next few years, increasing the Lodge's guest capacity once again.

L2. OFL Boiler Building/Housekeeping Office

This building was constructed in 1930 and was originally the "boy's dormitory" and linen house for the lodge. It was later converted to a boiler house for the lodge, and still houses the housekeeping office.[11]

L3. Columbine Dormitory

Opened in 1940 as the Cinderella Dormitory (girl's dorm) for the Old Faithful Lodge, this building is now a coed dorm with 31 rooms for 60 employees (mostly under the age of 21).

L4. OFL Employee Laundry Building

Built in 1925 as one of the guest cabins, this building now houses the laundry for the employees housed in the Columbine Dormitory and the cabins near the Lodge.

L5. OFL Location Manager's Cabin

This employee cabin, built in 1939 along with most of the existing cabins, is the residence of the Lodge's Location Manager during the summer and the Winterkeeper during the winter.

L6. Historic Preservation Crew Office

Built in 1939 as one of the guest cabins and later converted into a linen cabin for the housekeeping staff when this area was used for guests, this building now houses Xanterra's Historic Preservation Crew. The crew is charged with ensuring the historical aspects of the Inn, the Lodge, and the other buildings under their jurisdiction remain intact.

L7. OFL Storage Building

This building was also constructed in 1939 as one of the guest cabins. It has been converted into a storage building.

L8. Haynes Photo Shop Museum 📷

Constructed in 1927 just southwest of the Old Faithful Lodge, the building was expanded in 1936 and 1958, and then relocated to the site of the present day Snow Lodge in 1971 to allow for realignment of the road system within the Old Faithful development. The building contained a retail photo shop, a photo-finishing plant (which replaced the original plant in the area built in 1897), and living quarters for employees. The Haynes family operated the photo shop until they sold all of their assets to the Hamilton Stores franchise in 1967. From that point forward, it was operated as a satellite store or sat vacant.

In 2010, following the construction of the new Snow Lodge building, the entire structure (which by this point was a large T-shaped facility) was broken into two parts and relocated to the Government Area, where it sat abandoned until 2012.

In 2012-2013, the Yellowstone Park Foundation raised funds to have half of the building relocated back to its (approximate) original position between the Old Faithful Lodge and the Visitor Education Center (the other half was destroyed). It was converted into a museum showcasing the photography of Frank J. Haynes and his son Jack over the course of the 80+ years they operated their photo shops in the park.

Old Faithful Snow Lodge Area

S1. Old Faithful Snow Lodge 🛏 🍽 🛗 🧴 📷

The Old Faithful Snow Lodge is the newest hotel in the park, having been built in 1997-1999 to replace the original Snow Lodge, which was never designed to house guests in the first place (see below). The building sits on the footprint occupied by the old snow lodge and many of its cabins.

The Snow Lodge has 100 rooms, 80 of which have two queen beds, and 20 which have a single king sized bed. The rates for the 2014 season were $241 and $251 per night respectively. The lodge has a full service, 106-seat dining room, and the Geyser Grill, a fast food restaurant that seats 106. There's also a 63-seat Employee Dining Room and office space located in the lodge's basement. During the summer, you can rent bicycles from the gift shop, and in the winter you can rent ski equipment, snowshoes, and snowmobiles there as well. There's a guest laundry on the 2nd floor.

Guest Cabins

The Snow Lodge has 11 cabin buildings with 34 rooms, a holdover from the massive camper cabin complex that existed in this area prior to the removal of the old Snow Lodge. Five of these cabins were constructed in 1959 and are literal holdovers from a bygone era. These are known as "Frontier" cabins and rent for $105 per night in 2013. The other six "quad" cabin buildings were constructed in 1989 to replace the 16 that burned in the fires of 1988. These more modern rooms are marketed as "Western" cabins and in 2013 rented for $165 per night.

S2. Obsidian Dormitory

The Obsidian Dormitory was constructed in the late 1970s. It houses employees of the Old Faithful Snow Lodge, mostly older, more mature employees. The dorm has 50 rooms for 99 employees. It is occasionally used in the winter to house overflow guests from the Snow Lodge.

S3. Old Faithful Upper General Store

Built in 1929 during the Great Depression, the "Upper Store" replaced a small store constructed in 1923 to serve the campground that was located on the site of the present day eastern parking lot at the time. This is the largest general store in the park, and was originally known as the Basin Auto Camp, or BAC Store. The rear grill/soda fountain portion was added in 1953, and it has been remodeled on several occasions since, including in the mid-2000s when the interior was restored to its original appearance. The top floor is mostly employee dorm space. The store has 80 employees.

The building was designed by Robert Reamer, the architect of the Old Faithful Inn, and is open from early May to early October.

S4. "Four Seasons" Comfort Station [♦♦]

This comfort station was constructed in 1972 to provide restroom facilities when the old camper laundry and shower building was being converted into the Four Seasons Snack Shop (since removed; see below) for winter use. The building has been renovated a couple of times and is still used as a comfort station.

S5. YGS Dormitory

Opened in 1952, this building is a dormitory for Yellowstone General Store employees. It houses roughly 70 employees.

S6. YPSS Upper Service Station [⛽] [🔧]

The service station was constructed in 1927 to serve visitors staying at the Old Faithful Auto Campground, which, at the time was located on the site of the present day eastern parking lot immediately adjacent to the station. The facility was renovated in 1940 and is the primary repair center (including for RVs) for the Old Faithful area. The station is typically open from mid-May to mid-September. Propane is available here.

S7. CenturyTel Building

This building is the telephone central office switching center for the Old Faithful area. Notice the microwave dish at the rear of the building. From here, telecommunications traffic is bounced off a passive reflector (the green rectangular board you can see on the side of the hill to the northwest of the area), up to Mt. Washburn, and then into Mammoth. The building was constructed in 1980, and replaced an older building constructed in the 1960s.

S8. Old Faithful Post Office [✉]

Built in 1970, the Post Office Building was originally located between the Upper General Store and the old Snow Lodge. It was relocated to this site when construction of the new Snow Lodge was begun in 1997.

S9. Old Faithful Ranger Station/Clinic [🏠] [?] [✚]

Constructed in 1996, this building houses the ranger station for the Old Faithful District, as well as the area's clinic. The Ranger Station replaced older buildings used to house the law enforcement ranger staff (see below).

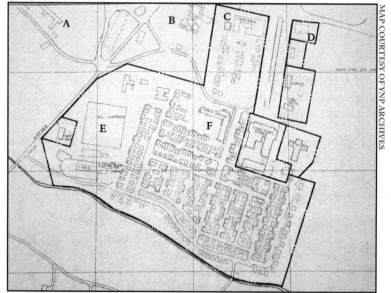

Plat of the Old Faithful Complex, Center Section, showing the Transportation Compound (E), the Camper Cabins Office & Cabins (F), ca. 1956.

The clinic replaced an old double-wide trailer that was situated across from the original Snow Lodge for many years (which itself had replaced the dispensary that served as the "clinic" in the Old Faithful Lodge for a period of time). The clinic is typically open from mid-May to early October, each season, and is staffed by three nurses and a physician's assistant. Old Faithful has two ambulances in service during the summer, one of which is based here at the clinic (the other is across the highway in the Government Area).

BUILDINGS NO LONGER PRESENT

Old Faithful Geyser Baths: Originally known as the Brothers Bathhouse and Plunge, this large structure housed a series of plunge pools and swimming pools. It was constructed in 1914-1915 on the large flat north of the present day front parking lot of the Old Faithful Inn, west of the little foot path that leads to the Upper Geyser Basin boardwalk from the parking lot.[12] In 1933, Mr. Brothers retired and sold the facility to Charles Hamilton, the park's store concessioner.

Hamilton refurbished the building and reopened it in 1934 as the Old Faithful Geyser Baths. It operated until the U.S. Public Health Service ordered it closed (for sanitation reasons) in 1950, and was razed the following year. The NPS itself had been trying to force Hamilton to close it

Museum of Thermal Activity at Old Faithful, ca. 1953. Today, the new Old Faithful Visitor Education Center sits on this spot.

for a number of years prior to this because they didn't believe an "unnatural" swimming pool was the right fit for a national park. Other, smaller pools in use throughout the complex were also shut down around this time.

Water for the bathhouse came from Solitary Spring, located to the north of Geyser Hill. The diversion of water from this spring caused it to undergo a transformation, however, and the pool is now known as Solitary Geyser because it does erupt from time to time (every 4-8 minutes).[13] The pool had 147 changing rooms and several "sand porches" for sunbathing. The original pool was 50' x 100', but was lengthened to 160' by Hamilton during the renovation.

Old Faithful Ranger Stations: There were at least three ranger stations at Old Faithful prior to the existing building (the joint ranger station-clinic). The first of these was located in the large oxbow in the Firehole River just northwest of where the Brothers/Hamilton Geyser Baths were located (see above). This structure and its related outbuildings dated back to the late 1880s, and were all removed in the early 1920s. The second ranger station was constructed in 1921 just southwest of the present day Old Faithful Lodge, in the woods across the walkway from the site of the (existing) refurbished Photo Shop. It was later used as a residence and then razed in 1965. The third building was constructed adjacent to the Museum of Thermal Activity (at location "B" on the diagram above). Following the demolition of the museum for the construction of the 1972 Visitor Center, the building was relocated to another part of the complex, and used until the existing ranger station was constructed.

Museum of Thermal Activity: The Museum of Thermal Activity was one of the four museums originally funded by the Laura Spelman Rockefeller Foundation in 1929. An 800-seat amphitheater was added in 1932. These are visible at location "B" on the diagram above. Both facilities were undersized from the outset, and were continuously overwhelmed with visitors wanting to learn how the area's thermal features functioned. It sat on the site occupied by the present day visitor center. The museum was torn down in 1970 to make room for the 1972 Visitor Center (the other three museums remain standing).

Old Faithful Visitor Center (1972): The Old Faithful Visitor Center replaced the museum and opened to the public in 1972. It was of modern design, but had several shortcomings such as ineffective use of space, technology that didn't function correctly, and a lack of insulation and other features that allowed it to handle the park's harsh winters very well. It's small auditorium was inadequate for anything other than small presentations given the size of the crowds that could be found in the area during the summer tourist season. The decision was made in the late 1990s to replace it. The building was razed in 2007, and the new Old Faithful Visitor Education Center was constructed on the same site, opening in 2010.

Old Faithful Cafeteria: Operated by the Yellowstone Park Company, this cafeteria was located in the large open field (now partially treed) just east/southeast of the present day OFVEC (location "C" on the diagram above). It was constructed in 1927-1928 and removed in 1970 to make way for the new traffic pattern that came with the redesign of the road system in and around the Old Faithful Development. The cafeteria was built to serve meals to the guests staying at the camper cabins complex south of here (on the site of the present day Snow Lodge and its cabins and behind the existing Upper General Store)

Yellowstone Park Improvement Company Tent Camp: This tent camp opened on the site of the present day Inn in 1883 (roughly on the site of what is today the West Wing), and was the first lodging facility of any type to be located in this section of the park. It consisted of a small office structure and several tents for guests.

Upper Geyser Basin "Shack" Hotel/Lunch Station: This small, relatively poorly built hotel was constructed in 1885, replacing the tent operation started in 1883 (see above). The hotel could accommodate approximately 50 guests. In 1891, the building was converted into a lunch station since the grand new Fountain Hotel located a few miles north of this area was much more preferable to guests for an overnight stay. This facility would

Old Faithful Hothouse, ca. 1917. Thermal heat was used to grow vegetables year round.

burn to the ground in 1894 and would be replaced shortly thereafter by another, smaller lunch station. The operators would add tent cabins to it in 1901, and the entire enterprise was removed in 1903 to make room for construction of the Old Faithful Inn.

Old Faithful Hothouse: This greenhouse was constructed in 1897 on the thermal field behind the existing Lower Service Station. It was used to grow fresh vegetables to feed those dining at the Old Faithful Inn. It was removed in 1941.[14]

Old Faithful Inn Men's Dorms: A large, eight-room, 90-person, U-shaped dormitory was built in 1913 to house the male staff for the Inn. The building was located on the bare ground inside the fenced area just to the southeast of the Laurel Dorm. Across the road from it was another 8-room dorm for 16 maintenance personnel that was built in 1926. When it was originally constructed, it used hot water from the thermal field upon which it is located to provide water for baths and heat. These buildings were at location "A" on the diagram above. The larger building was razed in 2010, while the smaller one was removed in 2009, due primarily to encroachment of thermal features.

Old Employee Pub: This small building, located adjacent to the Men's Dorm described above, was originally a paint and carpentry shop, but was converted for use as a recreation hall and pub at some point (post-1972). After the new pub was constructed in the Government Area, this building was used for storage. Constructed in 1913, it was razed in 2009.

Old Faithful Camper Cabins/Old Snow Lodge: The existing Snow Lodge replaced the "old Snow Lodge," which was never designed to house guests to begin with. In 1926, a Camper Services Building was constructed just south of the site of the Old Faithful Cafeteria (also no longer present; see above). This building served the over 400 "camper cabins" that populated the area around and south of the existing Snow Lodge and the Upper General Store. It burned in 1955.

Two years later, a new Camper Services Building was constructed just south of the site of the original one, on the site of today's Snow Lodge (the space occupied by the gift shop and the grill). The building included a registration desk, small lounge, and dining room on the ground floor, and 30 dorms rooms on the top floor for the female housekeeping staff. It was located at "F" on the diagram above.

In the winter of 1972 when NPS opened the park to winter visitation for the first time, this building was hastily converted into an itinerant Snow Lodge, with the dorm rooms being converted into guest rooms. The following year, the building was officially christened the Old Faithful Snow Lodge and became a two-season operation (employees were moved to cabins, and later to the Obsidian Dorm). It would remain in operation until the winter of 1996-1997, after which it was torn down to make room for the new lodge.

At the height of the camper cabins operation, more than 400 cabins were available to guests. In the 1960s, a great many of these would be transitioned to other areas of the park or torn down. In 1988, the fires that struck the Old Faithful area burned 16 of them. These were replaced with the 710-733 cabins marketed as "Western" cabins today. Cabins 700-709 are all that remain of the original cabins, and are marketed as the "Frontier" cabins.

YPTC Bus Barn/Transportation Complex: Where the western parking lot exists today (the large lot west of the Snow Lodge and north of the Ranger Station/Clinic, and Post Office, labeled as location "E" on the diagram above), there was a large transportation complex used by the Yellowstone Park Company (and its predecessors) to house and manage its bus fleet. It included a bus barn, offices, dormitories, and a mess hall for employees. All of these facilities were demolished in the early 1970s as the new traffic pattern was created throughout the Old Faithful development.

Four Seasons Snack Shop: Constructed in 1957 as a laundry and shower facility for guests staying in the old "Camper Cabins," this building was converted into a snack shop during the first winter the park was opened

(1972). As a result, it became known as the "Four Seasons" Snack Shop. In 1982, the laundry and shower facilities were removed, and it was converted into a permanent deli/snack shop, a purpose it served until it was closed and torn down in 1999 in preparation for the construction of the new Snow Lodge. Its satellite restroom facility remains in place.

Old Faithful Auto Campground: There have been three separate auto campgrounds at Old Faithful. The first was a small campground constructed in 1916 at the southeast corner of the Old Faithful Lodge cabin area (south end of the cabin area currently used for employee housing). It had a small, rectangular shed capable of housing 12 vehicles (people camped out of the back of their vehicles during this period), and quickly became overwhelmed with travelers wanting to camp there.

In 1920, the second campground was constructed south of the first one across what was then the main road into the development from West Thumb. This one was much larger and was capable of hosting as many as 350 vehicles. Over time, the NPS added streetlights and ten comfort stations. Within ten years, this campground, too, would become too small to accommodate all of the visitors who wished to camp in the park. It would be another two decades before additional facilities would be constructed, however. This campground existed entirely on the site of the present day East Parking Lot.

The third and final campground addition was begun in 1939, when the Civilian Conservation Corps (CCC) started work on a large addition that occupied land southeast of what is today the East Parking Lot. The CCC would be called away for other projects, however, and the campground would not be completed and opened to tourists until the 1949 summer season. If you take the long drive into the complex as if you were driving to the Old Faithful Lodge, as you go around the curve you're driving through what was the northwestern half of the campground.[15]

The campgrounds were removed in 1969 as a prelude to the reconfiguration of the traffic patterns around and throughout the Old Faithful development. Only a picnic area remains. Much of the infrastructure on this side of the development came about because of the presence of this campground, including the Upper Service Station and the large Upper General Store, which was known during the campground's presence as the Basin Auto Camp (or BAC) Store.

The campground had a bear feeding area that had existed since 1919, and was formalized in 1931. Known as the "Lunch Counter for Bears," hundreds of tourists would gather each evening to watch the bears feed on garbage from the area's restaurants and hotels. The practice of feeding the bears at Old Faithful ended in 1934. This was one of two sanctioned bear feeding areas in the park during this period. The other was at Canyon, south of what is today the Canyon Corrals. It was initially kept open because it wasn't near any developed areas, but it, too, would close in 1941.

OTHER FEATURES

The Ruin: The Ruin is an old geyserite deposit along the service road running between Lower Store and the West Parking Lot, south of what used to be the old men's dorm (east of Laurel Dorm). It is the 40-foot wide remnant of an old thermal pool/spring and is identifiable from the road by the large three-foot high rocks that form a ring around what was the edge of the pool.

Three Sisters Springs: Three Sisters Springs is a series of apparently interconnected hot springs located just off the east side of the road leading to the Lower Service Station, the Lower General Store, and the front parking lot of the Old Faithful Inn. In fact, the road itself is referred to by many locals as Three Sisters Road. There is a sewer pipe that runs underneath the road here that often cracks due to the heat, creating recurring problems for park road and maintenance crews.

East Lot Picnic Area: This picnic area is located along the southern edge of the East Parking Lot, in the forested area. There are seven tables (one of which is wheelchair accessible) as well as a vault toilet. Given the high volume of traffic in the Old Faithful area during the day, it is often difficult to find a free table here. 🌲 🚻

TRAILS

Upper Geyser Basin Trail: This mostly paved and boardwalked trail is between 1.5 miles (2.4 km) and 5 miles (8 km) long depending on which loops you take, and is easily the most heavily traveled trail in the park. The trail takes you through the most geyser-dense area on the planet, including Geyser Hill, and on to Riverside Geyser, Castle Geyser, Giant Geyser, and Beehive Geyser, some of the most popular features in the park. The paved/boardwalked section ends at Morning Glory Pool (there's a vault toilet there), but you can continue on a well-maintained dirt trail to Artemisia Geyser and then to Biscuit Basin if you're so inclined. A portion of the trail is paved and follows the original road that ran through the area before 1972. It is an approved bicycle path. 🚶 🚲

Observation Point Trail: This trail leads to the top of Observation Point, the small hill to the northeast of the Old Faithful Geyser. This is an excellent vantage point from which to get photos of the geyser with the Inn in the background, especially during the early morning hours when the sun is shining at just the right angle. Check at the Old Faithful Visitor Education Center for prediction and time your hike accordingly. Even though this is a short hike, be sure to take your bear spray with you, as bears are occasionally seen along this trail (as well as other wildlife).

Going up or coming back, you can take a side hike (about 3/10 of a mile) to Solitary Geyser. This geyser was originally a hot spring used to supply water to the Old Faithful Geyser Baths/Swimming Pool (see above). As a result of damage from that misuse, the pool now acts as a geyser rather and a true hot spring. 🚶

The Mallard Lake and the Kepler Ski Trails: These trails begin at the east edge of the employee cabin housing area east of the Old Faithful Lodge. The Mallard Lake Trail is a 6.5 mile (10.6 km, round trip) trail that takes you to Mallard Lake, also reachable via the Mallard Creek Trail on the road between Old Faithful and Madison Junction. The Kepler Ski Trail also begins from the trailhead, and follows what was the original road through the Upper Geyser Basin up to the parking area at Kepler Cascade. 🚶 ⛷

Appendices

Appendix A: Important Telephone Numbers

Appendix B: Location of Public Restrooms

Appendix C: Yellowstone Picnic Areas

Appendix D: Yellowstone Campgrounds

APPENDIX A
IMPORTANT PARK TELEPHONE NUMBERS

GENERAL NUMBERS

- **Emergencies**: Dial **9-1-1** for all emergencies (in park)
- Anonymous Crime Tip Line: 307-344-2132[a]
- 24-Hour Weather Reports: 307-344-2113
- 24-Hour Weather Forecast: 307-344-8401
- 24-Hour Road Conditions: 307-344-2117
- 24-Hour Lodging Status: 307-344-2114
- Main Park Switchboard: 307-344-7381
- Park Lost and Found: 307-344-2109
- Visitor Services Office: 307-344-2107
- Mammoth Jail: 307-344-2178

XANTERRA RESERVATIONS & INFORMATION

- Lodging Reservations: 307-344-7311
- Campground Reservations: 307-344-7901
- Human Resources Office: 307-344-5324

VISITOR CENTERS/MUSEUMS

- Mammoth: 307-344-2263
- Canyon: 307-242-2550
- Fishing Bridge: 307-344-2450
- Grant Village: 307-344-2650
- Old Faithful: 307-545-2750
- Old Faithful Geyser Predictions: 307-545-2751
- Madison: 307-344-2821
- West Yellowstone NPS Desk: 307-344-2876

BACKCOUNTRY OFFICES:

- Central Backcountry Office: 307-344-2160/3
- Mammoth: 307-344-2176
- Tower: 307-344-2817
- Canyon: 307-242-2503
- Bridge Bay: 307-242-2413
- Grant Village: 307-242-2609
- Snake River/South: 307-242-7209
- Old Faithful: 307-242-2703
- Bechler: 406-581-7071
- West Yellowstone: 307-344-2878

---

a. Do not use this line to report emergencies, as it is checked only during business hours.

Post Offices

- Mammoth: 307-344-7764
- Canyon: 307-242-7323
- Lake: 307-242-7383
- Grant Village: 307-242-7338
- Old Faithful: 307-545-7252

Service Stations

- Mammoth Service Station: 307-344-7731
- Tower Service Station: 307-344-7784
- Canyon Service Station: 307-242-7581
- Fishing Bridge Service Station: 307-242-7363
- Fishing Bridge Repair Garage: 307-242-7543
- Grant Village Service Station: 307-242-7364
- Old Faithful Lower Service Station: 307-545-7285
- Old Faithful Upper Service Station: 307-545-7286

General Stores/Gift Shops

- Mammoth General Store: 307-344-7702
- Mammoth Hotel Gift Shop: 307-344-5236
- Roosevelt General Store: 307-344-7779
- Tower General Store: 307-344-7786
- Canyon General Store: 307-242-7377
- Canyon Adventure Store: 307-242-7551
- Canyon Lodge Gift Shop: 307-242-3936
- Fishing Bridge General Store: 307-242-7200
- Lake General Store: 307-242-7563
- Lake Hotel Gift Shop: 307-242-3740
- Lake Lodge Gift Shop: 307-242-3836
- Bridge Bay Marina Store: 307-242-7326
- Grant Village General Store: 307-242-7266
- Grant Village Mini-Store: 307-242-7390
- Grant Village Lodge Gift Shop: 307-242-3436
- Old Faithful Lower General Store: 307-545-7282
- Old Faithful Upper General Store: 307-545-7237
- Old Faithful Inn Gift Shop: 307-545-4636
- Old Faithful Lodge Gift Shop: 307-545-4936
- Old Faithful Bear Den Gift Shop: 307-545-4824

HOTELS/LODGES

- Mammoth Hot Springs Hotel: 307-344-5600
- Roosevelt Lodge: 307-344-5272
- Canyon Lodge: 307-242-3900
- Lake Hotel: 307-242-3700
- Lake Lodge: 307-242-3800
- Grant Village Lodge: 307-242-3400
- Old Faithful Inn: 307-545-4600
- Old Faithful Lodge: 307-545-4900
- Old Faithful Snow Lodge: 307-545-4800

CAMPGROUNDS (XANTERRA)

- Canyon Campground: 307-242-3963
- Fishing Bridge RV Park: 307-242-3776
- Bridge Bay Camground: 307-242-3874
- Grant Village Campground: 307-242-3464
- Madison Campground: 307-344-5463

RESTAURANTS/DINING ROOMS

- Mammoth Dining Room: 307-344-5314
- Mammoth Terrace Grill: 307-344-5234
- Roosevelt Dining Room: 307-344-5411
- Canyon Lodge Dining Room: 307-242-3999
- Canyon Lodge Cafeteria: 307-242-3919
- Canyon Lodge Deli: 307-242-3922
- Lake Hotel Dining Room: 307-242-3899
- Lake Hotel Deli: 307-242-3719
- Lake Lodge Cafeteria: 307-242-3816
- Grant Village Dining Room: 307-242-3499
- Grant Village Lakehouse: 307-242-3424
- Old Faithful Inn Dining Room: 307-545-4999
- Old Faithful Inn Deli: 307-545-4622
- Old Faithful Lodge Cafeteria: 307-545-4916
- Obsidian Dining Room (OFSL): 307-545-4998
- Old Faithful Geyser Grill (OFSL): 307-545-4813

CLINICS

- Mammoth: 307-344-7965
- Lake: 307-242-7241
- Old Faithful: 307-545-7325

Activities/Tour Desks

- Mammoth Hotel Activities Desk: 307-242-5430
- Mammoth Hotel Tour Desk: 307-344-5603
- Mammoth Ski Shop (Winter Only): 307-344-5276
- Mammoth Corral Ticket Office: 307-344-5274
- Roosevelt Corral Ticket Office: 307-344-5212
- Canyon Activities Desk: 307-242-3909
- Canyon Tour Desk: 307-242-3981
- Canyon Corral Ticket Office: 307-242-3912
- Fishing Bridge RV Activities Desk: 307-242-3777
- Lake Hotel Activities Desk: 307-242-3708
- Lake Lodge Activities Desk: 307-242-3808
- Bridge Bay Campgrd Activities Desk: 307-242-3889
- Bridge Bay Marina: 307-242-3876
- Grant Village Tour Desk: 307-242-3408
- Old Faithful Inn Activities Desk: 307-545-4612
- Old Faithful Inn Tour Desk: 307-545-4608/9
- Old Faithful Lodge Activities Desk: 307-545-4902
- OF Snow Lodge Activities Desk: 307-545-4802
- OFSL Snowmobile Rentals: 307-545-4806

Yellowstone Association Bookstores

- Gardiner: 406-848-2400
- Mammoth: 307-344-2297
- Canyon: 307-242-2552
- Fishing Bridge: 307-242-7358
- Grant Village: 307-242-7694
- Old Faithful: 307-545-2752
- Madison: 307-344-2821
- Norris: 307-344-8973
- Yellowstone Institute (Gardiner): 406-848-2400

APPENDIX B
LOCATION OF PUBLIC TOILETS

The most critical facility most people will ever need in Yellowstone is a toilet. After you've been stuck in a bison jam for more than an hour, sometimes nature gets pretty insistent about wanting you to take care of business. And if you're not that familiar with the park, trying to find one in such an emergency can be quite frustrating. For that reason, I've created a list of all of the public toilets located in the park's front country.

There are three types of restroom facilities in the list below. There are those located in public buildings such as hotels, stores, visitor centers, etc. Those are listed simply as buildings. The second includes what are known as "comfort stations," which are basically brick/wood buildings complete with toilets, urinals, and sinks with running water (and occasionally even soap and toilet paper!).[a] These are listed as a "comfort station" or with "CS" after their name in these lists. The third is the vault toilet ("VT" in the list). These are the primitive, seat over a hole in the ground toilets common in parks and campgrounds around the country.

The list below includes 90 vault toilets, 88 comfort stations, and 33 public buildings where you can find restroom facilities of some type. The ones marked with asterisks (*) are only open during normal business hours of the facility. Otherwise, the remainder should be accessible 24 hours a day during the summer season.

For those located along the highways, you'll see parentheses with two distance measurements in them. These indicate distances from the last major junction, depending on which direction you're traveling from. For example, if you see "(3.0N/2.2S)," this means the restroom is located 3.0 miles from the last junction if you're headed FROM the north, and 2.2 miles from the last intersection if you're headed FROM the south.

NORTH ENTRANCE ROAD
- Boiling River Turnout VT (3.0N/2.2S)
- Mammoth Campground Roadside CS (8.3N/0.9S)

---

a. I'm only slightly kidding here. There's an old saying in the park that you can tell whether the NPS is responsible for a bathroom or it belongs to one of the park's concession operators. If you can read through the toilet paper, it's an NPS bathroom. It seems they buy the cheapest TP possible - it literally has holes in it in many cases.

MAMMOTH HOT SPRINGS

- Albright Visitor Center* (Basement Level)[b]
- Mammoth Hot Springs Hotel Lobby
- Mammoth Dining Room*
- Mammoth Terrace Grill*
- Yellowstone General Store*
- Mammoth Comfort Station

MAMMOTH TO TOWER JUNCTION ROAD

- Lava Creek Trailhead VT (4.4W/13.7E)
- Blacktail Patrol Cabin Service Road VT (6.7W/11.4E)
- Tower Service Station Recycle Lot VT (x2) (18.0W/0.1E)

ROOSEVELT/TOWER JUNCTION

- Tower Service Station*
- Roosevelt Lodge Lobby
- Roosevelt Corrals VT
- Yancey's Cookout Site VT (x2)

NORTHEAST ENTRANCE ROAD

- Northeast Entrance Station VT (0.4E/28.2W)[c]
- Warm Creek Picnic Area VT (1.5E/27.1W)
- Soda Butte Picnic Area VT (7.5E/21.1W)
- Pebble Creek Campground VT (x3) (9.7E/18.9W)
- Lamar "Hitching Post" Trailhead VT (x2) (14.3E/14.3W)
- Slough Creek Campground Ent VT (22.7E/5.9W)[d]

TOWER JUNCTION TO CANYON JUNCTION ROAD

- Tower Fall Store Comfort Station (2.4N/15.9S)[e]
- Chittenden Junction VT (8.7N/9.5S)[f]
- Dunraven Pass Trailhead VT (13.5N/4.8S)
- Sulfur Creek Overlook VT (13.9N/4.4S)
- Dunraven Picnic Area VT (15.8N/2.4S)
- Cascade Lake Picnic Area VT (17.0N/1.3S)

CANYON VILLAGE

- Canyon Visitor Education Center Lobby*

---

b. Currently, this is an exterior entrance located to the left and right of the front steps. Albright is undergoing renovation that will change the location of these facilities.
c. Toilet is in the woods on the south side of the road, outside the gate.
d. There are 4 additional VTs up the road in the campground
e. There are 3 additional VTs in the Tower Campground
f. There are 2 additional VTs at the parking area at the end of Chittenden Road

CANYON VILLAGE (CONTINUED)
- Yellowstone Adventure Store*
- Canyon General Store*
- Canyon Lodge Building Lobby*
- Canyon Camper Services Building
- Canyon Campground (17 Comfort Stations)
- Canyon Service Station*

CANYON VILLAGE TO FISHING BRIDGE
- Canyon Corral VT (0.9N/14.5S)
- North Rim Drive CS & VT (x3) (1.2N/14.2S)[g]
- Brink of the Upper Falls Drive CS (1.6N/13.8S)
- South Rim Drive CS & VT (x5) (2.3N/13.1S)[h]
- Mud Volcano Parking Lot VT (x4) (9.5N/5.8S)
- Nez Perce Ford Picnic Area VT (10.4N/5.0S)
- Cascade Picnic Area VT (10.6N/4.8S)
- LeHardy Picnic Area VT (11.3N/4.1S)

FISHING BRIDGE AREA
- Fishing Bridge General Store*
- Fishing Bridge Warming Hut Parking Lot VT
- Fishing Bridge Museum Comfort Station
- Fishing Bridge Camper Services Building
- Fishing Bridge RV Park Comfort Stations (x4)

EAST ENTRANCE ROAD
- East Entrance VT (x2) (0.2E/25.7W)
- Sylvan Falls Turnout VT (3.7E/22.2W)
- Sylvan Lake Picnic Area VT (8.9E/17.1W)
- Lake Butte Overlook VT (16.4E/9.5W)
- Sedge Bay picnic Area VT (18.1E/7.8W)
- Steamboat Point Picnic Area VT (19.6E/6.3W)
- Fishing Bridge Warming Hut VT (25.2E/0.7W)

LAKE VILLAGE
- Lake Hotel Lobby
- Lake General Store Comfort Station[i]
- Lake Lodge Lobby

g. The facilities are located at the first stop. Exiting requires you to go all the way back up to Canyon Village, however.
h. There's a comfort station and a VT at Uncle Tom's Trailhead, a VT at the Chittenden Bridge Picnic Area/Wapiti Lake Trailhead, and two VTs at Artist Point.
i. Comfort Station is located out "behind" the store to the east.

FISHING BRIDGE TO WEST THUMB ROAD
- Bridge Bay Ranger Station* (3.4N/17.2S)
- Bridge Bay Picnic Area/CG CS (x17) (3.4N/17.2S)[j]
- Gull Point Picnic Area VT (3.7N/16.9S)
- Sand Point Picnic Area VT (x2) (6.5N/14.0S)
- Contrasting Forest Picnic Area VT (9.8N/10.8)
- Fisherman's Access Picnic Area VT (12.7N/7.9S)
- Hard Road to Travel Picnic Area VT (13.8N/6.8S)
- West Thumb Basin VT (x4) (20.5N/0.1S)

GRANT VILLAGE
- Grant Village Mini Store*
- Grant Village General Store*
- Grant Village Lodge Registration Building
- Grant Village Dining Room*
- Lake House Restaurant*
- Grant Village Marina VT
- Grant Village Visitor Center
- Grant Village Camper Services Building
- Grant Village Picnic Area CS
- Grant Village Campground CS (x17)

SOUTH ENTRANCE ROAD
- South Entrance VT (x2) (0.2S/21.2N)
- Snake River Picnic Area VT (0.3S/21.1N)
- Lewis Falls Picnic Area/CG VT (x7) (11.3S/10.1N)
- Heart Lake Trailhead VT (14.2S/7.2N)
- Lewis Channel/Dogshead Trailhead VT (14.4S/7.0N)

WEST THUMB TO OLD FAITHFUL ROAD
- East Divide Picnic Area VT (3.7E/13.8W)
- DeLacy Creek Picnic Area VT (8.6E/9.6W)
- Spring Creek Picnic Area VT (12.0E/5.6W)
- Lone Star Trailhead VT (15.0E/2.6W)

OLD FAITHFUL AREA
- Lower Service Station*
- Lower General Store*
- Old Faithful Inn 1st & 2nd Floors
- Old Faithful Visitor Education Center*
- Old Faithful Snow Lodge Lobby

---

j. There is one comfort station at the picnic area, and 16 in the campground.

OLD FAITHFUL AREA (CONTINUED)

- Old Faithful Geyser Grill Lobby*
- Old Four Seasons Comfort Station
- Upper General Store*
- Old Faithful Warming Hut Comfort Station
- Old Faithful Lodge Lobby
- Old Faithful East Parking Lot Picnic Area VT
- Morning Glory Pool VT

OLD FAITHFUL TO MADISON JUNCTION ROAD

- Midway Geyser Basin Parking Lot VT (x2) (5.8S/10.1N)
- Whiskey Flats Picnic Area VT (6.2S/9.7N)
- Fountain Paint Pots Parking Lot VT (x2) (7.7S/8.2N)
- Nez Perce Creek Picnic Area VT (10.3S/5.6N)
- Firehole River Picnic Area VT (11.4S/4.5N)
- Firehole Canyon Swimming Area VT (x2) (15.3S/0.6N)[k]
- Madison Service Area Comfort Station (15.7S/0.2N)

WEST ENTRANCE ROAD

- West Entrance Station VT (x2) (0.3W/13.6E)
- Madison River Picnic Area VT (7.5W/6.4E)
- Madison Campground CS (x16) (13.7W/0.1E)

MADISON JUNCTION TO NORRIS JUNCTION

- Tuff Cliff Picnic Area VT (1.6S/11.8N)
- Iron Spring Picnic Area VT (5.3S/8.0N)
- Caldera Rim Picnic Area VT (6.2S/7.1N)
- Gibbon Meadow Picnic Area VT (10.2S/3.1N)

NORRIS JUNCTION TO CANYON JUNCTION ROAD

- Norris Geyser Basin Parking Lot CS/VT (x5) (0.0/11.6)
- Norris Meadow Picnic Area VT (0.5W/11.0E)
- Virginia Cascade Picnic Area VT (1.6W/9.9E)[l]

NORRIS JUNCTION TO MAMMOTH HOT SPRINGS ROAD

- Norris Camground CS (x4) (0.8S/20.1N)
- Beaver lake Picnic Area VT (7.5S/13.5N)
- Apollinaris Spring Picnic Area VT (9.9S/11.1N)
- Mid Willow Park Turnout VT (11.1S/9.9N)
- Indian Creek Campground VT (x8) (12.5S/8.5N)

---

k. These VTs are located one mile down the canyon drive, and are often closed.
l. VT is at the picnic area, which is near the end of the scenic road.

Norris Junction to Mammoth Hot Springs Rd (continued)
- Sheepeater Cliff Picnic Area VT (13.0S/7.9N)
- Mammoth Snowmobile Rental Hut VT (18.8S/2.1N)[m]
- Upper Terrace Drive VT (18.9S/2.0N)
- Mammoth Corral VT* (20.2S/0.8N)
- Mammoth Comfort Station (20.7S/0.2N)

Bechler Area
- Bechler Ranger Station VT
- Cave Falls Picnic Area VT

U.S. Highway 191
- None in the park

---

m. This VT is usually open but may be closed periodically during the summer.

Appendix C
Yellowstone Picnic Areas

There are 58 picnic areas in Yellowstone. This figure differs slightly from what is provided on the park's web site and literature, as well as many other guides to the park. This is because there are a small handful of "unofficial" picnic areas that exist in various places. They don't appear on the material, but they all have at least two or three picnic tables and are available for public use.

You are allowed to use camping stoves and charcoal grills to prepare food at these areas, but can only build fires in the NPS-provided grates. During fire season, there may be restrictions on starting fires. You are not permitted to camp in picnic areas. The only picnic area where water is available is the area located at Madison Junction (#45). When you depart, be sure to pick up all of your waste, including uneaten food, and dispose of it properly. This does not include feeding it to the cute little rodents or the ravens and other birds that hang out begging for food.

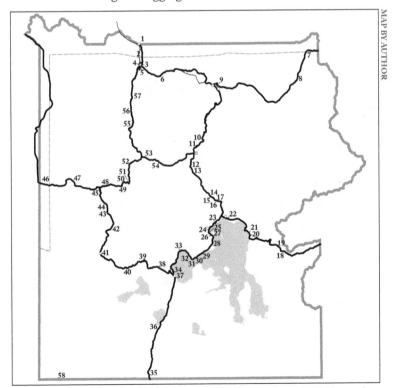

MAP BY AUTHOR

Location of picnic areas in Yellowstone. See the chart on the next two pages for details on each.

Map #	Picnic Area Name	Tables	Toilets[1]	Grills	Elevation	Location/Notes[2]
1	Arch Park	7	0	1	5280	N of the Roosevelt Arch
2	Gardiner River	2	N	0	5630	3.0S of Arch, 2.2N of MHS
3	Albright	4	N	0	6250	Across from Albright VC
4	Mammoth Store*	3	N	0	6280	In front of General Store
5	Mammoth Terraces	4	N	0	6280	Across from terraces
6	Lava Creek	5	VT	0	6570	4.4E of MHS, 13.7W of TJ
7	Warm Creek	7	VT	0	7290	1.5W of NE Ent, 27.1E of TJ
8	Soda Butte	4	VT	0	6970	7.5W of NE Ent, 21.1E of TJ
9	Yellowstone River	9	VT	0	6245	27.4W of NE Ent, 1.2E of TJ
10	Dunraven Road	12	VT	0	8340	15.8S of TJ, 2.4N of CJ
11	Cascade Lake Trail	16	VT	5	8040	17.0S of TJ, 1.3N of CJ
12	Chittenden Bridge	4	VT	0	7740	Wapiti Lake Trailhead
13	Otter Creek	8	0	0	7700	3.0S of CJ, 12.4N of FB
14	Nez Perce Ford	17	VT	0	7715	10.4S of CJ, 5.0N of FB
15	Cascade	6	VT	0	7730	10.6S of CJ, 4.8N of FB
16	LeHardy	6	VT	0	7723	11.3S of CJ, 4.1N of FB
17	North LeHardy Turnout*	2	0	0	7730	12.3S of CJ, 3.1N of FB
18	Eleanor Lake	2	0	0	8485	7.8W of E Ent, 18.1E of FB
19	Sylvan Lake	6+2	VT	0	8440	8.9W of E Ent, 17.1E of FB
20	Sedge Bay	3	VT	0	7750	18.1W of E Ent, 7.8E of FB
21	Steamboat Point	2	VT	0	7780	19.6W of E Ent, 6.3E of FB
22	Fishing Bridge	11	N	0	7753	Museum parking lot
23	Lake Village	2	0	0	7755	South of old Hatchery
24	Bridge Bay	23	CS	3	7760	Adjacent to the marina
25	Gull Point North*	2	0	0	7750	Bend E of north junction
26	Yellowstone Lake*	3	0	0	7770	3.9S of FB, 16.7N of WT
27	Gull Point	21	VT	0	7775	Bend E of south junction
28	Sand Point	18	VT	0	7800	6.5S of FB, 14.0N of WT
29	Spruce-Fir Exhibit	4	VT	0	7790	9.8S of FB, 10.8N of WT

* = "Unofficial" Picnic Areas that don't appear on park maps/literature
(1) VT = Vault Toilet(s), CS = Comfort Station (running water), N = Restrooms nearby
(2) Distance provided in miles from indicated junction

Map #	Picnic Area Name	Tables	Toilets[1]	Grills	Elevation	Location/Notes[2]
30	Dot Island*	4	0	0	7800	10.9S of FB, 9.7N of WT
31	Pumice Point	2	0	0	7775	11.9S of FB, 8.6N of WT
32	Fisherman's Access	3	VT	0	7775	12.7S of FB, 7.9N of WT
33	Hard Road to Travel	3	VT	0	7750	13.8S of FB, 6.8N of WT
34	West Thumb	5	VT	0	7795	East side of parking lot
35	Snake River	15	VT	8	6895	0.3N of S Ent, 21.1S of WT
36	Lewis Lake	9	VT	0	7800	End of CG entrance road
37	Grant Village	17	CS	12	7795	South side of campground
38	East Divide	14	VT	0	8355	3.7W of WT, 13.8E of OF
39	DeLacy Creek	9	VT	0	7995	8.9W of WT, 9.6E of OF
40	Spring Creek	10	VT	2	7960	12.0W of WT, 5.6E of OF
41	East Lot	7	VT	0	7375	East parking lot @ O.F.
42	Whiskey Flat	13	VT	1	7280	6.2N of OF, 9.7S of MJ
43	Nez Perce	12	VT	3	7173	10.3N of OF, 5.6S of MJ
44	Firehole River	12	VT	0	7155	11.4N of OF, 4.5S of MJ
45	Madison Junction	14	CS	0	6830	Behind comfort station @ MJ
46	Barn's Hole	2	0	0	6635	At end of road @ riverside
47	Madison River	7	VT	0	6760	7.5E of W Ent, 6.4W of MJ
48	Tuff Cliff	3	VT	0	6870	1.6N of MJ, 11.8S of NJ
49	Gibbon Falls	0	0	0	7025	4.4N of MJ, 8.9S of NJ
50	Iron Spring	0	VT	0	7180	5.3N of MJ, 8.0S of NJ
51	Caldera Rim	0	VT	0	7350	6.2N of MJ, 7.1S of NJ
52	Gibbon Meadows	9	VT	0	7350	10.2N of MJ, 3.1S of NJ
53	Norris Meadows	16	VT	4	7495	0.5E of NJ, 11.0W of CJ
54	Virginia Cascade	6	VT	0	7810	End of Virginia Cascade Dr.
55	Beaver Lake	9	VT	0	7410	7.5N of NJ, 13.5S of MHS
56	Apollinaris Spring	6	VT	0	7350	9.9N of NJ, 11.1S of MHS
57	Sheepeater Cliff	5	VT	0	7280	13.0N of NJ, 7.9S of MHS
58	Cave Falls	4	VT	0	6320	Cave Falls parking lot

* = "Unofficial" Picnic Areas that don't appear on park maps/literature
(1) VT = Vault Toilet(s), CS = Comfort Station (running water), N = Restrooms nearby
(2) Distance provided in miles from indicated junction

APPENDIX D
YELLOWSTONE CAMPGROUNDS

There are 11 campgrounds and an RV park in Yellowstone. Of these, five accept reservations and are operated by the park's primary concessioner, Xanterra. See the included chart on the next page for details about each, as well as the phone number to call to reserve a site. Note that, during the busy summer season (July-August), most, if not all, of these will fill early in the day (between 11AM and 2PM, generally). There are also over 300 backcountry campsites located throughout the park for hikers. You need to reserve these through the park's Backcountry Offices (see the park's website for specific details).

Note that it is illegal to camp anywhere other than one of the park's campgrounds. The rangers stop and check on every vehicle they find parked in parking lots, pullouts, and other areas where vehicles shouldn't be at night, so you'll only get disturbed (and may get a citation) if you try to camp illegally.

MAP BY AUTHOR

Location of campgrounds in Yellowstone. See the chart on the next page for details on each.

Map #	Campground Name	# of Sites	Reservations Accepted? (1)	Cost (2014)	Open	Elevation (2)	Bathrooms (3)	Showers/ Laundry	Dump Station	Generators (4)	Notes
1	Mammoth	85	N	$20.00	Year round	6050	CS	N*	N	Y	
2	Slough Creek	29	N	$15.00	Mid-June – Late Oct	6275	VT	N	N	N	
3	Pebble Creek	36	N	$15.00	Mid-June – Late Sept	6840	VT	N	N	N	
4	Tower	32	N	$15.00	Late May – Late Sept	6600	VT	N	N	N	30' or less
5	Canyon	272	Y	$25.50	Late May – Early Sept	7950	CS	S/L	Y	Y	
6	Fishing Bridge RV**	346	Y	$46.50	Mid-May – Mid-Sept	7765	CS	S/L	Y	Y	Hard sided units only
7	Bridge Bay	431	Y	$21.00	Late May – Early Sept	7780	CS	N	Y	Y	
8	Grant Village	425	Y	$25.50	Late June – Late Sept	7805	CS	S/L	Y	Y	
9	Lewis Lake	85	N	$15.00	Mid-June – Early Nov	7800	VT	N	N	N	25' or less
10	Madison	277	Y	$21.00	Early May – Mid Oct	6850	CS	N	Y	Y	
11	Norris	116	N	$20.00	Mid-May – End of Sept	7515	CS	N	N	Y	
12	Indian Creek	75	N	$15.00	Mid-June – Early Sept	7293	VT	N	N	N	

(1) For reservations, call 866-439-7375 (2) Elevation at entrance to campground (3) VT=Vault Toilets, CS=Comfort Stations, N=None (4) Generators permitted 8AM-8PM
* Showers available at nearby hotel ** Sites have water, sewer, and 50-amp electrical hookups

Notes

INTRODUCTION

1. This assertion is attributed to author/artist Frederic Remington, but is widely quoted by almost every park employee who's been around the park for more than a season.

PART I - ROAD LOGS: INTRODUCTION

1. Page 6, Mary S. Culpin, *A History of the Construction of the Road System in Yellowstone National Park, 1872-1966.*

2. This junction came to be known as "Prospect Point." It was given this name because the tourists always wondered what exciting prospects lay ahead of them regardless of which path they took (Whittlesey, *Wonderland Nomenclature*).

3. An existing manifestation of these surveys are the survey markers found all over the park from 1923. See my book, *Benchmark Hunting in Yellowstone National Park,* for more details on where to find these, and how they eventually led to the discovery that Yellowstone's ground rises and sinks as a part of the volcanic processes that make it the unique geologic marvel that it is.

4. You can find a copy of the current version of the agreement on FHWA's website at http://www.fhwa.dot.gov/agreements/headquarters/hfla1agr.htm.

NORTH ENTRANCE ROAD

1. See Whittlesey and Schullery's article in the Summer, 2003, edition of *Yellowstone Science* for elaboration on this, as well as a detailed explanation of the thought and engineering that went into its construction.

2. Lee Whittlesey, *Wonderland Nomenclature.*

3. Some sources, including Whittlesey in his *Wonderland Nomenclature* text, indicate that Dude Hill is the same as Cedar Terrace, the extinct terrace above the Mammoth Campground. In his abridged *Yellowstone Place Names* book, however, Whittlesey states that this hill is Dude Hill, and this hill is what the locals refer to as Dude Hill. The origin of the discrepancy is unknown.

MAMMOTH TO TOWER JUNCTION

1. Turkey Pen Road (and the identically named peak and creek) were named for a cabin built in the area by a prospector. The Turkey Pen Cabin was where Truman Everts was taken after his 37-day ordeal in the park's wilderness. The book, *Lost in the Yellowstone: Truman Everts's "Thirty-Seven Days of Peril"*, details his story.

2. From 1889 until 1893, the hospital was located in the old Camp Sheridan, and prior to that, medical treatment was rendered in one of the cabins near the camp. From 1894 to 1911, there was a second hospital that preceded this last one at Mammoth. It, too, was located in the new Fort Yellowstone. See the Mammoth Hot Springs Development section for more details on these structures.

3. Lost Lake is a small, seasonal lake found below the old Mammoth Powerhouse located in the Lower Mammoth Housing Area, so-named because it's "lost" much of the season when it's dry. There are at least two other lakes in the park with this name, including one near Roosevelt Lodge that is accessible via a short trail.

4. Page 34, *National Register of Historic Places Nomination Form for the Grand Loop Road Historic District.*

5. Raymond Guntz died on August 16, 1980, when he fell trying to get a better photo. He slipped and fell into the canyon sustaining fatal internal injuries. See Whittlesey's *Death in Yellowstone* for additional information.

6. Whittlesey, *Wonderland Nomenclature.*

NORTHEAST ENTRANCE ROAD

1. Page 47, Mary Shivers Culpin, *A History of the Construction of the Road System in Yellowstone National Park, 1872-1966.*

2. Whittlesey, *Wonderland Nomenclature.*

3. Ibid.

4. Page 66, Whittlesey, et. al., *Yellowstone Waterfalls and Their Discovery.*

5. Whittlesey, *Wonderland Nomenclature.*

6. Page 318, Mary Shivers Culpin, *A History of the Construction of the Road System in Yellowstone National Park, 1872-1966.* Interestingly, Whittlesey does not mention this in *Wonderland Nomenclature.*

7. Some sources inaccurately list Red's last name as Sowash, rather than Siwash.

8. The entry for this can be found on page 311 of the book.

9. Whittlesey, *Wonderland Nomenclature.*

10. Page 25, Mary S. Culpin, *For the Benefit and Enjoyment of the People: A History of Concession Development in Yellowstone National Park, 1872-1966.*

11. Whittlesey has a rather lengthy description of the squatter and his story in his unpublished *Wonderland Nomenclature*, as well as the much abridged version of the material published as *Yellowstone Place Names* (which is out of print, but can often be found on Amazon in used form).

12. Page 143, Fritz and Thomas, *Roadside Geology of Yellowstone Country.*

13. There is some disagreement over exactly how this area came to be known as Little America. Some claim it got its name from the fact that it gets so cold here, just like it does at a place in Antarctica known as Little America, and was named in its honor. Still others claim it was named for the shape of some (natural) landscaping in the area. Park historian Lee Whittlesey, in his unpublished document *Wonderland Nomenclature*, states the name came from the fact the American flag was raised daily at the old road camp that was in the area. However, many of the old CCC camps were informally known as Little Americas, and this seems to be the most logical reason behind the name in this author's opinion.

14. Whittlesey, *Wonderland Nomenclature.*

15. Page 109, Kenneth Baldwin, *Enchanted Enclosure.*

16. Page 138, Fritz and Thomas, *Roadside Geology of Yellowstone Country.*

TOWER JUNCTION TO CANYON JUNCTION

1. Page 252, Mary S. Culpin, *For the Benefit and Enjoyment of the People: A History of Concession Development in Yellowstone National Park, 1872-1966.*

2. Whittlesey, *Wonderland Nomenclature.*

3. The correct syntax for the name of this waterfall is Tower Fall, as it is a single waterfall. Both the singular and plural (Tower Falls) are used throughout park literature and historical documents, however.

4. Page 68, Robert Goss, *Yellowstone: The Chronology of Wonderland.*

5. Whittlesey, *Wonderland Nomenclature.*

6. Page 408, Diane Papineau, *Transforming Place at Canyon: Politics and Settlement Creation in Yellowstone National Park.* The practice continued until 1975 via the north road.

7. Page 172, Culpin and Rydell. *Managing the "Matchless Wonders." A History of Administrative Development in Yellowstone National Park, 1872-1965.*

CANYON JUNCTION TO FISHING BRIDGE JUNCTION

1. Page 35. Diane Papineau. *Transforming Place at Canyon: Politics and Settlement Creation in Yellowstone National Park.*

2. The story of the fire ran in the August 10, 1960, edition of the Wyoming State Tribune. It included the theorization from the story's author: "The Great Lady Chose Sudden Death: The Great Lady was outraged. She could not, she would not, accept the indignity of laborious, prolonged, and piecemeal destruction. She chose sudden death. And so the Canyon Hotel, the once grand edifice of Yellowstone National Park, a 950-room [sic] and superb example of luxurious living in another era, burned to the ground."

3. Page 119, Diane Papineau. *Transforming Place at Canyon: Politics and Settlement Creation in Yellowstone National Park.* Papineau also has several diagrams of the layout of the buildings, campgrounds, etc., that used to be in this area.

4. The concession companies disposed of their own trash apart from what NPS was doing, generally speaking, until after WWII. The NPS was largely burning their trash in several incinerators located around the park, while the concession companies were dumping it behind their facilities (sometimes burying it, but often not) or feeding it to the bears.

5. Page 194-195. Lee Whittlesey, *Death in Yellowstone.*

6. Park historian Lee Whittlesey has created a rough, hand-drawn map of this area and the location of the old roads. It is available in the park's library and archives at the HRC.

7. Whittlesey, *Wonderland Nomenclature.*

8. Chapter 2, Mary Shivers Culpin, *A History of the Construction of the Road System in Yellowstone National Park, 1872-1966.*

9. Pages 193-194, William Fritz and Robert Thomas, *Roadside Geology of Yellowstone Country.*

10. Pages 14-15, Thomas P. Bohannan, *Benchmark Hunting in Yellowstone National Park.*

11. Whittlesey, *Wonderland Nomenclature.*

12. Page 400, T. Scott Bryan, *The Geysers of Yellowstone.*

13. There is a map of the proposed layout of this new campground in the park's map archives. They're in the process of being renumbered as this is being written, so the specific numeric citation is not available. See the Finding Aid available in the HRC.

14. Page 198, Fritz and Thomas. *Roadside Geology of Yellowstone National Park.*

15. Landscape Alterations Map, 1870-1967 and data on old camps from the park's Spatial Analysis Center.

EAST ENTRANCE ROAD

1. Page 339, Mary Shivers Culpin, *A History of the Construction of the Road System in Yellowstone National Park, 1872-1966.*

2. Pages 115-116, Robert Goss, *Yellowstone: A Chronology of Wonderland.*

3. Page 50, Whittlesey, et. al., *The Guide to Yellowstone Waterfalls and Their Discovery.*

4. Whittlesey, *Wonderland Nomenclature*

5. Page 49, Whittlesey, et. al., *The Guide to Yellowstone Waterfalls and Their Discovery.*

6. He discusses this in the transcript of his 1993 tour with other park historians and officials. The transcript is available in the park's library.

7. Whittlesey, *Wonderland Nomenclature.*

8. Page 227, *Fritz and Thomas, Roadside Geology of Yellowstone Country.*

9. See pages 67-70 of Lee Whittlesey's *Death in Yellowstone* for an extensive recount of this heartbreaking story.

10. See the transcript of the Aubrey Haines 1993 tour of the park, Tape 12.

FISHING BRIDGE JUNCTION TO WEST THUMB JUNCTION

1. Whittlesey, *Wonderland Nomenclature.*

2. Ibid.

3. Some sources suggest this bridge was actually used to transport stage and even vehicular traffic. When you examine the bridge, however, it's clear this isn't feasible.

4. The other two included a second, 340-site campground at Grant Village (in the area currently occupied by the upper employee RV camp), and a 140-site campground along the Mesa Service Road (see the Old Faithful to Madison Junction section for information on the Mesa Service Road).

5. Different sources list either six, seven, or eight islands in the lake, depending upon how they're counted. The islands are Frank, Stevenson, Dot, Peale, Carrington, and Pelican Roost, plus the two small Molly Islands, Rocky and Sandy.

6. Whittlesey, *Wonderland Nomenclature.*

7. Some of the confusion may stem from the fact that this picnic area is located on an unnamed point in the lake directly across from Park Point. Park Point itself is located on the eastern shore of the lake.

8. Though this camp was located four miles north of West Thumb, this was Shaw and Powell's "West Thumb" camp.

9. Whittlesey, *Wonderland Nomenclature.*

10. Scott Bryan discusses this area and its features beginning on page 315 in his book, *The Geysers of Yellowstone* (4th Edition).

11. See page 302 for a map, and pages 312-315 of Scott Bryan's book for details on these features.

12. Page 215, Fritz and Thomas, *Roadside Geology of Yellowstone Country.*

SOUTH ENTRANCE ROAD

1. Page 357, Mary S. Culpin, *A History of the Construction of the Road System in Yellowstone National Park, 1872-1966.*

2. Pages 310-311, Lee Whittlesey, *Death in Yellowstone.*

3. Page 213. Fritz and Thomas, *Roadside Geology of Yellowstone Country.*

4. Page 67. Steve Pierce. *The Lakes of Yellowstone: A Guide for Hiking, Fishing, and Exploring.*

5. Whittlesey, *Wonderland Nomenclature.*

6. Ibid.

WEST THUMB JUNCTION TO OLD FAITHFUL

1. Page 233, Mary S. Culpin, *A History of the Construction of the Road System in Yellowstone National Park, 1872-1966.*

2. Though there is some confusion about the correct way to pronounce Shoshone, and many in the park pronounce it with two syllables, as *Shō shown.* The correct pronunciation according to most linguists is the three-syllable word as provided in the main text, however.

3. Lee Whittlesey, *Wonderland Nomenclature.*

4. Ibid.

5. Though many sources list the elevation of this pass as 8262 feet, recent three-dimensional mapping of the earth's surface by NASA and other agencies has revealed the actual highest elevation here at 8290 feet.

6. Whittlesey, *Wonderland Nomenclature.*

7. Ibid.

8. Page 151, Lee Whittlesey, *Death in Yellowstone.*

9. Page 26, Mary S. Culpin, *For the Benefit and Enjoyment of the People: A History of Concession Development in Yellowstone National Park, 1872-1966.*

OLD FAITHFUL TO MADISON JUNCTION

1. Figures are taken from the park's Thermal Features Database, provided by the Yellowstone Spatial Analysis Center. 2010.

2. Page 129, Scott Bryan, *The Geysers of Yellowstone.*

3. Ibid, page 129; page 142.

4. Page 35, Lee Whittlesey, et. al., *The Guide to Waterfalls of Yellowstone and Their Discovery.*

5. Lee Whittlesey, *Wonderland Nomenclature.*

6. Whittlesey, *Wonderland Nomenclature;* Scott Bryan, *The Geysers of Yellowstone,* pages 175-176.

7. There have been several "drill holes" drilled into the ground around the park since the late 1920s to study the underground systems that support the geysers and other thermal features. The Y-5 drill hole was dug in 1967 by the U.S. Geological Survey.

8. Whittlesey, *Wonderland Nomenclature*.

9. Ibid.

10. Ibid.

11. Page 216, Scott Bryan, *The Geysers of Yellowstone*.

12. Pages 3-4, Lee Whittlesey, *Death in Yellowstone*.

13. Pages 263-264, Lee Whittlesey, *Death in Yellowstone*.

14. Page 238, Scott Bryan, *The Geysers of Yellowstone*.

15. Whittlesey, *Wonderland Nomenclature*. No one knows for sure why this rocky point was given the name "Suicide Point," though it may have been perhaps because of the potential for use as a point from which one could jump in an attempt to commit suicide.

16. Ibid.

17. Ibid.

18. Page 309, Lee Whittlesey, *Death in Yellowstone*.

19. Page 199, et. seq., Fritz and Thomas, *Roadside Geology of Yellowstone Country*.

WEST ENTRANCE ROAD

1. Page 220, Mary S. Culpin, *For the Benefit and Enjoyment of the People: A History of Concession Development in Yellowstone National Park, 1872-1966*. This "new" road was still referred to as the Virginia City and National Park Free Road, however.

2. Ibid, page 50.

3. Memo from Asst. Superintendent Robert Haraden to the Chief Ranger and Chief of Maintenance, dated October 27, 1972. YNP Archives.

4. Marshall's Park is a large meadow through which the old road passed (the first you come to if you're traveling toward the southeast), named after the gentleman who built the Marshall Hotel. Buffalo Meadows is the next meadow you pass through, and was named because it was one of the places scouts looked for the last remaining buffalo in the early days of the park, per Lee Whittlesey, *Wonderland Nomenclature*.

5. Lee Whittlesey, *Wonderland Nomenclature*.

6. Ibid.

MADISON JUNCTION TO NORRIS JUNCTION

1. Page 221, Mary S. Culpin, *For the Benefit and Enjoyment of the People: A History of Concession Development in Yellowstone National Park, 1872-1966*.

2. Page 108, Fritz and Thomas, *Roadside Geology of Yellowstone Country*.

3. National Park Service, Yellowstone National Park, Thermal Features Database, accessed October, 2012.

4. Pages 113-116, Robert Goss, *Yellowstone: The Chronology of Wonderland*. Both camps were closed and removed with the consolidation of all of the camping companies into a single entity in 1917.

5. Whittlesey, *Wonderland Nomenclature.*

6. Ibid.

7. Ibid.

NORRIS JUNCTION TO CANYON JUNCTION

1. Page 274, Mary S. Culpin, *For the Benefit and Enjoyment of the People: A History of Concession Development in Yellowstone National Park, 1872-1966.*

2. Whittlesey, *Wonderland Nomenclature.*

3. Some sources state that a tornado was responsible for downing all of the trees in this area. The National Weather Service office in Riverton, Wyoming, however, states that there was no tornadic activity in or around the park at the time, and that the meteorological conditions at the time are indicative of a microburst. (Personal communication with the meteorological staff at RIW, November 13, 2013.)

NORRIS JUNCTION TO MAMMOTH HOT SPRINGS

1. There are some who believe the existing structure was designed by Robert Reamer, the architect who designed the Old Faithful Inn and several other important structures within the park. Many historians doubt this, however.

2. Information on number of features comes from the park's Thermal Features Database, accessed in October, 2012.

3. Information on the naming comes from Whittlesey's *Wonderland Nomenclature.* The figure for the number of features on One Hundred Spring Plain comes from the park's Thermal Features Database, accessed in October of 2012.

4. Whittlesey, *Wonderland Nomenclature.*

5. pH measurement and information about the number of features comes from the park's Thermal Features Database, accessed in October, 2012.

6. Whittlesey, *Wonderland Nomenclature.*

7. Pages 117-119, Fritz and Thomas, *Roadside Geology of Yellowstone Country.*

8. Whittlesey, *Wonderland Nomenclature.*

9. Mary S. Culpin, *Managing the "Matchless Wonders." A History of Administrative Development in Yellowstone National Park, 1872-1965.*

10. Ibid, page 92.

11. Ibid, page 125.

12. Ibid, page 92.

13. A recent document, the Environmental Analysis for the pending maintenance project for the reconstruction of the road between the Norris Campground and Golden Gate viaduct suggests this campground may have operated into the 1920s, though Culpin (*Managing the "Matchless Wonders."*) and Goss (*Yellowstone: Chronology*) both indicate it was abandoned in 1917 following the consolidation of the camping companies into a single entity.

14. U.S. Army Corps of Engineers, *Enchanted Enclosure: The Army Engineers and Yellowstone National Park, A Documentary History.*

15. Ibid, pp. 101-102.

16. Whittlesey, *Wonderland Nomenclature.*

17. Ibid.

18. Page 100, Culpin, *Managing the "Matchless Wonders." A History of Administrative Development in Yellowstone National Park, 1872-1965.*

19. Ibid, page 84.

20. Page 381, *"This Modern Saratoga of the Wilderness!": A History of Mammoth Hot Springs and the Village of Mammoth in Yellowstone National Park.*

21. Aubrey Haines refers to it as Boot Hill while leading a tour of the park for history and archeological staff in 1993 (as referenced in the transcript available in the park's library).

U. S. HIGHWAY 191

1. Whittlesey, *Wonderland Nomenclature.*

2. Ibid.

MISCELLANEOUS ROADS

1. Pages 307-308, Lee Whittlesey, *Death in Yellowstone.*

2. Whittlesey, *Wonderland Nomenclature.*

3. Page 88, Kenneth Baldwin, *Enchanted Enclosure.* The first road to Mammoth from Gardiner approached the village to the west of the Old Gardiner Road. It descended into the area via the road that is now known as the "Electric Substation Road," which today departs just to the west of the Delaware North Warehouse (behind the Lodgepole Dormitory) and has a rather steep incline up to the Mammoth North electrical substation.

4. Whittlesey, *Wonderland Nomenclature.*

5. Ibid.

6. Pages 190-191, Fritz and Thomas, *Roadside Geology of Yellowstone Country.*

7. Page 53, Mary S. Culpin, *A History of the Construction of the Road System in Yellowstone National Park, 1872-1966.*

8. Pages 132-133, Lee Whittlesey, *Death in Yellowstone.*

9. Page 201, Diane Papineau. *Transforming Place at Canyon: Politics and Settlement Creation in Yellowstone National Park.*

10. Robert Goss, *Yellowstone: The Chronology of Wonderland.*

11. Whittlesey, *Wonderland Nomenclature.*

12. Ibid.

13. Castle Geyser and the extinct White Pyramid Geyser cones, both in the Upper Geyser Basin, are larger.

14. Page 198, Scott Bryan, *The Geysers of Yellowstone.*

15. Ibid, pp 205-207.

16. Whittlesey, *Wonderland Nomenclature.*

17. Page 17, Lee Whittlesey, *Death in Yellowstone.* The term "ojo caliente" has been interpreted to translate as "warm spring" or "hot spring" by many. This is inaccurate.

18. Whittlesey, *Wonderland Nomenclature.*

PART II - DEVELOPMENTS: INTRODUCTION

1. Some people use the term "concessionaire," while others use "concessioner" or "concession operator." All three of these are legitimate terms and are interchangeable, and all have been used throughout the park's history. The author prefers the term "concessioner."

2. The first legislation restricting how closely concessioners could build to the park's sensitive features was the Sundry Civil Act of 1883. It stipulated that concession operators couldn't build any facility closer than ¼ mile from thermal features, waterfalls, etc. It was this same act that authorized the Department of Interior to call in the U.S. Army to provide security for the park, which it finally did in 1886. It also placed the U.S. Army Corps of Engineers in charge of the park's roads immediately upon its taking effect. Many of the concessioners failed to abide by the law, however, and in 1894 a new law was passed. The Hayes Act, as it was known, changed the distance requirement to ⅛ of a mile, which is where it remains to this day.

3. The federal law that governs these operations is known as the 1998 Concessions Management Improvement Act (PL 105-391). The standard concession contract is for ten years, though the Secretary of the Interior may authorize contracts of up to 20 years under certain circumstances, including those where significant capital improvements are required as a condition of the contract such as is the case in Yellowstone. Xanterra's new contract was for a term of 20 years because they're being required to invest millions of dollars to construct and improve several facilities.

4. A variety of sources were used to compile this time line. Primary sources included Robert Goss' *Yellowstone: The Chronology of Wonderland*, and Mary S. Culpin's *For the Benefit and Enjoyment of the People: A History of Concession Development in Yellowstone National Park, 1872-1966*, but also included material from Lee Whittlesey, Aubrey Haines, Leslie Quinn, and Gwen Petersen.

5. Some sources cite the name of this entity as the Yellowstone National Park Improvement Company (YNPIC).

GARDINER - NORTH ENTRANCE

1. Page 8, Lon Johnson, *Yellowstone Park Transportation Company Historic District.*

2. Ibid.

3. Ibid.

4. Ibid.

MAMMOTH HOT SPRINGS

1. Pages 81-82. Battle and Thompson. *Fort Yellowstone Historic Structures Report.*

2. Page 269. Lee Whittlesey, *"This Modern Saratoga of the Wilderness!": A History of Mammoth Hot Springs and the Village of Mammoth in Yellowstone National Park.*

3. Pages 93-94. Battle and Thompson. *Fort Yellowstone Historic Structures Report.*

4. Ibid. Pages 111-114.

5. Ibid. Page 119

6. Ibid. Page 152

7. Ibid. Page 165

8. Ibid. Pages 189-190

9. Ibid. Page 205

10. Whittlesey makes the claim that many of these wives were laundresses who'd been "cut" from the army in 1878. Page 220, *"This Modern Saratoga of the Wilderness!": A History of Mammoth Hot Springs and the Village of Mammoth in Yellowstone National Park.*

11. Lee Whittlesey. *A Brief History of the Mail Carrier's Residence at Mammoth.*

12. Page 289. Battle and Thompson. *Fort Yellowstone Historic Structures Report.*

13. Ibid. Page 68.

14. Ibid. Page 271.

15. Personal correspondence with Lee Whittlesey, September 28, 2011.

16. Lee Whittlesey. *Brief History of Haynes Picture Shop at Mammoth, Known in Recent Years as Hamilton Christmas Store.*

17. Page 92. Mary S. Culpin. *For the Benefit and Enjoyment of the People: A History of Concession Development in Yellowstone National Park, 1872-1966.*

18. Page 150. Whittlesey, in his draft manuscript, *"This Modern Saratoga of Wilderness": A History of Mammoth Hot Springs and the Village of Mammoth in Yellowstone National Park*, speaks of having been in the attic of this building prior to its being remodeled in 2009 and finding old Livingston (MT) newspapers from 1886. The newspaper had been used to "insulate" the attic, a common practice at the time.

19. Page 15. Front Range Associates. *National Register of Historic Places Nomination Forms: Mammoth Hot Springs, Yellowstone National Park.*

20. Most sources say the building was removed in 1949, but Culpin (*Concessions*, 2003) states that it was removed in 1950.

21. Technically, it was the second, as Norris had constructed a temporary cabin near the McCartney Hotel on Clematis Gulch to serve as his headquarters until the could get the blockhouse built.

22. Culpin provides two different dates for the removal of this building. In her work on the park's administration she says it was removed in 1941 (which agrees with most other sources), while her work on concessions states it was removed in 1942 (Page 87). Whittlesey, in his draft history of the Mammoth area (2010) states that this building was present until at least September of 1965 based on photographs of the time. The Weather Bureau left the park in 1941, so Culpin apparently conflates this information with the removal of the building.

ROOSEVELT - TOWER JUNCTION AREA

1. There are two versions of this story floating around. This version is taken from Robert Goss' *Yellowstone: A Chronology of Wonderland* (Page 104). Aubrey Haines, in *The Yellowstone Story, Volume II* (Page 242), states that, after the hotel burned, Dan lost all interest in running the place and neglected to pay his annual lease fee, and his rights were terminated (though he was compensated $1,000 for the property rights he lost). Goss used Haines' information, but also sourced information from memos at the park's archives, so it seems logical that his version more accurately reflects what actually transpired.

2. Page 104. Robert Goss. *Yellowstone: The Chronology of Yellowstone.*

3. Conoco had an exclusive contract to provide gasoline to the park from 1917 until the late 1960s when Sinclair assumed that right (and holds it to this day).

4. Page 92. Mary S. Culpin. *For the Benefit and Enjoyment of the People: A History of Concession Development in Yellowstone National Park, 1872-1966.*

CANYON VILLAGE AREA

1. Different sources list different figures for the number of cabins that opened when Canyon Village first began serving the public. Most list 117, including Robert Goss (Page 91, *Yellowstone: The Chronology of Wonderland*).

2. The story of the fire ran in the August 10, 1960, edition of the Wyoming State Tribune. It included the theorization from the story's author: "The Great Lady Chose Sudden Death: The Great Lady was outraged. She could not, she would not, accept the indignity of laborious, prolonged, and piecemeal destruction. She chose sudden death. And so the Canyon Hotel, the once grand edifice of Yellowstone National Park, a 950-room [sic] and superb example of luxurious living in another era, burned to the ground."

FISHING BRIDGE AREA

1. Page 23. Paul Schullery. *Nature and Culture at Fishing Bridge: A History of the Fishing Bridge Development in Yellowstone National Park.*

2. According to Schullery's history (Page 86), of the 305 cabins located at Fishing Bridge, 138 were removed in 1980, 52 in 1981 (along with the old cafeteria and a dormitory), 22 in 1982, and 44 were removed in 1984. There are five left (see the entry for the YPSS Employee Cabins). The remainder were removed over time for a variety of reason, including those destroyed by fires, condemned, and relocated for use in other areas of the park.

3. Ibid. Page 33.

4. Ibid. Page 57.

5. Ibid. Page 39.

6. Ibid. Page 39. There are conflicting dates about the construction of the garage and service station, though most only vary by a couple of years or so. The dates provided by Schullery seem to be the most commonly agreed upon.

7. Ibid. Page 34.

8. Ibid. Page 125.

LAKE VILLAGE

1. Pages 127, 130. Mary S. Culpin. *For the Benefit and Enjoyment of the People: A History of Concession Development in Yellowstone National Park, 1872-1966.*

2. Page 71. Aubrey Haines. *The Yellowstone Story, Volume II.*

3. Page 134. Robert Goss. *Yellowstone: The Chronology of Wonderland.*

4. B. B. Arnold wrote an excellent history of fishery operations in Yellowstone entitled, *A Ninety-Seven Year History of Fishery Activities in Yellowstone National Park, Wyoming.* It's interesting reading if you would like to know more about how these operations evolved and where the facilities were located. The report can be found in the Yellowstone National Park Library.

5. Page 93. Robert Goss. *Yellowstone: The Chronology of Wonderland.*

6. Section 8, page 5. National Park Service. *National Register of Historic Places Nomination Form: Lake Hotel.*

7. Some sources say this work was done in 1926.

8. Page 21. Barbara Dittl. *Plain to Fancy: The Story of the Lake Hotel.*

9. Ibid.

10. Section 8, page 6, *Nomination Form.*

11. Page 5. Sievert and Seivert. *Lake Area Fish Hatchery Historic Structures Report.*

12. The park's building database shows construction date of 1927. The reason for the disparity is unclear.

13. The uncertainty about the exact date this boathouse was constructed is discussed on pages 9-10 of the Lake Area Fish Hatchery Historic Structures Report. The writers postulate that the structure was built in 1930, but the park's building database indicates the construction date was 1941. This date apparently comes from the fact that this is the first year the boathouse appears on park maps. Obviously, it makes more sense that it would have been constructed along with all of the other hatchery facilities in the 1930 time frame, however.

14. Page 94. Robert Goss. *Yellowstone: A Chronology of Wonderland.* This information is also supported by an unpublished "Lake Lodge Timeline," by an unknown author (though presumably Lee Whittlesey).

BRIDGE BAY

1. There are occasional references to campgrounds at Bridge Bay in maintenance and "public health" related memos from the 1930s and 1940s in the park's archives.

GRANT VILLAGE - WEST THUMB

1. Page 113, Robert Goss, *Yellowstone, The Chronology of Wonderland.*

2. There is a bit of confusing information about this in many of the references. Goss gets it right, though it's not explicit, in his chronology. On p. 120 he states that Hamilton opened "another store and filling station in West Thumb" in 1917, and goes on to state that Hamilton "establishes small stores in auto campground at West Thumb..." (p121). Haines and Culpin make no mention of the original store established in the lunch station in 1917; they only make reference to the store built in 1924. He did *build* his first store at Thumb in 1924, but he'd been operating out of the abandoned lunch station for some time prior to that. This may confuse some researchers into believing that the 1917 date provided by Goss is inaccurate when it's not.

3. Aubrey Haines and Robert Goss both state that the cabins were transferred in 1928, while Culpin claims it was 1930. Given that everyone agrees the Gratiot camp existed for only one year in 1927, it would seem reasonable that 1928 was the correct year.

4. Page 168. Robin L. Smith. *A Case Study of the National Park Planning Process: Grant Village, Yellowstone National Park.*

5. Though there's little discussion of the marina in this book, it, too, would prove to be quite controversial. The marina was apparently conceived by engineers who'd not conducted a proper study of the lake. As a result, it was not designed well and silt accumulates to the point where it would be necessary to dredge the approaches almost continuously (especially after storms) to allow for its use commercially. It also received substantial damage during one of the park's heavy winters. Therefore, the marina was closed to all but canoes and small, non-motorized craft. The NPS does base a patrol boat here during the summer, however.

6. Page 361. Aubrey Haines. *The Yellowstone Story, Volume II.*

7. Pages 115-117. Robert Goss. *Yellowstone: The Chronology of Wonderland.*

OLD FAITHFUL AREA

1. Unpublished time line notes from Xanterra Parts and Resorts Interpretation Manager, Leslie Quinn. Copy obtained from the Yellowstone National Park Library and Archives.

2. Some sources say the building wasn't constructed until 1923. However, the park's buildings database, unpublished material from Leslie Quinn, as well as Mary Shivers Culpin (p. 132, *For the Benefit and Enjoyment of the People...*) all indicate the building was constructed in 1914.

3. Page 126, Mary S. Culpin, *For the Benefit and Enjoyment of the People: A History of Concession Development in Yellowstone National Park, 1872-1966.* YPTC entered into agreements with all of the store owners at that time (Whittaker, Pryor and Trischman, etc.) to operate service stations jointly at the various locations. When Charles Hamilton consolidated his ownership of the stores in 1953, he and the Yellowstone Park Company, YPTC's successor, continued to operate the service stations jointly until 2003, when they were spun off as a result of Delaware North's being awarded the general stores contract.

4. Page 3, Yellowstone Park Foundation, *Resource Brief: Old Faithful Historic District Overview.* This is the only source the author has seen asserting this claim.

5. Page 3, Yellowstone National Park, *Old Faithful Cabin Repurposing and Dormitory Construction: Environmental Assessment.*

6. Unpublished time line notes from Leslie and Ruth Quinn.

7. Ibid.

8. This figure comes from the park's buildings database, and represents its insurance value.

9. James R. McDonald, *Historic Structures Report: Old Faithful Lodge*, 1995.

10. Ibid.

11. Ibid.

12. Some sources say this building didn't open until 1923, but Culpin (*History of Concession Development...*) and the park's building database indicate it was constructed and opened in 1914.

13. Page 47, T. Scott Bryan, *The Geysers of Yellowstone*, 4th Edition.

14. Most sources indicate this building was removed in 1941, though the park's building database lists 1963 as its year of demolition. It does not show up on any maps of the era past 1941, however.

15. More details can be found in Karl Byrand, *Integrating Preservation and Development at Yellowstone's Upper Geyser Basin, 1915-1940.*

References

Baldwin, Kenneth. 1976. Enchanted Enclosure: The Army Engineers and Yellowstone National Park, A Documentary History. Office of the Chief of Engineers U.S. Army, Washington, D.C.

Battle, David G., and Erwin N. Thompson. 1972. Fort Yellowstone Historic Structure Report. National Park Service, Yellowstone National Park, Wyoming.

Bohannan, Thomas P. 2012. Benchmark Hunting in Yellowstone National Park. Hayden Press, New Castle, Delaware.

Bryan, T. Scott. 2008. The Geysers of Yellowstone, 4th Edition. University Press of Colorado, Boulder, Colorado.

Bullock, Jill. 2011. Postcard History Series: Yellowstone National Park. Arcadia Publishing. Charleston, South Carolina.

Byrand, Karl. 2007. Integrating Preservation and Development at Yellowstone's Upper Geyser Basin, 1915-1940. *Historical Geography*, Volume 35, pp. 136-159. Geoscience Publications, Baton Rouge, Louisiana.

Campbell, Reau. 1913. Campbell's Complete Guide and Descriptive Book of the Yellowstone Park. H. E. Klamer, Chicago, Illinois.

Corbin, Annalies, and Matthew A. Russell, ed. 2009. Historical Archeology of Tourism in Yellowstone National Park. Springer Media, New York, New York.

Culpin, Mary S. 2003. For the Benefit and Enjoyment of the People: A History of Concession Development in Yellowstone National Park, 1872-1966. National Park Service, Mammoth, Wyoming.

Culpin, Mary S. 1994. A History of the Construction of the Road System in Yellowstone National Park, 1872-1966. National Park Service, Denver, Colorado.

Culpin, Mary S., and Kiki L. Rydell. 2006. Managing the "Matchless Wonders." A History of Administrative Development in Yellowstone National Park, 1872-1965. National Park Service, Mammoth, Wyoming.

Dittl, Barbara, and Joanna Mallmann. 1987. Plain to Fancy: The Story of the Lake Hotel. Roberts Rinehart, Inc., Boulder, Colorado.

Fritz, William J., and Robert C. Thomas. 2011. Roadside Geology of Yellowstone Country, Second Edition. Mountain Press Publishing Company, Missoula, Montana.

Front Range Research Associates. 2000. National register of Historic Places Nomination Forms: Mammoth Hot Springs, Yellowstone National Park. Front Range Research Associates, Denver, Colorado.

Goss, Robert V. 2002. Yellowstone: The Chronology of Wonderland. Self-Published.

Haines, Aubrey L. 1996. The Yellowstone Story, Volume I. Revised Edition. University Press. Niwot, Colorado.

Haines, Aubrey L. 1996. The Yellowstone Story, Volume II. Revised Edition. University Press. Niwot, Colorado.

Haines, Aubrey L. Unknown Date, ca. 1967. Personal Notes Regarding Landscape Alterations Map. Author's personal collection.

James R. McDonald Architects, 1995. Historic Structures Report: Old Faithful Lodge, Yellowstone National Park. Missoula, Montana.

Johnson, Lon. 2001. Yellowstone Park Transportation Company Historic District: Determination of Eligibility for Listing in the National Register of Historic Places. Historic Research Associates, Missoula, Montana.

Marschall, Mark C., and Joy Marschall. 2008. Yellowstone Trails: A Hiking Guide, 30th Edition. Yellowstone Association, Yellowstone National Park, Wyoming.

National Park Service. 1967. Landscape Alterations Map, 1870-1967. National Park Service, Yellowstone National Park, Wyoming.

National Park Service. 1982. National Register of Historic Places Inventory Nomination Form for the Old Faithful Historic District. National Park Service, Denver, Colorado.

National Park Service. 2003. National Register of Historic Places Nomination Form for the Grand Loop Road Historic District. National Park Service, Yellowstone National Park, Wyoming.

Papineau, Diane Marie. 2008. Transforming Place at Canyon: Politics and Settlement Creation in Yellowstone National Park. Masters thesis, Montana State University, Bozeman, Montana.

Petersen, Gwen. 1985. Yellowstone Pioneers. Sequoia Communications, Santa Barbara, California.

Pierce, Steve. 1987. The Lakes of Yellowstone: A Guide for Hiking, Fishing, and Exploring. The Mountaineers, Seattle, Washington.

Schneider, Bill. 2003. Hiking Yellowstone National Park, Second Edition. Morris book Publishing, Guilford, Connecticut.

Schullery, Paul. 2010. Nature and Culture at Fishing Bridge: A History of the Fishing Bridge Development in Yellowstone National Park. National Park Service, Yellowstone Center for Resources, Mammoth, Wyoming.

Sievert and Sievert Cultural Resource Consultants. 2008. Lake Area Fish Hatchery Historic Structure Report. Helena, Montata.

Smith, Robert B., and Lee J. Siegel. 2000. Windows into the Earth: The Geologic Story of Yellowstone and Grand Teton National Parks. Oxford University Press, New York, New York.

Smith, Robin L. 1988. A Case Study of the National Park Planning Process: Grant Village, Yellowstone National Park. Master's Thesis, Ohio State University, Columbus, Ohio.

"Transcript of Aubrey L. Haines Forty-Hour Tour of Yellowstone National Park, August 9-13, 1993." n.d. Copy in library collection at the Yellowstone National Park Research Library and Archives.

Watry, Elizabeth A., and Lee H. Whittlesey. 2012. Images of America: Fort Yellowstone. Arcadia Publishing, Charleston, South Carolina.

Whittlesey, Lee H. 2010. A Brief History of the Mail Carrier's Residence at Mammoth, Building 2032. Unpublished manuscript, Yellowstone National Park Library and Archives Vertical File, Gardiner, Montana.

Whittlesey, Lee H. 2008. Brief History of Haynes Picture Shop at Mammoth, Known in Recent Years as Hamilton Christmas Store. Unpublished manuscript, Yellowstone National Park Library and Archives Vertical File, Gardiner, Montana.

Whittlesey, Lee H. 2014. Death in Yellowstone: Accidents and Foolhardiness in the First National Park, 2nd Edition. Roberts Rinehart Publishers, Boulder, Colorado.

Whittlesey, Lee H. 2010. "This Modern Saratoga of the Wilderness!": A History of Mammoth Hot Springs and the Village of Mammoth in Yellowstone National Park, Draft Manuscript. Yellowstone National Park, Mammoth, Wyoming.

Whittlesey, Lee H. 2006. Yellowstone Place Names, Second (Revised) Edition. Wonderland Publiching Company, Gardiner, Montana.

Whittlesey, Lee H., Paul Rubenstein, and Mike Stevens. 2000. The Guide to Yellowstone Waterfalls and Their Discovery. Westcliff Publishers, Englewood, Colorado.

Whittlesey, Lee H., and Paul Schullery. 2003. "The Roosevelt Arch: A Centennial History of an American Icon." *Yellowstone Science*, Summer 2003. National Park Service.

Whittlesey, Lee H. 1988. Wonderland Nomenclature. Unpublished manuscript.

Yellowstone Foundation. 1997. A Yellowstone Album: A Photographic Celebration of the First National Park. Roberts Rinehart, Dublin, Ireland.

Yellowstone National Park. 2001. Canyon Junction to Fishing Bridge Junction Road Resurfacing, Restoration, and Rehabilitation: Environmental Assessment. National Park Service, Mammoth, Wyoming.

Yellowstone National Park. 2001. Canyon Junction to Tower Junction Road Improvement: Environmental Assessment. National Park Service, Mammoth, Wyoming.

Yellowstone National Park. 2006. Canyon Rim Drives, Road Rehabilitation: Environmental Assessment/Assessment of Effect. National Park Service, Mammoth Wyoming.

Yellowstone National Park. 2012. Lake Area Comprehensive Plan: Environmental Assessment. National Park Service, Mammoth, Wyoming.

Yellowstone National Park. 1999. Madison Junction to Norris Junction Road Improvement: Environmental Assessment. National Park Service, Mammoth, Wyoming.

Yellowstone National Park. 1991. Nomination Form: Lake Hotel. Yellowstone National Park, Mammoth, Wyoming.

Yellowstone National Park. 1982. Nomination Form: Old Faithful Historic District. Yellowstone National Park, Mammoth, Wyoming.

Yellowstone National Park. 2012. Norris to Golden Gate Road Reconstruction: Environmental Assessment. National Park Service, Mammoth, Wyoming.

Yellowstone National Park. 2011. North Entrance/Park Street Improvement Plan. National Park Service, Mammoth, Wyoming.

Yellowstone National Park. 2012. Old Faithful Cabin Repurposing and Dormitory Construction: Environmental Assessment. National Park Service, Mammoth, Wyoming.

Yellowstone National Park. 2005. Old Faithful Visitor Education Center: Environmental Assessment. National Park Service, Mammoth, Wyoming.

Yellowstone National Park. 1992. Parkwide Road Improvement Plan: Yellowstone National Park, Wyoming. National Park Service, Denver, Colorado.

Yellowstone National Park. 2006. Stephens Creek Administrative Area: Environmental Assessment/Assessment of Effect. National Park Service, Mammoth, Wyoming.

Yellowstone National Park. 2009. Tower-Roosevelt Comprehensive Plan: Environmental Assessment. National Park Service, Mammoth, Wyoming.

Yellowstone National Park. 2004. Yellowstone Justice Center: Environmental Assessment. National Park Service, Mammoth, Wyoming.

Yellowstone Park Foundation, 2011. Resource Brief: Old Faithful Historic District Overview. Yellowstone Park Foundation, Bozeman, Montana.

Yellowstone Park Foundation. 2010. Resource Brief: Old Faithful Inn. Yellowstone Park Foundation, Bozeman, Montana.

Yellowstone Park Foundation. 2010. Resource Brief: Queen's Laundry Bathhouse. Yellowstone Park Foundation, Bozeman, Montana.

Index

C

CPSIA information can be obtained
at www.ICGtesting.com
Printed in the USA
LVHW040716100820
662719LV00004B/142